걸프 사태

대책 및 조치 5

_____

걸프 사태

대책 및 조치 5

| 머리말

  걸프 전쟁은 미국의 주도하에 34개국 연합군 병력이 수행한 전쟁으로, 1990년 8월 이라크의 쿠웨이트 침공 및 합병에 반대하며 발발했다. 미국은 초기부터 파병 외교에 나섰고, 1990년 9월 서울 등에 고위 관리를 파견하며 한국의 동참을 요청했다. 88올림픽 이후 동구권 국교 수립과 유엔 가입 추진 등 적극적인 외교 활동을 펼치는 당시 한국에 있어 이는 미국과 국제 사회의 지지를 얻기 위해서라도 피할 수 없는 일이었다. 결국 정부는 91년 1월부터 약 3개월에 걸쳐 국군의료지원단과 공군수송단을 사우디아라비아 및 아랍 에미리트 연합 등에 파병하였고, 군·민간 의료 활동, 병력 수송 임무를 수행했다. 동시에 당시 걸프 지역 8개국에 살던 5천여 명의 교민에게 방독면 등 물자를 제공하고, 특별기 파견 등으로 비상시 대피할 수 있도록 지원했다. 비록 전쟁 부담금과 유가 상승 등 어려움도 있었지만, 걸프전 파병과 군사 외교를 통해 한국은 유엔 가입에 박차를 가할 수 있었고 미국 등 선진 우방국, 아랍권 국가 등과 밀접한 외교 관계를 유지하며 여러 국익을 창출할 수 있었다.

  본 총서는 외교부에서 작성하여 30여 년간 유지한 걸프 사태 관련 자료를 담고 있다. 미국을 비롯한 여러 국가와의 군사 외교 과정, 일일 보고 자료와 기타 정부의 대응 및 조치, 재외동포 철수와 보호, 의료지원단과 수송단 파견 및 지원 과정, 유엔을 포함해 세계 각국에서 수집한 관련 동향 자료, 주변국 지원과 전후복구사업 참여 등 총 48권으로 구성되었다. 전체 분량은 약 2만 4천여 쪽에 이른다.

2024년 3월

한국학술정보(주)

| 일러두기

· 본 총서에 실린 자료는 2022년 4월과 2023년 4월에 각각 공개한 외교문서 4,827권, 76만 여 쪽 가운데 일부를 발췌한 것이다.

· 각 권의 제목과 순서는 공개된 원본을 최대한 반영하였으나, 주제에 따라 일부는 적절히 변경하였다.

· 원본 자료는 A4 판형에 맞게 축소하거나 원본 비율을 유지한 채 A4 페이지 안에 삽입 하였다. 또한 현재 시점에선 공개되지 않아 '공란'이란 표기만 있는 페이지 역시 그대로 실었다.

· 외교부가 공개한 문서 각 권의 첫 페이지에는 '정리 보존 문서 목록'이란 이름으로 기록물 종류, 일자, 명칭, 간단한 내용 등의 정보가 수록되어 있으며, 이를 기준으로 0001번부터 번호가 매겨져 있다. 이는 삭제하지 않고 총서에 그대로 수록하였다.

· 보고서 내용에 관한 더 자세한 정보가 필요하다면, 외교부가 온라인상에 제공하는 『대한 민국 외교사료요약집』 1991년과 1992년 자료를 참조할 수 있다.

| 차례

정 리 보 존 문 서 목 록

기록물종류	일반공문서철	등록번호	2021010239	등록일자	2021-01-28
분류번호	721.1	국가코드	XF	보존기간	영구
명 칭	걸프사태 : 대책 및 조치, 1990-91. 전11권				
생 산 과	중동1과/북미1과	생산년도	1990~1991	담당그룹	
권 차 명	V.10 해외건설 관련 대책				
내 용 목 차					

0001

이라크의 쿠웨이트侵攻에 따른

工 事 管 理 對 策

1990. 8. 3

建 設 部

0002

目 次

1. 事態現況

戰 況

- 90. 8. 2 새벽 2時 (韓國時間 08時) 탱크 350餘臺를 앞세운 이라크軍이 侵攻開始하여 數時間만에 首都 掌握

- 現在 이라크軍이 主要 政府廳舍 占領 및 王宮포위중이며 空港은 閉鎖狀態이고, 알사바 쿠웨이트王은 사우디로 逃避中

※ 事態進行經緯

- 90. 7.17 : 이라크 후세인大統領이 쿠웨이트의 原油盜掘에 대한 보복 시사

  7.18 : 이라크는 쿠웨이트에 대해 24億弗을 支拂해야 한다고 主張

- 7.20∼23 : Fahd 사우디國王 및 Mubarak 이집트大統領 등이 外交仲裁

  7.26 : OPEC에서 油價引上合意하여 이라크 要求中 一部를 수용

- 8. 1 : 사우디 젯다에서 이라크와 쿠웨이트間 直接會談을 했으나 決裂

- 8. 2 : 이라크가 쿠웨이트 侵攻

-2-

0004

- 現在까지 人命 및 現場被害는 없으나 勤勞者 3名이 宿所에

  未歸還

  1名은 泰國勤勞者와 함께 이라크軍 領內에 保護中인 것으로

  보이며, 送電線 工事現場 確認차 나갔던 2名도 이라크軍이

  保護中인 것으로 推定됨.

2. 建設進出現況

△ 쿠웨이트

- 1975.1 이후 現在까지 現代, 大林 등 17個 業體가 進出하여 128件 2,955 百萬弗을 受注·施工

- 現在는 現代가 4件 232 百萬弗을 施工中임.

  施工殘額 : 179 百萬弗

  人 力 : 韓國 333人, 外國 1,421人

  施工中인 現代建設工事現況 : 4件, 232 百萬弗

工 事 名	工事金額	工 期	工程(%)
순환도로인터체인지공사	46 百萬弗	88.2 - 91.7	70
순환도로미르갑구간공사	47 〃	89.6 - 91.6	42
수비야 송전선공사	94 〃	88.5 - 91.1	81
에가일라 貯水槽공사	45 〃	90.1 - 92.7	4

※ 이라크

- 1977.3 以後 現在까지 現代·三星등 14個業體가 進出하여 71件 6,439 百萬弗을 受注·施工

- 現在는 現代등 4個業體가 13件 2,280 百萬弗을 施工中임.

  施工殘額 : 804 百萬弗

  人 力 : 韓國 618人, 外國 1,262人

-4-

3. 事態發生後 措置事項

外務部

○ 8.2 僑民安全對策 緊急 訓令

- 쿠웨이트 및 이라크 주재공관에 대해 정확한 狀況을 早速 把握 報告하고 現地 僑民들의 安全에 만전을 기하도록 訓令

○ 現地 大使館의 報告에 의거 現地 僑民은 모두 무사함이 확인되었음을 發表

現地 大使館

○ 쿠웨이트 駐在 大使館은 韓國建設業體의 作業現場을 緊急點檢

○ 國境地帶 송전선 工事現場 勤勞者 74名에 대해서는 유사시 緊急 撤收토록 준비 지시

○ 他 現場에 대해서도 非常連絡網 構築과 現場別 安全保護機構를 設置토록 지시

-5-

| 建設部 |

O 非常對策班을 設置하여 外務部등 關係機關, 現地公館, 海外建設協會, 進出業體間 有機的 連繫와 신속한 對應

O 海外建設協會 및 進出業體에 대해서도 非常勤務體制를 갖추도록 하는 한편 勤勞者家族에 대해 安全無事함을 案內

O 現地進出業體에 대해 主副食 및 生必品의 최대한 確保를 指示

| 業體 |

O 現代建設 4個現場 勤勞者를 모두 쿠웨이트市內 宿所로 집결하여 待避

이 中 쿠웨이트市內 외곽에 있는 送電線工事現場 勤勞者는 쿠웨이트 全域이 同一한 狀況이므로 現場宿所로 復歸措置

O 工事를 中斷하고 外出등 個別行動 統制

-6-

4. 이번 事態가 現地工事에 미칠 影響 및 向後 措置計劃

○ 勤勞者·職員의 身邊安全에 최대의 力點을 두고 事態進展推移를 銳意 注視하면서 적절한 對應策 講究

事態推移	影響	措置計劃
戰鬪再開時	工事中斷 및 人名 被害 憂慮	• 安全地域 대피 및 철수 준비등 非常對策 講究 • 主副食등 生必品 確保
戰況不透明時 (現狀態)	工事繼續 困難 및 旣成金受領 隘路	• 安全地域 待機 및 工事 再開 準備 • 旣成金 受領對策 講究
終戰狀態의 經濟·社會 混亂時	工事代金 受領困難 및 遲延	• 安全措置 및 旣成金受領 對策 講究하여 工事 繼續

-7-

0009

5. 이라크 其他 周邊國家 現場에 미칠 影響 및 措置計劃

    ○ 現在로서는 이라크의 일방적인 優勢下에 있으므로 특별한 影響이 없을 것으로 보임

        • 다만 사우디등 親쿠웨이트 國家의 支援으로 事態가 擴大될 경우에는 施工中인 工事를 早期 完工한 후 철수하도록 하고 新規工事 受注도 당분간 抑制하는 등 別途對策 講究

    ○ 이후 美國·蘇聯 및 아랍圈의 움직임을 예의 蒐集 分析하는 등 關係部處와 긴밀히 協調하여 亦態發展에 따른 對應方案 講究

-8-

0010

〈 周邊國 建設進出現況 〉

單位 : 百萬弗

國 家	總 契 約		施 工 中		施工殘額	人力(名)	裝備(臺)
	件 數	金 額	件 數	金 額			
計	1,587	70,289	329	32,608	8,312	12,227	15,877
사 우 디	1,261	48,702	226	17,462	1,222	3,476	7,653
리 비 아	194	17,833	72	13,395	6,681	6,854	6,708
이 란	48	1,810	8	1,041	397	868	1,122
아랍에미리트	52	1,342	9	390	4	758	299
예 멘	32	602	14	320	8	271	95

-9-

0011

〈 周邊國　建設進出現況 〉

單位 : 百萬弗

國　　　家	總　契　約		施　工　中		施工殘額	人力(名)	裝備(대)
	件　數	金　額	件　數	金　額			
計	1,587	70,289	329	32,608	8,312	12,227	15,877
사　우　디	1,261	48,702	226	17,462	1,222	3,476	7,653
리　비　아	194	17,833	72	13,395	6,681	6,854	6,708
이　　　란	48	1,810	8	1,041	397	868	1,122
아랍에미리트	52	1,342	9	390	4	758	299
예　　　멘	32	602	14	320	8	271	95

0012

건 설 부

해건 30600-20176　　　(503-7416)　　　1990. 8. 6.
(3년)

수신　외무부장관

제목　이라크-쿠웨이트사태에 따른 건설공사 관리대책

　　　이라크와 쿠웨이트사태로 인한 진출업체의 건설공사에 대하여
근로자, 직원의 신변안전에 최대의 역점을 두고 사태 진전단계에 따라
신속한 대응책을 강구하여 피해를 최소화 하고자 쿠웨이트 및 이라크
공관장에게 다음 사항을 조사 보고토록 훈령하여 주시기 바랍니다.

　　　　　　　　　　　다　　　　음

　　　1.　이번 사태로 인한 각 공사현장의 시공 및 공사중단상황과
근로자 상황 및 조치한 내용

　　　2.　현상태 지속시, 전쟁 장기화 또는 전쟁확대시, 사태호전시등
사태진전 단계에 따라 현지 공사에 미치는 영향과 공사재개, 안전지역대피,
철수시의 수송수단 철수로 및 부상자 후송대책등에 대한 대책방안과 의견

　　　3.　공사기성금 수령 및 공사중단으로 인한 손실보전을 위한 조치
방안

　　　4.　미귀환근로자 석방 및 귀환을 위한 조치내용과 전망 및 대책

　　　5.　근로자 숙소 대기시의 안전 및 기타 교육, 공사현장 출퇴근시의
안전관리수칙, 비상식량비축, 비상연락체제등 안전관리에 관하여 조치한 실적

　　　6.　이라크, 사우디등 주변국의 현지공사에 미치는 영향과 이들을
통한 쿠웨이트내 공사관리 및 근로자 귀환방안 및 전망

　　　7.　기타 이번 사태로 인해 건설공사와 관련된 제반상황을 수시파악
보고. 끝.

접수일 1990. 8. 8

21844

0013

해건 30600-   1990. 8. 6.

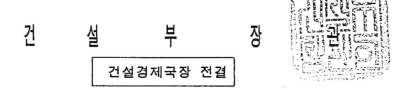

건 설 부 장
건설경제국장 전결

0014

건 설 부

해건 30600- ~~378   (503-7416)   1990. 8. 8

수신 외무부장관   김옥 (3년)

제목 이라크-쿠웨이트사태에 따른 조치

　　　이라크 . 쿠웨이트사태와 관련 현지와의 통신이 원활치 않아
상황파악이 어려운바 이의 신속한 정보수집과 효과적인 대책의 수립
및 지원을 위하여 건설관 주재 인근 공관인 사우디와 이란 주재 공관에
아래 사항을 조치하고 그 결과 보고토록 긴급 훈령하여 주시기 바랍니다.

　　　　　　　　　　아　　　　래

　　1.　이라크. 쿠웨이트 사태와 관련된 정보수집활동 강화

　　2.　양국 사태에 따른 주재국 해외건설 진출에 미칠영향 및 송
대책 검토

　　3.　사태의 장기화 또는 악화시 양국 진출 해외건설업체 지원
가능성 및 방안 검토.

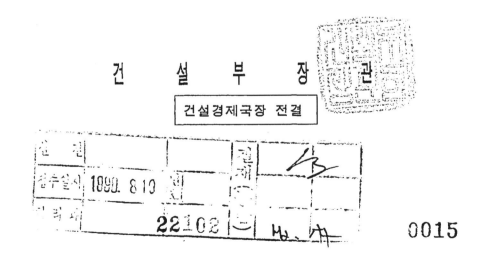

건 설 부 장 관

건설경제국장 전결

발 신 전 보

분류번호	보존기간

번 호 : WBG-0214   900809 1919 DY   종별 : _____ WKU -0199

수 신 : 주 수신처 참조 *대사/청령실*

발 신 : 장 관 (중근동)

제 목 : 건설공사 관리대책 훈령

　　　건설부는 이란.쿠웨이트 사태와 관련한 대응책을 강구코자 아래사항에 대한 조사보고를 협조요청하여 온바, 적의조치 바람.

　　　1. 이번 사태로 인한 각 공사현장의 시공 및 공사중단상황과 근로자 상황 및 조치한 내용

　　　2. 현상태 지속시. 전쟁 장기화 또는 전쟁확대시. 사태호 전등 사태진전 단계에 따라 현지 공사에 미치는 영향과 공사재개. 안전지역대피. 철수시의 수송 수단 철수로 및 부상자 후송 대책등에 대한 대책방안과 의견

　　　3. 공사기성금 수령 및 공사중단으로 인한 손실보전을 위한 조치 방안

　　　4. 미귀환근로자 석방 및 귀환을 위한 조치내용과 전망 및 대책

　　　5. 근로자 숙소 대피시와 안전 및 기타 교육. 공사현장 출퇴근시의 안전 관리수칙. 비상식량비축. 비상연락체제등 안전관리에 관한 조치한 실적

　　　6. 이라크. 사우디등 주변국의 현지공사에 미치는 영향과 이들을 통한 쿠웨이트내 공사관리 및 근로자 귀환방안 및 전망

　　　7. 기타 이번 사태로 인해 건설공사와 관련된 제반상황을 수시파악 보고. 끝.

　　　　　　　　　　　　　　　　(중동아프리카국장 이 두 복)

수신처 : 주 이라크. 쿠웨이트 대사

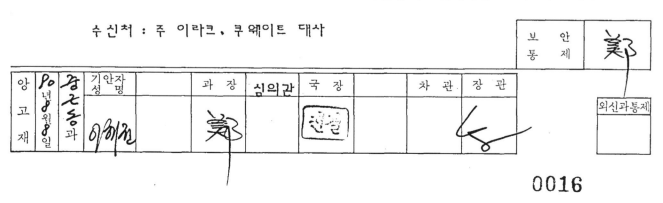

0016

발 신 전 보

분류번호 | 보존기간

번 호 : **WSB-0303**   900810 2215 FC   종별 : 긴급

WIR -0263

수 신 : 주 수신처 참조   대사!!총병씨!!

발 신 : 장 관   (중근동)

제 목 : 이라크.쿠웨이트 사태 관련 대책

건설부는 이라크.쿠웨이트 사태와 관련, 신속한 정보 수집과 효과적인 대책 수립 및 지원을 위하여 아래사항을 긴급 조치 (건설관) 후 그 결과를 통보해 줄것을 요청하여 왔는바, 적의 조치 바람.

- 아   래 -

1. 이라크.쿠웨이트 사태 관련 정보 수집 활동 강화

2. 동 사태가 주재국 해외건설 진출에 미칠 영향 및 대책 검토

3. 사태의 장기화 또는 악화시 양국 진출 해외건설업체 지원 가능성 및 방안 검토. 끝.

(중동아프리카국장   이 두 복)

수신처 : 주사우디, 이란 대사

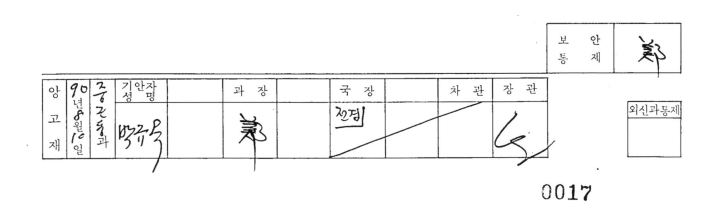

건   설   부

해건   30600- 20683   (503-7416)   1990. 8. 11
수신   외무부장관   (3년)
제목   이라크, 쿠웨이트 사태에 대한 조치

        1. 해건 30600-20176('90. 8.6)및 해건 30600-20378
('90. 8. 8) 관련입니다.

        2. 위 관련으로 이라크. 쿠웨이트사태에 대한 대책수립을 위하여
해당공관 및 인근 공관인 이라크. 쿠웨이트. 사우디. 이란공관에 사태의
진전상황, 영향과 이에 대한 대책 및 비상시의 철수계획과 지원방안에 대한
검토의견을 보고토록 요청하였으나 아직까지 보고가 없어 업무에 지장을
초래하고 있아오니 당해 공관에 조속 보고토록 하고 특히 이라크는 이라크에
진출하고 있는 외국건설업체의 동향을 조사보고토록 긴급 훈령하여 주시기
바랍니다.

            건   설   부   장   관

이락·쿠웨이트 궁사현황 및 사태에 대한 대책

1990. 8. 11.

현 대 건 설 (주)

0019

I. 한국정부의 대이락 경제제재와 당사의 문제점 및 의견
===

가. 현지 파견 한국인 현황 : 총 809 명

    1. 이라크   : - 직 원 : 144 (가족 8명 별도)
              - 근로자 : 358   계 : 502

    2. 쿠웨이트 : - 직 원 : 75 (가족 6명 별도)
              - 근로자 : 234   계 :309

나. 대 이라크, 쿠웨이트 채권및 자산 현황(단위 :USD 1,000)

    1. 이라크 : USD 995,107

      1) 어음 미수금 : USD 500,096
         - 만기도래후 미수령 : USD 93,491
         - 만기 미도래 :USD 406,605 (만기도래후 90.9.5.
                       재발행어음임)   91.1.5

    √2) 원유분 미수금 : USD 167,121 (매월 600,000BBL x
                       USD 20 = USD12,000,000 씩 수령중)

      3) 기성미수금 : USD 12,741

      4) 유보금   : USD 100,059 x

      5) 동원후 미시공분 : USD 8,991 x

      6) 재고 자재가액 : USD 2,007 x

      7) 보유장비 가액 : USD 8,179 x

          현금 소계 : USD 799,194

      8) 공사 관련 보증현황 : USD 195,913

    2. 이락 신규공사 (PROJECT 701)

      1) 계약금액 : USD 754,000

    √2) 선수금 : USD 67,400   (57.mil convert)

         A. 현지화 : USD 13,480 (8월초 수령예상)
         B. 어음 지급중 : USD 12,132 (기수령)
         C. 원유 : USD 41,788 (90.3/4분기 전액수령예정)

      3) 동원장비가액 : USD 50MIL

      4) 동원자재 : USD 5MIL

0020

3. 쿠웨이트 : USD 153,890

    1) 기성·미수금 : USD 42,034(확정 클레임
                          USD 10,200포함)

    2) 유보금 : USD 32,977 X

    3) 동원후 미시공분 : USD 8,125 X

    4) 재고 자재가액 : USD 918 X

    5) 보유 장비가액 : USD 3,929 X

    현금 소계 : USD 88,003

    6) 공사관련 보증 현황 : USD 65,887

다. 당사의 입장

한국정부가 공식적으로 대이라크 경제 봉쇄 제재를
가할경우 이라크로서는 대한국 대응조치를 취할
가능성이 있으며 이경우 이라크 및 쿠웨이트내의
한국 인원·재산에 대한 억류 또는 압류 조치를
배제할 수 없다는 것이 당사의 우려인바

이라크와 쿠웨이트에 상기와 같이 대규모의 인원
및 재산을 파견 유지하고 있는 폐사로서는 이러한
엄청난 결과를 감당할 수 있는 입장이 되지 못함을
양지하시고

아국정부로서는 이라크에 대하여 유연한 입장을
견지해 주실것을 희망하는 바 입니다.
부득이하여 정부가 경제제재 조치라는 불행한 결정을
할경우에는 당사는 도산이라는 심각한 상황에 처할
수 밖에 없는바 금번 사태와 관련한 WAR RISK에 대하여
정부가 정당한 보상조치를 해줄것을 요청하지 않을 수
없음을 양지하시기 바랍니다.

0021

II-1 공 사 현 황 (IRAQ)

(단위 : 천 미불)

現場名	發注處	工期	契約金額	工程率	人員				保有裝備	備考
					職員	勤務者	第三國人	計		
키르쿠 상수도 공사	상하수도청	85.11.11 - 90.12.10	102,919	92	19	76	367	462		
키르쿠-베이지-하디다 고속철도 공사	철도공사 시행청	82.08.26 - 87.09.30	694,909	100	11	42	44	97		
안무사일 화력발전소 공사	전력청	84.08.13 - 90.10.31	726,166	100	16	72	49	137		
수리 조선소 공사	군 공사국	42개월	754,089		52	125	23	200		
기타 현장			2,321,859		46	43	66	.155		
총 계			4,599,942		144	358	549	1,051	879	

0022

표-2. 공사대금 미수 및 보증현황 (IRAQ)

(단위 : 천ID)

현장명	계약고	신수금 미반제 기성회하	미수금 기성	미수금 유보금	미수금 전도금	계	보증현황 P/BOND	보증현황 AP/BOND	보증현황 기타	비고
키르쿡 상수도 공사	102,919	91,269	5,335	5,085	1,229	13,792	4,374	3,000	6,418	
키르쿡-베이지-하디다 고속 철도공사	694,909	675,430	1,264	18,215		15,579	15,579			
엠무사입 최미넬건소 공사	726,156	692,250	4,912	28,994		32,152	32,152			
수리조신소 공사	754,089				754,089	101,080	33,693	67,387		
기타 현장	2,321,859	2,275,012	1,229	44,918		33,310	11,484		21,826	
총계	4,599,942	3,734,171 / 0	12,741	97,212	755,318	195,013	97,282	70,387	28,244	

0023

II-3 이락 지역 인원 현황

現 場 名	職員	勤勞者	小 計	TCN	總 計
이락 사업본부	36(6)	1	37(6)	0	37(6)
알무사입 화력발전소	16	72	83	49	137
바이지 비료공장 공사	1	5	6	7	13
화루자 주택공사	0	2	2	2	4
하이파 주택공사	0	6	6	9	15
400KV 변전소 공사	6	22	28	23	51
키르쿡 상수도 공사	19	76	95	367	462
메디칼시티 병원공사	3	3	6	0	6
수리 조신소 공사	52	125	177	23	200
키르쿡.바이지.하디다 철도공사	11	42	53	44	97
요르단.시리아 고속도로 공사	0	4	4	25	29
計	144(6)	358	502(6)	549	1,051(6)

0024

II-4 工事 現況 (KUWAIT)

(1990.08.05 現在)

(UNIT : IISD)

現場名	發注處	工期	契約金額	工程率	人員 職員	人員 現勞者	人員 第三國人	保有裝備 (臺數)	備考
수비야 300KV 송전선 공사 (KT-300)	수전력성 (MEW)	88.05.09-91.01.08	86,074,000	91.00%	15	58	351	125	職員外家族 5人 별도
비럴 크유트 교저류 FF공사 (FAJIF)	공공사업성 (MPW)	87.09.22-90.06.07	13,060,000	100.00%	1	5	45	38	
제1 순환도로 - 3A단계 공사 (KIST)	공공사업성 (MPW)	88.02.10-91.07.13	34,128,000	71.58%	12	39	141	86	
미르카 집입도로 공사 (MIRQAB)	공공사업성 (MPW)	89.06.01-91.06.20	45,566,000	44.81%	22	72	453	166	
에기일라 지수소 공사 (KURES-3)	수전력성 (MEW)	90.01.02-92.07.01	45,319,000	5.02%	12	50	305	57	
아즈주르 배수단지 공사 (AZOUR)	수전력성 (MEW)	85.07.17-88.06.16	98,760,000	100.00%	3	6	0		
쿠웨이트 지점 (KWT JJ)					10	4	3		
總計				322,907,000		75	234	1,298	472

0025

Ⅱ-5. 工事代金 未受領 및 保證 現況 (KWT)

(UNIT: USD 1,000)

現場名	契約高	先受金 未反濟	既成取下	未受金 既成	未受金 留保金	殘工事	保證 現況 計	P-BOND	AP-BOND	其他	備考
수비야 300KV 송전선 공사 (KT-300)	86,074	(2,307)	47,099	13,197	18,007	7,774	13,293	8,747	4,546	-	기타 완공공사 현장 (미수금): FINTAS: 10,454 AZOUR: 1,938 KADIS: 313 KD 031: 5 계: 12,710
파힐 고속도로 교차로 공사 (FAJIF)	13,080	-	11,123	631	1,306	-	1,911	1,240	-	671	
제1순환도로 3A 단계 공사 (KIST)	34,128	(155)	21,428	1,320	3,057	8,323	6,225	3,207	2,005	1,013	
미르캅 전입도 공사 (MIRQAB)	45,586	(873)	18,462	2,021	2,784	24,209	7,491	4,534	2,645	312	
예가일라 계수조 공사 (KURES-3)	45,319	(8,670)	1,412	2,135	259	41,513	13,547	4,532	9,015	-	*선수금은 미반제분으로서 당사의 채무가 될 것임.
其他	318,223		298,052	12,710	7,461	-	23,420	12,823	770	9,827	
總計	542,370	(12,005)	395,573	32,014	32,874	81,909	65,887	35,083	18,981	11,823	

11-6 쿠웨이트 체류 인원 현황 (KUWAIT)

구분	한국인		삼국인	비고
현장명	직원	근로자		
KT-300	15	58	351	한국인 근로자 2명 (조준택 가성 반장, 노제항 가성공), 배국인 경비 3명 소제항 억음.
KURES-III	12	50	292	
KIST	12	39	141	김 영호 (정비반장)과 배국인 100여명 배아로 HTI.암 억음.
MIRQAB	22	72	453	
AZOUR KADIS	3	6	13	
FAJIF	1	5	45	
KWT JJ	10	4	3	
계	75	234	1,298	추가로 송출희망 김 진수 GJ (WEJA) 외 3인, 이 송일 SW (HEIN) 외 2인
	309			
총 계			1,298	총 인원 : 1,607 (외 기족 8인)

→ 工程事

III. 안전대책 및 철수계획
=====================================

가. 직원.근로자 신변안전대책

1. 쿠웨이트 :

[손글씨: 근로자 철수시 교섭진행중]

1) 간선도로등에 군인들의 검문.검색이 강화되어 있어 장소를 이동하는 것은 신변안전에 불리.
2) 따라서 모든 인원은 현재 대피중인 현장별 숙소내 대피하며 외부출입을 통제하고 안전교육 실시.
3) 유사시 지역적 위험성을 고려 숙소간 이동대피를 실시.

2. 이라크 :

[손글씨: 버스, 5명씩 동원기]

1) 현재 모든일이 정상적으로 이루어지고 있는 편이며 각 현장별 숙소에서 정상생활중이며 방공시설 보수 및 안전교육
2) 유사시(공습,미사일공격등) 지역별 위험성을 고려 현장간 이동방법으로 안전대피실시(예.알무사입 발전소 현장인원은 바그다드 지점으로 대피)
3) 야간에 인원외출을 통제.

나. 주.부식, 의료, 통신 대책

1. 쿠웨이트 지역

1). 주식 : 1 개월분 보유
2). 부식 : 1-2 주분 보유
3). 의료 : 자체 의무실 및 현지 약국을 통하여 비상 구급 약품의 확보 가능.
4). 통신 : 상업용 전화/텔렉스가 두절된 바, 바그다드 및 쿠웨이트의 아국 공관 무전교신 라인을 이용할 예정. (외무부의 협조 약속받음)

2. 이락 지역

1). 주식 : 2 개월분 보유
2). 부식 : 2 개월분 보유
3). 의료 : 현장별토 충분히 비상 구급약품 기확보됨.
4). 통신 : 폐사 바그다드 본부로 부터 1일 2-3회씩 서울 본사 대책본부로 전화 상황보고를 해오고 있으며, 또한 알무사이브 화력발전소 발주처인 전력청으로 부터 자기들의 텔렉스를 이용해도 좋다는 계의를 받음. (통신 보안 문제를 고려, 특별한 경우외에는 아직 이용치 않고 있음.)

0028

다. 직원 및 근로자 가족 위안 문제

　　폐사는 상기건에 관련하여 아래와 같은 조치를 취하고 있음.

　　1. 근로자 가족에 대한 조치.

　　　1). 근로자 가족에 대하여는 해외인력 관리부에서 주관하여, 실종
　　　　근로자 3명에 대해서는 직원을 해당 근로자 가족집에 방문토록
　　　　하여 위로하였으며, 매일 오전, 오후 한차례씩 전화로 사태 진전
　　　　사항을 통보해 줌.

　　　2). 나머지 근로자에 대해서는 가정마다 전화번호를 파악하여, 매일
　　　　사태 진전 사항을 통보해 주고, 폐사로 내방하는 가족에 대해서는
　　　　상담실을 설치, 운영하여 문의에 상세히 답변하고 있음.

　　　3). 8월 9일에 폐사 사장 명의로 위로의 편지를 발송함.
　　　　(일주일 단위로 편지예정)

　　2. 직원 가족에 대한 조치

　　　1). 각 소속 사업 본부별로 해당 직원의 가정에 매일 전화하여,
　　　　위로의 말과 함께 사태 진전사항, 수립중인 대피 및 철수 방안에
　　　　대해 개략적인 설명을 해주고 있음.

　　　2). 폐사로 내방하는 직원 가족에 대해서는 인사부/해외업무본부에서
　　　　상담 요원을 배치하여 문의에 상세히 답변하고 상황을 설명함.

라. 단계별 비상대책
----

　1. 쿠웨이트 인원철수계획

　　1) 시　기 :　1990.8.-
　　　　　　　　(이락정부의 철수승인후 착수)

　　2) 대상인원 :　직　원　　　　75 명
　　　　　　　　　기능직　　　234 명
　　　　　　　　　T C N　　1,298 명

　　　　　　　　　　　　　　1,607 명
　　　　　　　　　가　족　　　　8 명
　　　　　　　　　===============
　　　　　　　　　총　계 1,615 명

Third Country National
(이상시인체비)

0029

3) 예비점검

    A. 외무부 협조사항 - 통신시설 사용
                      - 현지 대사관 훈령 (이락정부 승인)

    B. 이락 정부승인

    C. 수송수단 점검   - 수송차량. BUS ( )대
                        전세비행기   ( )대

    D. 각 현장별 기자재 재고파악 및 안전보관 대책안수립

4) 철 수

    A. 조 편성 (6개조) - 1조 X 50명 X 6 대 =   300명
                        300명 X 6조   = 1,800명
                        (명단별표 참조)

    B. ROUTE 설정 (별지참조)
                - 육로 : KWT-BASRA-BAGDAD-AMMAN
                - 항로 : AMMAN-BKK-SEOUL

5) 사전준비물

    A. 개인소지품
    B. 식수/ 식염
    C. 비상식품/ 약품
    D. OIL

2. 이라크 인원대피 및 철수계획

  1) 대상인원 : 직 원   144명
               기능직   358명
               T C N   549명

                          1,051명
               가 족   6명
               =================
               총 계   1,057명

  2) 주요산업시설 공격시

    A. 1차 대피 : ALHUS현장은 IPOC으로 대피
    B. 2차 대피 : KIWAS,RAILN현장은 IPOC으로 대피

0030

3) 무웨이트 국경지역이 밀릴경우

바스라에 있는 NASRY 현장은 현장 소장 책임하에 바그다드로 대피가
필요한 경우 IPOC으로 대피하고 IPOC과 같이 행동함.

IRAQ Project operation center

4) 도심 공격시

가. 1차 대피 : 교민, IPOC과 협조 대피 (공관지침에 의거)
나. 2차 대피 : IPOC 캠프 인원은 KIWAS, RAILN 현장으로 대피

5) 철수의 경우

A. 국제 공항 재개시 : 바그다드 공항이용 철수

B. 공항 폐쇄시   : 상황 전개에 따라 즉시 대응

제 1루트 : 바그다드-베이치-모슬-터키국경 (약 510 KM)
제 2루트 : 바그다드-루트바-요르단 국경 (약 564 KM)

기타 필요한 루트는 공관 협조하에 결정한다.

C. 조편성 : 6개조 - 45명 x 4대 x 6조 = 1,080명

0031

V. 현장 철수시 제 예상의 고려 사항
=================================

문 제 점	대 비 책
1. 특별위험 발생으로 인하여 실제로 공사가 중지되고 있거나 (구웨이트), 공사 수행이 거의 곤란한 상태 이지만 (이란), 특별위험이 발생했음을 승인받을 발주처가 존재하지 않거나 (구웨이트) 또는 발주처가 이를 승인하지 않아 공사를 가동할 수 없으므로 (이란) 결국 공사의 시공자의 일방적인 철수가 불가피하는 경우 향후 발주처로부터 BONDS의 피의 비치는 순해 배상청구를 당할 위험성이 높음.	1. 향후 공사 재개시 또는 계약 해지시 특별위험 발생함을 입증할 수 있도록 현지 인지 우체국 등 관련기관을 통한 내용증명 우편 송부 또는 내용 확인을 득하도록 하고 교 이의 불가 시 한국대사관을 통한 특별위함 발생에 대한 사실 공증을 득한후 시신 발송하는 방법 강구.
2. UN의 TRADE EMBARGO 결의 및 한국의 경제 제재 조치 참가에 의하여 공사 지역의 인원/ 장비/자재의 투입이 불가능하므로 발주처로도 문제인 특별위함을 인정받지 못할 경우 공기지연으로 인한 상당한 경제적 손실이 예상됨.	2. 향후 사태가 완화될 경우 외교적, 법적인 모든 조치를 강구하여 발주처의 보증물수와 손해 배상 청구를 막도록 적극적으로 대처.
3. 향후 불가항력적으로 클레임 문제가 발생될 것으로 예견 되지만 특별위함을 인정받지 못할 경우 예견 피해의 경제적 손실이 예상됨.	3. 지금적인 클레임 근거자료 확보 및 유지.

국 경 및 현 장 간 거 리
============================

1. 국 경 까 지 거 리

   1) BGD - 요르단 국경   : 538 KM
   2) BGD - 루웨이브 국경   : 608 KM
   3) BGD - 터키 국경   : 516 KM
   4) 루웨이브 시내 -   : 125 KM
      이라크 국경

2. 루웨이브 현장에서 시내까지 거리

   1) KIST/MIRQAB   :   시내
   2) KIST 숙소   :   20 KM
   3) FAJIF 현장   :   25 KM
   4) KWT 지점   :   30 KM
   5) KURES-3 숙소   :   40 KM
   6) AZOUR 숙소/현장 :   70 KM
   7) KT-300 숙소/현장 :   50 KM

3. 이라크 현장에서 바그다드까지 거리

   1) BGD - AL MUSSAIB(ALMUS) :   62 KM
   2) BGD - BAIJI   (BAIFE) : 187 KM
   3) BGD - FALUZA   (FALUZ) :   58 KM
   4) BGD - KIRKUK   (KIWAS) : 275 KM
                       (RAILN)
   5) BGD - NASRY   (NASRY) : 580 KM
   6) BGD - RUTBA   (YOSY) : 413 KM
   7) BGD   (IPOC,IS-400,MECY)

0033

차 량 준 비 현 황

구분	현장명	대상버스	소형버스	지원차량(엠브런스,물차,트럭등)
쿠웨이트	쿠웨이트지점			앰;1 트;7
	아주루트 배수단지 공사	1		트;2
	파헬 고속도로.교차로 공사	6		트;9
	1번 순환도로 공사	2		트;14
	300KV 송전선 공사	4	2	앰;1 트;12
	미르칸 도로 공사	2	1	앰;2 트;17
	기타 현장	2		
	소 계	17	3	앰;4 트;61
이라크	이라크사업부 본부		2	앰;5
	암무사이브 화력발전소 공사	5	5	트;15
	키르쿡 상수도 공사	4	2	트;8
	북부 철도 공사	3	4	트;16
	701 수리조선소 공사		1	트;8
	기타 현장	19	3	트;2
	소 계	31	17	앰;5 트;72
	총 계	48	20	9 / 133

외 무 부

종 별 : 긴급

번 호 : BGW-0475

일 시 : 90 0811 1100

수 신 : 장관(건설부,노동부,중근동,기정)

발 신 : 주 이라크 대사

제 목 : 건설공사 관리대책

대:WBG-0214

1. 당관이 무선으로 수신한 쿠웨이트공관의 대호 건설공사 관리대책을 다음과 같이 보고함

가. 현재 이라크공관과의 무선봉신밖에 없으며 보고수단이 위하지 않아 자세한 보고는 불가함.

나) 사태발생이후 각 공사현장은 작업을 일체 중단하고 근로자는 숙소에서 안전대피중이며 현재까지 사망, 실종, 부상자는 없음

다. 당지의 사태가 종결되지 않아 주재국의 존립조차 예측할수없는 상황이므로 공사재개등의 판단은 불가하며 아국근로자 314 명을 포함한 총 1,640(현대소수 3 국근로자 포함)여명의 철수대책은 다각도로 모색중임

라. 현재 5 개공사 미수금은 약 7,000 천 쿠웨이트디나르로 추산되며 이에대한 대책은 사태의 추이에 따라 강구되어야할것임

마.) 비상식량은 3 주일분을 비축하고있으며 일부 현장에서는 차량및 부속품을 징발당한 사례가 있어 부식 약탈도 우려하고있음. 끝

(대사 최봉름-국장)

예고:90.12.31

건설부	장관	차관	1차보	2차보	중아국	정문국	정와대	안기부
노동부								

외 무 부

종 별 : 긴 급

번 호 : BGW-0474
일 시 : 90 0811 1100

수 신 : 장관(건설부,노동부,중근동,기정)

발 신 : 주 이라크 대사

제 목 : 건설공사 관리대책

대:WBG-0214

1. 대호 주재국 진출업체의 건설공사 관리대책을 다음과같이 보고함

가. 주재국에서 시공중인 공사는 현대의 키르쿡수도공사 1 건이며 인력투입이 가장많은 공사는 701 공사임. 여타공사는 대부분 소수인력만으로 하자보수중 인바 주요현장의 인력은 701 공사 144 명, 키르쿡상수도 94 명, 알무사이브발전소 72 명, 아브그레이브도로 60 명, 북철 (남광, 정우, 현대) 60 명등이며 지사 인력을 포함한 건설업체 전체인력은 647 명임

나. 발주처 감독등의 비상동원으로 하자보수작업이 중단상태에 있는 북부철도 공사의 사태와 마찬가지로 공사유관부서의 주요실무자 대부분이 사태후 자리를 비우고 있어 (동원으로 추정) 공사 대전연불협의 및 하자보수등의 정상추진이 불가능하거나 정체 상태에 있음

마. 공관 조치사항

1) 사태발생직후 외출금지, 경계강화, 비상연락체재 유지, 비상근무조 편성, 비상대피 또는 철수등 근로자 안전대책과 시설, 장비등 현장보호 및 손실보전 방안을 수립 실시토록 수차 지시 (회의, 공문등) 한바 있으며 특히 위험지역인 바스라소재 현장근로자에 대하여는 바그다드등 안전지역으로 철수를 긴급 지시 하였고 주요산업시설지역의 경우에도 바스라지역근로자 대피방안에 준하여 필요한 조치를 취할것을 지시하였음

2) 1 인 또는 소수인력이 주재하고있는 남광, 대림, 동아, 또는 거주가족에 대하여는 유효한 방법을 모색, 인접국으로의 철수 또는 귀국을 종용하였음

3)전면철수가 필요할경우 공항폐쇄 및 국경봉쇄로 현시점에서의 유일한 방법은 특별기 투입밖에 없으며 가능한 방안을 모색중에 있고 이 경우에 필요한 사전조치를

| 건설부 | 장관 | 차관 | 1차보 | 2차보 | 중아국 | 통상국 | 정문국 | 영교국 |
| 청와대 | 안기부 | 노동부 | | | | | | |

이행할것도 아울러 지시하였음

　라. 주변국의 현지공사에 미치는 영향평가등에 관하여는 각종 정보가 차단된 현
단계로서는 그 보고가 어려울것으로 자료되며 추후 보고위게임.

　마. 각 업체의 비상식량은 2 개월분이 비축되어 있으며 지금현재까지 부상등의
유고자는 없음. 끝

　　(대사 최봉름-국장)

　　예고:90.12.31 일반

PAGE 2

0037

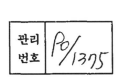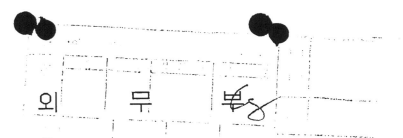

관리 번호	PO/1375

외 무 부

종   별 :

번   호 : BGW-0489   일   시 : 90 0813 0930

수   신 : 장관(건설부,노동부,중근동,기정)

발   신 : 주이라크 대사

제   목 : 건설공사 관리대책

연: BGW-0474

쿠웨이트 사태와 관련 이라크 아국 건설업체의 근로자 안전대피등 상황을 다음 보고함

1. 사태발발 이전까지는 발주처의 동의(SUPPORTING LETTER)하에 출국사증 취득이 가능 하였으나 최근 이제도가 강화, 8.10 을 전후하여 발주처의 동의가 없는 경우, 사증 취득이 불가능 한바, 이는 각 업체가 시공한 각종 시설중 자국 인력 또는 기술로 관리.운영이 어려운것은 동 시설을 시공한 제삼국 인력으로 하여금 관리.운영토록 하기 위하여 필요한 최소한의 인력을확보하기 위한 의도로 판단되며 따라서 사태가 악화될 경우라도 아국 인력의 전원 철수는 어려울 것으로 보임

2. 삼성은 쿠웨이트 국경 인접지역인 움.카슬의 부두공사 하자 보수를 위하여 상주하고 있던 근로자 4 명 전원을 8.10 바그다드 본부 캠프로 철수조치함

3. 현대도 바스라의 701 공사현장 인력(144 명)을 단계적으로 바그다드 캠프로 철수 시킬 계획임

4. 이미 출국비자를 취득하고있던 현대소속 근로자 5 명이 8.12 오전 요르단 국경을 통과 출국함

5. 상기 출국자를 제외하고 출장자등 일시 체류자를 포함한 8.12 현재의 주재국 실거주인원(휴가자 제외)는

가. 공관: 직원 12(고용원 5 포함), 가족 14, 계 26 명

나. 건설업체: 임직원 184, 근로자 438, 가족 18, 계 640 명(현대 쿠웨이트소속 근로자인수 이력 3 명제외)

다. 상사: 직원 4, 가족 12, 계 16 명

라. 대한항공: 직원 1, 가족 3, 계 4 명

건설부   1차보   2차보   중아국   통상국   청와대   안기부   노동부

마. 은행주재원: 직원 2, 가족 6, 계 8 명

바. 기타 유학생, 개별취업자, 강남필러(주)출장자등 교민 17 명과 그가족 2명등 19 명 등으로서 총 713 명임.끝

(대사 최봉름-국장)

예고:90.12.31

이라크·쿠웨이트 事態에 따른 建設 對策

90. 8. 15
가운 해외건설과

1. 現況

가. 進出現況 (첨부 1참조)

o 이라크 : 現代등 7개業體 進出, 施工殘額 776백만불, 人力 628名

(施工殘額中 754백만불은 現代의 701 수리조선소 工事

受注額으로 着工 準備 狀態)

o 쿠웨이트 : 現代等 3개業體 進出, 施工殘額 82백만불, 人力 313名

나. 未收金 現況 (첨부 2참조)

o 이라크 : 927백만불

- 旣成未收 32백만불, 留保金 125백만불, 어음 602백만불, 기타 168백만불

- 현대 790백만불, 삼성 73백만불, 남광 16백만불, 정우 43백만불, 한양 5백만불

o 쿠웨이트 : 65백만불 (現代)

- 旣成未收 32백만불, 留保金 33백만불

2. 考慮 事項

o 勤勞者 및 裝備 撤收 問題

- 撤收時期, 經費, 範圍, 方法等

o 旣 進行中인 工事中斷에 따른 事項

- 契約不履行에 따른 問題等

o 未收金 回收 問題

0040

3. 對策

o 勤勞者의 安全에 最優先 (撤收對策 別途資料)
- 撤收時期 및 方法等 撤收關聯 問題는 現地 公館長과 進出業體間 긴밀 協議 決定
    · 公館長은 勤勞者의 身邊安全考慮, 撤收問題에 대한 最終 決定權 행사
    · 단, 撤收에 따른 經濟的 損失등 모든 責任은 業體가 감수
- 化學戰 勃發 대비 (방독면 支援等)
- 아국업체 고용 第3國人 安全問題 考慮
- 事態의 隣近國家로 擴大 대비, 隣近國家滯留 勤勞者의 身邊安全對策 사전 講究

o 新規受注 禁止
- 현재 進行中인 工事는 事態進展에 따라 融通性있게 대처

o 事態惡化로 撤收 또는 工事 中斷時, 工事代金 收金등 事後 예상되는 問題에 대한 대비 철저
- 發注處와 協議, 不可抗力에 의한 措置임을 正式文書化하여 事後 法的 摩擦 소지등 最少化
- 不可抗力에 의한 措置임을 證明하는 기타 根據資料 確保 및 維持 努力
- 각 現場別 機資材 在庫 파악 및 安全保管 대책 수립
- 殘留 必須要員은 發注處와 계속 接觸, 관계 유지

o 未收金 回收問題는 發注處와 協議, 極少化 하도록 노력
- 未收金 回收遲延에 따른 해당 業界에 대한 國內 支援 대책등은 財務部, 建設部등 關係部處에서 講究

o 外國 進出業體의 動向 파악
- 이지역에서 建設受注를 하고 있는 여타 國家들의 對策動向 및 工事代金 受領등을 위한 共同步調 방안 검토등

0041

o 建設市場 多邊化

  - 契約額 기준 地域別 점유비율 (90년 上半期)·
    중동(93.1%), 아프리카(0.7%), 아세아(4.9%), 태평양 (1.3%)

o 勞動集約型 건설에서 技術集約型 건설로 轉換

o 施工爲主 건설에서 engineering 및 管理監督型 건설로 轉換

4. 參考事項 (旣措置事項)

가. 勤勞者 撤收問題

o 이라크 當局의 요르단을 통한 我國僑民撤收 許容 (陸路)에 따라 駐이라크,
  쿠웨이트 大使에게 下記事項指示
  - 短期滯留者, 婦女者, 幼兒등 非必須要員에 대한 出國許可 요청 (8.12)
  - 이라크정부와 出國許可 簡素化 방안, 輸送經路, 出國人士등 최단
    시일내 實現토록 協議 및 業體等과 協調하여 撤收時 後遺症과 事後
    法的 摩擦소지 최소화 대책 講究 (8.13)

---

o 僑民現況(8.13 現在)· 이라크 712名, 쿠웨이트 584名
  - 이라크   712名 (업체근로자 및 가족 640名, 주재상사원 및
               가족 26名, 공관원가족 26名, 기타 20名)
  - 쿠웨이트 584名 (업체근로자 및 가족 317名, 주재상사원 및
               가족 38名, 공관원 및 KOTRA 가족 40名,
               기타 189名 …
               ※ 사우디 國境通過 出國者 21名

0042

o 이라크·쿠웨이트 事態가 長期化 할 것에 대비, 주요 外國公館 및 關係機關등과 긴밀히 協調하여 非必須僑民을 조속 撤收토록 지시 (주사우디, 바레인, 카타르, UAE, 요르단대사)

  - 隣接國 僑民現況 : 사우디 6,091명, 바레인 498명, 카타르 88명, UAE 829명, 요르단 122명

o 駐 요르단 大使에게 下記事項 지시 (8.12)

  - 쿠웨이트와 이라크 거주 我國僑民이 무비자로 요르단 入國할 수 있도록 조치

  - 入國地點에 직원을 파견하여 구체적 對策을 樹立報告하고 시행에 만전을 기하도록 함

  - 到着僑民 狀況에 관하여는 수시 緊急 報告

나. 工事進行問題

o 8.11 關係部處 對策 會議에서 현재 進行中인 工事에 대해서는 業界의 自律的 判斷에 맡기고 政府로서는 新規受注만을 禁止키로 한다는 原則 合意

0043

아국업체 진출현황

구 분	업체명	공 사 명	계약금액 (백만불)	시공잔액 (백만불)	인 력 (명)	장 비 (대)
이라크	현 대	701 수리조선소	754	754	177	-
		키르쿡상수도	103	1.3	95	85
	삼 성	바그다드-아브 그레이브 도로	204	18	64	285
	정 우	이락철도 공사	101	0.7	11	31
		제 4 비료공장	46	1.5	14	42
	기 타	-	-	-	266 (현대 227 한양 31 남광 6 동아 2 대림 1)	873
	합 계		1,208	775.5	628	1,316
쿠웨이트	현 대	수비야 송전선	86	7.8	73	125
		제1 순환도로	34	8.3	52	86
		미르캅진입로	46	24.3	94	166
		에가일라 저수로	45	41.5	62	57
		기타	-	-	29	38
	기 타	-	-	-	3 (대림 2 효성 1)	-
	합계		211	81.9	313	472
총 계			1,419	857.4	941	1,788

※ 이라크 701 조선소 공사는 착공 준비중인 공사로 계약액 전액 시공잔액임.

0044

미수금 현황

(단위 : 천불)

구분	업체명	계	기성미수	유보금	어음	기타
이라크	현대	789,758	12,741	109,800	500,096	167,121 (원유)
	삼성	72,960	1,850	6,749	64,361	-
	남광	16,325	222	3,236	11,405	1,462 (이자)
	정우	43,289	17,535	-	25,754	-
	한양	5,134	106	5,028	-	-
	합계	927,466	32,454	124,813	601,616	168,583
쿠웨이트	현대	65,000	32,000	33,000		
총 계		992,466	64,454	157,813	601,616	168,583

※ 선투자비용은 제외되었음

0045

'90 건설진출 현황 ('90.6.30 현재)

(단위 : 천불)

지역별	진출현황		계 약 현 황				계약예정공사
	국 별	진출업체	누 계		1990		
	사우디	36	1,261	48,701,937	2	36,448	324,000
	리비아	6	194	17,832,643	1	4,671,842	1,115,500
	이락	6	71	6,441,486	-	2,400	1,000
	기다 (10개국)	16	443	9,040,226	4	319,541	119,000
	소계 (13개국)	44	1,969	82,016,292	7	5,030,231	1,559,500
아프리카	6개국	3	41	654,095	1	38,993	125,320
아세아	14개국	23	635	8,572,228	11	265,187	134,050
태평양	8개국	9	168	684,261	2	70,542	143,000
중남미	개국		12	52,456	-	-	-
합 계	41개국	50개사	2,825	91,979,332	21	5,404,953	1,961,870

0046

외 무 부

종 별 :

번 호 : LYW-0513

일 시 : 90 0820 1400

수 신 : 장관(통일,마그,중근동,해기)

발 신 : 주 리비아 대사

제 목 : 쿠웨이트 사태

연:LYW-0499,502,504,505

연호와 같이 주재국 정부는 쿠웨이트 사태에 대해 UN 을 통한 해결을 주장하고 있고, 아랍 연합군(미군대신 역할로)에도 적극 참여할 의사를 표명하고 있어 중도 내지 온건 입장을 취하고 있다고 판단되며, 당지는 금번 사태에도 불구하고 정치.경제적인 영향을 받지 않고 있으므로 정부의 쿠웨이트 사태, 관련 대책 추진시 당지 실정을 감안하여, 동대책으로 인하여 당지에서의 아측 이해 관계에 불이익이 생기 않도록 조치하여 주시기 바람

가. 정부 대책 추진시 걸프만 지역과 당지를 포함한 타 중동지역에 대한 대책을 분리하여 조치함으로서 걸프만 이외의 지역에 영향을 미치 않도록 하기 바람

나. 아국의 주 해외건설 시장인 당지에서의 건설활동은 정상적으로 이루어지고 있고, 국제 유가급등에 따른 주재국의 재정수입 증대가 예상되므로 시장 여건은 호전될 것으로 보임.특히 사우디, UAE 를 제외한 중동지역 OPEC 국가들이 쿼타를 준수하고 있으므로 주재국은 석유수입 증대로 인하여 아국 업체에 대한 공사대전의 원유지급을 확대할 것으로 보여 미수금이 감소할 것으로 예상되며 앞으로 공사수주도 증가할 것으로 전망됨

당지 진출건설업체는 교통부가 걸프사태 악화시 트리폴리 까지도 KAL 운항 정지 명령할 것이라는 보도에 우려를 표하고 있음. 특히 작년 KAL 사고시 아측의 일방적인 운항취소에 주재국은 큰 불만을 표시한바 있는데, 금번 사태로 인하여 당지로의 KAL 운항이 영향을 받게 되는 경우 상당한 마찰을 유발할 것으로 예상됨. KAL 운항 여부는 7 천명이 넘는 당지의 아국 근로자에게도 당지의 안정성과도 관련하여 심리적인 영향이 클 것으로 예상되므로 사태의 진행 여부에 불구하고 당지로의 KAL 운항은 정상적으로 이루어 지도록 조치하여 주실 것을 건의함.끝

통상국	장관	차관	1차보	2차보	중아국	중아국	정문국	청와대
안기부	공보처	대책반	교통부					

90.08.20 23:33
외신 2과 통제관 DO

0047

(대사 최필립-장관)
예고 90.12.31. 일반

impo 12 31
시기   (이)

0048

외 무 부

종 별 : 지 급

번 호 : BGW-0557

일 시 : 90 0821 1030

수 신 : 장관(건설,중근동)

발 신 : 주 이라크 대사

제 목 : 701공사착공 추진상황

대:WBG-0214

1. 5.20 수정 계약이 발효된 701 공사의 착공 기간은 계약 금액 (잠정계약액 25 백만 디나르를 제외한 계약액 210 백만 디나르)의 10 프로에 해당하는 선수금을 전액 수령한날로 부터 기산 토록 되어 있는바 현대는 지난 7.29 선수금 중 연불 공사 금액 해당액 12,130 천불의 지불 약정서를 수령한바있음

2. 현대는 8.13 주재국 으로 부터 착공기간 기산의 요건이 될 잔여선수금 55,257 천불(원유해당 선수금:41,780 천불, 현지화 해당선수금 13,477 천불)의 지불 통고를 받은바 있으나 쿠웨이트 사태로 인한 착공의 어려움과 수령원유 운송의 불가능 등의 이유 때문에 선수금의 수령을 하지못하고본사의 지침을 대기중임.끝

(대사 최봉름-국장)

예고:90.12.31

건설부   차관   1차보   2차보   중아국   통상국   정와대   안기부   대책반

PAGE 1

사본

건　설　부

해건　30600-2858　　　　(503-7416)　　　　1990.8.22
수신　외무부장관　　　　　　　　　　　　　(1년)
제목　관계부처 장관회의 결과 조치

　　8.9　관계부처 장관회의에서 결정된 대이라크 조치사항중 이라크.
쿠웨이트 건설공사 신규수주 금지와 관련하여 당부는 도급허가 업무처리지침
(해건 30600-14842, '90.6.15)에 의하여 전쟁중인 국가에 대하여는
도급허가 하지 않도록 되어 있을뿐만 아니라, 사태발생 즉시 도급허가를
중단토록 해외건설협회에 지시하였으며 또한 8. 5 대책회의시 이를 확인한바
있음을 통보하며 아울러 현재까지 동 양국에 대한 도급허가 실적이 없음을
통보합니다.

건　　설　　부　　장

건설경제국장 전결

0050

외 무 부

종 별 :

번 호 : SBW-0720   기밀   일 시 : 90 0825 1510

수 신 : 장 관(중근동, 경외, 건설부, 노동부, 기정, 국방부)

발 신 : 주 사우디 대사

제 목 : 진출 건설업체 직원 및 가족 신변안전 조치

대: WSB-348

1. 중동사태 발생 즉시 전 건설업체 직원, 근로자 및 가족의 신변안전을 위해 각건설업체와 대사관(건설관, 노무과)간에 비상연락망을 유지하고 계속 비상근무중에 있으며 유사시 대비 대사관에서 하달한 안전대책수립지침(사우디(건)90-506)에 의거 업체별로 철수, 공사 마무리 계획등 필요한 제반준비를 완료하여, 수시 각종정보를 긴밀히 교환하고 있고, 일단 유사시에는 비상연락 체계에 의하여 지체없이 안전지대로 대피할 수 있도록 만전을 기하고 있으며

2. 현재 주재국에는 현대건설등 29개사 총9,708명(아국직원 1,101. 근로자1,921. 삼국인6,686)이 근무하고 있으며 직원가족은 총 71세대 190명중 30가구 73명이 귀국하였고 잔여가족(41세대117명)은 귀국 준비중에 있음.

3. 특히 쿠웨이트 국경에 인접해 있는 동부지역의 극동, 대림, 삼성, 유원, 풍림, 현대산업, 신화등 7개사 16개 공사현장에는 2,182명(한국인 687명)이 근무하고 있는데 유사시 리야드 제다등 안전지역으로 긴급 대피할 수 있도록 계획을 수립 신변안전에 만전을 기하고 있음.

(대사 주병국-국장

중아국   차관   1차보   2차보   경제국   안기부   국방부   건설부   노동부
대책반
미주국

PAGE 1   90.08.25   23:09 CG
                                                          외신 1과 통제관

0051

걸프사태 : 대책 및 조치, 1990-91. 전11권 (V.10 해외건설 관련 대책)   57

외 무 부

종   별 : 지 급

번   호 : SBW-0731   일   시 : 90 0826 1410

수   신 : 장 관 (경아,중근동,노동부,건설부,기정)

발   신 : 주 사우디 대사

제   목 : 근로자 대피보고

1. 주재국에서 주베일-리야드간 송수관공사를 하고있는 현대산업개발 (소장: 박기원)에서는 주베일 산업공단에 가까운 고속도로부근에 주캠프를 설치하고 있었는바, 쿠웨이트사태로 인한 긴장이 고조됨에 따라 본사의 지시에 의하여, 총근로자 379명 (아국인 122, 삼국인 257) 중동캠프를 사용하고 있던 근로자 120명 (아 44, 삼 76)을 90.8.24.밤 리야드부근 캠프로 대피시켰음을 보고함.

2. 동현장은 84.2.22 착공한 123,593천불 규모의 공사로써 7월말 공정은 87.5프로임.끝

    (대사 주병국-국장)

경제국   중아국   안기부   건설부   노동부

PAGE 1

90.08.26   22:06 FC

외신 1과 통제관

0052

외 무 부

종   별 :

번   호 : SBW-0736   일   시 : 90 0827 1420

수   신 : 장 관(중근동, 경이, 건설부, 노동부, 기정)

발   신 : 주 사우디 대사

제   목 : 중동사태관련 업무동향 보고

　　주재국 진출 건설업체인 동산토건 지사(차장 정영균외 5명)가 90.8.27 카이로 동산토건지사로 잠정 철수함.끝

　　(대사 주병국-국장)

동	국 제 경 제 국	90 8 28 일	담 당	과 장	국 장	차관보	차 관	장 관
탑					√			

외 무 부

종 별 :

번 호 : SBW-0742   일 시 : 90 0828 1000

수 신 : 장 관(청와,중근동,노동부,건설부,기정)

발 신 : 주 사우디 대사

제 목 : 근로자 현황

연: SBW-711

8.27 현재 주재국에 진출한 아국업체의 아국인은 모두 3,112 명으로서, 8.20보다 184명 감소, 동산토건지사 (6명)가 카이로에 있는 지사로 대피한 외에는 근로 계약만료, 공사 종료에 따른 귀국자임 (업체별 현황 파편송부). 끝

(대사 주병국-국장)

공 람	국 제 경 제 국	90 년 8월 2일	담 당	과 장	국 장	차관보	차 관	장 관

경제국   중아국   안기부   건설부   노동부

외신 1과 통제관

0054

외 무 부

종 별 : 지 급

번 호 : SBW-0748   기협   일 시 : 90 0829 1100

수 신 : 장 관(중근동, 경협, 건설부,국방부,기정,노동부)

발 신 : 주 사우디대사

제 목 : 공사정보 긴급보고

중동사태관련 미공병단(C.O.E)발주 공사정보를 아래와 같이 입수 보고함.

1. 공사명: 미군막사 건설

2. 공사비:미상

3. 공기:약 6 개월

4. 공사내용: 미군용 BASE CAMP 약 6 개소, (1 개소당 5 천-1 만명 정도 수용)

5. 공사착수:90.9 월말 이전 착공예정, (9 월초:도면 및 시방서 배포, 9 월중순: 입찰, 9 월하순:계약체결)

6. 근무조건:-착공후 6 개월이내 필히 공사완료(인원, 장비, 자재의 집중부입, 야간작업등이 요구됨)

    -계약방식은 LUMP SUN 방식 혹은 COST FEE BASE 방식으로 하고 여건 변경시는 설계변경

    -공사대금은 미공병단에서 직접 지급

    -기타 BLOCK VISA, 공사추진 및 진행 절차등에 필요한 행정지원은 미공병단이 직접 사우디 국방항공성과 협조 최대지원

7. 추진현황

    미공병단 측은 공사의 시급성을 감안 과거부터 C.O.E 공사경험이 있는 아국업체인 **동아, 대림, 삼환, 유원, 극동, 한일**등 6 개업체와 **현지 1 개업체**의 의사타진(장비, 자재, 인력등 동원가능범위등)중에 있음.

8. 당관의견

    -미공병단 발주공사는 공사대금지급, 각종행정지원, 계약조건(COST BASE 혹은 LUMP SUM)이 유리하여 수익성이 양호한 것으로 보임.

    -의사타진 받고 있는 6 개사의 과다경쟁으로 인한 저가입찰등의 사례는 억제되어야

중아국   차관   1차보   2차보   경제국   청와대   안기부   국방부   건설부
노동부

할것임 (6 개 내외 공구가 될것이므로 6 개업체 각기 1 개 공구씩 수주토록 해건협에서 조정하여 도급허가 하는 방안이 좋을것임)

-중동사태로 인한 인력확보 문제에 어려움이 예상되므로 아국인력 송출등의문제에 대한 관계기관과의 협의가 요구됨.

-예측불허의 중동 사태와관련 인력. 장비투입등 신변 및 재산 안전문제는 사전 고려되어야 할것임.끝

(대사 주병국-국장)

예고:90.10.31 일반 1

일반문서로께분류(90.10.3))

PAGE 2

0056

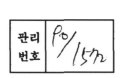

관리
번호 PO/157

＋   ＋

외   交   부

조사무관

종   별 : 지급

번   호 : BGW-0687   일   시 : 90 0906 1200

수   신 : 장관(건설,기정,중근동)

발   신 : 주 이라크 대사

제   목 : 90년도 연불협의 추진상황

1. 각사의 90 년도 공사대전 연불협의 추진상황을 다음과같이 보고함

가. 현대:90 년도 말까지의 기간도래 어음 120 백만불,90 년중 신규기성액 60 백만불, 기간중 발생이자 47 백만불등 도합 227 백만불의 공사대전을 대상으로 어음 120 백만불중 26 백만불과 이자 47 백만불등 73 백만불은 원유로 수령하고, 어음잔액 94 백만불은 3 년거치 3 년 분할상환하는것으로 그리고 신규기성 60백만불은 4 년 6 월거치 3 년 6 월 분할상환하는것을 내용으로 연불에 대한 실무협의를 8.30 완료하였으며, 협약체결을 대기중임. (건설공사대전과는 별개로 수출입은행의 알. 무사이브화력발전소 기자재금융상환액 37 백만불은 원유로 수령키로 협약체결 예정임)

나. 삼성:90 년말까지 기간도래어음 15,673 천불, 기간중이자 5,573 천불, 신규기성 1,334 천불, 유보금 1,375 천불등 도합 23,955 천불을 대상으로 연불협의중이며 8.28 주재국으로부터 전액 원유수령을 제의받고 있는바 원유수령에 대한 실현가능한 방법, 절차, 시기등 구체적인 사항에 대하여 계속 협의중임

다. 기타 남광, 대림, 동아, 정우, 한양등의 공사대전 수령협의는 사태후 사실상 중단 상태임

2. 현대 및 삼성의 연불협약이 체결된다하드라도 원유수송 봉쇄때문에 원유수령 해당액의 미수금에 대한 수령처리까지는 상당기간이 소요될것으로 보임.끝

(대사 최봉름-국장)

예고:90.12.31

건설부   2차보   중아국   정와대   안기부

PAGE 1   90.09.06   18:51

외신 2과 통제관 BT

0057

페 灣事態에 따른
工事管理 現況과 對策

90. 9

建 設 部

現　況

△　이라크・쿠웨이트　建設進出現況

- 兩國에서 ’75年 以後 總 199件 , 94億弗의 工事를 受注하였고, 現代는 이라크 및 쿠웨이트에서, 三星,漢陽,正友,南光은 이라크에서 施工中에 있으나 經濟制裁措置로 인한 資材,裝備 搬入 不能으로 大部分 工事 中斷狀態임

- 現在 施工殘額은 9個 現場에 8.4億弗로서 273名의 人力과 1,788臺의 裝備가 남아 있음

	總受注	施工中	施工殘額	人員	裝備
計	9,396百萬弗	1,419	837	273名 (941)	1,788臺
이라크	6,441	1,208	755	273 (628)	1,316
쿠웨이트	2,955	211	82	- (313)	472

　　　* ( )는 事態發生時 人員임

△　債權등 資産現況

- 事態發生時 我國業體가 가지고 있던 債權은 總 992百萬弗相當임 (쿠웨이트 72, 이라크 920)

    * 未收金 :　　　　　　　　　　　 67百萬弗
     留保金 :　　　　　　　　　 168 ”
     工事代金으로 받은 어음 : 598 ”
     原油未船積分등 其他: 159 ”

- 債權外에도 裝備 및 資材殘存價格 43百萬弗과 工事用 預置金등 25百萬弗 相當의 資産이 있음

- 債務現況은 601百萬弗相當(쿠웨이트117, 이라크 484)으로

    契約履行保證등 各種保證 281百萬弗 ,
    現地金融 282百萬弗 ,
    外上買入金등 38百萬弗임

6 - 1

0059

當面 課題

△ 人力撤收의 限界

- 勤勞者 身邊安全에 最優先 力點을 두고 撤收를 推進한 結果 9.6 現在 總 941名中 668名이 撤收하여 273名이 殘留하고 있음

- 이라크는 우리業體가 施工한 施設의 試運轉 및 維持管理를 위한 必須 要員의 殘留를 要求하면서 Supporting Letter 發給을 遲延시키고 있고 비자發給도 어려운 形便임

- 發注處 許可없이 現場撤收時는 契約違反으로 發注處로부터 保證没收, 債權回收不能등 問題發生 憂慮

△ 業體의 資金壓迫

- 금번 事態로 工事代金受領, 留保金解除, 어음決濟등의 遲延으로 인하여 今年末까지 進出業體는 金融償還등 所要資金 約 1,700 億원의 調達에 蹉跌이 豫想됨

- 滿期到來 現地金融에 대한 償還延期, 新規 借入, 保有資産處分에 의한 自體調達등으로 現地所要 1,000億원의 確保는 可能하나 외상機資材代, 撤收費用등 700餘億원의 國內所要資金이 不足한 實情임

- 發注處로부터 工事代金의 一部를 原油로 支給하겠다는 通報를 받았으나 經濟制裁措置등으로 인하여 現實的으로 受領不可

△ 業體 追加負擔 費用發生

- 進出業體는 금번 事態로 인하여 工事代金 및 未收金受領 遲延에 따른 金融費用과 人力撤收에 따른 費用등을 追加 負擔하게 되었으며

- 또한 工事中斷에 따른 裝備, 資材등 資産의 毁損, 流失이 不可避하여 相當한 被害가 豫想됨

  ※ 事態가 好轉되지 않을 時 쿠웨이트의 境遇 債權 및 資産은 損失化가 憂慮됨

6 - 2

0060

對 策

△ 人力撤收 支援

- 全面撤收를 原則으로 함. 다만, 發注處가 우리業體의 繼續管理를 바라고 있으므로 我國의 長期的 經濟利益保全등 諸般事項 勘案 最少人力만 殘留하면서 伸縮性있게 對處

    工事中斷 및 撤收의 不可避性과 事態鎭靜時 即刻 工事再開 意思가 있음을 發注處등 關係機關에 通報, 協助要請

    進出業體는 能動的으로 撤收를 推進토록 하고 政府는 外交交涉을 통한 Supporting Letter 및 비자發給등 必要한 支援을 함

    未撤收 人力에 대하여는 生必品을 充分히 確保토록 하고 非常連絡網을 構築하면서 狀況惡化時 즉각 緊急待避토록 措置

    工事現場 撤收時에는 裝備,資材등 資産의 毁損과 流失 防止를 위하여 移動禁止裝置를 하던지, 現地人을 雇傭하여 管理를 委託하는등 損失 極小化에 最大한 努力

    ※ 이라크 總 殘留人員 273名中 現代建設이 9.10 - 9.25까지 123名을 撤收할 計劃으로 있어 向後 殘留豫定人員은 150名임

△ 業體에 대한 資金支援

- 滿期到來 現地金融등에 대하여는 償還延期 또는 新規借入 承認을 하도록 하고

- 國內不足資金에 대하여는 國內金融機關에서 支援對策 講究

△ 追加費用 補塡對策

- 工事現場撤收나 工事中斷 및 遲延에 대하여는 發注處,監督技術會社 및 資材供給者등에게 特別危險으로 인한 不可抗力狀況을 書面通報하여 免責등 損失 最少化 措置

- 금번 事態로 인한 追加 費用發生에 대하여는 證憑資料를 確保하여 事態가 正常化된 後 클레임을 提起하고

- 政府는 外交채널을 통하여 發注國에 工事中斷 및 撤收의 不可避性을 說得시키고 工事代金 및 未收金 支拂을 促求

6 - 3

0061

1. 國別 進出現況

單位 : 百萬弗

國別	業體名	契約額		施工殘額	人員		裝備 (臺)	備考
		件數	金額		當初	現在		
計		9	1,419	837	941	273	1,788	
쿠웨이트	現代建設	4	211	82	293		434	
	其 他				20		38	
	小計	4	211	82	313		472	
이라크	現代建設	2	857	755	499	215	85	
	三星綜合	1	204	-	64	39	116	
	正友開發	2	147	-	25	2	10	
	其 他				40	17	1,105	
	小計	5	1,208	755	628	273	1,316	

6 - 4

0062

2. 債權등 資産現況

△ 債權등 資産現況

單位:百萬弗

業體別	債權					其他 資産			
	계	未收金	留保金	어음	其他	計	資材	裝備	其他
計	992	67	168	598	159	68	22	21	25
(쿠웨이트)	72	32	34	-	6	19	9	5	5
現代	65	32	33	-	-	18	9	5	4
其他	7	-	1	-	6	1	-	-	1
(이라크)	920	35	134	598	153	49	13	16	20
南光	15	-	3	12	-	-	-	-	-
三星	74	3	7	64	-	4	1	3	-
正友	43	9	8	26	-	3	-	-	3
漢陽	12	-	5	-	7	9	1	2	6
現代	765	19	104	496	146	33	11	11	11
其他	11	4	7	-	-	-	-	-	-

△ 債務 現況

單位 : 百萬弗

業體名	計	保證			金 融	未支給金등
		先受金	履 行	其 他		
計	601	91	146	44	282	38
(쿠웨이트)	117	19	36	12	32	18
現代	117	19	36	12	32	18
(이라크)	484	72	110	32	250	20
南光	3	-	3	-	-	-
三星	13	-	9	-	-	4
正友	11	-	7	-	3	1
漢陽	5	-	1	4	-	-
現代	452	72	90	28	247	15

6 - 5

0063

3. '90. 業體別 資金需給 現況

單位 : 億원

區分	業體名	計	月　　別					備　　考
			8月	9	10	11	12	
所要資金	計	1,691	209	759	252	138	333	現地金融償還, 機資材購入貸金 現場維持管理· 工事費, 撤收費
	三星	101	17	24	17	13	30	
	正友	86	-	86	-	-	-	
	現代	1,504	192	649	235	125	303	
資金調達	計	982	161	158	235	125	303	現地金融償還 延期및 新規 借入
	三星	-	-	-		-	-	
	正友	-	-	-		-	-	
	現代	982	161	158	235	125	303	
不足額	計	709	48	601	17	13	30	
	三星	101	17	24	17	13	30	
	正友	86	-	86	-	-	-	
	現代	522	31	491	-	-	-	

6 - 6

0064

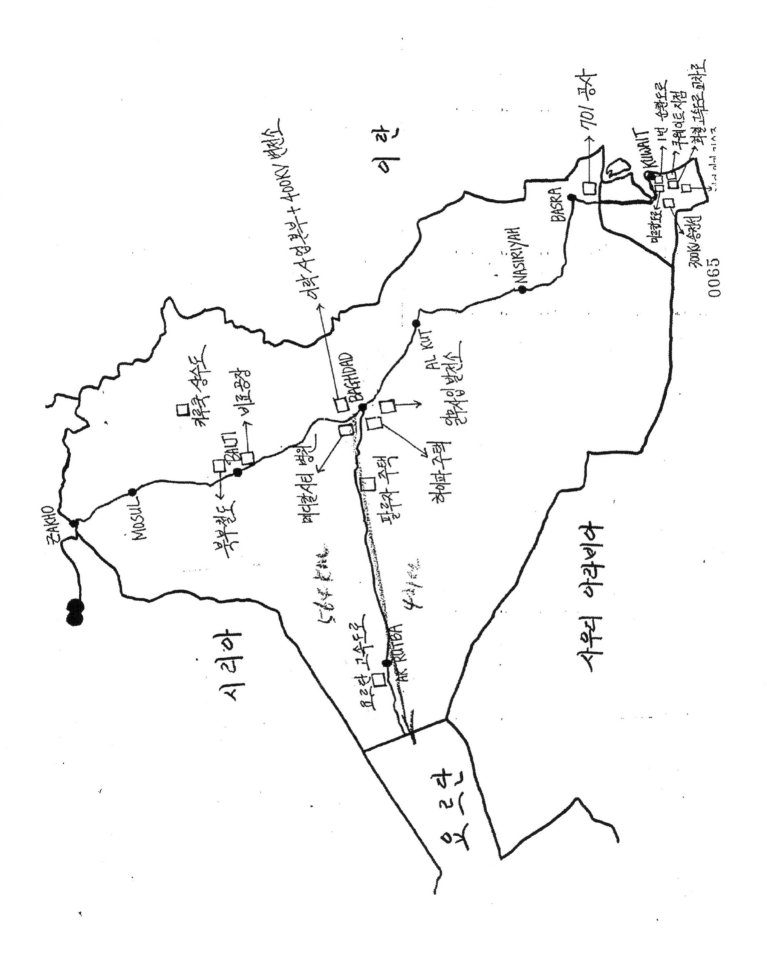

3. 參考圖面

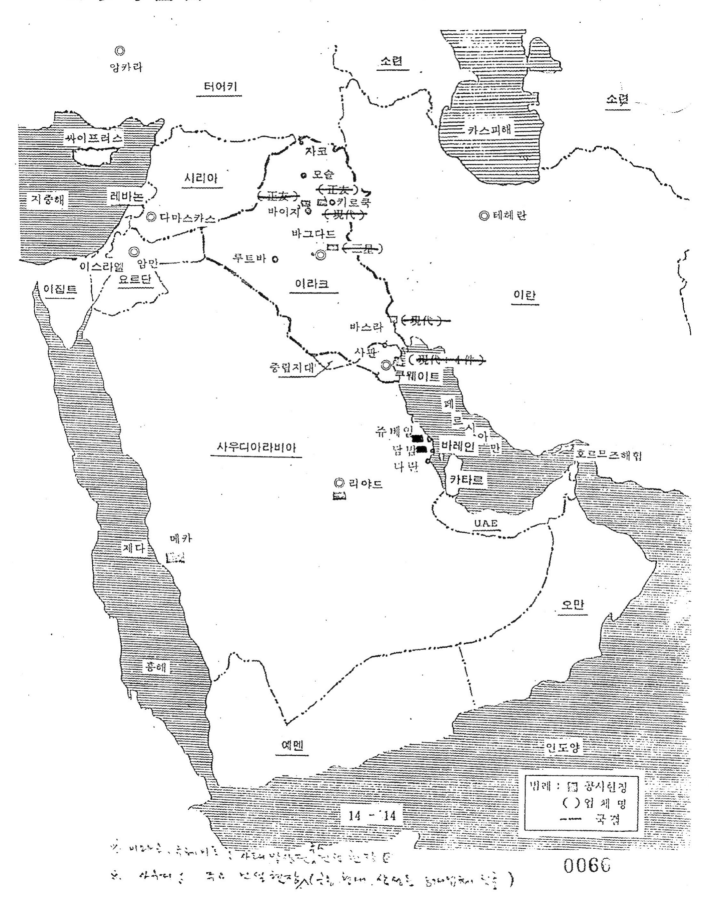

14 - '14

※ 범례: ◨ 공사현장
　　　 ( ) 업체명
　　　 --- 국경

※. 이라크, 쿠웨이트 : 사태 발생전(?)현재 현황 ◨
※. 사우디 : 각종 건설현장(주택, 항만, 시설등 현재진행 현황)

Ⅱ. 교민신변 안진 대책

1. 교민 분포도

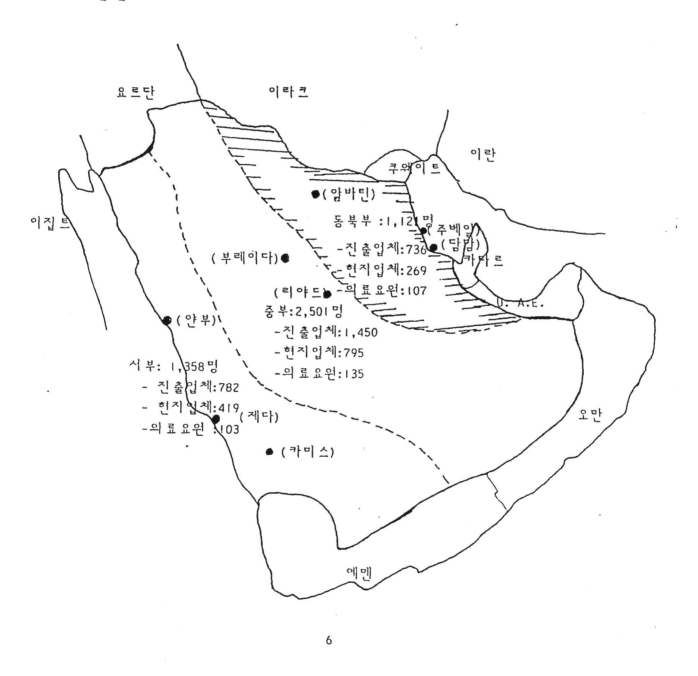

요르단 　이라크

이란

쿠웨이트

이집트

● (암바틴)

동북부 : 1,12?명
- 진출입체 : 736
- 현지입체 : 269
- 의료요원 : 107

주베일
(담맘)
카타르
U. A. E.

(부레이다) ●

(리야드) ●

중부 : 2,501명
- 진출입체 : 1,450
- 현지입체 : 795
- 의료요원 : 135

(얀부) ●

서부 : 1,358명
- 진출입체 : 782
- 현지입체 : 419 (제다)
- 의료요원 : 103

오만

● (카미스)

예맨

6

0067

기안용지 상단 여백의 손글씨 메모

기 안 용 지

분류기호 문서번호	기협	(전화 :)	시 행 상 특별취급	
보존기간	영구·준영구. 10. 5. 3. 1.		장 관	
수 신 처 보존기간				
시행일자	1990.9.14			

보 조 기 관	국장	전결	협 조 기 관	대책반장 아중동국장 심의관 통상1과장	문 서 통 제	
	과장					
기안책임자		홍성화			발 송 인	

경 유 수 신 참 조	건설부장관	발 신 명 의	

제 목	대이라크 경제제재 조치

　

1. 이라크, 쿠웨이트사태에 따른 UN안보리의 대이라크

경제제재 조치 결의안 661호와 관련, 주한 미국 대사관은 별첨

NONPAPER 에서와 같이 외국 계약자들에 의한 이라크내 노동용역

(lobour services) 제공은 노무자들이 이라크의 강압에 의해 체류

하고 있지 않는한, 동 결의안을 위반하는 것이라면서 각국 정부가

대이라크 경제제재 조치의 효과를 증진시키기 위하여 상품과 같이

service 제공도 엄격하게 규제하여줄 것을 희망하여 왔는 바,

0068 　 /계속...

1505-25(2-1) 일(1)갑
85. 9. 9. 승인 　 "내가아낀 종이 한장 늘어나는 나라살림" 　 190mm×268mm　인쇄용지 2급 60g/㎡
가 40-41 1990. 2. 10.

74 　 걸프 사태 대책 및 조치 5

귀부 업무에 참고하시기 바랍니다.

　　2. 상기관련 이라크 진출 아국 건설업체 들의 공사내용,

공사별 진행현황 및 전망, 대책등에 대해 당부로 회보하여

주시기 바랍니다.　　끝.

첨부 : NONPAPER 1부.　 끝.

예고 : 1990.12.31 일반.

0069

1505-25(2-2) 일(1)을
85. 9. 9. 승인　　"내가아낀 종이 한장 늘어나는 나라살림"　　190㎜×268㎜　인쇄용지 2 급 60g/㎡
가 40-41 1989. 12. 7.

NONPAPER ON IRAQ SANCTIONS: SERVICES

We believe that in the spirit of UNSCR 661 and to achieve the goals it seeks, economic restrictions against Iraq must be applied rigorously and comprehensively. In this context, services as well as goods must be denied to Iraq.

Paragraphs 3B, 3C and 4 of UNSCR 661 prohibit the provision of virtually all services to Iraq or Kuwait by virtue of the prohibition on activities to support trade or to facilitate the flow of financial or economic resources to Iraq and Kuwait.

The provision of services to Iraqi-flagged, -owned or -controlled vessels and aircraft or to vessels and aircraft carrying goods to and from Iraq is clearly contrary to UNSCR 661 since it would promote the export, supply, or transshipment of goods and/or facilitate making available funds to Iraq. In this context, insurance services which support the import or export sectors of the Iraqi economy are also clearly prohibited.

The provision of labor services by foreign contractors in Iraq, when workers are remaining without coercion, in many cases clearly violates resolution 661. Workers in the oil and other export industries, in transportation and even in construction are facilitating Iraqi exports and imports.

More importantly, the provision of these and other services in Iraq delay the day when the crisis will be resolved, and undermine the best possibility for a peaceful outcome.

If host country believes a particular service might not be covered by UNSCR 661, the burden is on the country to make its case. We would be prepared to consult bilaterally on such cases. Ultimately, we believe the appropriate body to make a determination is the Security Council or its designee, and US Sanctions Committee, with the service withheld pending the outcome.

The US legal adviser has agreed that a broad range of services are covered by resolution 661. Furthermore, he notes the purpose and object of resolution 661 was to prevent exports and imports and to deny to Iraq access to financial and economic resources.

We hope all governments will regulate services as strictly as goods to strengthen the impact of resolution 661 and enhance the prospects or achieving its goals.

007C

GENERAL GUIDANCE ON INTERCEPTION PLAN AND NOTICE TO MARINERS

- A. BASIS OF OPERATIONS. THE GOVERNMENT OF KUWAIT HAS, IN THE EXERCISE OF ITS INHERENT RIGHT OF INDIVIDUAL AND COLLECTIVE SELF-DEFENSE, REQUESTED A NUMBER OF GOVERNMENTS TO TAKE SUCH MILITARY OR OTHER STEPS AS ARE NECESSARY TO ENSURE THAT ECONOMIC MEASURES DESIGNED TO RESTORE KUWAITI RIGHTS ARE EFFECTIVELY IMPLEMENTED. (RESOLUTION 661 OF THE UN SECURITY COUNCIL SPECIFICALLY AFFIRMS THE INHERENT RIGHT OF INDIVIDUAL OR COLLECTIVE SELF-DEFENSE, IN RESPONSE TO THE ARMED ATTACK BY IRAQ AGAINST KUWAIT, IN ACCORDANCE WITH ARTICLE 51 OF THE UN CHARTER.) IN PARTICULAR, THE GOVERNMENT OF KUWAIT HAS REQUESTED THE UNITED STATES TO COORDINATE AND COMMENCE MULTINATIONAL NAVAL OPERATIONS TO INTERCEPT MARITIME TRADE WITH IRAQ AND KUWAIT THAT IS PROHIBITED BY RESOLUTION 661. THE UNITED STATES HAS AGREED TO THESE REQUESTS.

- THE ENFORCEMENT OF THE SANCTIONS PROVIDED IN RESOLUTION 661 DEPENDS PRIMARILY ON THE ACTIONS OF NATIONAL AUTHORITIES TO PREVENT PROHIBITED SHIPMENTS FROM ENTERING OR LEAVING THEIR TERRITORIES. INTERCEPTION OPERATIONS WILL REINFORCE THESE NATIONAL ACTIONS AND VIGOROUS DIPLOMATIC EFFORTS TO MAKE THESE SANCTIONS EFFECTIVE. ALL SUCH INTERCEPTION OPERATIONS WILL BE CARRIED OUT IN ACCORDANCE WITH ACCEPTED PRINCIPLES OF INTERNATIONAL LAW.

- B. TRADE TO BE INTERCEPTED. AMONG OTHER THINGS, UNSC RESOLUTION 661 ESTABLISHES MANDATORY SANCTIONS AGAINST: (1) THE EXPORT OF ALL COMMODITIES AND PRODUCTS ORIGINATING IN IRAQ OR KUWAIT AFTER THE DATE OF THE RESOLUTION (AUGUST 6); AND (2) THE EXPORT TO IRAQ OR KUWAIT OF ANY COMMODITIES OR PRODUCTS, WHATEVER THEIR STATE OF ORIGIN, EXCEPT FOR "SUPPLIES INTENDED STRICTLY FOR MEDICAL PURPOSES, AND, IN HUMANITARIAN CIRCUMSTANCES, FOODSTUFFS . . . . ." THESE SANCTIONS APPLY NOTWITHSTANDING ANY CONTRACT ENTERED INTO OR LICENSE GRANTED BEFORE THE DATE OF THE RESOLUTION. ACCORDINGLY, THE FOLLOWING TRADE WILL BE INTERCEPTED:

I. SHIPMENTS FROM IRAQ OR KUWAIT. THE INTERCEPTION OPERATIONS WILL PREVENT THE MARITIME SHIPMENT OF ALL COMMODITIES OR PRODUCTS ORIGINATING IN IRAQ OR KUWAIT, REGARDLESS OF PORT OF EMBARKATION OR TRANSSHIPMENT POINT. THIS WILL INCLUDE ALL PRODUCTS PRODUCED IN IRAQ OR KUWAIT FROM MATERIALS PRODUCED ELSEWHERE.

0071

CONFIDENTIAL

- II. SHIPMENTS FROM IRAQ OR KUWAIT. THE
INTERCEPTION OPERATIONS WILL PREVENT THE MARITIME
SHIPMENT OF ALL COMMODITIES OR PRODUCTS TO IRAQ OR
KUWAIT (WHATEVER THEIR DECLARED FINAL DESTINATION), OR
TO OTHER PORTS IN THE REGION FOR TRANSSHIPMENT TO IRAQ
OR KUWAIT, EXCEPT FOR SUPPLIES INTENDED STRICTLY FOR
MEDICAL PURPOSES. THE BURDEN WILL BE ON THE SHIPPER TO
ESTABLISH THE BONA FIDE CHARACTER OF SUCH SHIPMENTS.
MEDICAL SUPPLIES WILL ONLY BE PERMITTED TO PASS IF AN
APPROPRIATE REQUEST HAS BEEN RECEIVED FROM THE
AUTHORITIES OF THE COUNTRY OF EXPORT OR AN APPROPRIATE
INTERNATIONAL HUMANITARIAN ORGANIZATION, CERTIFYING THE
PRECISE QUANTITY AND TYPE OF SUPPLIES INVOLVED AND THE
MEDICAL PURPOSES FOR WHICH THEY ARE INTENDED. THE
SHIPMENT OF FOODSTUFFS WILL NOT BE PERMITTED AT THIS
TIME.

- C. METHOD OF INTERCEPTION. INTERCEPTION WILL BE
ACCOMPLISHED BY NAVAL FORCES STATIONED IN THE VICINITY
OF THE STRAIT OF HORMUZ, AND OTHER CHOKE POINTS, PORTS
AND PIPELINE TERMINALS AS NEEDED. THE NAVAL UNITS OF
EACH PARTICIPATING COUNTRY WILL ACT UNDER NATIONAL
COMMAND, UNDER OVERALL COORDINATION BY THE UNITED
STATES IN ACCORDANCE WITH THE REQUEST OF THE GOVERNMENT
OF KUWAIT.

- NOTICE OF INTERCEPTION OPERATIONS WILL BE
PUBLISHED AS SOON AS POSSIBLE IN INTERNATIONAL NOTICE
TO MARINER'S AND PROMULGATED IN OTHER APPROPRIATE
CHANNELS, INCLUDING LOCAL MARINE BROADCASTS. SPECIAL
LIAISON WILL BE ESTABLISHED WITH STATES IN THE AREA,
STATES WHOSE FLAG VESSELS CONDUCT SUBSTANTIAL
OPERATIONS IN THE AREA, AND OTHER APPROPRIATE
AUTHORITIES, WITH THE OBJECTIVE OF OBTAINING
INFORMATION AND COOPERATION FROM THESE GOVERNMENTS AND
MINIMIZING DISRUPTION TO LEGITIMATE MARITIME COMMERCE.

- COMMERCIAL SOURCES, INTELLIGENCE SOURCES,
MILITARY AND NAVAL ASSETS, AND OTHER MEANS WILL BE USED
TO IDENTIFY SHIPS THOUGHT TO BE CARRYING CARGO TO OR
FOR IRAQ OR KUWAIT. SHIPS ENTERING OR LEAVING THE
INTERCEPTION AREAS WILL, AS APPROPRIATE, BE ASKED TO
PROVIDE APPROPRIATE IDENTIFICATION AND INFORMATION AS
TO THEIR ORIGIN OR DESTINATION AND THEIR CARGO. THIS
INFORMATION WILL BE NORMALLY OBTAINED BY RADIO
COMMUNICATION BETWEEN THE INTERCEPTION VESSEL AND THE
SHIP SEEKING TO ENTER OR LEAVE THE AREA.

- IF THE INTERCEPTION VESSEL IS UNABLE TO OBTAIN
ADEQUATE INFORMATION IN THIS MANNER, IT WILL BOARD THE
SHIP AND CONDUCT SUCH INSPECTION OF RECORDS OR CARGO AS
MAY BE NECESSARY OR (IF NECESSARY FOR OPERATIONAL
REASONS) ESCORT THE SHIP TO A NEARBY PORT FOR SUCH

CONFIDENTIAL

0072

INSPECTION. WHERE NECESSARY, THE INTERCEPTION VESSEL WILL CONTACT THE LIAISON AUTHORITIES OF THE INTERCEPTION FORCE OR APPROPRIATE NATIONAL AUTHORITIES TO CONFIRM INFORMATION PROVIDED BY THE SHIP. WARSHIPS, AUXILIARIES, AND OTHER SHIPS THAT ARE STATE-OWNED OR OPERATED AND USED ONLY ON GOVERNMENT NONCOMMERCIAL SERVICE ENJOY SOVEREIGN IMMUNITY AND ARE NOT SUBJECT TO BOARDING AND INSPECTION. THEY MAY, HOWEVER, BE INTERCEPTED AND DIVERTED.

- ONCE THESE INQUIRIES OR SEARCH IS COMPLETED, THE SHIP IN QUESTION WILL NOT BE PERMITTED TO PROCEED UNLESS THE COMMANDER OF THE INTERCEPTION VESSEL IS SATISFIED THAT THE INTERCEPTED VESSEL IS NOT IN VIOLATION OF THE SANCTIONS REGIME.

- RATHER THAN BE SUBJECT TO A SEARCH, INTERCEPTED SHIPS WILL BE PERMITTED TO TURN AWAY FROM THE INTERCEPTION AREA, IN WHICH CASE THE INTERCEPTION FORCE WILL NOT INSIST ON THE ABOVE PROCEDURES OR TAKE FURTHER ACTION AGAINST THE SHIP.

- D. ENFORCEMENT OF INTERCEPTION. TO THE MAXIMUM POSSIBLE EXTENT, INTERCEPTION WILL BE ENFORCED WITHOUT THE USE OF FORCE. OTHER METHODS WILL BE USED TO INDUCE A SHIP TO PROVIDE NECESSARY INFORMATION, TO SUBMIT TO NECESSARY INSPECTION OR TO REFRAIN FROM PROCEEDING ON ITS INTENDED COURSE, INCLUDING RADIO AND VISUAL COMMUNICATIONS, MANEUVERS BY THE INTERCEPTION VESSEL, AND WARNING SHOTS. WHERE NECESSARY THE MINIMUM PROPORTIONATE FORCE NEEDED TO COMPEL COMPLIANCE WILL BE USED, INCLUDING BOARDING OPERATIONS OR DISABLING THE SHIP. ANY HOSTILE ACTION BY THE SHIP WILL BE COUNTERED BY NECESSARY AND PROPORTIONATE FORCE.

- E. COORDINATION. THE UNITED STATES, IN RESPONSE TO THE REQUEST IT HAS RECEIVED FROM THE GOVERNMENT OF KUWAIT, IS COMMUNICATING WITH ALL OTHER STATES WHO HAVE BEEN ASKED BY THE GOVERNMENT OF KUWAIT TO PARTICIPATE IN THIS MULTINATIONAL EFFORT, FOR PURPOSE OF COORDINATING THE VARIOUS NATIONAL FORCES. WE WILL BE WORKING WITH THESE OTHER NATIONS TO ESTABLISH APPROPRIATE MECHANISMS FOR COORDINATION, INCLUDING THE ESTABLISHMENT OF CHANNELS FOR COORDINATION OF INFORMATION ON MARITIME TRAFFIC AND APPROACHES TO GOVERNMENTAL AUTHORITIES, FOR OPERATIONAL COORDINATION, AND FOR LOGISTICAL ARRANGEMENTS.

CONFIDENTIAL

0073

외　무　부

종　별 : 지　급

번　호 : BGW-0726　　　　　　　　　　일　시 : 90 0915 1200

수　신 : 장관(건설,노동,기정,중근동,기재,정일)

발　신 : 주 이라크 대사

제　목 : COE 발주공사

대:WBG-437

1. 일부발주처에서는 아국업체의 의사와는 관계없이 필수요원이라고 간주할경우 출국동의를 기피하거나 거부하고있으나 기타 아국인력에 대하여는 지금까지 주재국의 우호적인 협조하에 철수를 진행중에있음

2. 미국, 영국등 주요서방제국과 일본등 파병을 하거나 강력한 경제 제재조치를 취한 국가에 대하여는 적대국으로 간주, 이들 국민을 주요산업시설 또는 호텔에 분산억류중에 있으며 방글라, 파키스탄등 회교국으로서 파병을 결정한 국민에 대하여도 소매상에서조차 식품등 생필품의 판매를 거부하는등 완전히 적대시하고 있는 실정임

3. 이러한 분위기에서 아국업체가 사우디내 미군막사 건설공사에 참여할경우, 이. 이전중 쌓아온 아국업체의 대주재국 신임도가 크게 손상될것임은 물론이고, 나아가 아국이 군사시설을 지원했다는 이유로 적대국으로 간주, 현재 진행중인 공사의 시공관리, 또는 사태진정후의 신규수주 활동등에 많은 지장이 초래될것이며 또 지금까지 우호적인 협조하에 진행중인 아국교민(9.15 현재 206 명 잔류)의 철수도 그안전이 더이상 보장될수 없을것이며 사태가 악화될경우 우호국의 입장에서 적대국으로 반전 아국교민에 대한 인질억류 가능성도 전혀 배제할수 없기때문에 동 공사에 대한 아국업체의 참여는 명분과 실리면에서 전혀 고려대상이 될수없으며 바람직스럽지 못한것으로 사료됨

4. 뿐만아니라 군사대치가 지속되고있는 전쟁위험지역인 사우디에서 건설공사를 시행할경우 막대한 인력손실의 위험부담을 져야하는바 이에대하여도 충분한 고려가 있어야 할것임.끝

(대사 최봉름-차관)

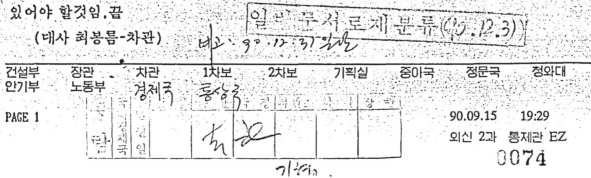

건설부	장관	차관	1차보	2차보	기획실	중아국	정문국	청와대
안기부	노동부	경제국	통상국					

PAGE 1　　　　　　　　　　　　　　　　　　　90.09.15　19:29

외신 2과 통제관 EZ

0074

외 무 부

종 별 : 지 급

번 호 : SBW-0835

일 시 : 90 0915 1400

수 신 : 장관(중근동,경이,건설부,기정,노동부)

발 신 : 주 사우디 대사

제 목 : C.O.E 발주 공사 관련 보고

연:WSB-398

1, 연호 관련 아래보고함

가. 공사참여 필요성

-동 공사는 공사여건이 양호하여 그수익성 보장이 거의 확실시 되고 있고 앞으로 상당량(최소한 10 억불 이상)의 공사 물량이 계속해서 발주될 전망임.

-COE 측은 동공사의 시급성을 감안 적격업체 선정을 위한 P.Q 신청을 아국 11 개업체를 비롯한 영, 독, 이태리, 불, 일, 대만, 필등 세계각국의 수십개 업체로부터 이미 이를 받아 현재 그 심사가 계속중이며 근간 최종 적격업체가 확정되어 입찰초청장이 발급되어 질것임.

-이러한 일련의 상황을 판단해 볼때 우리업체의 동공사 참여는 이를 권장하는것이 좋을것으로 사료됨.

나. 이라크측 반응

-동공사에 참여하는 경우 이라크측의 반응을 고려하지 않을 수는 없겠으나 유엔 안보회결의의 경제제재 조치에 우리정부가 이미참여 결정을 발표하였음을 감안할때 우리업체의 COE 공사참여는 민간차원의 공사수주 행위로 보아야할것이며 우리업체의 동공사 참여를 제지해야할 필요성은 없을것으로 보여짐.

다. 공사수주시 유의사항

-COE 공사관련 우리업체의 수주활동 상황은 일체 대외비로 보안이 유지되어야 할것임(신문보도금지등)

-인력(최소한 800 명)자재(프리훼이브, 천막등)등 장비확보가 계약일로부터1 개월 이내에 동시에 해결되어야 하기때문에 이에대한 특별대책이 필요할것임.

-전쟁위험에 대비한 수익성과 안전성 보장등이 계약전에 검토되어야할것임.끝

중아국   차관   2차보   경제국   정와대   안기부   건설부   노동부

PAGE 1

(대사 주병국-국장)
예고:90.12.31 까지

일반문서로 재분류(90.12.31)

암 호 수 신

종 별 : 지 급

번 호 : SBW-0853

일 시 : 90 0919 1100

수 신 : 장 관(중근동, 경이, 건설부)

발 신 : 주 사우디 대사

제 목 : 공사 정보보고

연:SBW-847

0. 미공병단측의 군막사시설 공사에대한 현장설명(9.19) 주요내용파악보고

가. 규모:5 천명숙소 6 개소(6 개지역)

나. 계약방식:일괄계약(FIXED LUMP SUM)

다. 입찰서 제출마감:9.25(화),

라. 조건

-이행보증: 계약액의 10%

-기타보증(AP, B, 유보금)은 없음

-재원:미정부

-지불화폐:사우디리알

-관급자재:없음

-공기:104 일.끝

(대사 주병국-국장)

중아국   경제국   건설부

PAGE 1

건 설 부

해건 30600-80   (503-7396)   1990. 9. 28

수신 외무부 장관

제목 대이라크 경제제재

1. 통일 2065-1250('90. 9. 17)의 관련입니다.

2. 위관련 당부 소관사항에 대하여 다음과 같이 통보하오며, 이라크 건설 관련 대책에 대하여는 원활히 추진되도록 적극 협조하여 주시기 바랍니다.

다   음

가. 대이라크 경제제재 조치에 대한 검토의견

정부가 8.9 국무총리주재 관계부처 장관회의에서 대이라크 경제 제재 조치의 일환으로 양지역에서 건설공사를 수주하지 않기로 한 조치와 전쟁중인 국가에 대하여는 도급허가하지 않도록 되어 있는 당부의 도급허가업무처리지침 (해건 30600-14842, '90. 6. 15)에 의하여 사태발생과 동시 수주가 중지 되었으며 사태발생이후 해외건설협회에 수차 확인 지시한 바 있어 현재까지 도급허가 실적이 없는 상태로 별도의 조치가 불요함.

나. 이라크 건설진출현황 및 대책

(1) 진출현황 ('90. 9. 25 현재)

단위 : 백만불

구분	공사명	계약액	시공잔액	인원	공정(%)
계	5 건	1,208	755	74	
현대	701 수리조선소	754	754	20	-
	키르쿡 상수도공사	103	1	20	98.8

0078

해건 30600- 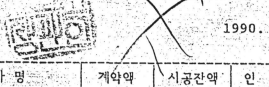 1990. 9. 28

구분	공 사 명	계약액	시공잔액	인 원	장비(%)
삼성	바그다드-아브그레이브 간 도로공사	204	-	32	100
정우	북부철도공사	101	-	2	100
	제 4비료공장 공사	46	-	-	100

* 하자보수중인 공사현장 및 지사 요원 82명 제외.

　　　(2) 공사 추진현황

　　　　　· 키르쿡 상수도공사는 최소 인력으로 마무리 작업중이나
외자재 반입불가로 시공 중단상태임.

　　　　　· 착공준비중이던 701 수리조선소 착공을 유보중임.

　　　　　· 기타 완공공사 하자보수기간에 있는 공사는 최소인력
으로 마무리작업 및 행정처리중에 있으나 공사는 거의 중단상태임.

　　　(3) 전　망

　　　　　· 이라크는 우리업체가 시공한 시설의 시운전 및 유지
관리를 위한 필수요원의 잔류를 요구하면서 출국확인서 발급을 지연시키고 있고 비자
발급에 이락측의 까다로운 심사로 인력 철수에 한계가 있음.

　　　　　· 금번 사태로 공사대금수령, 유보금 해제, 어음결제등의
지연으로 금년말까지 진출업체는 금융상환등 소요자금 약 1,700억원의 조달에 차질이
예상됨 (미수금등 920백만불의 채권보유).

　　　　　· 진출업체는 금번 사태로 인하여 공사대금 및 미수금
수령지연에 따른 금융비용과 인력철수에 따른 비용등을 추가 부담하게 되었으며 또한
공사중단에 따른 장비, 자재등 자산의 훼손, 유실이 불가피하여 상당한 피해가
예상됨.

0079

(4) 대 책

　　o 인력철수지원

　　　　· 공사중단 및 철수의 불가피성과 사태진정시 즉각
공사재개 의사가 있음을 발주처등 관계기관에 통보, 협조 요청

　　　　· 진출업체는 능동적으로 철수를 추진토록 하고
정부는 외교교섭을 통한 출국확인서 및 비자발급등 필요한 지원을 함.

　　　　· 미철수인력에 대하여는 생필품을 충분히 확보토록
하고 비상연락망을 구축하면서 상황 악화시 즉각 긴급 대피토록 조치

　　o 업체에 대한 자금지원

　　　　· 만기도래 현지금융등에 대하여는 상환연기 또는
신규 차입승인을 하도록 하고,

　　　　· 국내 부족자금에 대하여는 국내 금융기관에서
지원대책 강구

　　o 추가비용등 손실보전대책

　　　　· 공사현장 철수나 공사중단 및 지연에 대하여는
발주처, 감독 기술회사 및 자재공급회사에게 특별위험으로 인한 불가항력 상황을
서면 통보하여 면책등 손실 최소화 조치

　　　　· 이번 사태로 인한 추가비용 발생에 대하여는
증거자료를 첨부하여 사태가 정상화된 후 클레임을 제기하고,

　　　　· 정부는 외교채널을 통하여 발주국에 공사중단 및
철수의 불가피성을 설득시키고 공사대금 및 미수금 지불을 촉구

0080

해건 30600-   1990. 9. 28

　　　　　ㅇ 장기대책

　　　　　　　• 중동지역 공사는 전쟁위험 경우를 감안 근로자 안전
대책을 강구하고 위험부담을 반영하여 수익성이 확실한 공사를 선별수주

　　　　　　　• 선진국 및 동구권등 신시장 개척으로 시장다변화 추진

　　　　　　　• 수주전략은 노동집약형에서 기술집약형으로 시공위주에서
엔지니어링 및 관리감독형으로 전환.

예고문 : 1990. 12. 31 에일 반문서에
　　　　의거 일반문서로 재 분류됨.

　　　　　　　　　　　접 수 필 (1990. 12. 31.)

　　　　　　　건　　설　　부　　장　　관

　　　　　　　　　　　　　　　　　　　　　0081

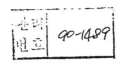

건   설   부

해건 30600-130   (503-7416)   1990.10.30
수신 외무부장관
참조 통상국장
제목 대이라크 경제제재

1990. 12. 31. 에 대고문에
의거 일반문서도 재분류됨

　1. 통일 2065-2525('90.10.17) 관련입니다.
　2. 위관련 유엔 안보리결의 661호 (대이라크 경제제재)의 이행상황에
관한 질의서중 당부 소관사항인 이라크, 쿠웨이트로 부터 건설수주 중지에
대한 답변서를 첨부와 같이 송부합니다.

첨부 : 안보리결의 661호 이행조치에 관한 질문에 대한 답변. 끝.

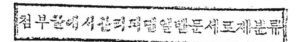

첨부물에서관리대형일반문서로재분류

전 결			결재 (공람)
접수일자	1990. 11. 2	번호 446	
처 리 과			

건   설   부   장

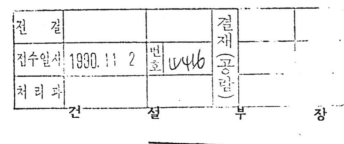

건설경제국장

0082

안보리 결의 661호 이행조치에 관한 질문에 대한 답변
===

1. 법률적 체재

    a) 귀국이 안보리결의 661호의 이행조치를 취하기 위한 법률적 기반은?

    답) 해외건설촉진법에 (법률 제 3316호) 근거하여 행정지도하고 있음

    Ans) The Korean government advises and guides Korean
          contractors to abide by the U.N sanction according
          to the relevant provisions of the "Overseas
          Construction Promotion Law".

2. 강제집행

    a) 귀국은 개인 또는 기업에 의한 안보리 결의 661호 위반을 방지하기
       위하여 어떠한 강제조치 (벌금,압류,몰수등)를 시행하고 있는가?

    답) 별도의 강제조치는 없으나 정부의 지도에 적극 호응하고 있음

    Ans) There is no specific punishment-directive
          against the contractors.
          All the contractors, however, faithfully
          respect the government guideline so far.

0083

3. 기   타

   a) 안보리 결의 661호를 이행하는데 있어서 귀국에게는 어떠한
       문제점이 있는가 ?

   답) 아국은 이라크와 쿠웨이트에 5개 건설업체 941명의 인원이
        진출하여 9건의 공사를 시공중에 있었으며 제재조치로 인한
        보복 조치가 있을 경우 인명의 안전위험 및 직.간접 피해가
        15억불에 이를 것으로 추정되고 있음

   Ans) When the Persian Gulf crisis broke out, 5 Korean
         contractors and 941 construction workers were
         involved in 9 projects.
         Because of U.N sanction and expected retaliations
         by Iraqi authorities, Korea might suffer from
         project losses amounted to 1.5 billion U.S. dollars,
         and security burdens of Korean construction
         workers and employees as well as other indirect
         losses.

   b) 안보리 결의 661호를 이행함에 있어서 동 결의 채택 이전에
       계약이 체결되었거나 허가 부여된 사안에 대해서 귀국은 어떠한
       조치를 취했는가 ?

   답) 시공중인 공사를 중단 철수중에 있음

   Ans) Because of the U.N. sanction, all the projects
         have been suspended and the withdrawal is in
         process now.

0084

매일경제신문　91.1.10.

페灣태풍 海外건설 타격

건설업계 戰雲지역 공사受注 중단

근로자 철수·안전대책 부심
동남아·蘇시장 진출총력
發注금액 작년비 20~30% 줄듯

페르시아灣에 전쟁위기를 발부할것으로 전망했으나 페灣사태로 발주규모가 개업체가 13개현장에 진척, 공사를 진행하고 있다.

이에따라 국내해외건설업계는 올 한해동안 中東지역으로부터 26억8천만달러에 달하는 각종 건설공사를 수주할것으로 내다봤으나 페르시아灣사태로 수주활동이 위축되면서 이중 20~30%가량 수주물량이 줄어들것으로 전망하고 있다.

정부와 업계는 中東지역에의 수주활동에 이같은 차질이 예상됨에 따라 대신 東南亞·美國·蘇聯등지에서의 수주활동을 강화해 나가기로 했다.

특히 日本 건설시장에 대한 진출을 확대하고 美國시장에 대해서는 소규모 개발형 공사와 국내현지법인의 발주공사에 적극참여·수주물량을 늘려나갈 계획이다.

또 국교수립을 계기로對蘇진출을 한층 강화하고 인도네시아 말레이시아를 중심으로한東南亞에 대한수주 활동도 활발히펴기로했다.

국내업계가 현재 추진중인 주요 해외건설공사는 現代의 리비아 라스라누프 석유화학단지조성(4억6천8백만달러) 雙龍建設의 인도네시아 신산부프 관용빌딩공사(1억8천2백만달러)와 인도네시아인 터컨티넨탈호텔건립(7천만달러) 등이다.

이때문에 올 해외건설수주는 연초부터 벽에 부서는 잠정적으로 수주활동을 중단키로 했다.

업계는 현재 이라크에서의 공사를 전면중단하거나 철수작업을 진행중이며, 이라크국경과 비교적 가까운 거리에 위치해있는 라비아부지역에 쿠웨이트 담만등 사우디아라비아에 대해서도 수주활동을 가능한 자제해나갈 방침이다.

페르시아灣에 전쟁위기가 점차 높아지자 국내 건설업계는 中東건설공사 수주를 포기하거나 상담을 중단하고 전쟁우려 지역 근로자의 철수및 안전대책에 비상이 걸렸다.

현대 大宇등 건설업계는 日本 東南亞건설시장을 대상으로 수주활동을 강화하고 蘇聯등 北方圈에 대한 진출확대를 모색하며 해외건설수주의 전략을 바꾸는등 대책마련에 부심하고 있다.

건설부에 따르면 올해에 사우디아라비아 이라크이랍등 中東지역국가들은 2백억달러수준의 각종공사에는 현재 極東建設·韓逸사우디아라비아동부지역에는 현재...

외 무 부

종   별 :

번   호 : SBW-0079   일   시 : 91 0113 2000

수   신 : 장 관(중근동,재무부,한은,건설부,기정)

발   신 : 주 사우디 대사

제   목 : 걸프사태관련 건설업체 재무관리지도

1. 최근 걸프사태와 관련하여 향후 전쟁발발등으로 사태가 악화될 경우 우리

   건설업체의   재무관리상   발생될수있는   문제점에   대한   대책을   사전에
강구함으로서건설공사 미수금 발생 및 전쟁피해로 인한 손실을 최소화 할수있도록
다음사항에

   대사항에 대한 처리지 침을 시달하였음

   가. 공사 시공상의 불이익 예방대책

   나. 공사 미수금의 적기회수 대책

   다. 전시 회계처리등 재무관리대책

2. 상세내용은 파편 송부위계임

   (대사 주병국-국장)

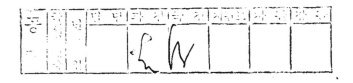

중아국   2차보   경제국   안기부   재무부   건설부   친은

건 설 부

해외 30600- **1263**   (503-7396)   1991. 1. 17

경유 외무부 장관   (1년)

수신 수신처 참조

제목 페만전쟁 발발에 따른 해외건설 조치

'91. 1. 17 페만전 발발에 따라 중동지역 해외건설에 대한 조치사항을 다음과 같이 통지하오니 진출인력의 안전과 효율적 공사 수행을 위한 업체 지도에 만전을 기하여 주시기 바랍니다.

다   음

1. 대상지역

사우디, 리비아, 이란, 카탈, 예멘, U.A.E, 바레인, 오만, 요르단, 이집트

2. 조치내용

가. 현장투입 인력안전 우선, 사태 악화에 따른 안전지대로의 철수 및 대피를 위한 비상대책 수립 철저

나. 신규공사 수주 억제, 다만 발주처가 요청하는 긴급한 공사, 수익성이 있는 공사는 사전에 건설부와 협의후 수주

다. 시공중공사 완공위주 시행

라. 각현장과 본사와의 24시간 연락망 유지

마. 사태 악화에 대비 인력 안전보호를 위한 대피 또는 철수에 대비하여 발주처와 사전 협의 철저.

0087

해외 30600-　　　　　　　　　　　　　　　　　　　　1991. 1. 17

건　설　부　장　관

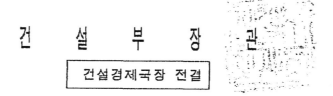

건설경제국장 전결

수신처 : 주사우디아라비아, 리비아, 이란, 카탈, 예멘, 아랍에미레이트,
　　　　　바레인, 오만, 요르단, 이집트대사.

0088

주 이 란 대 사 관

이란(건) 0II12 -24   I99I. I. 22

수 신 : 외무부장관(사본:건설부장관,노동부장관)

참 조 : 중동아국장,국제경제국장

제 목 : 아국 건설업체 노무관리 현황검토보고

　　　아국 건설업체의 건설현장 노무관리 현황 (4/4)을 별첨과같이 검토

보고합니다.

첨 부 : 아국 건설업체 노무관리 현황 검토 (4/4). 끝.

　　　　주 　이 　란 　대

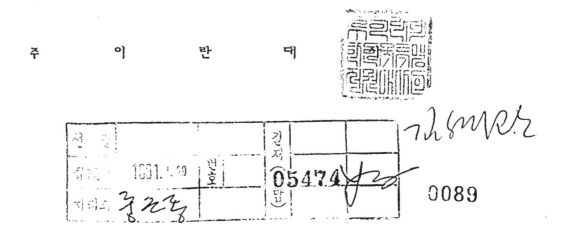

0089

아국 건설 업체 노무관리 현황 검토 보고

1991. I. 22

주 이 란 대 사 관

0090

아국 건설 업체 노무관리 현황 검토(4/4)

I. 인원현황

가. 총 괄(90. 12. 31현재)

(단위: 명)

업체명	계	한 국 인			현 지 인			제3국인
		소 계	임직원	기능직	소 계	사 원	기능직	기능직
계	3,490	798	232	566	2,624	111	2,513	68
대 림	1,212	388	94	294	756	37	719	68
대 우	1,237	270	67	203	967	30	937	
신 화	959	118	56	62	841	42	799	
쌍 용	82	22	15	7	60	2	58	

✻ 제3국인 = 필리핀인

나. 한국인과 현지인과의 대비(월말기준)

(단위: 명)

구 분	10 월		11 월		12 월	
	인력수	%	인력수	%	인력수	%
계	3,707	100.0	4,264	100.0	3,490	100.0
한 국 인	811	21.9	807	18.9	798	22.9
현 지 인	2,836	76.5	3,398	79.7	2,624	75.2
제3국인	60	1.6	59	1.4	68	1.9

0091

다. 아국 인력 입, 출국 대비

(단위: 명)

구 분	I0 월	II 월	I2 월
월 초 인 력	80I	8II	802
입 국 인 력	63	53	7I
출 국 인 력	53	62	75
	(I8.9)	(-I4.5)	(-5.3)
월 말 인 력	8II	802	798

＊(　) 내는 출국 인력 대비 입국 인력의 증가율(%)

바. 전년 동기 인력 대비 (월말 기준)

(단위: 명)

연 도 ＼ 월	I0	II	I2
89	868	863	978
90	8II	807	798
증 가율(%)	-6.6	-6.5	-I8.4

＊ 전년동기 대비 월평균 인력 ~~II.9%~~ I0.L% 증가추세

0092

2. 노사 협의회 운영등

　가. 운영내용

　　(1) 일　자 : 매월 1회 (주로 하순)

　　(2) 장　소 : 각 현장 캠프사무실

　　(3) 참석자 : 노사 협의회 대표 전원

　　(4) 주요 토의 사항 (발췌)

　　　· 건강관리 철저

　　　　- 환절기 건강관리 수칙 주지

　　　　- 아침식사 개선 (카스테라 → 식빵)

　　　· 후생복리 철저

　　　　- 매점 판매 물품 능향

　　　　- 세탁물 건조대 보수등

　　　　- 식당 세척대등 보수, 청결유지

　　　· 안전관리 철저

　　　　- 동절기 대비 화재예방 대책

　　　　- 동절기 안전사고 예방

　　　· 정서 함양

　　　　- 비디오 테이프 증량 및 질 향상

　　　　- 연말 연시 행사 (노래, 장기자랑 등)

　　　　- 식사 시간 음악 방송

　　　· 준법 정신 함양

　　　-무 면허 운전 금지

　　　-무단외출 금지

　　　· 기타 사항

　　　　- 현지인과의 지속적인 관계 개선

　　　　- 현지인 근무의욕 고취방안

0093

(5) 주요 이행 사항

- 건강관리 : 음주 행위 금지, 아침식사 개선등
- 안전교육 : 동절기 화재 예방, 안전사고 방지
- 정서함양 : 도서실 확장 및 도서량 증량
- 체력단련 : 중추절 체육 대회(배구등)
- 준법정신 함양 : 휴식시간, 외출 버스시간 엄수
- 기타사항 : 크리스마스 카드판매, 연말연시 행사실시등

나. 임금 지급 현황 : 체불 노임없음

다. 사고발생에 대한 진료실적없음.

0094

3. 기타사항 (일반진료)

구 분	계	10 월	11 월	12 월
계	3,609	1,349	1,177	1,163
내 과	2,060	819	691	550
외 과	559	196	157	206
치 과	79	18	33	28
안 과	43	19	17	7
기 타	948	297	279	372

4. 검토의견

가. 국내 인력의 고임금 및 해외근무기피 현상으로 국제 경쟁력 약화 및
   효율적 시공관리에 애로있음. 따라서 수주증대 및 적정공정 추진상
   현지 또는 제3국 인력의 증가 불가피함.

나. 다국적인을 고용, 공사 추진의 경우, 의사소통·감정처리·근로자간 화
   합문제등 노무관리에 특단의 노력 필요함.

0095

아국 건설 업체 현장별 인원 현황(90. 12. 31 현재)

현 장	계	한 국 인			현 지 인			제3국인 (필리핀) 기능직
		소 계	임직원	기능직	소 계	사 원	기능직	
	3,490	798	232	566	2,624	111	2,513	68
대 립	1,213	388	94	294	756	37	719	68
- 본 부	33	10	6	4	23	23	-	
- KANGAN	714	223	44	179	491	10	481	
- SHAHID RAJAI	465	155	44	111	242	4	238	68
대 우	1,237	270	67	203	967	30	937	
- 본 부	54	24	16	8	39	20	10	
- LOT 6	6	1	1	-	5	1	4	
- LOT 4B	808	164	16	138	644	5	639	
- AHWAZ	369	81	24	57	289	4	284	
신 화	959	118	56	62	841	42	799	
- 본 부	7	3	2	1	4	3	1	
- AROMATICS	952	115	54	61	837	39	798	
쌍 용	82	22	15	7	6	2	58	
- 본 부	4	2	2	-	2	1	1	
- KHARG	78	20	13	-	58	1	57	

0096

건 설 부

해건 30600-*1939*   (503-7416)   1991. 1. 23.

수신 외무부 장관   (1년)

제목 걸프사태에 따른 공사관리 대책

　　　1. 최근 걸프사태는 장기화 조짐을 보이는 가운데 이라크의 공격권이
점차 확대되어 가고 있습니다. 따라서 걸프지역 전역(사우디아라비아, 이라크
, 바레인, 카타르, U. A. E)에서 시공중인 공사에 대하여 만약의 위험발생에
대비, 철수 또는 안전지역으로의 대피등 진출인력의 안전조치와 대발주처
관계등의 계약관리, 기자재와 시설등의 공사현장 관리등 종합적인 공사관리
대책이 절실히 요구되는바, 해당 공관으로 하여금 근로자 신변안전에 최우선
역점을 두되, 손실을 최소화할 수 있는 각 현장별 공사관리 대책을 수립
시행토록 하고 그 내용을 보고토록 지급 훈령하여 주시기 바랍니다.

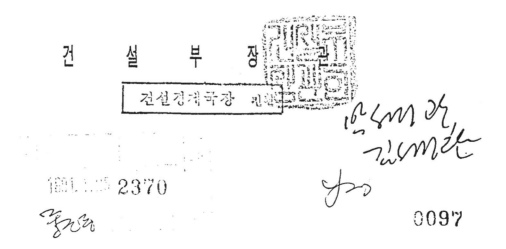

건 설 부 장

건설경제국장

1991. 2370

0097

Ⅱ 工事中斷에 따른 問題點및 對策

〈91.1.31〉

1. 當面課題 및 對策

當 課 題	對 策
ㅇ 工事現場 資産保存 및 管理	ㅇ 保存管理에 最善
· 旣成 ~ 來畢 施工物資 및 ~ 材·裝備	· 現在 狀況에 對한 寫眞記錄 維持와 現地人 委託管理, 盜難防止施設裝置 등으로 資材·裝備 및 施設物의 遺失 防止
· 宿舍등,什器등 支援施設	· 證憑確保를 위한 對發發建設 監理社에 行政措置
	〈旣措置〉 · 工事管理對策 關文指示 6回 · 關聯業體 對策會議開催 5回
ㅇ 施工業體의 資金 壓迫	ㅇ 政府次元에서 關係機關과 協議, 支援 方案마련
· 旣成金受領, 留保金解除, ~ 濟등 遲延	· 滿期到來 現地金融의 期間延長 또는 新規借入 許可
· 現地金融 滿期 到來	· 撤收費用,外上搬資材代등 國內發生 費用을 國內金融에서 支援
· 撤收費 등 追加費用 發生	
ㅇ 進出人力 및 工管理	ㅇ 사우디東部地域을 中·西部로 待避
· 不要不急한 人力 撤收	· 東部地域待避人員을 包含한 中部 人員을 狀況에 따라 西部로 待避,또는 撤收
· 現場管理 必須要 ~ 의 安全 對策	〈旣措置〉 · 防護面 確保와 安全管理 指示 6回 · 關聯業體 對策會議 2回

0098

4 - 2

2. 戰後課題 및 對策

戰 後 課 題	對 策
◦ 追加費用 處理 (不可抗力 認定與否) ・施工物量被爆時 原狀復舊費 ・資材·裝備遺失 또는 損壞 에 따른 被害額 ・人力撤收 및 再動員 費用	◦ 工事中斷이 契約上 不可抗力 條項에 따른 것임을 說得시키고 事態鎭靜후 迅速한 工事再開를 保障하여 施工者 로서의 성실한 姿勢堅持하고 ◦ 事態鎭靜후 追加費用은 契約條件 및 國際補償關聯 法規에 依據 클레임提起 ・專門 國際辯護士 活用과 與件이 같은 外國業體와 共同으로 對處 效果的으로 損失補塡 推進 ※이라크進出 外國業體:23個國 95個社 ・政府次元 外交經路를 통한 積極支援 ・國際司法裁判所에 提訴
◦ 工事 再着工 ・物價上昇에 따른 諸費用 增加와 工事期間 不足 ・發注處의 代金支撥能力 不足으로 資金運用에 蹉跌 ・人力求得難	◦ 徹底한 事前對備로 損失 最少化 ・發注處 및 監理社와 協議,契約 變更 推進 ・原抽受領등 方案 講究 ・제3국人力(中國人力등) 屈備擴大推進 및 管理監督型으로 工事遂行 패턴 轉換 推進

4 - 3

0099

Ⅲ. ●向後 中東建設市場의 展望과 三●戰略

1. 市場展望

○ 短期的으로는 中東情勢의 緊張持續에 따른 軍事費支出의 增大와 發注
中斷, 延期, 取消등 投資 優先順位의 變動으로 油價上昇에도 不拘하고
中東建設市場은 크게 萎縮될 것으로 豫想되나

○ 長期的으로는 油價引上에 따른 中東産油國의 收入增大로 建設發注量은
多少 擴大될 것으로 展望됨

　- 사우디, 리비아, 이란등에서 軍事施設과 石油探掘, 送油, 貯油施設,
　　石油化學플랜트, 都市基盤施設部門의 發注 增加

　- 이라크, 쿠웨이트에서는 戰後 復舊事業 活潑

2. 對應戰略

○ 國別 分野別 優先順位에 따라 選別 參與하되, 發注國의 財政狀態, 工事
收益性등에 대하여 綜合的으로 事前檢討

　· 쿠웨이트

　　海外逃避資産(1,500~3,000억불 推定)과 石油資源이 豊富하므로 優先的
　　으로 石油生産, 貯油, 精製施設 및 石油化學施設 復舊工事에 參與

　· 사우디, 리비아, 이란등 周邊國

　　石油收入 增大로 軍事施設擴充에 注力할 것이므로 軍事施設關聯工事와
　　石油化學플랜트, 都市基盤施設 關聯工事에 參與

　· 이라크

　　8年間의 對이란戰 및 걸프戰爭으로 代金支拂能力에 限界가 있을
　　것이므로 愼重을 期하되

　　世界銀行등 國際金融機關의 復舊資金支援工事와 金融調達能力이 있는
　　先進國 業體와 共同參與가 可能한 分野에 參與

○ 工事遂行方式을 旣存의 "直接施工" 爲主에서 "管理監督型"으로 轉換을
推進하여 危險 輕減

4 - 4

0100

건 설 부

해건 30600-3849   (503-7416)   1991. 2. 12.

수신 외무부장관

제목 걸프지역 해외건설 공사관리대책

1. 해건30600-1939('91. 1. 23)의 관련입니다.

2. 걸프전쟁이 예상외로 장기화되고 전황이 지상전 임박등으로
긴박해지고 있음에 비추어 사우디아라비아전역, UAE, 카탈, 바레인, 오만등
걸프만전역이 이라크의 공격권이 될 위험성이 높아지고 있는 실정입니다.

3. 이에 따라 현지주재 공관장(사우디아라비아, UAE, 카탈, 바레인,
예멘) 으로 하여금 상황을 예의 분석하여 비상사태의 발생이 우려될 경우
에는 현지 진출업체들로 하여금 즉시 공사를 중단하고 인력을 철수함과
동시에 공사현장의 장비자재등에 대한 안전 보존대책의 강구와 계약상의
분쟁요인을 사전에 철저히 방지할 수 있도록 공사중단에 따른 대발주처
행정조치 준비에 만전을 기하도록 지도감독 체제를 강화토록 긴급훈령
하여 주시기 바랍니다. (끝)

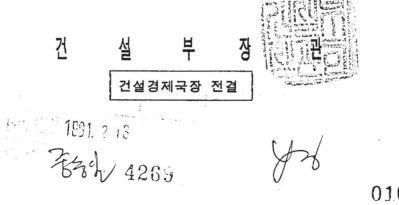

건 설 부 장

건설경제국장 전결

분류번호	보존기간

발 신 전 보

번   호 : WAE-0137 · 910218 1808 AO   종별 :

수   신 : 주 수신처 참조   ///대사.//총영사

발   신 : 장 관 (중근일)

제   목 : 진출 근로자 철수 문제

WQT -0070   WBH -0094
WOM -0070   WJO-180

     걸프전쟁과 관련, 귀 주재국 진출 아국 건설업체 근로자들의 철수에 따라
업체별로 입은 피해가 있는지 여부 및 앞으로 수주에 미칠 영향등 관련사항을
파악 보고 바람. 끝.

                                        (중동아국장   이 해 순)

수신처 : 주 UAE, 카타르, 바레인 대사
                    , 오만, 요르단

예 고 : 91.6.30. 까지

19ㅣ. 6.30 에 예고문에
의거 일반문서로 재분류됨

보안통제	7ㄴ

앙 고 재	91년 월 18일	기안자 성명	과 장	심의관	국 장	차 관	장 관	외신과통제
	중동 과	이종순	7ㄴ	여	전결		74	

0102

정 리 보 존 문 서 목 록					

기록물종류	일반공문서철	등록번호	2021010240	등록일자	2021-01-28
분류번호	721.1	국가코드	XF	보존기간	영구
명 칭	걸프사태 : 대책 및 조치, 1990-91. 전11권				
생 산 과	중동1과/북미1과	생산년도	1990~1991	담당그룹	
권 차 명	V.11 기타				
내용목차	1. 걸프사태 명칭 조정, 1991 2. 한국의 지원에 대한 각국 반응, 1991 3. 화학전 대비 훈련시범 교육 출장, 1990.12.25-91.1.5 ★ 출장자 : 박종순 외무부 중근동과 서기관, 황기수 비상계획관실 예비군 중대장 ★ 출장지 : 사우디아라비아, 아랍에미리트연합국, 바레인, 카타르, 이라크, 요르단				

0001

1. 걸프사태 명칭 조정, 1991

더맑은 마음을, 더밝은 사회를, 더넓은 미래를

분류기호 문서번호	출근동720 -22	협 조 문 용 지 (720-2327)	결 재	담 당	과 장	국 장
시행일자	1991. 1. 19.					(서명)
수 신	수신처 참조	발 신	걸프사태대책본부장			
제 목	페만사태 명칭 조정					

금후 "페만사태", "페만전"은 "걸프사태", "걸프전"으로 조정

지칭키로 하였음을 알려 드립니다.

첨 부 : 관련자료 1부. 끝.

수신처 : 각 실국(과)장, 외교안보연구원장

0003

더맑은 마음을, 더밝은 사회를, 더넓은 미래를

분류기호 문서번호	종로동 720 _22	협조문용지 (720-2327)	결 재	담 당	과 장	국 장
시행일자	1991. 1. 19.					
수 신	수신처 참조	발 신	걸프사태대책본부장 (서명)			
제 목	페만사태 명칭 조정					

금후 "페만사태", "페만전"은 "걸프사태", "걸프전"으로 조정

지칭키로 하였음을 알려 드립니다.

첨 부 : 관련자료 1부. 끝.

수신처 : 각 실국(과)장, 외교안보연구원장

0004

페만사태 명칭 조정

1. 금후 페만사태, 페만전은 걸프사태, 걸프전으로 조정 지칭키로 함.

2. 명칭 조정 사유
   - 과거 이란(페르시아)이 중동지역의 최강국이었던 관계로
     페르시아만(Persian Gulf)으로 호칭
     - 일부 지도에는 아직도 페르시아만으로 표기
   - 아랍 국가들은 "아라비아만"(Arabian Gulf)으로 호칭하며,
     페르시아만으로 지칭하는데 거부감을 갖고 있음.
   - 따라서, 중립적인 표현인 걸프(the Gulf)로 지칭하는 것이 타당함.
   - 현재 미국 및 구주 각국은 모두 "걸프"라는 명칭을 사용중이며
     (예 : 미 CNN 방송은 War in the Gulf 라는 Headline 사용),
     다만 일본은 "灣岸" 이라고 호칭

3. 시행 방안
   - 오랫동안 국내 언론등에서 페만이라는 용어를 사용해와서
     급작스러운 명칭 변경에 어려움이 있음을 감안, 명칭 조정은
     시간을 두고 서서히 시행, 완결시키도록 함.
   - 금 1.19. 외무장관 기자 간담회에서 상기 명칭 변경 사유를
     설명하고 협조를 당부한바 있음.

0005

발 신 전 보

번   호 : AM-0021   910119 1155 FK 종별 : _____

수   신 : 주 전 재외공관장   대사// 총영사//

발   신 : 장 관 (중근동)

제   목 : 걸프사태 명칭 조정

	분류번호	보존기간

      종래 "페만사태", "페만전"의 명칭은 앞으로 "걸프사태", "걸프전(쟁)"
으로 조정 지칭키로 하였으니 시행 바람. 끝.

                    (중동아국장   이 해 순)

앙고재	기안자 성명	과 장	국 장	차 관	장 관

발 신 전 보

WIR-0076   910122 1421   BX

번   호 : _____   종별 : _____

수   신 : 주 이 란   대사. 송영사////

발   신 : 장 관   (중근동)

제   목 : 걸프사태 명칭 변경

연 : AM-0021

1. 주한 이란 대사는 금 1.22. 중동아국장에게 전화를 걸어 연호 명칭
변경에 대해 (금일자 코리아 헤럴드 보도) 유엔문서나 OPEC 문서에 까지
"페르시아만"이라고 되어있는 명칭을 한국정부가 "걸프"라고 변경한 것은
이해하기 어려우며 양국 우호협력을 위해 노력해온 자신의 본국에 대한 입장이
대단히 난처해 질 것임과 양국관계에 영향을 미칠 가능성에 대해 우려를 표명하고
명칭 환원을 검토해 줄것을 요청함.

2. 이 국장은 명칭 변경은 많은 나라의 관행을 따른 것임과 아국 언론에
흔히 "페만"이라고 표기됨으로서 발음상 듣기에 좋지않아 바꾼데 불과한 것을
가지고 한.이 양국간의 관계까지 거론하는 것은 적절치 않으며 양국간의 우호
협력관계를 증진코자 하는 정부의 입장에는 추호의 변화도 없다고 대응하고 다만
대사의 관심은 유의하겠다고 답하였으니 참고 바람.

/ 계속 . . .

3. 코리아 헤럴드 기사전문은 다음과 같음.

'PERSIAN GULF' OUT, 'GULF' IN

THE GOVERNMENT HAS DECIDED NOT TO USE THE WORD "PERSIAN GULF" ANY MORE.
INSTEAD, IT WILL REFER TO IT AS "THE GULF."

FOREIGN MINISTRY OFFICIALS SAID THE "PERSIAN GULF" WAS NAMED AFTER
PERSIA, FORMER OFFICIAL NAME OF IRAN, AS THE KINGDOM USED TO BE THE MAIN
POWER IN THE MIDDLE EAST.

BUT OTHER MIDDLE EAST COUNTRIES DON'T LIKE THE NAME AND CALL IT "THE
ARABIAN GULF."

"THE GOVERNMENT DECIDED TO USE A NEUTRAL NAME 'THE GULF,' CONSIDERING
THE DISSENTION, "A MINISTRY OFFICIAL SAID.

THEREFORE, THE ONGOING CONFLICT IN THE AREA WILL BE DUBBED THE "WAR IN THE
GULF" INSTEAD OF "WAR IN THE PERSIAN GULF" IN GOVERNMENT PAPERS, HE SAID.

THE OFFICIAL ALSO RECOMMENDED THAT NEWS ORGANIZATIONS USE THE SAME
EXPRESSION. 끝.

(중동아국장   이 해 순)

예 고 : 1991. 6. 30. 일반

0008

In the name of God

January 23,1991
No. /99ユ

The Embassy of the Islamic Republic of Iran presents   its
compliments to the Ministry of Foreign Affairs of the Republic
of KOrea and has the honour to inform the latter that the Korea
Herald, an English language daily newspaper on page 2 of its
Tuesday, January 22, 1991 edition published a matter titled
"Persian Gulf out, Gulf in" and said that the Government of the
Republic of Korea has decided not to use the word "Persian Gulf"
any more and will refer to it as The Gulf.

The paper quoted officials of the MInistry of Foreign Affairs
that, The Persian Gulf was named after Persia, former name of
Iran, but other MIddle East countries do not like this name and
the Government decided to use a neutral name in its papers.

This Embassy wishes to remind the esteemed Ministry that some
geographical names have roots in histories of nations and could
not be changed or disparaged by the will of others. For further
information of the above-mentioned officials of the Ministry, the
United Nations' Secretariat and its office of Legal Affairs in
different occasions clarified and reaffirmed the name of Persian
Gulf. The latest document in this regard is ST/CS/SER.A/29 dated
January 10, 1990 stated that "THE STANDARD GEOGRAPHICAL DESIGNATION
FOR THE BODY OF WATER LYING BETWEEN THE ISLAMIC REPUBLIC OF IRAN

0009

EMBASSY OF THE ISLAMIC
REPUBLIC OF IRAN
SEOUL

AND THE ARABIAN PENINSULA IS PERSIAN GULF. HOWEVER, IN DOCUMENTS, PUBLICATIONS AND STATEMENTS EMANATING FROM ALL MEMBER GOVERNMENTS OR INTERGOVERNMENTAL ORGANIZATIONS THE TERMINOLOGY OF THE ORIGINAL SHOULD BE RETAINED."

Noting this fact that the Republic of Korea is seeking a full membership of the world body, the relevant authorities, specially those who decided to change an official and historic name are invited to consider the realities of the United Nations and are expected to correct the guidance to the Korean Mass Media which will be in the interest of friendly and excellent political and economical relations between our countries.

The Embassy of the Islamic Republic of Iran avails itself of this opportunity to renew to the Ministry of Foreign Affairs of the Republic of Korea the assurances of its highest consideration.

Wishing the oppressed victory over the oppressors.

Ministry of Foreign Affairs
Republic of Korea
Seoul

0010

'Persian Gulf' out, 'Gulf' in

The government has decided not to use the word "Persian Gulf" any more. Instead, it will refer to it as "the Gulf."

Foreign Ministry officials said the "Persian Gulf" was named after Persia, former official name of Iran, as the kingdom used to be the main power in the Middle East.

But other Middle East countries don't like the name and call it "the Arabian Gulf."

"The government decided to use a neutral name 'the Gulf,' considering the dissention," a ministry official said.

Therefore, the ongoing conflict in the area will be dubbed the "war in the Gulf" instead of "war in the Persian Gulf" in government papers, he said.

The official also recommended that news organizations use the same expression.

Letters to the Editor

Persian Gulf in

To the Editor:

In reference to the item published in Jan. 22 issue of The Korea Herald: "Persian Gulf Out, Gulf In" on Page 2, we would like to remind you that the first secretary of this embassy sent you a letter in this regard on Aug. 9, 1990 which was published on Aug. 18, 1990. Frankly we did not expect such a pungent matter to be put forth again in your popular and prudent paper.

For your further information once again we are referring to the Document No. ST/CS/SER.A/29 dated Jan. 10, 1990 of the secretariat of the United Nations:

"The standard geographical designation for the body of water lying between the Islamic Republic of Iran and the Arabian Peninsula is the Persian Gulf. However, in documents, publications, and statements emanating from a member government or intergovernmental organizations, the terminology of the original should be retained."

The historical name of this gulf, even on the stone plate belonging to Achaemenian era, 522-485 B.C., was the Persian Gulf and the claim of a number of Iran's neighboring countries has absolutely no historical value and is unworthy of discussion. Furthermore the wills or claims of other countries could not be a rational base for changing or disparaging the historical names.

This embassy has strongly protested to the Ministry of Foreign Affairs of the Republic of Korea against the decision and will insist that the neutral position for the Republic of Korea which is seeking the full membership of the United Nations is to honor the world body's recommendation and use only the standard and historical name of Persian Gulf.

It would be appreciated if you once again kindly consider the contents of the said document and urge the relevant staff of your paper to use the correct term "Persian Gulf."

Embassy of the Islamic
Republic of Iran,
Seoul

0011

	분류번호	보존기간

발 신 전 보

번   호 : _____   종별 : 긴 급

수   신 : 주   유엔   대사. 총영사

발   신 : 장   관 (중근동)

제   목 : 걸프사태

주한 이란 대사관으로부터 전부의 '걸프사태' 용어사용과 관련 시정을 요구하여 왔는바,

1. 본부 업무에 필요하니 90.1.10자 유엔 사무국 문서(ST/CS/ SER A/29)를
FAX 송부 바람.(분량이 많을 경우는 걸프 해역의 지명에관한 부분만 FAX 송부코,
문서 자체는 파편 송부)

2. 상기와 관련, '페르시아만'이라는 지명을 사용하는데 대한 유엔 사무국의
공식 입장이 있는지 여부 및 동내용을 파악보고바라며, 아울러 해당산하기구 (지명
표준화위원회등)의 관련결정사항 및 토의현황에 대해서도 파악 보고 바람. 끝.

2. 상기와 관련

(중동아국장 이 해 순)

앙고재	91년1월2일	중근동과	기안자성명 조재룡		과 장		국 장		차 관	장 관	보안통제	
												외신과통제

0012

관리
번호 이-
      1007

<table>
<tr><td>분류번호</td><td>보존기간</td></tr>
<tr><td></td><td></td></tr>
</table>

발 신 전 보

WUN-0166   910127 2248   CF

번   호 : _____   종별 : 긴 급

수   신 : 주   유엔   대사 . 총영사

발   신 : 장 관   (중근동)

제   목 : 걸프사태

1. 주한 이란 대사관은 정부의 '걸프사태'용어 사용과 관련 시정을 요구해
왔는바, '페르시아만'이라는 지명을 사용 하는데 대한 유엔 사무국의 공식
입장이 있는지와 해당산하기구 (지명표준화위원회등)의 관련결정사항에 대해서도
파악 보고 바람.

2. 상기와 관련, 90.1.10자 유엔 사무국 문서(ST/CS/ SER.A/29)를
FAX 송부 바람.(분량이 많을 경우는 걸프 해역의 지명에관한 부분만 FAX 송부코,
문서 자체는 파편 송부.)   끝.

(중동아국장 이 해 순)

예 고 : 91.6.30.일반

<table>
<tr><td>보 안
통 제</td><td>7h</td></tr>
</table>

<table>
<tr><td rowspan="3">앙
고
재</td><td rowspan="3">91
년
1
월
29
일</td><td rowspan="3">중
근
동
과</td><td>기안자
성 명</td><td></td><td>과 장</td><td>심태환</td><td>국 장</td><td></td><td>차 관</td><td>장 관</td><td rowspan="3">외신과통제</td></tr>
<tr><td rowspan="2">조재옥</td><td></td><td rowspan="2">7h</td><td rowspan="2">영</td><td rowspan="2">전계</td><td></td><td rowspan="2"></td><td rowspan="2">발간</td></tr>
<tr><td></td></tr>
</table>

0013

The ruins of Persepolis from the south, showing the terrace and retaining walls. The apadana of Darius I, of which 13 stone pillars are still standing, and the propylaeum of Xerxes, marked by two pillars, are at the top left.
By courtesy of the Oriental Institute, University of Chicago

plete, are richly ornamented with reliefs. About eight miles north by northeast, on the opposite side of the Pulvār, rises a perpendicular wall of rock in which four similar tombs are cut at a considerable height from the bottom of the valley. This place is called Naqsh-e Rostam (the Picture of Rostam) from the Sāsānian carvings below the tombs, which were thought to represent the mythical hero Rostam. That the occupants of these seven tombs were Achaemenian kings might be inferred from the sculptures, and one of those at Naqsh-e Rostam is expressly declared in its inscriptions to be the tomb of Darius I, son of Hystaspes, whose grave, according to the Greek historian Ctesias, was in a cliff face that could be reached only by means of an apparatus of ropes. An inscription beside the entrance to Darius' tomb describes his character and states that God had given him two special qualities, wisdom and activity. The three other tombs at Naqsh-e Rostam, besides that of Darius I, are probably those of Xerxes I, Artaxerxes I, and Darius II. Xerxes II, who preceded Darius II, reigned for a very short time and could not have obtained so splendid a monument; still less could Sogdianus (Secydianus), who usurped his brother's throne and reigned for less than a year. The two completed graves behind Takht-e Jamshīd probably belong to Artaxerxes II and Artaxerxes III. The unfinished one might be that of Arses, who reigned at the longest two years, but is more likely to be that of Darius III, the last of the Achaemenian line, who was overthrown by Alexander the Great.

BIBLIOGRAPHY. E. FLANDIN and P. COSTE, Voyage en Perse, 2 vol. (1851); F. STOLZE, Persepolis: Die Achaemenidischen und Sasanidischen Denkmäler und Inschriften von Persepolis (1882); G. PERROT and C. CHIPIEZ, Histoire de l'art dans l'antiquité, vol. 5 (1890; Eng. trans., History of Art in Persia, 1892), with a description of the platform and the Propylaeum of Xerxes at Persepolis; G.N. CURZON, "Persepolis and Other Ruins," in Persia and the Persian Question, vol. 2 (1892); F. SARRE and E. HERZFELD, Iranische Felsreliefs (1910); A. SAMI, Persepolis, 6th ed. (Eng. trans. 1970); D.N. WILBER, Persepolis: The Archaeology of Parsa Seat of the Persian Kings (1969), with full bibliography of works on Persepolis.

(R.N.S.)

Persian Gulf

The Persian Gulf (known to the Arabs as the Arabian Gulf) is the shallow marginal sea of the Indian Ocean that lies between the Arabian Peninsula and southeast Iran. The sea has an area of 92,500 square miles (240,000 square kilometres). Its length is 615 miles, and its width varies from a maximum of 210 miles to a minimum of 35 miles in the Strait of Hormuz. It is bordered on the north, northeast, and east by Iran, on the northwest by Iraq and Kuwait, on the west and southwest by Saudi Arabia, Bahrain, and Qatar, and on the south and southeast by the United Arab Emirates and part of Oman. The term

Persian Gulf is often used to refer not only to the Persian Gulf proper but also to its outlets, the Strait of Hormuz and the Gulf of Oman, which open into the Arabian Sea. This article deals with the Persian Gulf alone (see also TIGRIS–EUPHRATES RIVER SYSTEM).

Physiography. The Iranian shore is mountainous, and there are often cliffs; elsewhere a narrow coastal plain with beaches, intertidal flats, and small estuaries borders the gulf. The coastal plain widens north of Būshehr on the eastern shore of the gulf and passes into the broad deltaic plain of the Tigris, Euphrates, and Kārūn rivers. Cliffs are rare on the Arabian shore of the gulf, except around the base of the Qatar Peninsula and in the extreme southeast around the Strait of Hormuz. Most of the Arabian shore is bordered by sandy beaches, with many small islands enclosing small lagoons.

The gulf is very shallow, rarely deeper than 300 feet, although depths exceeding 360 feet are found at its entrance and at isolated localities in its southeastern part. It is noticeably asymmetrical in profile, with the deepest water occurring along the Iranian coast and a broad shallow area, which is usually less than 120 feet deep, along the Arabian coast. There are numerous islands, some of which are salt plugs or domes and others merely accumulations of coral and skeletal debris.

The Persian Gulf receives very small amounts of riverborne sediment except in the northwest, where the Tigris, Euphrates, and Kārūn, together with other small streams, empty into the gulf. The rivers reach their peak flow in spring and early summer, when the snow melts in the mountains; disastrous floods sometimes result. There are some ephemeral streams on the Iranian coast south of Būshehr, but virtually no freshwater flows into the gulf on its southwest side. Large quantities of fine dust are, however, blown into the sea by predominant northwest winds from the desert areas of the surrounding lands. Biological, biochemical, and chemical processes lead to the production of considerable calcium carbonate in the form of skeletal debris and fine mud. The deeper parts of the Persian Gulf adjacent to the Iranian coast and the area around the Tigris–Euphrates Delta are mainly floored with gray-green muds rich in calcium carbonate. The shallower areas to the southwest are covered with whitish-gray or speckled skeletal sands and fine carbonate muds. Often the sea floor has been hardened and turned to rock by the deposition of calcium carbonate from the warm, salty waters. Chemical precipitation is abundant in the coastal waters, and sands and muds are produced that mix with the skeletal debris of the local sea life. These sediments are thrown up by the waves to form coastal islands that enclose lagoons. The high salinities and temperatures result in the precipitation of calcium sulfate and sodium chloride to form extensive coastal salt flats.

0014

The Persian Gulf.

Geology. The present-day Persian Gulf, together with its northwestern continuation now infilled by the deposits of the Mesopotamian rivers, is thought by some to be the remains of a once much larger northwest-to-southeast-aligned basin of deposition that existed throughout a large part of geological history. In this basin many thousands of feet of sediments accumulated, consisting mostly of limestone and marls (loose, crumbling earthy deposits containing calcium carbonate), together with evaporites and organic matter, which ultimately produced the area's vast oil resources.

Climate. The gulf has a notoriously bad climate. Temperatures are high, though winters may be quite cool at the northwestern extremities. The sparse rainfall occurs mainly as sharp downpours between November and April and is higher in the northeast. Humidity is high. The little cloud cover is more prevalent in winter than in summer. Thunderstorms and fog are rare, but dust storms and haze occur frequently in summer. The wind blows predominantly from a north–northwest direction —the so-called *shamāl* (Arabic: "north wind")—is seldom strong, and rarely reaches gale force. Squalls and waterspouts are common in autumn, when winds sometimes reach speeds of 95 miles per hour in as little as five minutes. Intense heating of the land adjacent to the coasts leads to gentle offshore winds in the mornings and strong onshore winds in the afternoons and evenings.

Hydrography. The small freshwater inflow into the gulf is mostly from the Tigris–Euphrates–Kārūn rivers. The water temperatures range from 75° to 90° F (24° to 32° C) in the Strait of Hormuz to 60° to 90° F (16° to 32° C) in the extreme northwest. These high water temperatures and a low influx of freshwater result in evaporation in excess of freshwater inflow; high salinities result, ranging from 37 to 38 parts per thousand in the entrance to 38 to 41 parts per thousand in the extreme northwest. Even greater salinities and temperatures are found in the waters of the lagoons on the Arabian shore. The tidal range varies from about four to five feet around Qatar and increases to ten to 11 feet in the northwest and nine to ten feet in the extreme southeast. When onshore winds are strong, the level of the coastal waters, particularly in the southern gulf, may rise by as much as eight feet, causing extensive flooding of the low coastal plains. Tidal currents are strong (five miles per hour) in the entrance of the gulf but elsewhere—except between islands or in estuaries and lagoon entrances—rarely exceed one to two miles per hour. The wind affects local currents and may sometimes even reverse them.

Waves rarely exceed ten feet in height and are largest in the southern gulf. The swell from the Indian Ocean affects only the water at the entrance of the gulf; when it is

opposed by wind, very turbulent result. The general circulation pattern appears to be caused by water entering from the Indian Ocean, evaporating, becoming denser, and sinking to flow out into the Indian Ocean beneath the inflowing open ocean water.

The waters of the area support many plants and animals, but the high temperatures and salinities lead to a diminution in the variety of forms; many Indian Ocean forms penetrate only a small way into the gulf.

Economic resources. Until the discovery of oil in Iran in 1908, the Persian Gulf area was important mainly for fishing, pearling, the building of dhows (Arab lateen-rigged boats), sailcloth making, camel breeding, reed-mat making, date growing, and the production of other minor products, such as red ochre from the islands in the south. The arid lands surrounding the gulf produced little else and, except for the rich alluvial lands of the Mesopotamian plain, supported a small population of fishermen, date growers, and nomads. Today these traditional industries have declined, and the economy of the region is dominated by the production of oil. The Persian Gulf and the surrounding countries produce approximately 31 percent of the world's total oil production and have 63 percent of the world's proved reserves. The area has been explored only in a preliminary way, and there are still fewer drill holes in the area than are put down in a single month in the United States. Offshore exploration below the shallow waters of the gulf has revealed the presence of large reserves of oil and gas. These discoveries have led to numerous legal wrangles between states about exact territorial limits. Large quantities of oil are refined locally at Ābādān, in Iran, in Bahrain, and elsewhere, but most of it is exported to northwestern Europe and other parts of the world as crude oil.

Other exploitable mineral deposits appear to be rare, but only cursory surveys have been made; exploration was actively being pursued in the area in the early 1970s.

Fishing is becoming highly commercialized. The traditional pearl-fishing industry has declined since the introduction of the Japanese cultivated pearls in the 1930s. Large fishing industries have been set up in Kuwait, Qatar, and Bahrain; in 1968, 10,000 tons of prawns were exported by Kuwait.

There has always been a considerable sea trade carried on by local craft between the Persian Gulf and Africa and India; this is now completely dominated by an incessant flow of large tankers that carry oil from the large marine terminals at Khārk Island, Kuwait, Dhahran, Bahrain, Musay'īd, az̧-Z̧annah, and Dās Island to all parts of the world. The heavy traffic and the offshore oil installations have produced many hazards, despite the use of a system of radio-navigational stations.

Prospects for the future. The Persian Gulf area will probably remain an important source of world oil for a long period. The abundance of cheap power should make it possible to set up local extractive industries using raw materials that are too low grade to be exploited elsewhere: a large aluminum-smelting plant is already being constructed in Bahrain. This abundance of cheap power should also allow the exploitation of the highly saline coastal lagoon waters for chemicals such as magnesium, sodium, and chlorine. Although large underground reserves of freshwater have been found in the area, the general lack of freshwater and the unfavourable climate make agriculture difficult. The vast oil wealth, however, should make it possible to develop solar desalination plants to overcome this problem.

BIBLIOGRAPHY. G. EVANS, "Persian Gulf," in R.W. FAIRBRIDGE (ed.), *Encyclopedia of Oceanography*, pp. 689–695 (1966), a general review of the geology and physiography of the gulf; "The Recent Sedimentary Facies of the Persian Gulf," *Proc. R. Soc.*, Series A, 259:291–298 (1966), a general review of the oceanography and marine geology; N.L. FALCON, "The Geology of the North-East Margin of the Arabian Basement Shield," *Advmt. Sci.*, 24:31–42 (1967), an excellent general review of the geological development of the area, with references; GREAT BRITAIN, HYDROGRAPHIC OFFICE, *Persian Gulf Pilot* (rev. periodically), an invaluable source of meteorological, oceanographical, navigational, and local physiographic detail.

(G.EV.)

become a matter ███ us dispute since the discov ███

The large natural harbour of **Kuwait** was a terminus of the route through Iraq, and was considered at one time as a possible base for a railway across northern Arabia. Now an oil port, Kuwait is a wealthy state which imports most needs. Water is acquired from wells or through distilling sea-water.

The island of **Bahrain** and the nearby peninsula of **Qatar** used to exist on pearling and dhow trading, but their economies now rely overwhelmingly on the mining and export of oil, through Manamah, Umm Said and several specialized terminals. Further east, **Abu Dhabi** draws oil both from inland and fr ███ ore, and trades through th ███ of Dubay.

In spite of wide exploration, **Oman** has found oil only at one small field – that of Jebel Fahud on the western or desert slope of the mountains. The main Omani range, the Jebel Akhdar, an offshoot of the fold mountains of Makran on the other side of the Gulf of Oman, meets the coast between a series of deep inlets, on one of which lies the port of Muscat. The mountains trap a modest winter rainfall and grow winter grains and fruit trees. The high plateau edge that backs the bay of Dhufar on the south coast, by contrast, gets rain in summer from the monsoon winds, and grows a cover of shrubs, including the frankincense bush. On the plateau crest are summer meadows where the Qara and Mahra tribes graze cattle.

Further west along the south coast is the state of **South Yemen**, formerly the British Colony and Protectorate of Aden. Here too the plateau meets the Indian Ocean in a high edge where a moderate summer monsoon rain nourishes the myrrh bushes and supplies a number of coastal oases. Further inland lies the wide dust-covered plateau of the Jols, desolate and dissected by ravines. Beyond is the vale of Hadhramawt watered by one of the few permanent streams of Arabia, where the inhabi-

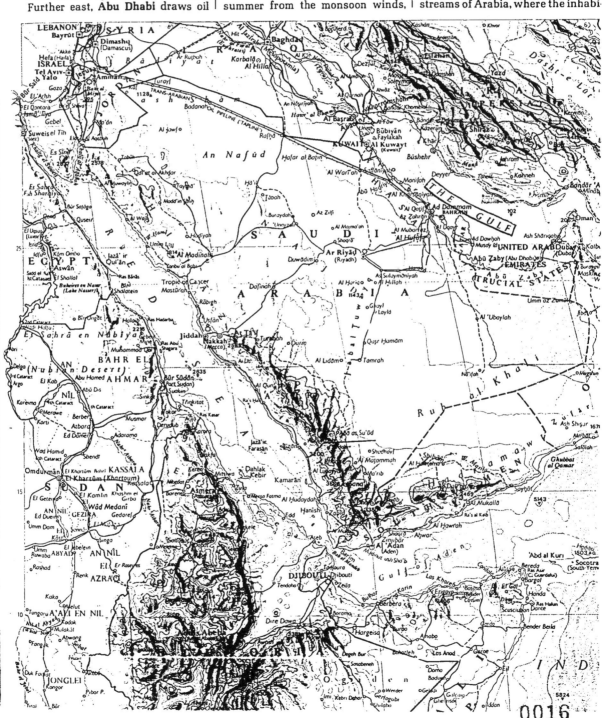

THE GULF WAR

Unleashing Desert Storm

FROM OUR CORRESPONDENTS IN THE MIDDLE EAST

SADDAM HUSSEIN'S "mother of battles" started on cue, though it did not follow the Iraqi dictator's script. The UN's deadline for Iraq's withdrawal from Kuwait came and went at midnight New York time on January 15th. About 19 hours later, under cover of night, aircraft from the American, British, Saudi and Kuwaiti air forces dropped thousands of tons of bombs on military targets throughout Iraq. The attacks were co-ordinated with the firing of hundreds of ground-hugging cruise missiles from allied warships.

The allied air forces claim that they did not lose a single aircraft in the first wave of overnight raids, although both British and American aircraft were lost in subsequent sorties. French aircraft joined the fray a little later, and four were damaged. The early evidence is that the bombers found their targets. By Thursday evening Tel Aviv, which Mr Hussein had vowed to make his first target in any war, was still untouched. Israel reported that most of the fixed launchers for ground-to-ground missiles in western Iraq appeared to have been knocked out, but it remained on alert.

Mr Bush announced the transformation of Operation Desert Shield into Operation Desert Storm in a brief television speech. The aim, he said, was to liberate Kuwait under the mandate of the UN, not to conquer Iraq—although Iraq's nuclear and chemical-weapons plants would be destroyed. During the waiting period, the president claimed, Mr Hussein had tried to add an atomic bomb to his chemical arsenal. From Baghdad's television station, a defiant Mr Hussein vowed that Iraq would fight on.

The next steps

The main question for the allies is how long to keep up the air attack on Iraq's forces before sending in the ground troops. One school of thought, which consists of some senior airmen and almost nobody else, holds that the air attack should go on for a long time, perhaps for several weeks, with fighter-bombers, cruise missiles and B-52s, in the belief that eventually the soldiers could walk in and occupy the rubble. The idea of victory through air power alone, with few casualties on the attacking side, has long beguiled military planners. It has not yet happened.

The allied air offensive started with a high "surge" of attacks. They will have to cut back within a few days, to something below the "steady" rate, in order to catch up on maintenance. One thing is certain: General Norman Schwarzkopf must be allowed to make decisions on the air war unencumbered by the detailed orders for air attacks that Lyndon Johnson often forced on his commanders, sometimes disastrously, during the Vietnam war.

Great convoys of American and British troops have, over the past week, been moving north and west from their bivouacs and training areas. As the UN deadline drew near and was passed, they advanced to holding areas only a few miles from the positions near the frontier from which they could launch an attack.

The precise positions are secret. Just before the deadline expired, armoured and mechanised units were strung along the east-west road from Abu Hadriyah in the east to a point some 25 miles (40km) west of Hafr-al-Batin. American marines anchor the eastern end of the road, as they have done since they arrived in August. The strike force at

0017

발 신 전 보

WIR-0110　　910128 1509　DP　　　종별 : 긴급

번　　호 :

수　　신 : 주 이 란 　대사·총영사

발　　신 : 장 관 (중근동)

제　　목 : 걸프사태 용어 사용

연 : AM-0021, WIR-0076

　　　外信 보도에 의하면 주재국 정부는 1.23. 귀지주재 외국 특파원에게
'페만'용어 사용을 촉구하고 '걸프'용어 사용시 法的 조치를 취하겠다고 경고
했다고 하는바, ~~사실 여부~~ 확인 보고 바람. 연호에 이어 주한 이란대사관은
별첨 구상서를 본부에 송부해 왔는 바 금 1.28. 제1차관보는 주한
이란 대사를 불러 본부입장을 설명할 예정임. 상세는 추보하겠음.
첨부 : 상기 구상서.
　　　　　　　　　　　　　　　　　　　　　　　　(중동아국장 이해순)

예 고 : 91.6.30. 일반

앙고재	91년 1월 28일 중근동과 조래용	기안자 성명		과장 7h	국장 전11m	차관	장관	외신과통제

0018

**EMBASSY OF THE ISLAMIC
REPUBLIC OF IRAN
SEOUL**

In the name of God

January 23,1991
No. /99ユ

~~The Embassy of the Islamic Republic of Iran presents its~~ ~~compliments to the Ministry of Foreign Affairs of the Republic~~ ~~of Korea and~~ has the honour to inform the latter that the Korea Herald, an English language daily newspaper on page 2 of its Tuesday, January 22, 1991 edition published a matter titled "Persian Gulf out, Gulf in" and said that the Government of the Republic of Korea has decided not to use the word "Persian Gulf" any more and will refer to it as The Gulf.

The paper quoted officials of the MInistry of Foreign Affairs that, The Persian Gulf was named after Persia, former name of Iran, but other MIddle East countries do not like this name and the Government decided to use a neutral name in its papers.

This Embassy wishes to remind the esteemed Ministry that some geographical names have roots in histories of nations and could not be changed or disparaged by the will of others. For further information of the above-mentioned officials of the Ministry, the United Nations' Secretariat and its office of Legal Affairs in different occasions clarified and reaffirmed the name of Persian Gulf. The latest document in this regard is ST/CS/SER.A/29 dated January 10, 1990 stated that "THE STANDARD GEOGRAPHICAL DESIGNATION FOR THE BODY OF WATER LYING BETWEEN THE ISLAMIC REPUBLIC OF IRAN

0019

AND THE ARABIAN PENINSULA IS PERSIAN GULF. HOWEVER, IN DOCUMENTS, PUBLICATIONS AND STATEMENTS EMANATING FROM ALL MEMBER GOVERNMENTS OR INTERGOVERNMENTAL ORGANIZATIONS THE TERMINOLOGY OF THE ORIGINAL SHOULD BE RETAINED."

Noting this fact that the Republic of Korea is seeking a full membership of the world body, the relevant authorities, specially those who decided to change an official and historic name are invited to consider the realities of the United Nations and are expected to correct the guidance to the Korean Mass Media which will be in the interest of friendly and excellent political and economical relations between our countries. ··· (후략)

~~The Embassy of the Islamic Republic of Iran avails itself of this opportunity to renew to the Ministry of Foreign Affairs of the Republic of Korea the assurances of its highest consideration.~~

~~Wishing the oppressed victory over the oppressors.~~

Ministry of Foreign Affairs
Republic of Korea
Seoul

0020

'걸프' 용어사용 관련 말씀자료 (Ⅰ)

o 지역 명칭에 관하여 관계국간 이견이 있음을 우리는 알고 있음.

o 역사적으로 페르시아만이라고 불리우고 있으나 아랍국가들이 유엔 지명 표준화위원회에 이의를 제기한 바 있음.

o 아국도 동해가 일부지도상에 일본해로 표기되어 있어서 유사한 문제를 가지고 있음.

o 우리정부가 '걸프'라고 호칭하는 것은 불편부당한 중립적 입장에서 적절한 용어라고 생각하였기 때문임.

o 현재 유엔지명 표준화 위원회에서의 토의기록 구득을 아국공관에 지시 하였으며 상세한 배경 등을 검토하여 보겠음.

첨부: 지명업무 담당 국제기구 현황 자료 1부.   끝.

0021

지명업무 담당 국제기구

91.1.28.

1. 유엔지명 표준화 회의(UN Conference on the Standardization of Geographical Names)

   o   65.7.15. 유엔 경사리 결의 의거 하기 목적으로 설치
       - 지명의 로마자 표기 통일
       - 지명 표준화를 위한 국제협력 및 자료 교환

   o   1967년 이래 매5년마다 유엔 사무총장 주관 회의 개최

2. 유엔지명 전문가그룹(UN Group of Experts on Geographical Names)

   o   68.5.31. 유엔 경사리 결의 의거 "유엔 지명표준화 회의" 보조
       기관으로 설치, 매2년마다 회합

   o   89.5.17-26 최근 회합시 36개국(남.북한 포함) 71명 참가

   o   지역 및 언어를 기준으로 19개 분과위 설치 운영
       - Arabic Division(알제리아, 예멘, 이집트, 이라크, 죠르단,
         레바논, 리비아, 쿠웨이트, 모로코, 사우디아라비아, 수단 소속)
       - Asia East Division(남.북한, 일본 소속)등

3. 유엔사무국 기술협력 개발부 주최 3개지역 지도제작 회의

   o   비정기적으로 다음 3개지역별 지도 제작자 회의 개최
       - 아프리카
       - 아시아.태평양
       - 미주

0022

4. 참고

   ○ 유엔은 International Map of the World on the Millionth Scale을
     매년 보고서로 발간하여 각종 정부의 지도 출판을 조정

   ○ 유엔은 또한 지도제작 지식 보급과 시사문제 토론의 장으로 정기적인
     bulletin을 발간.   끝

0023

'걸프' 용어사용 관련 말씀자료 (II)

o 우리정부가 '걸프'라고 호칭하는 것은 동 지역 지명표기에 대한 아국의
   공식입장과는 무관한 것으로서 금번 사태에 당면하여 아국이 동 사태를
   표현한 것에 불과한 것임.

   * 동 지역 지명표기에 대한 아국 공식 입장 문의시 답변

      - 아국도 동해가 일부 지도상에는 일본해로 표기되어 있어서 호칭상의
        어려움을 겪고 있음. 귀측이 관심을 가지고 있는 동 지명문제는
        일반국제관례 및 유엔관련기구에서 사용하는 명칭을 존중하는 것이
        합리적일 것으로 생각하며, 아국도 이러한 방향에서 관련자료를
        수집하여 계속 검토하도록 하겠음.

o 이러한 배경에 비추어 동 문제로 인하여 기존 양국관계가 영향을 받지
   않기를 희망함.

0024

면 담 요 록

1. 일   시 : 1991. 1. 28.(월)   15:30-15:55
2. 장   소 : 제1차관보실
3. 면 담 자 : 제 1차관보

     Fereidoun Entezari 주한 이란 대사

4. 면담내용

     차관보 : 현대 근로자 9명의 이란 입국과 관련한 이란 정부의 협조에 감사함.

     걸프해역 지명에 관한 귀관 Note와 1.27.자 코리아 헤럴드 독자
     투고란 기고문등 관련, 귀관 Note에 대한 공식 회신은 수일내
     하겠지만 우선 아국 정부 입장을 구두로 설명코자 함.
     한국 언론에서 "Gulf War"라는 용어를 사용하는데 대해 귀측에서
     다소 오해가 있는듯 한데, 이에대한 우리 정부 입장은 다음과 같음.

     1) 한국 언론의 "걸프전쟁(사태)" 용어 사용은 지리적, 역사적
         배경 및 유엔등 국제기구에서 사용하는 걸프 해역의 지명을
         변경하는 것과는 전혀 무관하며, 아국 정부는 동 해역을
         지칭하는 지명을 바꿀 의도는 없음.

     2) 분쟁 당사자는 물론 국제사회에서 대부분 "페르시아만 전쟁"이
         아닌 "걸프전쟁"이라는 용어를 사용하고 있으며, 우리는
         단순히 국제사회의 통례를 따르는 것뿐임.

     3) 금번 사태를 어떻게 지칭하느냐의 문제는 한.이란 양국 관계와는
         아무런 관련이 없으며, 양국간 기존 우호 협력관계를 강화해
         나가려는 아국 정부의 입장에는 변동이 없음.

         이상 이번 우리 정부의 조치에 관해 귀측의 오해가 없기를
         바람.(talking points 수교)

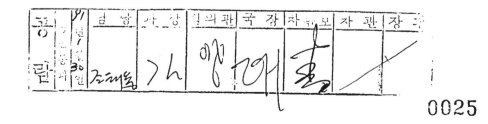

0025

우리로서는 걸프해역 지명을 둘러싼 아랍-이란의 의견 대립에
개입할 생각이 없으며, 또한 "Gulf War"라는 표현은 어디까지나
금번 분쟁을 지칭하는 것일뿐 걸프 해역의 지명이나 지위문제와는
무관함. 일본을 포함한 모든 국가에서 "Gulf War"라는
표현을 사용하고 있음. 아마도 전쟁이 사우디, 쿠웨이트,
이라크에 국한되고 이란은 당사국이 아니기 때문에 "Gulf
War"라는 표현을 사용하는지도 모름.
또한가지는 귀국인 1명(Mr. Yazdan Panadh)이 외환관리법 위반
혐의로 수사받고 있는 문제임.

대　사 : 많은 이란인들이 서울을 방문하고 있는데 일부 이란 사람들은 한국법
규정에 대한 이해가 없어 종종 그러한 사례가 발생함. 차관보께서
말씀하신 Mr. Panadh는 동경에서 $15,000을 바꾸어 서울에 가지고
들어왔다가 출국 과정에서 문제가 되어 법원에서 $4,000 벌금형을
받았음. 또한 최근 이란인 2명도 서울에서 미화를 바꾸었다가
출국 과정에서 외환 관리법 위반으로 조사를 받았음.
이러한 사례가 한국법을 위반한 범법행위라는 점은 명백함. 다만
한국어나 경우에 따라 영어도 못하는 외국인의 입장에서는 한국법
규정을 잘 몰라서 본의아니게 이러한 위법 행위를 저지르는 경우가
있음.
미화를 숨겨나간 것이 아니고 세관에서 소지 액수를 밝힌 경우에는
범법 의도가 없다는 점에서 정상이 참작되었으면 함.
이란에서 일하는 한국 근로자들이 이란 국내법을 잘 몰라서 위법
행위를 범하는 경우에도 관대하게 처리하고 있음.

차관보 : 여행객이 외화를 어느한도 이상 소지하고 있을 경우 세관에 신고
해야함은 상식임. 예컨대 미국에서는 $5,000 이상이면 신고해야
하는것으로 알고 있음.

대　사 : 그들이 첫번째 한국 방문이어서 잘 몰랐던것 같음.

차관보 : 한가지 분명히 하고싶은 것은 이란인 개인의 국내법 위반 사건
처리 문제는 양국간 우호 협력 관계와는 전혀 관련이 없다는 것임.
다만 양국간의 가까운 관계를 고려, 외무부에서는 검찰이 동사건
처리에 있어 최대한 정상을 참작하도록 협조를 요청 하였음.

0026

대 사 : 배려에 감사드림.

최근 이란인의 한국내 처우와 관련 다소 좋지않은 사례도 있는것
같음.

본인은 3년간 주한대사로 있으면서 양국관계 증진을위해 노력해
오고 있는데, 한국에 왔던 이란인들이 귀국하여 이런저런 이야기를
하게되면 양국관계에 좋지않은 영향을 미칠수 있어 안타까움.

이란인들의 위법 사례는 외환을 밀반출 하려다 적발된 것이
아니고 정정당당히 세관에 신고했는데 액수가 많아 문제가 생긴
것임을 참작해 주시기 바람.

차관보 : 세관에서의 외환 관리법 위반 조사는 특정 국적인을 대상으로
한것이 아니고 내국인, 외국인 모두에게 공평히 적용되는 것임.

재차 강조하지만 외국인 개인의 국내법 위반 사건과 양국 관계와는
엄연히 별개의 문제이므로 혼동이 없기 바람.

대 사 : 잘 알겠음.

"걸프사태" 지칭 문제와 관련 친절한 설명에 감사드림.

다만 본인으로서는 다소 의문이 있으며, 예컨대 Gulf of Oman에서
전쟁이 있다면 한국측에서 같은 조치를 할 것인지 궁금함.

차관보 : 가상적인 질문에는 논평 할수 없음.

대 사 : 언론이라면 다른 문제이나 정부 차원에서 명칭 변경 조치를
했다는데 놀람을 금할수 없음.

걸프해역 명칭 문제는 우리로서는 매우 민감한 사안이며, 솔직히
우리가 이라크와 8년동안 싸우면서 많은 희생을 감수한 것도
이라크측이 페르시아만이라는 지명을 바꾸려고 했기 때문임.

차관보 : 금번 분쟁 당사국이나 CNN등 모든 언론에서 Gulf War라는 표현을
사용하고 있음.

대 사 : 그것은 아마도 TV 화면이 작아서 짧은 제목을 써야할 필요 때문일
것임.

차관보 : 우리로서는 걸프 해역의 지명을 둘러싼 논쟁에 개입하지 않겠다는
입장이며, 다만 금번사태를 걸프 전쟁으로 지칭키로 한것은
보편적 국제 관행을 따르는것 뿐이니 오해 없기 바람.

0027

대 사 : 페르시아만이라는 명칭은 오랜 역사적 배경이 있음.

차관보 : 다시 말하지만 걸프해역 지명 문제는 이번 조치와 아무런
관련이 없음.
만약 우리가 페르시아만을 아라비아만으로 바꾸어 부르기로 했다면
귀측에서 항의를 제기할 권리가 있을 것이나, 이번일은 어디까지나
세계적으로 금번 사태를 Gulf War라고 지칭하고 있는 관례에 따른
것이므로 그 이상으로 확대해석 할 필요가 없음.

대 사 : 유엔 문서에도 페르시아만이라는 용어를 쓰고 있으며 3천년 전부터
그렇게 불리어온 역사적 근거도 있음.
부쉬 미 대통령도 페르시아만이라는 지명을 쓰고 있고 다만 현지 미군
사령관들이 잘 몰라서 아랍만이라고 부르는 경우는 있음.
우리로서는 페르시아만 지명 문제가 우리의 영토보전문제
(integrity)와 100% 관련되는 문제임.

차관보 : 우리로서는 걸프 해역의 지위문제에 개입코자 하는 의도가
전혀 없음. 이번일은 어디까지나 금번 전쟁을 어떻게 지칭하느냐
하는 문제이며 지명 문제와는 무관함.

대 사 : 상세한 설명에는 감사하나, 본인으로서는 이 문제가 매우 중요한
문제이며 한국측의 입장을 납득키 어려움.

차관보 : 세계 다수 국가들이 모두 Gulf War라고 부르고 있는데, 그러면
예를 들어 일본등 다른 나라에도 항의를 제기 했는지?

대 사 : 다른 나라에서는 정부에서 언론에 어떤 명칭을 사용하도록 한 것은
아닌 것으로 알고 있음. 특히 한국은 이란과 아주 가까운 나라인데
이러한 일이 생겨 본인으로서는 놀랍고 불행한 마음임.

차관보 : 다시 말하지만 우리가 Gulf War라는 표현을 쓰는것은 금번 사태를
지칭함에 있어 중립적인(unbiased) 입장에서 국제적인 통례를
따르는 것일뿐, 걸프해역의 지위를 바꾸려는 것이 아니며 아무런
정치적 의미가 없음.
따라서 귀측에서 불필요한 오해가 없기를 기대함.
아울러 이란인의 외환관리법 위반 사건 처리는 양국간의 가까운
관계를 감안 최대한 호의적 고려를 할것임.

대 사 : 배려에 감사드림. 장시간 면담을 허락해 주셔서 감사함.   끝.

0028

o With regard to your Embassy's Note of Jan. 23, the Foreign Ministry is going to make an official reply in the form of a diplomatic note in a few days. In the meantime, I wish to provide you with an oral explanation on the subject.

o Recently the Korean government has asked the Korean media to use the term "Gulf War" instead of "Persian Gulf War" concerning the current war in the Gulf area. Concerning this measure, it appears that there is some misunderstanding in your country. In this connection, we wish to point out the following facts :

First, the current use of the term "Gulf War" by the Korean media has nothing to do with the issue of changing the term designating the gulf area located between Iran and the Saudi peninsula for any geographical or historical background or for any consideration of international practices as seen in such international organizationa as the UN. In this connection, we wish to make it clear that we have no intention to change the term designating that particular area.

91. 1. 28 제1차한불, 주한이란대사 면담시 Talking Points

0029

Second, not only the participants of the current conflict but also a vast majority of the international community are presently using the term "Gulf War" instead of "Persian Gulf war" to designate the conflict. The Korean government is simply following what the international community is doing.

Third, the use of the term is totally irrelevant to the Korean government's position on Korea-Iran relations. There is no change in the position of the Korean government to further enhance the existing ties of friendship and cooperation between the two countries.

0030

o   We understand that an Iranian national, Mr. Yazdan Panadh, has been indicted by the Seoul District Prosecutor's Office on charges of violating the Foreign Exchange Law.

o   The case concerns violation of Korea's domestic law and, as such, it has nothing to do with the bilateral relations between Iran and Korea.

o   In view of the close ties of friendship and cooperation between our two countries, however, the Korean government is willing to provide all possible consideration under the existing law. We hope that you will understand such position of our government.

0031

長 官 報 告 事 項

報 告 畢

1991. 1. 28.
中 近 東 課

題 目 : '걸프事態', '걸프戰爭' 用語使用에 대한 駐韓 이란 大使館의 是正要請

駐韓 이란 大使館은 政府의 '걸프事態', '걸프戰爭' 用語使用에 대해 當部에
是正을 要請하여 왔는바, 關聯 事項과 措置計劃을 아래와 같이 보고합니다.

1. 經 緯

○ 1.19 當部는 종래 '페만사태', '페만전쟁'을 '걸프사태', '걸프전쟁'으로
  指稱키로하고 各 部處 및 言論에 通報.

○ 1.22 코리아 헤럴드는 用語變更에 대한 記事를 2면에 2단으로 揭載 (별첨1)

○ 동일 駐韓 이란 大使는 中東阿局長에 電話를 걸어 口頭抗議하고 是正要請
  - 中東阿局長은 용어 변경은 國際慣例에 따른 中立的表現을 채택한
    것으로서 대 이란 友好協力關係의 增進 이라는 정부의 입장과는
    전혀 無關한 것임을 설명.
  - 또한, 我國言論은 '페르시아만'이 아닌 '페만'표현을 쓰고 있는바,
    우리말의 語感上으로도 좋지않은 것이 變更理由중의 하나임.

○ 駐韓이란 大使館 , 1.27자 코리아 헤럴드 讀者 投稿欄에 寄稿文 揭載
  (별첨2)

○ 1.27 當部는 駐韓이란 大使館의 1.23자 구상서 접수 (별첨3)

참고 │ 이란 정부, 1.23 이란주재 외국 특파원에 '페만'용어 사용촉구 및
'걸프'용어 사용시 대응조치 경고

0032

이란側의 主張

o   '페만'표현은 歷史的 根據가 있는것으로서 任意로 바꿀수 없으며
    유엔 事務局도 이 표현을 수차 確認한바 있음.

o   韓國이 유엔 加入을 추진하고 있는만큼 關係當局은 유엔의 慣行을
    존중하여 언론에 대한 지침을 訂正해 주기 바라며, 이는 韓.이 兩國間의
    우호적이며 돈독한 政治.經濟關係에 利益이 될것임.

我側의 對應

가. 駐韓 이란 大使館에 대한 回信(구상서)

o   '걸프사태', '걸프전쟁'의 용어 사용은 다수 국가의 慣例를 따라
    중립적 표현을 쓰겠다는 趣旨에 立脚한것임.

o   또한 상기 용어 변경은 금번 '事態'에 대한 表現方法의 問題이며,
    '地名'表記에 대한 아국의 公式 立場과는 관련이 없음.

o   더구나 韓.이란 關係에 대한 정부의 입장과는 전혀 無關하며,
    兩國의 既存友好 協力關係를 강화해 나가겠다는 政府의 立場에는
    변함이 없음.

나. 상기 回信 송부후 적당한 때에 第 2次官補(非常對策本部長)가 주한
    이란 대사를 招致하여 我國 立場 說明.

다. 주 유엔 대표부에 '페만'용어 사용 관련 유엔 事務局 및 관련 傘下機構
    (地名 標準化 委員會)의 공식 입장등 파악 보고 지시(1.27 기조치)

| 參考 | 今番 事態 呼稱 및 地名 表記 |

o   세계 언론 매체 및 미국등의 전황 브리핑에서 대부분 'Gulf War',
    'War in the Gulf' 등으로 지칭, 일본에서는 '만안' 사용

o   역사적으로는 'Persian Gulf'표현이 많이 사용되어 왔으며,
    많은 지도에도 같은 표기가 발견되나, 일부 지도에는 'the Gulf'
    로 표기 (예:Philips Illustrated Atlas of the World)

o   아랍국에서는 'Arabian Gulf'로 지칭

添 附 : 1. 코리아헤럴드 1.22자 관련기사

         2. 주한 이란 대사관 1.27자 코리아 헤럴드 독자투고문

         3. 주한 이란 대사관 구상서.   끝.

0033

발 신 전 보

번   호 : WIR-0117   910129 0953 FK   종별 : 긴급

수   신 : 주 이란 대사 .총영사

발   신 : 장 관 (중근동)

제   목 : 걸프사태 용어사용

연 : WIR-0110

1. 연호, 제 1차관보는 금 1.28 주한 이란 대사를 불러 '페만사태(전쟁)' 대신 '걸프사태(전쟁)'으로 지칭키로한데 대한 아측 입장을 아래요지로 설명하였으니 참고 바라며 (수일내 문서로 공식회신 예정), 귀 주재국측에서 표제관련 문의등이 있는 경우 이를 참작 대응 바람.

   ㅇ 한국 언론의 '걸프사태(전쟁)'용어 사용은 지리적, 역사적 배경 및 유엔등 국제기구 ~~의명사용하는~~ 걸프해역의 지명을 변경하는 것과는 전혀 무관하며, 아측은 동 해역을 지칭하는 지명을 바꿀 의도가 없음.

   ㅇ 분쟁 당사국은 물론 국제사회에서 대부분 '페만전쟁'이 아닌 '걸프전쟁'이라는 용어를 사용하고 있으며, 한국 정부는 단순히 국제사회의 통례를 따르는것 뿐임.

   ㅇ 용어 사용 문제는 한.이란 양국 관계와는 아무런 관련이 없으며 양국간 기존 우호협력관계를 강화해 나가려는 아국정부 입장에는 변동이 없음.

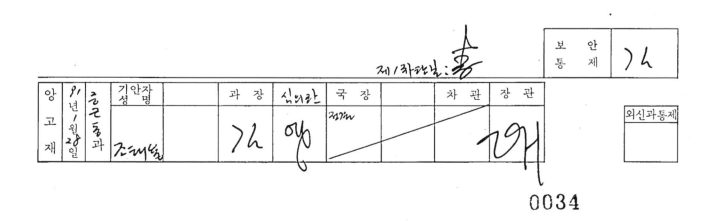

제 1차관보 : 홍

	보 안 통 제	가

앙 고 재	91 년 1 월 28 일	중근동과	기안자 성명 조대식		과 장 가	심의관 신의환 예	국 장 조기능		차 관	장 관 김	외신과통제

0034

2. 현대건설측은 주한 이란 대사관이 최근 이란인 1명이 $15,000을
공지 출국하려다 외환 관리법 위반혐의로 구속 수사중임을 알리면서 이라크
잔류 근로자의 이란 입국 협조를 들어 현대측이 검찰당국에 선처를 부탁해
줄것을 요청하여 왔다고 당부에 통보해 왔음.
이와 관련, 제 1차관보는 상기면담시 주한이란대사에게 이란민간인의 국내법위반
사건 처리문제는 양국관계와는 아무런 관련이 없음을 분명히 하고, 다만 양국간의
가까운 관계를 고려 관계당국이 현행법하에서 최대한 정상을 참작 동 사건을 처리
토록 하겠다고 언급하였으니 참고바람. 끝.

(중동아국장 이 해 순)

예 고 : 91.6.30.일반

0035

외 무 부

종 별 : 지급

번 호 : UNW-0206

수 신 : 장관(중근동)

발 신 : 주 유엔 대사

제 목 : 걸프사태

일 시 : 91 0128 1800

대:WUN-0166

1. 대호, 유엔 공보국에 따르면, 유엔문서에는 PERISIAN GULF 를 사용하도록 되어있으나, 실제로는 편의상 GULF 로 표기하는 예가 종종 있다고함.(별전 2 유엔 공보처 정오 브리핑 자료참조)

2. 또한 지명 표준화 위원회측도 공식 지명관련 결정사항은 없다고함.

첨부:1.ST/CS/SER.A/29, 2. 유엔 공보처 정오 브리핑자료:UNW(F)-043

끝

(대사 현홍주-국장)

예고:91.6.30 일반

중아국

Secretariat

ST/CS/SER.A/29
10 January 1990

ORIGINAL: ENGLISH

EDITORIAL DIRECTIVE

Prepared by Editorial Control at the request of the Chief Editor

To: Members of the staff

Subject: USE OF THE TERMS "PERSIAN GULF" AND "SHATT AL-ARAB"

1.   The term "Persian Gulf" is used in documents, publications and statements emanating from the Secretariat as the standard geographical designation for the body of water lying between the Arabian Peninsula and the Islamic Republic of Iran, thus following longstanding conventional practice. Equally, Shatt al-Arab is used rather than Darvand Rud or Darvand River.

2.   However, in documents, publications and statements emanating from a Member Government or intergovernmental organization, the terminology of the original should be retained.

3.   In cases of doubt, staff members are requested to contact the Chief Editor, who will then issue a ruling in consultation with the Office of the Secretary-General and the Office of Legal Affairs.

90-00567 1412h (E)

3-1

0037

<u>FOR INFORM ||||| N OF UNITED NATIONS SECRETARI— |||LY</u>

21 January 1991

<u>DPI DAILY PRESS BRIEFING</u>

François Giuliani began today's noon briefing by announcing the following appointments of the Secretary-General: at 11 a.m., Prime Minister Juan Carlos Hurtado Miller of Peru. He said they had discussed developments related to the Persian Gulf situation, and the Prime Minister had also informed the Secretary-General of his Government's efforts in the economic and social fields. At noon, the Secretary-General had met with the Permanent Representative of Luxembourg, Jean Feyder, in his capacity as President of the European Economic Community (EEC), at the Ambassador's request.

Later today, continued Mr. Giuliani, the Secretary-General would meet, at 3:30 p.m., with the Permanent Representative of Zaire, Bagbeni Adeito Nzengeya, in his capacity as President of the Security Council, to review the bilateral consultations the President had had this past weekend and also to assess the status of a number of issues before the Council; at 4 p.m., the Permanent Representative of Ecuador, Jose Ayala Lasso, in his capacity as Co-ordinator of the Non-Aligned Caucus in the Security Council; at 4:30 p.m., the Permanent Representative of India, Chinmaya R. Gharekhan, at the Ambassador's request; and at 5:30 p.m., the Permanent Representative of Kuwait, Mohammad Abulhasan, at the Ambassador's request.

Mr. Giuliani informed correspondents that the President of the Security Council had had the following meetings scheduled for today: at approximately 12:30 p.m., the Permanent Representative of Qatar, Hassan Ali Hussain Al-Ni'Mah, to brief the President on the meeting of the Gulf Co-operative Council, held this past weekend. Before 1 p.m., he was scheduled to meet a representative of the United States; and Ambassador Lasso of Ecuador, Co-ordinator of the Non-Aligned Caucus in the Council. Mr. Giuliani added that the President had indicated that, in addition to the situation in the Persian Gulf, he was also discussing possible Council action on Liberia. He said further details on Liberia were not available because the Council, at this point, had not yet had any consultations.

Mr. Giuliani drew attention to a situation report from the Office of the United Nations Disaster Relief Co-ordinator (UNDRO) on the emergency humanitarian situation in the Persian Gulf region, copies of which were available in room 378.

Asked if the Secretary-General had any comment on the shooting this weekend in Latvia, Mr. Giuliani said no, he did not believe so.

Had the Security Council President indicated whether formal consultations were expected today on the Persian Gulf situation? Mr. Giuliani said no.

Did the Secretary-General have any reaction to the "parading of allied prisoners of war" -- and their statements -- by Iraqi authorities"? Mr. Giuliani said the Secretary-General "obviously expects all the parties in that conflict to strictly abide by the provisions of the Geneva Conventions".

* *** *

3041B

3-2

0038

18 January 1991

DPI DAILY PRESS BRIEFING

François Giuliani opened today's DPI briefing with details of the Secretary-General's appointments for the day.

At 10:30 a.m., said Mr. Giuliani, the Secretary-General had met with the Foreign Minister of Indonesia, Ali Alatas. They had, as would be expected, discussed the situation in the Gulf. The Foreign Minister had informed the Secretary-General how the Co-Chairmen of the Paris Peace Conference on Cambodia (France and Indonesia) intended to continue their efforts. The question of East Timor had also been discussed.

At 11 a.m., he continued, the Ambassadors of the Nordic countries had called on the Secretary-General to discuss both the humanitarian aspects of the Gulf conflict and what help their countries could provide, if necessary. The Nordic idea concerning a peace-keeping force for Kuwait in the post-crisis end had also been discussed. As correspondents were aware, contingency planning along those lines had been going on for quite some time, he added.

At 11:30 a.m., the Permanent Representative of the United States, Thomas Pickering, had, at his own request, called on the Secretary-General. He was followed, at noon, also at his own request, by the Permanent Representative of China, Li Daoyu. (It was later announced over the public address system that additional appointments had been arranged for the Secretary-General to receive the Permanent Representatives of France and the Soviet Union at 3:30 p.m. and 4 p.m., respectively.)

Mr. Giuliani went on to say that when he had arrived at his office this morning, the Secretary-General had telephoned the Permanent Representative of Israel to convey his deep regret about the Iraqi missile attack on his country last night. Correspondents would recall that the Secretary-General, on his arrival at the Secretariat entrance, had expressed regrets about the incident, firstly, because it could widen the conflict since Israel was not part of the coalition ranged against Iraq, and secondly, because the attack had been directed at civilian targets.

Mr. Giuliani said the Secretary-General had also been asked what his message to the Government of Israel was, and how he expected Israel to respond. He had replied that he expected the Israeli Government to be as patient as possible. The transcript of his remarks was available in room 378.

As far as the President of the Security Council was concerned, and to anticipate correspondents' questions, Mr. Giuliani said Ambassador Bagbeni Adeito Nzengeya of Zaire had been having bilateral meetings with Council members although no formal or informal sessions were envisaged for the time being. The President had asked members of the coalition to keep the Council informed about the situation in the Gulf as required under paragraph 4 of Security Council resolution 678 (1990). He said the United States, the United Kingdom, France, Saudi Arabia and Kuwait had written the President in that

(more)

30408

3-3

0039

발 신 전 보

WMEM-0015 910129 0952 FK 종별: 지급

번 호 :

수 신 : 주 ~~수산청 참조~~ 전국동지역운한지방 대사//총영사 (이란제외)
이라크, 쿠웨이트

발 신 : 장 관 (중근동)

제 목 : 걸프사태 용어사용

연 : AM-0021

연호 국내에서 금번사태를 걸프사태(전쟁)으로 지칭키로한데 대하여, 주한이란

대사관측은 '페만사태(전쟁)'라는 용어를 계속 사용해 줄것을 요청하여 왔는바,

제1차한보가 금1.28 주한이란대사를 불러 설명하고 ~~아에 대한~~ 아국 입장을 아래 통보하니 참고 바람.

ㅇ 한국 언론의 '걸프사태(전쟁)'용어 사용은 지리적, 역사적 배경
및 유엔등 국제기구 ~~에 만해해 따른~~ 이미 사용하는 걸프해역의 지명을 변경하는 것과는 전혀
무관하며, 아측은 동 해역을 지칭하는 지명을 바꿀 의도가 없음.

ㅇ 분쟁 당사국은 물론 국제사회에서 대부분 '페만전쟁'이 아닌
'걸프전쟁'이라는 용어를 사용하고 있으며, 한국 정부는 단순히 국제사회의
통례를 따르는것 뿐임.

ㅇ 용어 사용 문제는 한.이란 양국 관계 와는 아무런 관련이 없으며
양국간 기존 우호협력관계를 강화해 나가려는 아국정부의 입장에는 변동이 없음.

(중동아국장 이 해 순)

~~수신처 : 주 사우디, 카타르, 바레인, 오만, UAE 대사~~

예 고 : 91.6.30.일반

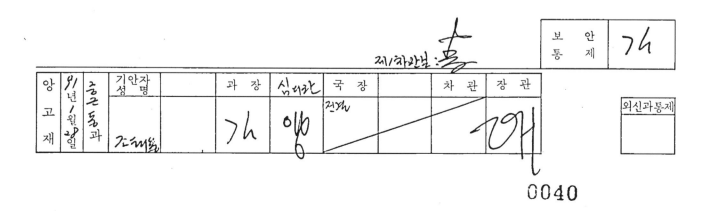

제1차한님 :

보 안 통 제	74

기안
성명	과 장 심대관	국 장	차 관	장 관	외신과통제
91년 1월 28일 중근동과 조해률	74 엽	전겸		74

0040

외 무 부

관리
번호 이-1006

종 별 :

번 호 : IRW-0091   일 시 : 91 0129 1400

수 신 : 장관(중근동)

발 신 : 주 이란 대사

제 목 : 걸프사태 용어사용

대호관련 당관 파악내용을 아래보고함.

1. 주재국 MINISTRY OF CULTURE AND ISLAMIC GUIDANCE 는 1.22 당지주재 외국특파원에게 향후 뉴스 DISPATCH 시 GULF 대신 THE PERSIAN GULF 를 사용할것을 정식 요청하며 위반시 의법조치하겠다고 밝혔음(당지 영자지 1.22 자 KAYHAN INT'L 지보도)

2. 당관이 당지 일본언론(요미우리및 아사히)특파원과 접촉한바에의하면 이들 특파원들은 1.22 주재국 정부로부터 전화로 상기 사실을 통보받았으며 금 1.29 이를 정식 통보하는 문서를 접수하였다고 설명하였음.

3. 참고로 일본대사관 담당에의하면 당지 개최 페만세미나(1.21-22)관련 주재국에 공한 송부시 PERSIAN GULF 를 사용하였더니 외무부에서 정식 항의하였던적이 있다고 언급하였음. 끝

(대사정경일-국장)

예고:91.12.31 까지

長 官 報 告 事 項

報告畢

1991. 1.31.
中 近 東 課

題 目 : '걸프' 地名에 대한 유엔 用例 및 이란政府 動向

駐유엔 大使 報告에 의하면 "(Persian) Gulf" 地名關聯 유엔 次元의 公式

決定事項은 없으며, 한편 이란政府는 同國 駐在 外國 特派員들이 '걸프'라는

用語를 使用할 경우 依法 措置하겠다고 警告하는등 敏感한 反應을 보이고

있음을 報告 드립니다.

1. 유엔의 用例 (駐유엔 大使 報告)

- ○ "(Persian) Gulf" 지명 관련 "유엔 지명 표준화 위원회"의 공식 결정사항은 없음. (동 지명에 대한 유엔 차원의 국제적 합의 부재)

- ○ 유엔 사무국 내부 문서인 문서작성 지침에는 "Persian Gulf"를 사용하도록 되어 있으나 실제로는 편의상 "Gulf"라고 표기하는 예가 종종 있음.

- ○ 또한 회원국 제출 문서등 유엔에 접수된 외부문서에 대해서는 어떻게 표기 되었든(예 : Arabian Gulf) 동 표기를 유엔 임의로 수정하지 말도록 상기 문서작성 지침에 명시

2. 이란 政府 動向 (駐이란 大使 報告)

- ○ 1.22. 이란 문화.회교지도부(Ministry of Culture and Islamic Guidance)는 이란 주재 외국 특파원에게 향후 기사 송고시 "Persian Gulf"를 사용토록 정식 요청하고 위반시 의법조치 하겠다고 경고

- ○ 이란 주재 일본 대사관에 의하면, 이란측에 보낸 공한에서 "Gulf"라는 용어를 사용했더니 외무부에서 정식 항의한 사례도 있음. 끝.

담 당	과 장	심의관	국 장	차관보	차 관	장 관
조재룡						

0042

(Draft)

ODZ 91-53

    The Ministry of Foreign Affairs presents its compliments to the Embassy of the Islamic Republic of Iran and, with reference to the latter's Note No. 1992 dated January 23, 1991, has the honour to ~~inform~~ ~~the latter of the official position of the Government of the Republic of~~ ~~Korea concerning the use of the term "Gulf War" by the Korean media~~ ~~referring to the ongoing conflict in~~ the Middle East ~~and around Iraq.~~

    ~~In this regard, the Ministry has the honour to~~ point out the following; First, the current use of the term "Gulf War" ~~by the Korean media~~ has no bearing on the question of changing the geographical name desingnating the gulf area located between Iran and the ~~Saudi~~ Arabian peninsula ~~(for any geogra-~~ ~~phical or historical background or for any consideration of international~~ ~~practices as observed in such international organizations as the United~~ ~~Nations.)~~ In this connection, the Ministry wishes to make it clear that the Korean Government had no intention to ~~change~~ review the geographical name designating that particular area.

Second, a vast majority of the international community as well as the parties to the current conflict are presently using the term "Gulf War" instead of "Persian Gulf War" to designate the conflict. The Korean Government is simply following ~~what is apparently the practice of the~~ ~~international community.)~~ the terms generally used by the international community.

Third, the question of designating the present conflict is totally irrelevant to the Korean Government's position on Korean-Iranian rela- tions. The Ministry wishes to assure the Embassy that there is no change in the position of the Korean Government to further enhance the existing ties of friendship and cooperation between the two countries.

    The Ministry avails itself of this opportunity to renew to the Embassy the assurances of its highest consideration.

Seoul, January 30, 1991

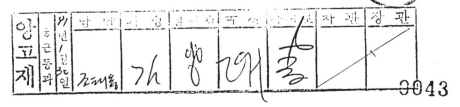

0043

ODZ 91-53

The Ministry of Foreign Affairs presents its compliments to the
Embassy of the Islamic Republic of Iran and, with reference to the
latter's Note No. 1992 dated January 23, 1991, has the honour to point
out the following :

First, the current use of the term "Gulf War" has no bearing on the
question of changing the geographical name desingnating the gulf area
located between Iran and the Arabian peninsula. In this connection, the
Ministry wishes to make it clear that the Korean Government had no intention to review the geographical name designating that particular area.

Second, a vast majority of the international community as well as the
parties to the current conflict are presently using the term "Gulf War"
instead of "Persian Gulf War" to designate the conflict. The Korean
Government is simply following the terms generally used by the international community.

Third, the question of designating the present conflict is totally
irrelevant to the Korean Government's position on Korean-Iranian relations. The Ministry wishes to assure the Embassy that there is no change
in the position of the Korean Government to further enhance the existing
ties of friendship and cooperation between the two countries.

The Ministry avails itself of this opportunity to renew to the
Embassy the assurances of its highest consideration.

Seoul, January 31, 1991

0044

2. 한국의 지원에 대한 각국 반응, 1991

0045

	분류번호	보존기간

발 신 전 보

AM-0029   910130 2346 DP

번   호 :   종별 :

수   신 : 주 전재외 공관장 ~~대사·총영사~~

발   신 : 장   관   (미북)

제   목 : 대미 추가 지원 발표관련 테러 활동 대처

WHG-133 WNM-72
~~WPD-127~~ WSV-303
WYG-117 WCZ-88
WAG-41 WRL-73
WRM-97 WMG-50

연 : AM-12.

1. 연호 정부의 추가 지원이 발표되고 아국이 특히 군 수송기를 지원키로 결정함에 따라 ~~본부문서능~~ 일부 친이라크 테러 단체에 의한 대 아국민 및 시설등에 대한 테러 가능성이 있을 것으로 우려됨.

2. 따라서 귀관은 본부에서 연호로 이미 지시한 바에 따라 주재국 당국과의 긴밀한 협조하에 필요한 대비책을 강구하기 바람.

3. 또한 아국의 추가 지원에 대한 귀주재국 정부 및 언론등 반응이 있으면 수시 보고바람.   끝.

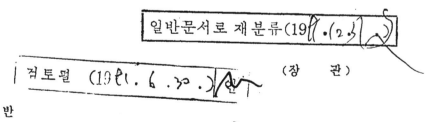

일반문서로 재분류(1991.12.   )

검토필 (1991. 6. 30.   )

(장   관)

예 고 : 91.12.31.일반

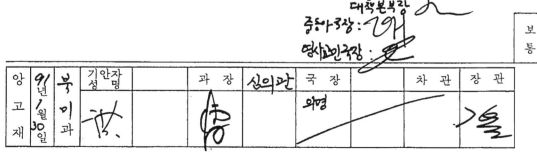

대책본부장
중동아국장 :
영사교민국장 :

		보 안	통 제	

앙고재	91년 1월 30일	북미과	기안자 성명		과 장	심의관	국 장 외명		차 관	장 관		외신과통제

0046

발 신 전 보

	분류번호	보존기간

번 호 : AM-0030   910130 2351 DP   종별 :

수 신 : 주전재외 공관장 ▦▦▦▦▦ 대사 총영사

발 신 : 장 관 (미북)

제 목 : 걸프전 관련 아국의 추가 지원

　　　　정부는 걸프사태와 관련 다국적군 특히 미국에 대하여 2억 8천만불의 추가
지원을 제공키로 결정하고 이를 1991.1.30(수) 18:15(서울시간) 다음과 같이
공식발표 하였음.

1.　정부는 지난해 8.2. 걸프 사태가 발생한 이래 무력에 의한 침략은 용인될 수
　　없다는 국제 정의와 국제법 원칙에 따라 유엔 안보 이사회 결의를 지지하고
　　이의 이행을 위한 국제적 노력을 지원하여 왔음. 이러한 입장에서 정부는
　　지난해 9.24. 다국적군 및 주변국 경제 지원을 위해 2억 2천만불의 지원을
　　발표한 바 있으며 또한 지난 1.24. 사우디에 군 의료 지원단을 파견한 바 있음.

2.　그러나 유엔을 비롯한 전세계 평화 우호국들의 노력에도 불구하고 지난 1.17.
　　걸프 전쟁이 발발하여 중동 지역은 물론 전세계의 평화 및 안정에도 큰 위협이
　　되고 있으며, 더우기 이번 전쟁이 예상보다 오래 계속될 조짐이 나타남에 따라
　　다국적군은 이에 따른 막대한 전비와 재정 수요에 직면하게 되었음.

/계속/

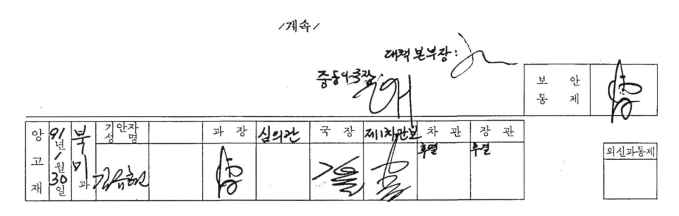

0047

3. 이에 따라 정부는 다음과 같은 추가 지원을 제공키로 결정하였음.

　o 추가 지원 규모는 2억8천만불로함.

　　- 이중 1억7천만불 상당은 국방부 재고 군수물자 및 장비 제공으로 하고 나머지 1억1천만불은 현금 및 수송 지원으로 함.
　　(구체적 집행 용도 및 내역은 한.미 양국간 협의를 거쳐 결정 예정)

　　- 금번 추가 지원은 다국적군 특히 미국을 위한 것이며 주변국 경제 지원은 불포함.

　　- 아국의 총 지원 규모는 금번 추가 지원으로 작년 약속액 2억2천만불을 포함, 총 5억불이됨.

　o 상기 지원과는 별도로 국회의 동의를 받아 후방 수송 지원 목적을 위하여 군 수송기(C-130) 5대를 파견키로 원칙적으로 결정하였으며, 이를 위한 기술적인 사항은 아국 국방부와 주한 미군간에 협의 예정임.　끝.

(장　관)

0048

걸프戰 關聯 한국 정부의 追加 支援 決定

公式 發表

1991. 1. 30.

18:15

1. 政府는 지난해 8.2. 걸프 事態가 發生한 이래 武力에 의한 侵略은 容認될 수 없다는 國際 正義와 國際法 原則에 따라 유연 安保 이사회 決議를 支持하고 이의 履行을 위한 國際的 努力을 支援하여 왔음. 이러한 立場에서 政府는 지난해 9.24. 多國籍軍 및 周邊國 經濟 支援을 위해 2億2千万弗의 支援을 發表한 바 있으며 또한 지난 1.24. 사우디에 軍 醫療 支援團을 派遣한 바 있음.

2. 그러나 유연을 비롯한 全世界 平和 愛好國들의 努力에도 불구하고 지난 1.17. 걸프 戰爭이 勃發하여 中東 地域은 물론 全世界의 平和 및 安定에도 큰 威脅이 되고 있으며, 더우기 이번 戰爭이 예상보다 오래 계속될 조짐이 나타남에 따라 多國籍軍은 이에 따른 막대한 戰費와 財政 需要에 직면하게 되었음.

0049

3. 이에 따라 정부는 다음과 같은 추가 지원을 제공키로 결정하였음.

ㅇ 追加 支援 規模는 2億8千万弗로함.

　－ 이중 1億7千万弗 相當은 國防部 在庫 軍需物資 및 裝備 提供으로
　　하고 나머지 1億1千万弗은 現金 및 輸送 支援으로 함.

　　　※ 具體的 執行 用途 및 內譯은 韓.美 兩國間 協議를 거쳐 決定

　－ 今番 追加 支援은 多國籍軍 특히 美國을 위한 것이며 周邊國 經濟
　　支援은 不包含.

　－ 我國의 總 支援 規模는 今番 追加 支援으로 昨年 約束額 2億2千万弗을
　　包含, 總 5億弗이됨.

ㅇ 上記 支援과는 別途로 국회의 동의를 받아 軍 輸送機(C-130) 5대를 派遣키로
　원칙적으로 결정하였으며, 이를 위한 기술적인 사항은 아국 國防部와 駐韓
　美軍間에 협의 예정임.

0050

걸프戰 關聯 多國籍軍에 대한

追加 支援 決定 說明 資料

91. 1. 30.

外 務 部

1. 追加 支援 決定 背景

o 今番 걸프戰爭은 유엔 安保理의 決議에 立脚, 유엔 歷史上 最大의 會員國이
參與하고 있는 國際社會의 對이라크 膺懲戰인 바, 우리의 積極的 支援 및
參與는 우리의 國際 平和 維持 의지 과시등 國際的 位相 提高에 크게
기여

o 걸프戰爭으로 인한 450億弗 정도의 막대한 戰費 및 軍需 物資 需要 增加에
따라 國際的으로 多國籍軍에 대한 追加 支援 必要性 增大

o 日本 政府가 90億弗, 獨逸이 55億弗의 寄與金을 多國籍軍에 追加로 提供
하고 있고 國際的으로도 多國籍軍의 막대한 戰費를 國際社會가 分擔해야
된다는 與論이 일어나고 있음에 비추어, 我國으로서도 우리의 伸張된
國際的 地位等을 감안, 應分의 寄與를 할 필요가 있음.

- 1 -

0051

° 多國籍軍 活動에 參與 및 支援에 대한 美國 및 世界의 耳目이 集中되어 있어 追加 支援時 國際社會에서 우리의 發言權等 立地 强化에 效果가 클 것으로 期待됨.

 - 걸프 戰爭 終了後 各國의 支援에 대한 評價 效果 長期間 持續 豫想

 * 美國內 與論은 걸프 戰爭에 대해 81%라는 壓倒的인 支持 表明

2. 考慮 事項

① 安保的 考慮事項

° 이라크의 武力侵略을 단호히 응징하고자 하는 유엔을 中心으로한 國際 社會의 努力을 적극 支援하므로써 韓半島의 有事時 國際社會의 共同 介入을 통한 平和 回復 期待 및 이라크에 대한 成功的인 膺懲時 韓半島 에서 武力 挑發 可能性 豫防 效果 期待

° 韓.美 安保協力 關係 鞏固化

 - 能動的이고 自發的인 支援을 통하여 我國이 信賴할 수 있는 友邦이라는 認識을 美國 朝野에 提高시키므로써 韓.美 安保協力 關係는 물론 全般的인 韓.美 友好關係 强化에 寄與

 * 걸프戰 終了後 美國은 友邦國의 對美支援 實績을 통해 美國의 對友邦國 關係를 再評價하려는 움직임(현재 美國 議會 및 一般 與論은 日本. 獨逸을 "자기들이 필요할 때만 美國을 친구로 대하는 國家-fair weather ally-라고 批判)

- 2 -

0052

② 經濟 通商的 考慮 事項

○ 걸프戰 終了後, 安定된 原油 供給 確保 및 戰後 復舊事業 參與 等 對中東
  經濟 進出 基盤 마련

○ 걸프戰의 早速 終結을 위한 國際的인 努力을 支援하므로써 걸프事態가
  我國 經濟에 미치는 影響을 最小化 하는데 寄與
  - 事態가 長期化 되어 國際原油價가 上昇할 경우, 我國 經濟에 미치는
    影響 深大(原油價가 배럴당 10弗 上昇時 年33億弗 追加 負擔 發生)

③ 外交的 考慮 事項

○ 6.25 事變時 유엔의 도움을 받은 國家로서 對이라크 共同制裁에
  관한 유엔 決議에 적극 참여해야 할 道義的 의무 履行

○ 我國의 伸張된 國威에 副應하여 國際 平和 維持 努力에 一翼 담당
  - 我國의 支援이 微溫的일 경우, 經濟的 利益만 追求한다는 國際的
    非難 可能性 考慮
  - 追加 支援이 自發的인 것이므로 多國籍軍側이 어느정도 評價하는
    水準에서의 支援 必要

- 3 -

0053

ㅇ 걸프戰 終了後 對中東 外交 기반 强化 布石의 일환

　　- 長期的인 觀點에서 사우디, 이집트, UAE 等 中東 友邦國들과의 關係
　　增進을 위한 重要한 投資

　　　　· 우리의 主要 原油 導入線이자 建設 輸出 市場이라는 점 및 其他
　　　　經濟的 活動 餘地等을 감안

　　- 戰後 樹立될 쿠웨이트, 이라크 兩國 政府와의 즉각적인 關係 强化
　　基盤 마련

④ 支援 規模 關聯 考慮

　　ㅇ 우리의 自發的 支援으로서 伸張된 國力에 알맞는 우리의 성숙한 모습을
　　國際的으로 과시

　　ㅇ 우리의 醫療支援團 派遣 等을 고려

　　ㅇ 財政 支援 規模는 적정한 수준에서 검토

添 附 : 1. 多國籍軍 派遣 現況

　　　　2. 各國의 支援 現況

　　　　　　가. 經濟 支援

　　　　　　나. 醫療 支援　　　　　끝.

- 4 -

0054

多國籍軍 派遣 現況

91. 1. 30. 現在

國 家	軍事力 派遣 및 參戰	備 考
美 國	◦ 兵 力 : 492,000 名 ◦ 탱 크 : 2,000 臺 ◦ 航空機 : 1,300 臺 ◦ 艦 艇 : 60 隻 (航空母艦 7隻)	
GCC (6個國)	◦ 兵 力 : 150,500 名 ◦ 탱 크 : 800 臺 ◦ 航空機 : 330 臺 ◦ 艦 艇 : 36 隻	사우디, 쿠웨이트, 바레인, 오만, UAE, 카타르
英 國	◦ 兵 力 : 35,000 名 ◦ 탱 크 : 170 臺 ◦ 航空機 : 72 臺 ◦ 艦 艇 : 16 隻	

國 家	軍事力 派遣 및 參戰	備 考
프랑스	o 兵 力 : 10,000 名 o 탱 크 : 40 臺 o 航空機 : 40 臺 o 艦 艇 : 14 隻	
이집트	o 兵 力 : 35,000 名 o 탱 크 : 400 臺	
시리아	o 兵 力 : 19,000 名 o 탱 크 : 300 臺	
파키스탄	o 兵 力 : 7,000 名	6千名 追加派遣 豫定
터 키	o 兵 力 : 5,000 名 o 艦 艇 : 2 隻	國境配置 約10万名
방글라데시	o 兵 力 : 2,000 名	3千名 追加派遣 豫定

0056

國 家	軍事力 派遣 및 參戰	備 考
카나다	○ 兵 力 : 2,000 名 ○ 航空機 : 24 臺 ○ 艦 艇 : 3 隻	
모로코	○ 兵 力 : 1,700 名	
세네갈	○ 兵 力 : 500 名	
니제르	○ 兵 力 : 480 名	
이태리	○ 航空機 : 8 臺 ○ 艦 艇 : 6 隻	
濠 洲	○ 艦 艇 : 3 隻	
벨기에	○ 艦 艇 : 3 隻	
네델란드	○ 艦 艇 : 3 隻	
스페인	○ 艦 艇 : 3 隻	
아르헨티나	○ 兵 力 : 100 名 ○ 艦 艇 : 2 隻	

0057

國 家	軍事力 派遣 및 參戰	備 考
그리스	ㅇ 艦艇 : 1隻	
포르투갈	ㅇ 艦艇 : 1隻	
노르웨이	ㅇ 艦艇 : 1隻	
체 코	ㅇ 兵力 : 200名	
總計 (總 28個國)	ㅇ 兵力 : 760,480名 ㅇ 탱크 : 3,710臺 ㅇ 航空機 : 1,774臺 ㅇ 艦艇 : 154隻	※ 蘇聯은 艦艇 2隻을 參戰 目的이 아니라 觀察 目的으로 派遣

0058

各國의 支援 現況

가. 經濟 支援

國 家	戰爭 勃發 前	戰爭 勃發 後
日 本	. 40億弗(20億弗 : 多國籍軍 支援, 20億弗 : 周邊國 支援)	. 90億弗(對美 現金 支援)
獨 逸	. 20.8億弗(33億 마르크)	. 10億弗(1億6千7百万弗의 이스라엘 支援額 및 1億4百万 弗의 英國軍 支援額 包含) . 55億弗(對美 支援)
E C	. 19.7億弗	
英 國	. EC 次元 共同 步調	
불 란 서	"	
이 태 리	. 1.45億弗(1次 算定額), "	
벨 기 에	. EC 次元 共同 步調	. 1億1千3百5拾万 BF
네 덜 란 드	"	. 1億8千万弗(戰前 支出 包含)
스 페 인	"	
폴 투 갈	"	
그 리 스	"	

0059

國　家	戰爭 勃發 前	戰爭 勃發 後
카 나 다	. 6千6百万弗	
노르웨이	. 2千1百万弗	
濠　洲	8百万弗(難民救護)	
G.C.C.國	. 사 우 디 : 60億弗 . 쿠 웨이트 : 50億弗 . U.A.E. : 20億弗	. 사 우 디 : 135億弗 . 쿠 웨이트 : 135億弗

0060

나. 醫療 支援

國 家	内 譯
美 國	. 사우디 담맘港에 病院船 2隻 派遣(1,000 病床) . 사우디 알바틴에 綜合 醫療團 運營 (專門醫 35 名, 350 病床)
英 國	. 野戰病院 派遣(醫師 200名, 400 病床) (有事時 對備 約 1,500名의 追加 軍 醫療陣 派遣 準備中)
濠 洲	. 2個 醫療團 派遣 檢討中
방글라데쉬	. 2個 醫務 中隊 300名 派遣
카 나 다	. 野戰病院 派遣(醫療陣 550名, 225 病床)
던 마 크	. 軍 醫療陣 30-40名 · 英國軍에 配置
헝 가 리	. 自願 民間醫療陣 30-40名 英國軍에 配置
체 코	. 自願 醫療陣 150名 派遣
파키스탄	. 1個 醫務 中隊 100名 派遣
오스트리아	. 野戰 엠블란스 1臺 派遣
필 리 핀	. 民間 醫療支援團 270名 派遣

0061

國　家	內　譯
폴란드	. 病院船 1隻 派遣 準備中
뉴질랜드	. 民間 醫療陣 50名 , 바레인 駐屯 美 海軍 病院에 勤務 . 軍 醫療團 20名 追加 派遣 決定
싱가폴	. 醫療支援團 30名 , 英國軍 病院에 勤務
벨기에	. 民.軍 自願 醫療 支援團 50名 派遣 . 醫療 裝備 支援(野戰 寢臺 2,800個, 앰블란스 1臺, 負傷兵 護送用 航空機 2臺)

0062

관리 번호	91-164

외 무 부

종 별 : 지 급

번 호 : USW-0418

일 시 : 91 0125 1553

수 신 : 장관(미북, 중근동, 미안, 아일)

발 신 : 주 미 대사

제 목 : 걸프 사태 관련 아국 지원 내용 보도

1. 금 1.25 자 USA TODAY 지의 " ALLIES' CONTRIBUTIONS UNDER SCRUTINY" 제하의 기사(FAX 편 기 송부)에 실린 도표에 따르면, 걸프 사태 관련 아국 지원 약속 총액이 1 억 2 천만불로 되어 있는바, 이와관련 당관은 동기사를 작성한 SHAREN JOHNSON 기자를 접촉, 아국의 지원 액수는 전선국에 대한 경제 지원 1 억불을 포함, 총 2 억 2 천만불이라는점을 설명하고, 관련 상세 자료를 송부함.

2. 한편 USW(F)-0310 로 FAX 송부한 별첨 금일자 NYT 지의 일본측 추가 지원 관련 사진 해설 기사는 작일 발표된 추가 지원 90 억불을 포함, 걸프 사태 관련 일본측 지원 약속 총액이 110 억불이라고 보도함으로서 전기 USA TODAY 지에 보도된 아국 지원 약속 액수와 마찬가지로 전선국에 대한 경제 지원 액수 20 억불을 누락 시켰는바, 최근 당지 언론과 미 행정부 관련부서에서는 금번 사태 관련 제 3 국의 대미, 대 전선국 지원 내용이 복잡, 다기해짐에 따라 내부적인 MISCOMMUNICATION 등으로 인해 여사한 혼란상을 빈번히 노정시키고 있는 형편임을 참고로 첨언함.

(대사 박동진-국장)

91.12.31 일반

미주국   아주국   미주국   중아국

수신 장관 (미북, 중근동, 一반, 아이)
발신 주미대사
제목 첨부. (1매)

Japan's Pledge to Gulf Effort Is Praised
Prime Minister Toshiki Kaifu, foreground, and members of his party during convention yesterday in Tokyo. Mr. Kaifu's announcement that Japan would contribute $9 billion to the allied forces fighting Iraq and supply aircraft for evacuating refugees was hailed by United States officials as "significant." The new pledge brings Japan's total to $11 billion

- 91. 1. 25.
- NYT 지

→ 전선중에 대한
격주 기원은
의역한 약속임.

0064

관리 번호	91-29

외 무 부

종 별 :

번 호 : UNW-0233

일 시 : 91 0130 1720

수 신 : 장관 (국연,미북,기정)

발 신 : 주 유엔 대사

제 목 : 걸프사태 관련 추가지원

대: AM-0030

연: UNW-0142

대호 걸프사태 관련 아국 추가지원 내역 (추가경비 지원 및 수송단 파견)도연호 고려에 비추어 유엔사무총장 및 안보리 의장에게 본직 서한으로 통보코자하는바 별도 본부지침 있을시 지급 회시바람. 끝

(대사 현홍주-국장)

예고:91.6.30. 일반

예고문에 의거 일반문서로		서명
재분류19 91 6 30		

국기국   장관   차관   미주국   정와대   안기부

PAGE 1

갓

외 무 부

종 별 :

번 호 : UNW-0235   일 시 : 91 0130 1800

수 신 : 장 관(미북,국연,해기,기정)

발 신 : 주 유엔 대사

제 목 : 걸프전 관련 추가지원

　　대: AM-0030

　　당대표부는 1.30 대호 내용을 프레스 릴리스로작성, 각국대표부, 유엔사무국 및 외신기자 대상배포한바, 동자료 별전 송부함.

　　첨부: FAX 1 매: UNW(F)-052

　　끝

　　(대사 현홍주-국장,관장)

미주국 안기부	장관 공보처	차관	1차보	2차보	국기국	정문국	정와대	종리실
		중아국						

PAGE 1

REPUBLIC OF KOREA
PERMANENT OBSERVER MISSION TO THE UNITED NATIONS
866 UNITED NATIONS PLAZA, SUITE 300, NEW YORK, N.Y. 10017. TEL: 371-1280

No. 04/91   30 January 1991

PRESS RELEASE

KOREA PROVIDES ADDITIONAL CONTRIBUTION OF
280 MILLION US DOLLARS AND TRANSPORTATION AIRCRAFTS
TO MULTINATIONAL FORCES

materiel

The Government of the Republic of Korea announced, on 30 January 1991, that it will make an additional contribution of US$ 280 million in financial and material support to the multinational coalition forces in the Persian Gulf region.

Together with the initial contribution of US$ 220 million, which was announced on 24 September 1990, the Republic of Korea's contribution to date totals US$ 500 million. In addition, the Republic of Korea sent, on 24 January 1991, a 154-member medical support group to Saudi Arabia.

military transport planes or aircraft

The Republic of Korea has also decided to dispatch five transportation aircrafts (C-130) to Saudi Arabia, by mid-February, to be used for transport of supplies inside Saudi Arabia. This decision is subject to the approval of the National Assembly.

These measures further represent the firm and sincere commitment of the Government of the Republic of Korea to help implement the resolutions of the Security Council.

relevant */adopted by*

1 - 1

0067

영23시보 김

외 무 부

관리번호 91-241

종 별 :

번 호 : CNW-0144   일 시 : 91 0130 1830

수 신 : 장 관(미북,중근동)

발 신 : 주 카 나 다 대사

제 목 : 걸프전 관련 아국의 추가지원 반응

대 : AM-0029. 30

1. 1.30. 외무부 WATERFALL 북아과장은 대호 아국 정부의 추가지원 내용 설명에 대해 카 정부는 한국정부의 금번 추가지원 조치를 크게 환영한다고 하면서 상세 내용을 관련 부서에도 전달 하겠다고 말하였음.

2. 한편 당관은 금번 추가지원 발표 관련 대 테러 경계대책 일환으로 주재국 외무부와 협조 당관 전직원 외교관 차량 번호판을 일반차량 번호판으로 교체토록 추진중임. 당지 미국, 영국, 호주, 일본등 다국적군 참여국 및 주요 지원국들은 이미 상기 조치를 취한바 있음. 끝

(대사 - 국장)

예고문 : 91.12.31. 일반

일반문서로 재분류 19(12.31.)

검 토 필 (19 . .)

미주국   차관   1차보   중아국   정와대   안기부

91.01.31   09:35
외신 2과   통제관 BT

0068

외 무 부

종   별 :

번   호 : IDW-0019   일   시 : 91 0131 1600

수   신 : 장관(미북,구일)

발   신 : 주 아일랜드 대사

제   목 : 걸프전 관련 아국지원

대:AM-0029

1.31 일자 THE IFISH TIMES 는 한국이 걸프전과 관련, 다국적군의 전비로서2 억 8 천만불을 추가지원하는 외에 5 기의 C-130 대로 구성된 군수송단을 지원 예정이라고 AFP 기사를 인용, 보도하였음. 끝.

(대사 민형기-국장)

미주국   차관   1차보   2차보   구주국   청와대   안기부   국방부

외 무 부

종   별 :

번   호 : CSW-0081   일   시 : 91 0131 1620

수   신 : 장관(미북,중근동,미남)

발   신 : 주 칠레 대사

제   목 : 대미 추가지원 관련 기사

대:AM-0029

당지 최대 일간 EL MERCURIO 지 1.31. 자는 '서울의 다국적군에 대한 추가 지원'
제하에, 대호건에 관한 서울발 UPI 통신을 논평없이 인용 보도하였음. 끝

(대사 문창화-국장)

미주국	차관	1차보	2차보	미주국	중아국	청와대	안기부

PAGE 1   91.02.01   04:55

외 무 부

종 별 :

번 호 : ARW-0089   일 시 : 91 0131 1600

수 신 : 장관(미북, 해공, 기정)

발 신 : 주 아르헨티나대사

제 목 : 대미추가 지원

　　당지 1.31.자 BUENOS AIRES HERALD 지는 UP 를인용, 국제면에 1단기사로 한국정부가 현금 1억 1천만불과 물자 1억 7천만불 상당 도합 2억 8천만불 및 150명의 병력을 포함하는 5대의 수송기를 연합군측에 추가 지원키로 결정하였다고 논평없이게재 하였음을 보고함.

　　(대사 이상진-국장)

| 미주국 | 장관 | 차관 | 1차보 | 2차보 | 중아국 | 청와대 | 총리실 | 안기부 |
| 공보처 | 대책반 | | | | | | | |

외신 1과 통제관

0071

원 본

외 무 부

종 별 : 지 급

번 호 : YMW-0093

일 시 : 91 0131 1400

수 신 : 장 관(중근동,미북,기정) (千희신)

발 신 : 주 예멘 대사

제 목 : 대미 추가 지원관련

대:AM-0029,30

1. 대호, 아국 추가 지원 결정(군 수송기 및 2 억 8 천만불 지원)에 대한 주재국 언론반응은 1.31. 현재 없는것으로 파악되고 있음.

2. 노구찌 일본 대사에 의하면 일본 정부의 군 수송기 5 대 지원 계획과관련 주재국 외무성에 동 계획으로 인하여 주재국내의 일본인 신변안전에 위협을 받지 않을까 우려를 표시하였던바, 외무 담당 국무장관 DALI 는 동 군 수송기가 난민 수송이라는 비군사 목적에 한정한다는 점을 확인하고 우려할 필요가 없다는반응을 보였다고함.

3. 한. 미 양국간의 협의 결과 아국 군 수송기의 사용용도가 걸프 전쟁의 군수물자 수송등 직접 군사 지원일 경우 주재국내 아국인에 대한 비판 여론뿐만아니라 테러 가능성 있다고 사료되오니 대외적으로 동 협의 결과가 발표되기전에당관에 알려주시기 바람. 끝.

(대사 류 지호-국장)

예고:91.12.31. 일반

91 6 30.

미주국장과 상의후 답 려주겠음.

중아국	장관	차관	1차보	2차보	미주국	청와대	총리실	안기부

91.02.01   19:24

외신 2과 통제관 BA

0072

주 국 련 대 표 부 COPY

주국련(공) 35260-*068*   1990. 1. 31.

수신 장관

참조 수신처 참조

제목 걸프전 관련 추가지원

1. UNW-0235의 관련입니다.

2. 연호관련 당대표부의 프레스릴리스를 별첨과 같이 송부합니다.

첨 부 : 동자료 1부. 끝.

주 국 련 대 사

수신처 : 해외공보관장, 국제기구조약국장, 정보문화국장, 미주국장

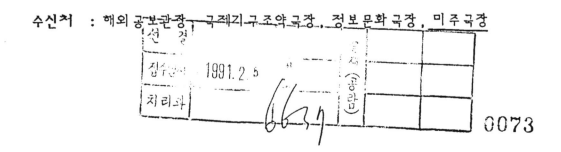

REPUBLIC OF KOREA

PERMANENT OBSERVER MISSION TO THE UNITED NATIONS
866 UNITED NATIONS PLAZA, SUITE 300, NEW YORK, N.Y. 10017. TEL: 371-1280

No. 04/91   30 January 1991

<u>PRESS RELEASE</u>

<u>KOREA PROVIDES ADDITIONAL CONTRIBUTION OF</u>

<u>280 MILLION US DOLLARS AND TRANSPORTATION AIRCRAFTS</u>

<u>TO MULTINATIONAL FORCES</u>

The Government of the Republic of Korea announced, on 30 January 1991, that it will make an additional contribution of US$ 280 million in financial and material support to the multinational coalition forces in the Persian Gulf region.

Together with the initial contribution of US$ 220 million, which was announced on 24 September 1990, the Republic of Korea's contribution to date totals US$ 500 million. In addition, the Republic of Korea sent, on 24 January 1991, a 154-member medical support group to Saudi Arabia.

The Republic of Korea has also decided to dispatch five transportation aircrafts (C-130) to Saudi Arabia, by mid-February, to be used for transport of supplies inside Saudi Arabia. This decision is subject to the approval of the National Assembly.

These measures further represent the firm and sincere commitment of the Government of the Republic of Korea to help implement the resolutions of the Security Council.

0074

외 무 부

종 별 :

번 호 : KNW-0138　　　　　　　　　일 시 : 91 0201 1300

수 신 : 장관(미북,아프이,정일,기정)

발 신 : 주 케냐 대사

제 목 : 걸프전 관련 아국의 추가지원

　　　대 AM-0029

　　　당지 KTN 방송은 1.30 저녁 뉴스시간에 CNN 의 WAR IN THE GULF 보도중 한국은
걸프전 관련 2 억 8 천만불 지원 요지의 자막 보도함. 끝

　　　(대사 이동익-국장)

　　　예고 91.12.31 일반

일반문서로 재분류(1991.12.5)

검 토 필 (19)

미주국　　중아국　　정문국　　안기부

외 무 부

종 별 :

번 호 : BHW-0084

일 시 : 91 0201 1600

수 신 : 장관(미북,중근동)

발 신 : 주 바레인 대사

제 목 : 걸프사태

대:AM-0029

주재국의 AL-AYAM 반관영 아랍어 일간지는 금 2.1 1 면 3 단기사로 동경발 KUNA(쿠웨이트 통신)을 인용, 한국이 쿠웨이트로 부터 이라크를 축출하기 위한 다국적군의 군사 노력을 지원하기 위해 2.8 억불의 전비를 추가 부담하고, 5 대의 군수송기 및 150 명의 비전투 요원을 파견키로 결정하였다고 보도함. 끝.

(대사 우문기-국장)

예고:91.6.30 일반

| 미주국 | 차관 | 1차보 | 2차보 | 중아국 | 안기부 | 국방부 |

외 무 부

종   별 :

번   호 : TTW-0022　　　　　　　　　　일   시 : 91 0201 1130

수   신 : 장관(미북,미중,중근동)

발   신 : 주 트리니 다드대사

제   목 : 주재국의 걸프사태 반응

　　대:AM-29

　　1. 주재국 정부와 언론은 금일까지 대호 아국의 대미 추가지원 발표에 대해언급이 없음

　　2. 표제사태관련, 주재국에서는 주재국 군경의 대테러 비상경계.순찰을 강화한 가운데, 최근 미대사관 앞에서 소수인원의 반전시위를 제외하고는, 테러 움직임과 같은 북이동향은 없으며, ROBINSON 수상은 주재국 최대 연례행사인 카니벌은 예정대로 2.11-12 간 개최될 것이라고 강조하였음. 끝

　　(대사 박부열-국장)

　　예고:91.12.31 일반

일반문서로 재분류(1991.12.31.)

검 토 필 (1991.6.30)

미주국　　2차보　　미주국　　중아국

외 무 부

종 별 :

번 호 : JOW-0142 일 시 : 91 0202 1300

수 신 : 장 관(중근동,대책본부,미북,기정)

발 신 : 주 요르단 대사

제 목 : 걸프전 관련 아국 추가지원

대:AM-0030

연:JOW-0134

1. 아국정부의 대다국적군 추가지원 내용이 1.30.및 2.1. 2차에 걸쳐 주재국 TV에크게 방영 되었으며 동추가지원, 군수송기 파견및 TEAMSPIRIT 관계 사항등 아측에 불리한 내용들이 주재국 언론에 연속 보도되고 있는바 이에 주재국 일부 언론계인사및 친한인사들은 아랍의 우호국인 한국이 구태여 타국보다 앞장서서 아랍인들의 감정을 자극할 필요가 있는가하고 앞으로의 사태진전에 우려를 표명하고 있음

2. 걸프전쟁이 장기화되고, 서방및 아국의 대다국적군 지원사실에 대한 주재국 특히 팔레스타인 인들의 반서방 감정과 함께 반한 감정이 고조될시 아국공관및 교민들도 테러대상에 포함될 가능성이 있을것인바, 가능한한 이라크나 아랍인들의 감정을 자극하는 내용의 보도는 안전차원에서 뿐만아니라 대아랍 국익차원에서도 신중히 다루어줌이 요망됨

3. 최근 미국의 CITIBANK, 영국의 BRITISH BANK OFMIDDLE EAST및 프랑스 문화원등 서방기관에 대한 과격 테러분자들의 총격및 폭발사고가 있었는바, 앞으로도 계속적인 테러행위가 예상되며 걸프전쟁의 추세와 각국의 대응여부에 따라 테러대상 국가및 기관도 증가할 것으로 전망됨

(대사 박태진-국장)

중아국	장관	차관	1차보	2차보	미주국	정와대	총리실	안기부

외   무   부

관리번호 91-281

종   별 :

번   호 : AEW-0085   일   시 : 91 0202 1300

수   신 : 장관(미북,중근동,기정)

발   신 : 주 UAE 대사

제   목 : 대미 추가지원

대:AM-0029,12

1. 대호, 소직은 금 2.2. 주재국 외무부 정무국장을 방문, 대호 내용을 설명하였는바, 동인은 금번 추가지원등 한국정부의 조치에 대하여 GCC 회원국의 일원으로서 사의를 표하고 주재국 정부는 대테러등에 만전을 기하고 있다고 말하였음.

2. 한편 당지언론은 1.31. 한국 280 백만불 추가지원이라는 제하의 서울 로이터발 외신을 인용 보도함. 끝.

(대사 박종기-국장)

91.6.30 일반

미주국	장관	차관	1차보	2차보	중아국	청와대	안기부

PAGE 1

91.02.02   23:25
외신 2과 통제관 FI
0079

관리	
번호 71-285	원 본

외 무 부

종 별 : 지 급

번 호 : YMW-0099

일 시 : 91 0202 1730

수 신 : 장 관(미북,중근동,기정)

발 신 : 주 예멘 대사

제 목 : 대미추가 지원 발표 관련 테러 활동 대처

대:WMEM-0010, AM-0029, AM-0012

연:YMW-0040,0092,0093

1. 소직은 2.2 주재국 외무성으로 AL-AZEEB 정무 담당 차관보를 방문, 대호 대미 추가 지원 결정 내용을 설명하고, 1.31. 발생한 주예멘 미국 대사관 총격사건과, 다국적군에 비군사적인 지원만을 하고 있는 주 예멘 일본 및 터키 대사관저에서의 수류탄 폭발 사건등에 비추어 당관 및 주재국내 아국민의 안전에 대한 우려를 표시하였음.

2. 이에대해 AL-AZEEB 차관보는 동 사건이 발생된데 대해 주재국 정부로서 유감스럽게 생각하며 유사 사고가 재발하지 않도록 범인 체포에 최선의 노력을 경주하고 있으나, 다국적군이 이락 침공에 대한 주재국 국민의 증오 감정을 진정시키는데 어려움이 있음을 이해해 달라고 말하면서 당관의 우려를 공안당국에 알려 보호조치를 강화하도록 하겠다는 반응을 보였음. 그러나 아국의 금번 추가 지원이 아국 교민의 안전에 별도 영향을 주지 않을것이라는 언급은 하지 않았음.

3. 한편 동 차관보는 유엔이 안보리 결의안 및 안보리 소집등 문제 취급에 있어서 편파성을 보였다고 비난하고 주재국은 걸프 전쟁 종결을 위한 비동맹권의 협력을 모색하기 위해 이란 및 쏘련(DALI 외무담당 국무장관), 알제리아(YUSUF SHAHARI 국회 부의장), 중국(TABET 국회 담당 국무상), 유고(AL-ARASHI 내각담당 국무장관), 인도(HAMDI 지방행정담당 국무장관)에 대봉령 북사를 파견중에 있다고함.

동 차관보는 특히 독일의 이스라엘에 대한 무기지원 결정은 중동 지역 문제를 더욱 복잡하게 한다고 비난하였음.

4. 교민안전은 2.2 일 현재 이상없음.(현 잔류 교민 182 명). 끝.

(대사 류 지호-장관)

미주국	장관	차관	1차보	2차보	중아국	영고국	청와대	총리실
안기부								

PAGE 1

예고:91.12.31. 일반

일반문서로 재분류(19[ ].12.31. 2)

검토필(19[ ].6.3. [서명])

관리번호 91/126

외 무 부

종 별 :

번 호 : CZW-0089 일 시 : 91 0202 1800

수 신 : 장관(중근동,동구이,정일)

발 신 : 주 체코 대사

제 목 : 걸프사태 추가지원

대:AM-29

1. 최참사관은 2.1 BACEK 의전장 및 SOUKUP 아주국장대리를 각각 면담, 공관.관저 보안대책(24 시간 경비경찰 파견)을 재요청함(당관노트 전달).

2. 의전장은 당관의 수차 보안대책 요청을 알고있다하고 경찰당국에 다시 협조요청하겠으나, 경찰의 인력과 사정이 매우 어려운 사정이라 부언함.

3. 국장대리는 한국의 다국적군지원등 내용과 보안대책 요청을 차관 및 걸프사태대책반 전하고, 남북한 대립상황도 설명, 경찰지원이 제공되도록 노력하겠다 하였음.끝.

예고: 년말

외 무 부

관리
번호 91-242

종 별 :

번 호 : QTW-0038   일 시 : 91 0202 1245

수 신 : 장관(미북)

발 신 : 주 카타르 대사

제 목 : 대미 추가지원 관련

    1. 본직은 2.2. 10:00-11:40 간 주재국외무성의 HUSSAIN ALI AL-DOSARI GCC
국장과 ALI HUSSAIN MUFTAH 정무국장을 각각 방문하고, 대호 추가지원에 관하여
군의료단과 공군수송부대등의 파견과 5 억불 규모의 지원결정은 아국이 미, 일, 독등
경제대국과 일부 아랍국가를 제외한 유일한 재정적 지원국임을 강조 , 남북대치
상황하에서 최선의 기여임을 설명하였음.

    2. 이에 대하여 양국장은 각각상부에 보고할것이라고 전제 하면서
이라크의쿠웨이트 침공에 대한 신속한규탄 및 경제 제재참가조치에 이어 금번
지원결정등 한국정부의 적극적이고 명쾌한 지지에 감사한다고 답변하였음.

    끝

    (대사 유내형-장관)

    예고:91.12.31 일반

인반문서로 재분류(1991.12.31.)

검 토 필 (1991.6.3)

미주국   장관   차관   1차보   2차보   중아국

PAGE 1   91.02.04   15:48

                                        외신 2과   통제관 BA

                    0083

외　무　부

관리
번호 91-304

종　별 :

번　호 : AGW-0078　　　　　　　　　일　시 : 91 0203 1210

수　신 : 장관(비상대책반,미북,기정)

발　신 : 주 알제리 대사

제　목 : 걸프전

　　　연 AGW-0076 , 대 AM-0029

　　1. 2.3(일) 12:00 현재 당지교민 신변안전 이상없음.

　　2. 당지 주요 일간지 HORIZONS 지는 2.3 자에 쿠웨이트, 사우디, 일본, 독일등 제국의 다국적군 전비부담내용기사를 통해 UAE, 대만, 한국도 도합 15 억불을 지원하였다고 보도함.

　　3. GHOZALI 장관은 걸프전 발발직후 다국적군 가담국가대사와 주요재정 지원국인 일본, 독일대사를 외무부로 초치, 유감을 표시한바 있고, 주재국언론도 29 개 참전국내용과 일본, 독일의 전비지원을 비난하는 기사를 게재한 사실에 비추어 아국의 추가지원내용이 알려질경우 주재국정부의 불만표시가능성이 없지않음.

　　4. 2.3 시위는 진정되고 있으며 주재국언론도 전쟁이 다소 소강상태(PAUSE RELATIVE)에 들어가고 있다고 보도하고 전쟁의 외교적 해결모색을 위한 GHOZALI 장관의 이란방문과 외교적활동을 부각 보도한바 동장관은 이란에 이어 벨기에와 불란서도 방문할 예정이라함. 끝

　　(대사 한석진-대책본부장)

　　예고 1991.6.30 일반.

예고문에의기 일반문서로
재분류19 91 6.30 서명

중아국	장관	차관	1차보	2차보	미주국	안기부

관리 번호	91-291

원 본

외 무 부

종 별 :

번 호 : JDW-0047 일 시 : 91 0204 1120

수 신 : 장관(미북,중근동)

발 신 : 주 젯 다총영사

제 목 : 대미 추가지원 발표

대:AM-0029

1. 대호관련, 당지 영자 일간 SAUDI GAZETTE 지는 1.31 및 2.3 자 경제및 걸프전 속보난에서 "SEOUL AID TO GULF WAR UP", "S.KOREA TO HELP IN WAR" 제하의 서울발 기사를 게재함.

2. 또한 아랍어 일간 OKAZ 지도 2.3 자 국제정치난에서 "DISCUSS WAYS TO ASSIGN THE SHARE OF THE FUNDS FOR THE ALLIED FORCES AT WASHINGTON MEETING" 제하의 기사를 서울 연합통신을 인용, 보도함. 끝.

(총영사 김문경-국장)

예고:91.12.31 일반

일반문서로 재분류(19$\,$|·|2.3| $\cdot$

검 토 필 (19$\,$|·|3.6|

미주국 차관 1차보 2차보 중아국

관리
번호 91-362

외 무 부

종 별 :

번 호 : TNW-0084

일 시 : 91 0208 1300

수 신 : 장관(미북,중근동,마그,기정동문)

발 신 : 주 뮈니지 대사

제 목 : 군수송기 지원

대:AM-0029

1. 주재국 일간지 "LA PRESSE"지는 2.8 자 해외 단신란에 "LA COREE AUSSI"라는 제하, 한국이 걸프전쟁 다국적군 지원을 위해 군수송기 5 대와 150 명의 비전투요원을 U.A.E 에 파견 예정이며, 지난주에는 다국적군 재정 지원을 위해 2.8 억 불을 제공키로 발표한 바 있다고 보도함.

2. 당관 이우정 1 등서기관은 2.8 오전 외무부 아세아국 KHALED KAAK 부국장을 면담, 한국전 당시 UN 16 개국이 안보리 결정에 따라 우리를 도운 사실과 견주어 금번 아국의 다국적군 지원은 아국의 국제적 의무 이행의 일환이라고 설명하였음. 끝.

(대사 변정현-국장)

예고:91.6.30 일반

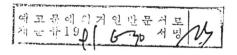

예고문에의거 일반문서로
재분류함 1991. 6. 30 서명

미주국   차관   1차보   2차보   중아국   중아국   안기부   국방부

3. 화학전 대비 훈련시범 교육 촉장,
1990. 12. 25 - 91. 1. 5

분류기호 문서번호	중근동 720-	기 안 용 지	시 행 상 특별취급	
보존기간	영구.준영구 10. 5. 3. 1	차 관	장 관	
수 신 처 보존기간		찬첢		
시행일자	1990. 12. 11.			
보조 기관	국장 / 심의관 / 과장	협조 기관	제1차관보 기획관리실장 미주국장 국제경제국장 영사교민국장 비상계획관 총무과장	문서통제 발송인
기안책임자	최형찬			

경유
수신 건 의
참조

발신명의

제목   걸프사태 관련 화학전 대비 훈련 시범 교육차 직원 출장

　　　1. 최근 걸프사태는 이라크측과 반이라크 진영의 군사적 대치로

긴장이 고조되고 있는 가운데 평화적으로 해결될 움직임도 보이고 있으나

이라크측이 쿠웨이트로 부터 철수하지 않을시, 미국을 포함한 다국적군의

대이라크 무력 공격 가능성도 농후하며, 만일 다국적군이 공격할 경우에

이라크측의 화학무기 사용 가능성도 배제할수 없는 실정입니다.

　　　2. 이에 대비하여 본부에서는 이라크의 화학전 공격시 피해가

예상되는 걸프 6개지역 주재 공관 및 동 가족에 대한 화학전 대비 훈련

시범과 현지 교민안전 실태 파악을 위해 아래와 같이 직원 출장을 건의

하오니 재가하여 주시기 바랍니다.

　　　　　　　　　　　　/ 계속 . . .

0088

- 아   래 -
1. 출 장 자 : 중근동과   박종순 서기관
비상계획관실   황기수 예비군 중대장 (별정직 5급)
2. 출장지역(중동 6개국) : 바레인, 카타르, UAE, 사우디, 요르단, 이라크
3. 출장기간 : 90.12.24-91.1.5.
4. 소요예산 : $ 11,940
가. 항공료 : $ 6,172
○ 여행구간 : 서울→바레인→카타르→UAE→사우디→요르단 →이라크→요르단→서울
- 박종순 서기관   : $ 3,086
- 황기수 별정직 5급 : $ 3,086
나. 채재비 : $ 2,968
○ 일 비 : $ 20 × 14일 × 2인 = $ 560
○ 숙박비 : (UAE) $ 66 × 2박 × 2인 = $ 264 (기타 5개국) $ 50 × 11박 × 2인 = $ 1,100
○ 식 비 : (UAE) $ 42 × 3일 × 2인 = $ 252 (기타 5개국) $ 36 × 11일 × 2인 = $ 792
/ 계속 . . .

0089

다. 활동비 : $ 100 × 14일 × 2인 = $ 2,800

5. 지변항목 :

　　가. 영사교민 국외여비 : $ 9,140 (항공료 및 체재비)

　　나. 정무활동, 해외경상이전비 : $ 2,800 (활동비)

　　　(대외무상원조, 해외경상이전비로 우선 지출하고 예산 확보시

　　　여입 조치 예정)

　　첨 부 : 항공운임증명서 1부. 끝.

0090

대 한 항 공 KOREAN AIR

FARE CERTIFICATE
항공운임증명서

	DATE : 일 자 90/12/11
TO. : 수신 M . O . F . A .	NO : 발행번호 9012-00-055

PASSENGER NAME : 여행자 성명	01 PERSON
CLASS : 등 급	ECONOMY CLASS
ROUTING : 구 간	SE/BAH/DOH/AUH/RUH/AMM/BGW/AMM/DXB/BKK/SEL 　　KE　　　　　　　　　　　　　　　　　　KE
FARE : 운 임	GRg　　　GROSS AMT : USD 3,430
	NET AMT : USD 3,086

THIS IS TO CERTIFY THAT THE ABOVE MENTIONED FARE IS CORRECT AND TRUE ACCO-
RDING TO INT'L TRAVEL TARIFF AND REGULATION. 상기요금은 국제항공여행요금표 및 규정에 의거
틀림없음을 증명합니다. 단, 정부 및 해당국의 요금 및 환율변경등의 사유로 변경되어질 수 있읍니다.
공무해외여행부 일부인(VALIDATION)이 없는 것은 무효입니다.

GTR

VALIDATION

PREPARED BY : _____

G. T. R. SERVICE OFFICE, SEOUL

KAL-SM-008
1981.1.4 등록

0091

190mm×265mm 모조70g/㎡
(90. 7. 1/16,000 매)

一般豫算檢討意見書

1990 . 12. 12.   중 근 동   課

事 業 名	'페'만 사태관련 화학전대비 면목출장		
支 辨 科 目	細 項	目	金 額
	1311	213	$9,140.00
	1211	341	$2,800.00

檢 討 意 見

主 務	1. 영사면만, 국외여비에서 집행 (활동비 $2,800은 관련 경비 배정시 추가통제 예정) 2. 정부활동, 해외경상이전에서 집행 (추가통제 .12.18 ~)
擔 當 官	″
調 整 官	″ 0092

분류기호 문서번호	중근동 720- 342 ( )	협 조 문 용 지	결	담당	과장	국장
시행일자	1990. 12. 11.		재	~~서명~~	전결	7ん
수　신	영사교민국장 (여권1과장)	발 신	중동아프리카국장			(서명)
제　목	여권 발급 및 출국 신고 협조 의뢰					

　　　최근 걸프사태와 관련, 화학전 대비 훈련 시범 및 걸프지역

체류교민 안전 실태파악차 직원 2명이 아래와 같이 중동지역을

출장 예정인바, 동 인들의 여권 발급, 출국신고, 비자 노트등

필요 조치를 취하여 주시기 바랍니다.

　　　　　　　　　　- 아 　 　 레 -

　　1. 출장자 인적 사항

　　　 o 박종순 서기관 (중근동 과)

　　　　　 생년월일 : 1948. 12. 28.

　　　 o 황기수 별정직 5급 (비상계획관실)

　　　　　 생년월일 : 1942. 8. 18.

　　2. 출장지 : 걸프 지역 6개국 (사우디, 요르단, 바레인,

　　　　　　　　　　　　　　　　/ 계 속 ....

UAE、카탈、이라크)

3. 출장 예정 일자 : 90. 12. 25 - 91. 1. 7.

4. 비자 노트 필요 방문국 : UAE、사우디、이라크. 요르단끝.

0094

분류기호 문서번호	중근동 720-344	(	)	협조문용지	결 재	담당 *(서명)*		각장 2L
시행일자	1990. 12. 13.							
수 신	서무계장		발 신		중근동과장			
제 목	직원 해외 출장							

최근 걸프사태와 관련하여 걸프지역 주재 공관원 및 가족을

대상으로하는 화학전 대비 훈련 시범교육 및 걸프지역 체류 교민

안전 실태 파악차 직원 2명이 아래와 같이 중동지역을 출장 예정

인 바, 업무에 참고 바랍니다.

                              - 아   래 -

    1. 출장자 인적 사항

        ㅇ 중근동과 박종순 서기관

        ㅇ 비상계획관실 황기수 별정직 5급

    2. 출장지 : 걸프지역 6개국 (사우디, 요르단, U.A.E,

                바레인, 카타르, 이라크)

    3. 출장 예정 기간 : 90. 12. 25 -91. 1. 8. 끝.

                                                0095

1505 - 8 일 (1)
85. 9. 9 승인 "내가아낀 종이 한장 늘어나는 나라살림"   190㎜×268㎜ (인쇄용지 2급 60g / ㎡)
                                            가 40-41 1990. 7. 9.

화학전 훈련 시범 요원 출장 소요 경비

1. 출 장 자 : 비상계획관실 황기수 중대장 (별정직 5급)

2. 출장지역(중동6개국) : 바레인, 카타르, UAE, 사우디, 요르단, 이라크

3. 출 장 기 간 : 15박 16일

4. 총소요경비 : $ 6,382

5. 소요경비 내역

　가. 항 공 료 : $ 3,086

　　ㅇ 여행구간 : 서울 → 바레인 → 카타르 → UAE → 사우디
　　　　　　　　　→ 요르단 → 이라크 → 요르단 → 서울

　나. 체 재 비 : $ 1,696

　　ㅇ 일 비 : $ 20 × 16일 = $ 320

　　ㅇ 숙박비 : (UAE) $ 66 × 2박 = $ 132
　　　　　　　　(기타 5개국) $ 50 × 13박 = $ 650

　　ㅇ 식 비 : (UAE) $ 42 × 3일 = $ 126
　　　　　　　　(기타 5개국) $ 36 × 13일 = $ 468

　다. 활 동 비 : $ 1,600

　　ㅇ $ 100 × 16일 = $ 1,600

0096

발 신 전 보

	분류번호	보존기간

번   호 : WJO-0533   901215 1328   AO종별 : 지급

수   신 : 주 요르단   대사. 총영사 (정신구 영사)

발   신 : 장 관   (중근동 과장)

제   목 : 업 연

　　　1. 걸프사태 관련 화학전 대비 시범 훈련 교육 및 교민 안전실태 파악차
아래 직원 2명이 91.1.1-1.5. 이라크 및 귀지 출장 예정(1.1. 09:55 RJ 607편
귀지 착)임.

　　　(성명, 생년월일, 여권번호, 발급일자 순)

ㅇ PARK JONG SOON   48.12.28.　　　　　　　　90.12.12

ㅇ HWANG KI SOO   42.8.18.　　　　　　　　90.12.12.

　　　2. 본부에서는 귀지발 이라크 출장 항공편 예약이 불가하니 귀지 및
바그다드간 왕복 항공표(1.1. 이라크 입국, 1.3. 귀지 착) 구입을 협조 바라며
결과 지급 회시하여 주시기 바람.

동 항공료는 출장 직원편 후불 예정이니 우선 귀관에서 입체 구입 바람.　끝.

		보안통제	71

앙고재	90년 월 일	기안자 성명	과 장	국 장	차 관	장 관		외신과통제
	중근동		전결			71		

외 무 부

종 별 :

번 호 : JOW-0674   일   시 : 90 1216 1600

수 신 : 장 관(중근동과장)

발 신 : 주 요르단 대사

제 목 : 업연

대: WJO-0533

1. 대호 직원출장과 관련 아래 일정으로 항공편 예약하였음

91.1.1 13:30(IA170) 암만 출발

91.1.1 15:00 바그다드 도착

91.1.3 11.00(IA169) 바그다드 출발

91.1.3 12:30 암만도착

2. 상기 항공요금(2인)은 JD 335.200(507 상당)임

중아국

90.12.17   02:08 BX

외신 1과 통제관

0098

발 신 전 보

번   호 : WSB-0577   901218 1138 FK 종별 : 지급

WBH -0175	WQT -0137
WAE -0285	WJO -0539
WBG -0604	

수   신 : 주 수신처 참조   /대사://총영사/

발   신 : 장   관 (중근동)

제   목 : 화학전 대비 시범 직원 출장

연 : WSB-0518, WBH-0162, WQT-0123, WAE-0261, WJO-0479, WBG-0569

　　　　1. 걸프지역 전쟁 발발 가능성에 대비, 본부는 연호 기지급된 화학
장비 사용 시범 교육과 체류교민의 안전 실태 파악을 위해 아래 일정으로
직원 2명을 출장시킬 예정임.

　　　　2. 상기 관련, 호텔 TWIN 1실 예약 바라며, 출입국 및 체제기간중 제반
편의 제공 바람.

　　　　3. 출 장 자

ㅇ 중근동과 박종순 서기관(PARK JONG SOON)

ㅇ 비상계획관실 황기수 예비군 중대장 (HWANG, KI SOO)

　　　　4. 일 정

ㅇ	KE 801	25 DEC	SEL/BAH	1710/0050
ㅇ	GF 161	27 DEC	BAH/RUH	1240/1350
ㅇ	GF 168	29 DEC	RUH/AUH	2030/2300
ㅇ	GF 233	30 DEC	AUH/DOH	1740/1730
ㅇ	RJ 607	1 JAN	DOH/AMM	0700/0955

(1.1-3. 이라크; 1.3-5. 요르단 예정)

ㅇ	EK 924	5 JAN	AMM/DXB	1830/2330
ㅇ	BA 35	6 JAN	DXB/HKG	0130/1215 . 끝.

수신처 : 주 사우디, 바레인, 카타르, UAE, 요르단, 이라크 대사

　　　　　　　　　　(중동아국장   이 해 순)

보	안	
통	제	

앙고재	90년12월14일 중근동과 박금숙	기안자 성명		과장 7ㅏ	심의관 %	국장 전결		차관	장관 서명	외신과통제

0099

발 신 전 보

번   호 : WBH-0176   901218 1142 FK   종별 : ___

WQT -0138

수   신 : 주 바레인, 카타르 대사. 총영사

발   신 : 장 관 대비 (중근동)

제   목 : 화학전 시범 직원 출장

연 : WBH -0175
    WQT -0137

　　　1.　연호 출장 관련, 아국에 귀 주재국 상주공관이 없고 출장이 임박한점을
감안, 동인들이 입국 사증을 귀지 공항 도착시 받을수 있도록 사전 조치하고
결과 보고 바람.

　　　2.　출장자 인적사항(성명, 생년월일, 여권번호, 발급일자순)
o　PARK JONG SOON, 48.12.28. ▓▓▓▓▓, 90.12.12.
o　HWANG KI SOO, 42.8.18. ▓▓▓▓▓, 90.12.12.　　끝.

(중동아국장   이 해 순)

앙고재	90년 12월 14일 중근동과	기안자 성명 박규옥	과장	심의관	국장	차관	장관	보 안 통 제	
								외신과통제	

0100

발 신 전 보

	분류번호	보존기간

번   호 : WJO-0540   901218 1143 FK 종별 : _____

수   신 : 주 요르단   대사. 총영사/

발   신 : 장 관   (중근동)

제   목 : 화학전 시범 직원 출장

연 : WJO-0539

　　연호, 본부에서는 직원 2명의 귀지발 이라크 출장 항공편 예약이 불가하니
귀지 및 바그다드간 왕복 항공표(1.1. 이라크 입국, 1.3. 귀지 도착)를 구입 협조
바라며 결과 지급 회시 바람. 동 항공료는 출장 직원편 후불 예정이니 우선 귀관에서
입체 구입 바람. 끝.

　　　　　　　　　　　　　　　　(중동아국장   이 해 순)

	보 안	
	통 제	

앙고재	90년 12월 14일 중근동과	기안자성명 백규옥		과장	심의관	국장 전결		차관	장관

외신과통제

0101

외 무 부

종 별 :

번 호 : BHW-0286

일 시 : 90 1218 1230

수 신 : 장관(중근동)

발 신 : 주바레인대사

제 목 : 직원 출장

대: WBH-0176

대호, 조치함.끝.

(대사 우문기-국장)

중아국

90.12.18   21:17 DQ

외신 1과 통제관

0102

분류기호 문서번호	중근동 720- 348	협조문용지 ( )	결 재	담당 박충옥	각장 전결	국장 (서명)
시행일자	21990. 12. 18.					
수　신	총무각장 (외환)	발신	중동아프리카국장			
제　목	경비 지불 의뢰					

별첨 재가를 득한 아래 경비를 지불의뢰 하오니 조치하여

주시기 바랍니다.

- 아　　　래 -

1. 금액 :

   ○ 항공료 : $ 6,172

   ○ 체재비 및 활동비 : $ 5,768

2. 지불처 :

   ○ 항공료(암만-바그다드 왕복 오금 제외)

   대한항공 : $ 5,618

   ○ 암만-바그다드 왕복 항공료(걸프사태로, 현지에서만

   항공권 구입 가능)

/계 속 ...0103

1505 - 8 일 (1)
85. 9. 9 승인 "내가아낀 종이 한장 늘어나는 나라살림"　190㎜×268㎜(인쇄용지 2급 60g / ㎡)
가 40-41 1990. 7. 9.

걸프사태 : 대책 및 조치, 1990-91. 전11권 (V.11 기타) 211

박종순 서기관(중근동과) : $ 277

황기수 별정직 5급 (비상계획관실) : $ 277

○ 체재비 및 활동비

박종순 서기관 : $ 2,884

황기수 별정직5급 : $ 2,884

3. 지변 과목 : 영사교민, 국익어비 및 정무활동 해외

경상 이전비

첨 부 : 원칙 재가 문서 사본 1부. 끝.

0104

분류기호 문서번호	중근동 720-	기 안 용 지	시 행 상 특별취급	
보존기간	영구.준영구 10. 5. 3. 1	차 관	장 관	
수 신 처 보존기간		전결		
시행일자	1990. 12. 11.			

보존 기관	국 장		협 조 기 관	제1차관보 기획관리실장	문 서 통 제
	심의관			미주국장 국제경제국장	
	과 장			영사교민국장 비상계획관	
기안책임자	최 형 찬			총무과장	발 송 인
경 유			발신명의		
수 신	건 의				
참 조					
제 목	걸프사태 관련 화학전 대비 훈련 시범 교육차 직원 출장				

　　1. 최근 걸프사태는 이라크측과 반이라크 진영의 군사적 대치로

긴장이 고조되고 있는 가운데 평화적으로 해결될 움직임도 보이고 있으나

이라크측이 쿠웨이트로 부터 철수하지 않을시, 미국을 포함한 다국적군의

대이라크 무력 공격 가능성도 농후하며, 만일 다국적군이 공격할 경우에

이라크측의 화학무기 사용 가능성도 배제할수 없는 실정입니다.

　　2. 이에 대비하여 본부에서는 이라크의 화학전 공격시 피해가

예상되는 걸프 6개지역 주재 공관 및 동 가족에 대한 화학전 대비 훈련

시범과 현지 교민안전 실태 파악을 위해 아래와 같이 직원 출장을 건의

하오니 재가하여 주시기 바랍니다.

　　　　　　　　　　／ 계속 ...

0105

- 아   래 -

1. 출장자 : 중근동과   박종순 서기관

                비상계획관실   황기수 예비군 중대장 (별정직 5급)

2. 출장지역(중동 6개국) : 바레인, 카타르, UAE, 사우디, 요르단,

        이라크

3. 출장기간 : 90.12.24-91.1.5.

4. 소요예산 : $ 11,940

    가. 항공료 : $ 6,172

        ○ 여행구간 : 서울→바레인→카타르→UAE→사우디→요르단

                →이라크→요르단→서울

        - 박종순 서기관   : $ 3,086

        - 황기수 별정직 5급 : $ 3,086

    나. 체재비 : $ 2,968

        ○ 일 비 : $ 20×14일×2인 = $ 560

        ○ 숙박비 : (UAE) $ 66×2박×2인 = $ 264

                    (기타 5개국) $ 50×11박×2인 = $ 1,100

        ○ 식 비 : (UAE) $ 42×3일×2인 = $ 252

                    (기타 5개국) $ 36×11일×2인 = $ 792

                / 계속 . . .

0106

니. 활동비 : $ 100 × 14일 × 2인 = $ 2,800

5. 지변항목 :

가. 영사교민 국외여비 : $ 9,140 (항공료 및 체재비)

나. 정부활동, 해외경상이전비 : $ 2,800 (활동비)

(대외무상원조, 해외경상이전비로 우선 지출하고 예산 확보시

여입 조치 예정)

첨 부 : 항공운임증명서 1부. 끝.

대 한 항 공 K☉REAN AIR

FARE CERTIFICATE
항공운임증명서

DATE :
일 자   90/12/11

TO :
수신   M . O . F . A .

NO :
발행번호   9012-00-055

PASSENGER NAME : 이행자 성명	01 PERSON
CLASS : 등 급	ECONOMY CLASS
ROUTING : 구 간	SE/BAH/DOH/AUH/RUH/AMM/BGW/AMM/DXB/BKK/SEL KE KE
FARE : 운 임	GRg GROSS AMT : USD 3,430
	NET AMT : USD 3,086

THIS IS TO CERTIFY THAT THE ABOVE MENTIONED FARE IS CORRECT AND TRUE ACCO-
RDING TO INT' L TRAVEL TARIFF AND REGULATION. 상기요금은 국제항공여행요금표 및 규정에 의거
틀림없음을 증명합니다. 단, 정부 및 해당국의 요금 및 환율변경등의 사유로 변경되어질 수 있읍니다.
공무해외여행부 일부인(VALIDATION)이 없는 것은 무효입니다.

GTR

VALIDATION

PREPARED BY :

G. T. R. SERVICE OFFICE, SEOUL

KOREAN AIR

0108

KAL-SM-008

190mm × 265mm 모조70g/m²

一般豫算檢討意見書

1990 . 12. 12.   중로동   課

事 業 名	"페"만 사태관련 화학과대비 관물총장		
支辨科目	細 項	目	金 額
	1311	213	$9,140.⁰⁰

檢 討 意 見

主 務	영사민만, 국회여비에서 정함 (환동비 $2,800을 반영 경비 배정시 추기통제 예정)
擔 當 官	"
調 整 官	

0109

화학전 대비 시범 직원출장 참고자료

1990. 12. 24.

주 바 레 인 대 사 관

0110

I

목　　　　　차

2

0111

1. 바레인 개관

- O 국 명 : State of Bahrain

- O 면 적 : 693 평방킬로

- O 인 구 : 49만명(89년도) - 현지인 32.5만명, 외국인 16.5만명

- O 군사력 : 5천명(경찰력 2,500명 포함)

- O 국가원수 : H.H. Shaikh Isa bin Salman Al Khalifa

  The Amir of the State of Bahrain

- O 민 족 : 아랍족 (25% 는 이란계)

- O 언 어 : 아랍어 (영어가 널리 통용됨)

- O 종 교 : 이슬람교 (순니파, 시아파가 각각 50%)

- O 기 후 : 열대성 기후 (다습한 혹서)

  (평균기온) 12 - 2월 : 섭씨 16.1도, 3 - 5월 : 25.1도

  6 - 9월 : 섭씨 33.5도, 10 - 11월 : 28.7도

- O 화폐단위 : 바레인 디나(BD 1 = $ 2.65 , $ 1 = BD 0.3755)

- O GDP 총액 : 37억불(1986년말 기준)

- O 주요공항 : 무하르락(Muharraq) 국제공항, 아미리(Amiri) 공군 비행장.

- O 주요항만 : 미나살만(Mina Salman)

3

2. 바레인 체류 아국민 수 (90.12.23 현재)

　　가. 총 체류자 수 : 335 명

　　나. 현황

기관명	직원	가족	근로자	계
대사관	3	11	0	14
외환은행	8	20	0	28
한일은행	4	15	0	19
현대건설	17	4	43	64
영진공사	21	0	121	142
대 우	2	3	0	5
대한항공	6	0	0	6
한인교회	1	3	0	4
한국학교	1	3	0	4
동양식품	3	2	0	5
아세아식품	3	6	0	9
한국제과	1	2	0	3
개별취업	7	7	0	14
코 취 단	5	0	0	5
BAPCO	2	7	0	9
기타(현지인부인)	0	4	0	4
합 계	84	87	164	335

4

0113

3. 긴급사태 발생시 비상대책

    가. 공관 안전대책 :

      (1). 비상시 공관장이 필요하다고 판단되는 경우, 공관내 주차된 차량 피격에 의한 공관내 배전실의 화재발생 위험등을 고려, 모든 차량은 공관 외부에 주차토록 조치.

      (2). 또한, 공관장의 판단하에 통신 기자재는 지상층의 안전한 곳으로 이동 조치.

    나. 교민 안전대책 :

      (1). 비상연락망 정비 : (별첨 1. 연락망 참조)

        - 당지내 모든 아국 체류민들의 경우, 차량편으로 15-20분이내 직접 연락 가능

      (2). 화학전 관련 사항 :

        - 12.10, 4/4분기 홍보대책 기관장 회의시, 본국정부로 부터의 체류민에 대한 방독면 지원이 어려운 실정임을 설명하고 현지에서 판매되고 있는 방독면 구입 권고.

        * 외무부의 공관 직원및 가족에 대한 방독면 지원 사실은 체류민들의 동요를 우려 일체 불언급

        - 동 방독면 현재 각자 보관중

    나. 교민 긴급 철수 계획 :

      * 별첨 "중동 분쟁지역 긴급 대피 한국민 구호 및 재 바레인 한국민 철수 계획" 참조. (별첨 2. 계획참조)

5

0114

4. **12.24 현재 주재국 주요 동향**

    가. 지난 12.21경부터 당지에서는 91.1.12을 전후하여 주재국 공항이 금번사태 해
        결시 까지 무기한 폐쇄될 예정이라는 말이 유포되기 시작하면서, 주재국민들
        중 일부가 가족들을 해외로 일단 대피시키기 위해 미,영,불 서방국가의 입국
        사증을 신청하고 있는 것으로 전해짐. (별첨 3. 신문사본 참조)

    나. 이에 관련 당관이 12.24 현재까지 확인한바에 따르면 지난 11.19 사우디 항공
        당국이 비상사태 발생시 이지역을 비행하는 민간항공기들에 대한 사전 안전
        지침을 통보한바 있으며, 91.1.15 유엔 안보리 최종 철수시한이 다가옴에 따
        라 별첨 3 GULF DAILY NEWS의 12.23일자 보도와 같이 만약의 사태등에 대비
        일부 항공사들이 1.10일 이후 예약을 받지 않고 있음으로 인해 동 안전지침이
        과장되어 그와 같은 소문으로 번지고 있는 것으로 판단됨.

    (별첨 4. 지시문 참조)

6

0115

5. <u>주요국가의 자국민 비상대책</u>

　가. 미 국

　　(1). 체류자 수 : 약 1,000 명

　　(2). 대책 :

　　　- 당지 미국 대사관에 의하면, 사태발생 초기의 걸프지역 여행 자제

　　　　권고및 가족등 비필수 요원의 철수 권고가 아직 유효함.

　　　- 12.15, Schwarzkopf 미 중동군 사령관등이 당지 체류 미국인에 대해

　　　　정세 브리핑 (6항 상세 참조)

　나. 영 국

　　(1). 체류자 수 : 약 4,000 명

　　(2). 대책 :

　　　- 11.27, 걸프지역내 영국인 가족등 비필수 요원들은 크리스마스 휴가후

　　　　사태 해결시까지 영국에 계속 잔류하도록 권고.

　　　* 91.1.15, 유엔 안보리 최종 철수시한등과 관련, 상당수가 90.12월말

　　　　및 91.1월초 출발 항공편을 예약중인 것으로 전해지고 있음.

　다. 일 본

　　(1). 체류자 수 : 약 100 명

　　(2). 대책 :

　　　- 당지 일본 대사관에 의하면, 8.10자 비필수 요원 철수 권고가 유효하

　　　　다는 입장이며, 12.23 현재 본국 정부로부터 별도의 지시는 없다고 함

　　　- 8.2 사태 발생이래 대부분이 철수한 상태로서 일부 필수요원만이 귀환

　　　　한 상태임.

　　　- 사태 발생전 : 약 400 명 체류.

　라. 불란서

　　(1). 체류자 수 : 약 260 명

　　(2). 대책 :

　　　- 12.1, 본국 정부로부터 당지내 비필수 요원들을 91.1월 첫째주까지

　　　　철수하도록 지도하라는 지시를 접수함.

7

6. 미국 정부의 자국민에 대한 정세 브리핑

가. 정부측 참석자 :

   주 바레인 미국대사

   미 중동 통합군 사령관(Schwarzkopf)

   미 걸프주둔 해군 지휘관(중장)

   미 해병대 장교(대령) 1명

나. 참석인원 : 약 500 명

다. 일 시 : 90.12.15, 16:00

라. 장 소 : BAPCO(바레인 국영 석유공사) CLUB

마. 요 지 (무력사용시 바레인의 안보 관련 사항)

   (1). 육전 :

      - 이라크 지상군의 바레인 접경지역 또는 바레인 자체에 대한 직접적
        위협 가능성은 거의 없음.

      - 근거 : 이라크는 쿠웨이트내에 미군등 다국적군 공격에 대비 대전차
        방어용 참호를 구축한바, 사우디등에 대한 지상군 공격을 위해서는
        이라크 자신이 동 참호를 다시 원상으로 환원하여야 할 것임.

   (2). 해전 :

      - 매우 미미한 이라크 해군력 및 걸프지역내 다국적군의 해군 화력등을
        감안할때, 이라크 해군의 바레인 접근은 거의 상상할 수 없는 일임.

   (3). 공전 :

      - 공군력에 있어서도 미국등을 위시한 다국적이 이라크에 비해 압도적
        으로 우세함.

      - 다만, HAWK등 미사일에 의한 위협요소를 전혀 배제할 수는 없으나, 현
        재 사우디 동부 유전지대 및 걸프 해상의 대공 미사일망등을 고려해
        볼때, 이라크의 미사일 공격에 의한 바레인의 피습 위험도가 높다고
        보기는 어려움.

      - 결론적으로, 무력 충돌시에도 바레인 피격 가능성은 있으나 위험도가

8

0117

그다지 높지 않다고 판단되며, 크리스마스 휴가등을 위해 본국 일시
방문시 가족들은 본국 정부에 남겨두는 것이 좋을것으로 사려됨.

첨 부 : (1). 바레인 비상 연락망 1부.

(2). 중동 분쟁지역 긴급 대피 한국민 구호 및

재 바레인 한국인 철수 계획 1부.

(3). GULF DAILY NEWS 기사 사본 1부.

(4). 사우디아라비아 항공교통및 항법보조시설 보안통제 지시문 사본 1부.

(5). 안전지출 및 긴급 파기계획 1부.끝.

9

0118

(별첨2)

中東 紛爭地域 緊急待避 韓國民 救護

및

在바레인 韓國民 撤收 計劃

1990. 8. 11.

駐 바 레 인 大 韓 民 國 大 使 館

0119

目　　　次

1

0120

1. 目　　　　的

本 計劃은 무웨이트 事態와 關連, 中東 紛爭地域으로 부터 當地로 待避해오는 我國 僑民에 對한 宿所, 食糧, 醫療, 入國便宜 등의 緊急 救護를 提供하고, 事態發展에 따라 必要하게되는 境遇 駐在國內에 滯留하고있는 我國民을 希望에 따라 外國에 安全하게 待避시키기 위한 것임.

2. 實施段階의 區分

本計劃은 狀況의 進展에 따라 다음 3 段階로 區分 施行한다.

가. 第 1 段階 (備蓄 段階)

1990.8.11 10:00를 期해 本計劃書 "5.다.(1).項"(8페이지)의 宿所, 食糧, 醫藥品, 燃料等 物資의 準備 및 備蓄을 開始한다.

나. 第 2 段階 (救護 段階)

中東紛爭地域으로부터 바레인에 緊急待避하는 我國民이 바레인에 入國하는 瞬間에 第 2 段階로 突入한다.

다. 第 3 段階 (撤收 段階)

本國政府로부터 撤收指示가 下達되거나, 戰鬪가 바레인 接境國家 領土內에서 大規模로 展開된다던가, 바레인 領土內의 軍事目標物이 外國軍에依해 空襲 또는 砲擊等 攻擊을 받게 된다던가, 周邊國家에서 化生放戰이 展開된다던가 또는 바레인의 治安이 崩壞되어 放火, 掠奪이 恣行된다던가 하는 境遇에는 第 3 段階에 進入한다.

3. 編　　　　成

가. 本 計劃의 目標를 效率的으로 成就하기 위하여, 1990.8.5. 11:00時에 駐바레인 韓國大使가 緊急 召集한 "在바레인 韓國機關長會議"에서 決議된바에 따라 "中東紛爭地域 緊急待避韓國民保護 및 在바레인 韓國人撤收 對策委員會"(以下 委員會)를 다음과 같이 編成한다.

나. 委員會는 "備蓄救護段階"와 "撤收段階"에 따라 各己 다음과 같이 編成한다.

2

0121

(1). 僑胞 救助 段階

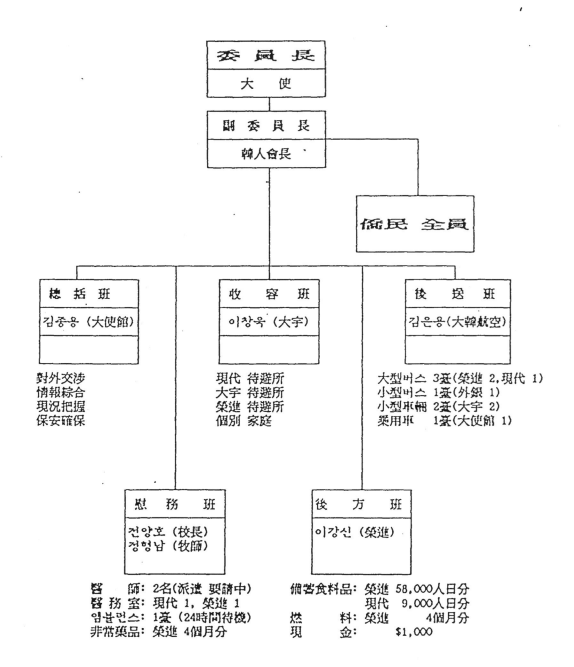

```
                        ┌─────────────┐
                        │  委 員 長   │
                        ├─────────────┤
                        │   大  使    │
                        └──────┬──────┘
                        ┌──────┴──────┐
                        │  副委員長   │
                        ├─────────────┤
                        │  韓人會長   │───────────────┐
                        └──────┬──────┘        ┌───────┴───────┐
                               │               │  僑民 全員    │
                               │               └───────────────┘
        ┌──────────────────────┼──────────────────────┐
  ┌───────────┐         ┌───────────┐          ┌───────────┐
  │  總 括 班 │         │  收 容 班 │          │  後 送 班 │
  ├───────────┤         ├───────────┤          ├───────────┤
  │김종용(大使館)│       │이창욱(大宇) │        │김은용(大韓航空)│
  └─────┬─────┘         └─────┬─────┘          └───────────┘
```

總括班	收容班	後送班
對外交涉 情報綜合 現況把握 保安確保	現代 待避所 大宇 待避所 榮進 待避所 個別 家庭	大型버스 3臺(榮進 2, 現代 1) 小型버스 1臺(外銀 1) 小型車輛 2臺(大宇 2) 乘用車 1臺(大使館 1)

```
        ┌───────────┐                    ┌───────────┐
        │  慰 務 班 │                    │  後 方 班 │
        ├───────────┤                    ├───────────┤
        │전양호(校長) │                    │이강신(榮進) │
        │정형남(牧師) │                    └───────────┘
        └───────────┘
```

慰務班	後方班
醫 師: 2名(派遣 要請中) 醫務室: 現代 1, 榮進 1 엠뷸런스: 1臺(24時間待機) 非常藥品: 榮進 4個月分	備蓄食料品: 榮進 58,000人日分 　　　　　　　現代 9,000人日分 燃　　料: 榮進　4個月分 現　　金: $1,000

3

0122

<u>(2). 撤收 段階</u>

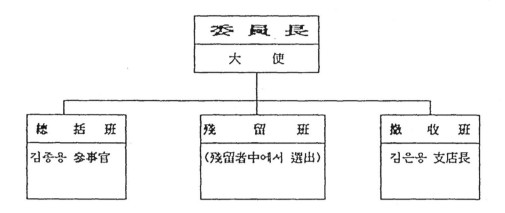

4. 用語의 定義

本 計劃書에서 解釋上의 混亂을 防止하고, 統一을 期하기 爲하여 다음과같이 定義한다.

가. <u>待　　避:</u>

中東事態와 關聯하여 바레인 以外의 國家로부터 戰亂을 避하여 駐在國 "바레인" 으로 緊急待避
하여오는것을 意味한다. 따라서 本計劃書에서는 流入 의 槪念이다.

나. <u>撤　　收:</u>

我國人이 中東事態와 關聯하여, 避亂을 目的으로, 本國 또는 第3國으로 가기 爲하여 駐在國 "바
레인" 으로부터 出國 하는것을 意味한다. 따라서 流出 의 槪念이다.

5. 備蓄,收容段階의 任務

가. <u>總 括 班</u>

<u>(1). 對外 交渉</u>

(가). 外國으로부터 駐在國에 緊急待避하는 我國民에 대한 駐在國 政府의 入國許可를
한다.

4

0123

(나). 駐在國에 緊急 待避하여온 我國民이 適正 範圍內에서 換錢을 可能케 하도록 努力한다.

(다). 必要한 境遇, 我國 民間 및 軍用 航空機, 船舶의 出入港 및 離着陸을 確保한다.

(라). 其他 駐在國政府 및 公共機關에 대한 交涉에 임한다.

(2). 情報 蒐集

(가). 委員長의 各種 主要 措置 및 決定에 必要한 諜報, 情報를 蒐集, 報告한다.

(나). 모든 在바레인 韓國人 및 韓國企業體는 本件 計劃의 成功的인 施行에 有關한 情報를 入手하였을 때에는 이를 委員會에 提供하여야 한다.

(3). 現況 把握

(가). 中東 紛爭地域으로부터 駐在國에 到着하는 緊急待避 我國民의 다음에 關한 現況을 別添(1): "緊急待避者收容 現況報告" 樣式에 따라 每日 18:00現在로 把握하여 委員長에게 當日中에 書面報告 한다.

- 當日 到着 待避人員數
- 當日 現在 到着 累計 總計
- 待避所別 收容 人員 現況
- 當日 出國者 現況
- 當日 現在 出國者 累計 總計
- 健康狀態
- 滯留 希望期間別 現況

(나). 備蓄物資의 出庫狀況을 把握하고 記錄을 維持하여 後日의 淸算에 對備한다.

(4). 其他 事項

(가). 大宇.榮進에서 動員되는 5名의 差出人力을 適所에 適切히 配置한다.

(나). 本 計劃의 立案으로부터 執行이 完了될때까지 必要한 保安에 最善을 다한다.

나. 收容班

(1). 分 類

中東紛爭地域으로부터 待避하여온 我國民을 다음과 같이 3個 範疇로 分類한다.

(가) 個別 家庭 收容 對象者

家族同伴, 特히 父母 또는 子女 同伴者

5

0124

(나) 業體別 收容 對象者

　　當地에 支店(事務所,駐在員) 또는 現場이 維持되고있는 業體所屬 待避者

(다). 無緣故 收容 對象者

　　上記 ″個別 家庭 收容 對象者″와 ″業體別 收容對象者″에 속하지 않는 待避者.

(2). 配　　　置

(가). 個別 家庭 收容 對象者

　　　ㄱ. 當地 到着 順序에따라 收容 家庭을 定한다.
　　　ㄴ. 收容順序는 다음表에 依據 한다.(가나다 順序)

1.	大使 官邸	
2.	김동원	外換銀行 支店長
3.	김동원	東洋食品 代表
4.	김종용	參事官
5.	김지호	代表
6.	박승규	副領事
7.	백광현	榮進公社 次長
8.	이강신	榮進公社 支店長
9.	이두흥	韓一銀行 支店長
10.	이창욱	大宇 支店長
11.	임창호	大林 支店長
12.	전양호	韓國學校 校長
13.	정형남	韓人教會 牧師

(나). 業體別 待避所 收容 對象者

　　　ㄱ. 當地에 所在하는 待避者 所屬 또는 緣故業體에 配當한다.
　　　ㄴ. 所屬 또는 緣故業體의 收容能力이 不足한 경우에는, 該當者를 無緣故 收容 對象者로 看做, 待避所를 配當한다.

(다). 無緣故 待避所 收容 對象者

　　　ㄱ. 當地 到着 順位 01番부터 60番까지는 榮進公社 待避所에 配當한다.
　　　ㄴ. 當地 到着 順位 61번부터 360번까지는 大宇 待避所에 配當한다.
　　　ㄷ. 當地 到着 順位 361番부터는 現代 待避所에 配當한다.
　　　ㄹ. 無緣故 收容 對象者中, 當地 到着 順位 361番부터 現代待避所에 配當함에 있어서, 現代待避所가 業體別收容對象者의 收容으로 因하여 그收容能力을 超過하는

6

0125

境遇가 發生하면, 이때에는 榮進 待避所와 大宇 待避所에 照會하여, 그間에 收容能力再生여부에따라 이들 超過되는 待避者는 榮進 待避所또는 大宇 待避所에 適切히 配當한다.

(3). 收 容

(가). 記 錄

ㄱ. "個別 家庭 收容 對象者"를 收容한 各 家庭은 收容即時 別添(2): "待避家族 身上報告書"를 作成하여 每日 17:00까지 總括班에 報告한다.
ㄴ. 業體別 收容對象者를 收容한 業體別 待避所는 別添(3): "業體別待避者 收容現況 報告書"를 作成하여 每日 17:00까지 總括班에 提出한다.
ㄷ. "無緣故 收容 對象者"를 收容한 待避所는 別添(4): "無緣故對避者 收容 現況 報告書"를 作成하여 當日分을 每日 17:00까지 總括班에 提出한다.

(나). 寢臺, 寢具 支給

ㄱ. 業體別待避所는 必要한 寢臺, 寢具의 支給.指定을 自體 處理한다.
ㄴ. 無緣故對避者를 收容한 待避所는 對避者에게 物品을 支給하였을때에는 1人當 1枚 原則에 따라 別添(5)의 "物品支給 및 經費 請求書"를 作成하여 當日分을 綜合, 每日 17:00까지 總括班에 提出한다.
ㄷ. 個別家庭收容對象者를 收容한 家庭은 1家族當 1枚原則에 따라 別添(5): "物品 支給 및 經費 請求書"를 作成하여 當該日 17:00까지 總括班에 提出한다.

(4). 寢 食

(가). 各待避所(榮進.大宇.現代.各家庭)는 別添 (6): "物品 請求書"를 作成하여 總括班에 提出한다.
(나). 總括班은 接受된 上記 "物品 請求書"에 基礎하여 別添(7): "物品 出庫 要請書"를 作成, 發給하며, 備蓄場(榮進備蓄場,現代備蓄場)은 "物品 出庫 要請書" 提出者에게 "物品 出庫 要請書"에 記載된 品目의 所定量을 支給한다.
(다). 各 備蓄場은 每日 17:00시 現在로 別添(8): "日日 備蓄品 支給現況 報告書"를 作成하여 當日中 總括班에 提出한다.
(라). 總括班은 每日 18:00時 現在로 別添(9): "日日 出庫要請書 發給現況 報告書"을 作成하여 每日 19:00時 까지 委員長에게 報告한다.

다. 後 方 班

(1). 바레인 進出 我國 企業이 本計劃의 成功的인 執行을 爲하여 本委員會에 自進支援 提供하는
다음의 人的,物的 資源中, 人力을 除外한 各種 物品 및 現金을 管理한다.

摘 要	築進公社	大宇	現 代	外銀	大使館	合 計
差出 人力	2名	3名				5名
看 護士	1名		1名			2名
保有宿泊施設	60名分	300名分	550名分			910名分
備蓄 食料品	580名 X 100日		300名 X 30日			67,000人日
無線 通信機						
醫 藥 品	4個月分					4個月分
버스(大型)	2臺		1臺			3臺
버스(小型)				1臺		1臺
小 型 車		2臺				2臺
救 急 車	1대					1臺
乘 用 車					1대	1臺
燃 料	4個月分					4個月分
現 金					$1,000	$1,000

(2). 總括班이 發給한 物品出庫要請書에따라 備蓄品을 支給한다.
(3). 他 企業場所에 保管되어있는 備蓄品도 一括 管理한다.

라. 撤 收 班

(1). 撤收段階(第 3段階)에 突入하였을때 緊急撤收가 圓滿히 이루어 질수있도록 하기 爲하여,
現在의 第 1段階 및 第 2段階 期間中 緻密한 觀察과 經驗을 蓄積한다.
(2). 緊急撤收必要時에 投入 할수 있는 特別機便의 確保에 萬全을 期한다.
(3). 不時의 緊急撤收에 對備하여 後方班과 緊密한 聯絡網을 維持하여 必要한 車輛便이 確保되
도록 한다.
(4). 緊急撤收時의 特別條件(攜帶貨物制限等)을 緊急撤收 對象者에게 周知 시켜둔다.

8

마. 慰 務 班

(1). 韓國學校는 放學 期間中 與否에 關係없이, 緊急對避者 子女가 相當數에 到達하면, 이들을 爲한 學校特別活動班을 編成.指導한다.

(2). 韓人敎會는 對避者들의 信仰生活上의 希望을 最大限 受容할수있도록 努力하고, 期待에 副應토록 最善을 다한다.

(3). 慰務班은 重患者發生境遇에 對備하여, 駐在國 綜合病院과 必要한 協助關係를 樹立.維持한다.

(4). 慰務班의 活動에 따르는 經費의 後日淸算을 위하여, 適切한 "活動 및 經費 報告書"를 總括班에 提出하여 둘것을 勸告한다. 報告書의 樣式과 報告週期는 慰務班의 裁量에 委任한다.

6. 撤收段階의 任務

撤收段階에 突入하면, 本計劃書의 "3.나.(1)項"(3페이지)의 備蓄.救護段階의 委員會는 自動的으로 解散되고, "3.나.(2)項"(4페이지)의 撤收段階의 撤收委員會로 改編된다.

가. 總 括 班

(1). 撤收優先順位를 "6.나.(3).(가)項"(10페이지)의 標準에 따라 定하고, 對象者를 姓名別로, 連絡處.交通手段등이 包含된 名單을 作成 維持한다.

(2). 殘留班員의 正確한 名單을 作成 維持한다.

나. 撤 收 班

(1). 撤收의 區分

撤收는 다음과 같이 3個로 區分한다.

(가). 自意 撤收

駐在國으로부터의 海外旅行이 全혀 自由스러운 段階에서 自身의 決定에 따른 撤收.

(나). 勸告 撤收

政府나 大使館의 勸告에 依하되 自身의 選擇과 決定에 따른 撤收.

(다). 强制 撤收

政府나 大使館의 命令 指示에 따른 撤收.

9

0128

(2). 自意 및 勸告 撤收

"自意撤收" 및 "勸告撤收"하는 撤收者가 必要로하는 便宜를 可能한限 提供한다.

(3). 强制 撤收

(가). 撤收 優先順位

强制撤收段階에서는 委員會의 撤收能力을 總動員하며, 紛爭地域으로부터의 待避者이
거나, 從來부터 바레인에서 居住하여오고있는 撤收者이거나를 不問하고 다음의 撤收
優先順位에 따라 撤收하며, 撤收優先順位는 嚴守되어야 한다.

　　　　　1. 年少者
　　　　　2. 老弱者
　　　　　3. 年少者를 同伴하는 婦女子
　　　　　4. 同伴 年少者가없는 婦女子
　　　　　5. 勤勞者
　　　　　6. 自營業者
　　　　　7. 進出業體 職員
　　　　　8. 進出業體 任員
　　　　　9. 委員會 委員
　　　　　10. 大使館 職員
　　　　　11. 大　使

(나). 撤收 手段

ㄱ. 空港閉鎖 以前

- 航空便에 依한 撤收를 原則으로 한다.
- 航空便 確保는 大使館과 大韓航空의 共同責任 事項이다.
- 大韓航空 바레인 支店은 最終 航空便에 關하여는 最大限의 時間餘裕를 두고
  大使館에 通報하여야 한다.

ㄴ. 空港閉鎖 以後

- 現代所有 船舶便을 利用, 最短 時間內에 安全海域으로 脫出한다.
- 撤收船舶便의 出港場所는 原則的으로 現代시멘트 埠頭로하되, 當時 狀況이 必
  要로 하는 境遇, 大使의 決定에따라 出港地點을 大使館 맞은便에 位置하고있
  는 MARINA CLUB 埠頭로 變更할수있다.

(다). 撤收 節次

ㄱ. 確保된 撤收手段 收容能力範圍內에서, 上記 "撤收優先順位"를 參酌, 該當 撤收
   者를 指名하여 大使館에 集結시킨다.

10　　　　　　　　　　　　　0129

ㄴ. 大使館에 集結된 撤收者들을 當該 撤收手段이 位置하는 場所까지 案內, 搭乘 시킨다.

다. 殘 留 班

(1). 殘留班員은 自己自身의 責任下에 殘留하는것임으로, 그 結果에 對하여도 當然히 自身이 全的으로 責任진다.
(2). 殘留班員은 希望하는 境遇, 大使館에 集結하여 宿食,生活할수있다.

7. 業體別 特別任務

가. 榮進公社는 空港, 港灣內 勤務 人員을 活用, 待避者의 到着 與否를 把握하여 大使 및 韓人會長에게 通報한다.
나. 大韓航空은 空港 勤務 人員을 活用, 待避者의 到着 與否를 把握하여 大使 및 韓人會長에게 通報한다.

8. 限時的 身分 變更 措置

가. 大使가 本計劃의 撤收段階突入을 宣言하면, 그 瞬間부터, 準戰時로 規定되고, 撤收航空便 또는 船舶便이 離陸 또는 出港할때까지의 期間中, 大使는 限時的으로 本計劃關聯 委員會構成員과 機關長會議構成員에 對하여는 그 本來의 所屬과 身分의 如何를 不問하고 大韓民國 準公務員으로 看做하고 指揮한다.
나. 撤收段階에서는 撤收와 關聯된 大使의 指示는 最優先的으로 施行되어야하며, 受命者는 自身의 所屬企業의 利益보다 撤收의 完遂를 優先시켜야한다.

9. 外國人 雇傭員의 撤收

가. 大使館, 各企業體에 雇傭되여있는 外國人雇傭員의 撤收는 原則的으로 本計劃의 對象이 되지 아니한다.
나. 다만, 我國民의 撤收에 時間的으로나 收容能力에있어 아무런 支障이없고, 所要費用全額을 外國人雇傭員自身이 全額 自擔하고, 바레인에서 가장 가까운 地點까지만 運送하여 준다는 前提下에 人道的 見地에서 不得已한경우에는 大使의 決定에따라 例外措置할수도 있다.
다. 外國人雇傭員의 撤收支援은 어떠한 境遇에도 最終目的地가 韓國이어서는 絕對不可하며, 또한 駐在國 政府에의한 合法的 出國許可와 入國目的地政府의 入國許可가 事前에 있어야한다.

11   0130

10. 發　　效

가. 本計劃의 備蓄段階는 1990年8月11日 10:00時를 期해 發效한다.

나. 本計劃의 救護·收容段階는 大使가 救護·收容을 必要로하는 緊急待避者의 發生을 認知하고, 救護·收容段階突入을 宣言할때에 發效한다.

다. 本計劃의 撤收段階는 大使가 撤收段階突入을 宣言할때에 發效한다.

라. 大使에依한 救護·收容段階宣言과 撤收段階宣言은 文書 또는 口頭로 한다.

本計劃에 言及되어있는 모든 部署의 長과 關係者 全員은 本計劃의 完遂에 最善의 努力을 다할 것을 命함.

1990年 8月 11日

駐바레인 大韓民國 大使　禹 文 旗

12

0131

別 添 目 錄 表

긴급대피자 수용현황보고서
(總括班用)

1990. . . 17:00현재

발　신: 총괄반장
수　신: 주바레인 대한민국 대사

금일도착대피자: 　　　명...(도착자누계　　　명)
금일출발철수자: 　　　명...(출국자누계　　　명)

금일현재잔류자: 　　　명..(영진대피소　　　명)(수용누계　　　명)
　　　　　　　　　　　　　(대우대피소　　　명)(수용누계　　　명)
　　　　　　　　　　　　　(현대대피소　　　명)(수용누계　　　명)
　　　　　　　　　　　　　(각 가 정　　　명)(수용누계　　　명)

대피희망기간별현황:.........1 - 3일　　　명
　　　　　　　　　　　　　4 - 7일　　　명
　　　　　　　　　　　　　8 - 14일　　　명
　　　　　　　　　　　　　15 - 30일　　　명
　　　　　　　　　　　　　30일 이상　　　명

건강상태: _____

금일 수용자 명단: (별첨한 다음 각종 보고서 참조)

　　　별첨(1): 가족대피자　 수용보고서 1부
　　　별첨(2): 무연고대피자 수용보고서 1부
　　　별첨(3): 업체별대피자 수용보고서 1부

보 고 자: _____

총괄반장: _____ (인)

14

0133

가족대피자 수용보고서
(各家庭用)

1990. . . 17:00현재

수용장소: _____ 씨댁 (TEL _____)

대피가족상황: 세 대 주 명: _____

주 민 등 록 번 호: _____ .

국 내 주 소: _____ (TEL _____)

소 속 기 업 명: _____

전(前) 체 류 지: _____

바 레 인 도 착 일: 1990. . .

출 국 예 정 일: 1990. . .

동반가족명단

번호	성 명	성별	관계	주민 등록 번호	비 고
1					
2					
3					
4					
5					
6					
7					

보고자: _____ (인)

15

0134

(별첨 3)

업체별 대피자 수용보고서

1990.   .   . 17:00 현재

업체명: _____

수용자 명단:

번호	성 명	주민등록번호	출국예정일	국 내 주 소	비 고
01					
02					
03					
04					
05					
06					
07					
08					
09					
10					
11					
12					
13					
14					
15					

(15명을 초과할때에는, 본 양식용지를 추가 사용한다)

소 속: _____
직 위: _____
성 명: _____ (인)

16   0135

무연고대피자 수용보고서

1990.　　.　.17:00현지

<u>수용장소</u>: (영진대피소) (대우대피소) (현대대피소)

전일잔류인원:＿＿＿＿＿명
금일수용인원:＿＿＿＿＿명
금일출국인원:＿＿＿＿＿명
현재 인원:＿＿＿＿＿명

번호	성 명	주민등록번호	출국예정일	국 내 주 소	비 고
01					
02					
03					
04					
05					
06					
07					
08					
09					
10					
11					
12					
13					
14					
15					

(15명을 초과할때에는 본 양식용지를 추가 사용한다)

소　속:＿＿＿＿＿＿＿
직　위:＿＿＿＿＿＿＿
성　명:＿＿＿＿＿＿(인)

0136

물품지급 및 경비 청구서

1990. . .

발 신: 영진대피소, 대우대피소, 현대대피소, (세대주)_____
수 신: 주바레인 대한민국대사
참 조: 총 괄 반 장

중동분쟁지역 긴급대피 아국민 구호와 관련, 아래에 기명.서명한 본건 신청인 책임하에 수용하고있는 긴급대피자를 위하여 아래와 같이 물품 잊 경비를 청구하니 이를 지급하여 줄것을 요청합니다.

(금액단위: 원)

번호	품 목 명	단 가	수 량	총 액	비 고
1					
2					
3					
4					
5					
6					
7					
8					

소 속:_____

직 책:_____

성 명:_____(서명)

18

0137

물품 청구서

1990.   .   .

수신: 주 바레인 대한민국 대사

중동분쟁지역 긴급대피 아국민 구호와 관련, 아래 물품을 지급하여 주시기 바랍니다.

번호	물 품 명	단 가	수 량	금액총액	비 고
01					
02					
03					
04					
05					
06					
07					
08					
09					
10					

위 청구인

소 속:_____

성 명:_____(서명)

19

0138

(별첨 7)

물품 출고 요청서

1990.   .   .

발 신: 총 괄 반 장
수 신: 후 방 반 장

중동분쟁지역 긴급대피 아국민 구호와 관련, 아래 물품을 본 요청서 소지인에게 출고하여 주시기 바랍니다.

번호	출고요청품목	단 가	수 량	금액총액	비 고
_01_					
_02_					
_03_					
_04_					
_05_					
_06_					
_07_					
_08_					
_09_					
_10_					

총괄반:

성 명: _____ (인)

비축품지급 일일 현황보고서

1990. .

수신: 주 바레인 대한민국 대사

중동분쟁지역 긴급대피 아국민 구호와 관련, 1990. . . 현재 비축품지급 일일현황 보고서를 아래와 같이 제출합니다.

번호	비축품명	총비축고	전일총잔고	금일지급고	금일총잔고	비고
01						
02						
03						
04						
05						
06						
07						
08						
09						
10						

소 속: 후   방   반

직 위: 반   장

성 명: _____(인)

21   0140

출고요청서발급 일일 현황보고서

1990. . .

수신: 주 바레인 대한민국 대사

중동분쟁지역 긴급대피 아국민 구호와 관련, 1990. . . 현재 일일 출고 요청서 발급 현황을 아래와 같이 보고합니다.

연번	발 급 대 상	물 품 명	수 량	출 고 지	비축잔고	비 고
01						
02						
03						
04						
05						
06						
07						
08						
09						
10						

첨부: 일일 출고 요청서 사본 부

소속: 총   괄   반

성명: _____(인)

22   0141

 حرمات الخليج العربي للملاحة

Arabian Gulf Aviation Services

ARABIAN GULF AVIATION SERVICES (AGAS) is pleased to announce the immediate availability in Manama and limited quantity of:

GERMAN CIVIL RESPIRATORS

A NATO TESTED GAS MASK FOR RESPIRATORY PROTECTION AGAINST CHEMICAL GASES FROM CHEMICAL WEAPONS. PROVIDES COMPLETE PROTECTION TO THE EYES, NOSE, THROAT, LUNGS AND FACIAL SKIN.

Price is BD__32___ per unit (cash only) including new respirator and new canister - each with warranties. _THERE IS NO OBJECTION TO THE IMPORTATION OF THESE MASKS BY AGAS INTO BAHRAIN FROM THE MINISTRY OF INTERIOR,PUBLIC SECURITY,CIVIL DEFENSE DIR._

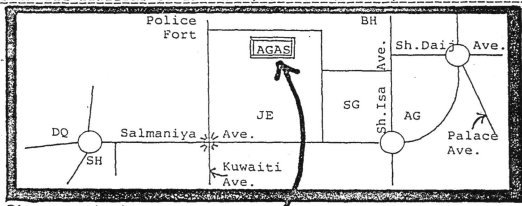

Please contact:

Arabian Gulf Aviation Services (AGAS)
House # 641, Road # 919
(Behind Japanese Embassy).
P.O. Box 2414
Manama, Bahrain.
Tel: 277700 _ 485651
Fax: 270555 - 324244

Map not to scale
Key to Map:
AG = Andalus Garden
SG = Salmaniya Garden
SH = Salmaniya Hospital
DQ = Dairy Queen
BH = Bristol Hotel
JE = Japanese Embassy

NOTE: FOR IMMEDIATE RESERVATIONS PLEASE SEND US AFAX.

P.O. Box 2414 - Tel.: 277700 - Fax: 270555 - Manama - Bahrain - Arabian Gulf

ص.ب: ٢٤١٤. تليفون: ٢٧٧٧٠٠. فاكس: ٢٧٠٥٥٥. المنامة. البحرين. الخليج العربي

0142

Gulf Daily News · Sunday, 23rd December 1990 Page 5

Flights heavily booked a UN deadline draws nea

By Soman Baby

ISLAND residents are flocking to book airline seats to beat the January 15 deadline set by the United Nations for Iraq's withdrawal from Kuwait.

Major international airlines operating through Bahrain said yesterday their flights were fully booked during the week preceding January 15.

Cathay Pacific said it had stopped giving confirmed bookings to passengers intending to travel out of Bahrain after January 10.

Gulf Air said its reservation staff was swamped with calls from people who wanted to make bookings between January 8 and 15.

A spokesman for the airline said flights to London were fully booked until January 15.

"Only a few seats are available in business and first class in the last week of December," said the spokesman.

Flights to Bombay are open till January 8, but they are full between January 9 and 15. Seats are available from January 16."

K V N Nair, Air India's airport and customer relations manager, said a few seats were available until January 8 and after January 17.

Adel Ali, British Airways' Bahrain manager, said the airline's flights from the island were "fairly full" until January 10 because of "festive pressure".

"For people who are unable to get seats confirmed on specific dates, we offer alternatives.

"However, we waitlist people and try to confirm seats as far as possible."

Robert Atkinson, Cathay Pacific's Bahrain-based general manager for the Middle East and India, discounted rumours that the airline was temporarily suspending its operations.

"We have no plans to suspend operations unless a situation develops forcing us to do so.

"However, we have decided to put a cap on confirmed bookings after January 10.

"There have been frantic bookings resulting in duplication and even triplication in reservations," said Mr Atkinson.

He said the airline had provisionally stopped giving confirmed bookings to passengers who wanted to fly after January 10.

A spokesman for KLM, which operates a weekly Bahrain-Dhahran-Amsterdam flight, said the flights were full until January 10.

(별첨 4)

제목 : 사우디아라비아 SCATANA RULE
=======================================

SCATANA (SECURITY CONTROL OF AIR TRAFFIC AND AIR NAVIGATION AIDS FOR SAUDI
ARABIA) : 사우디아라비아 항공교통 및 항법보조시설 보안통제 RULE

- 목적 : 사우디 영공내에서 전쟁 또는 DEFENCE EMERGENCY 기간중, 운항중인
항공기가 위협지역을 회피할 수 있도록 그 상황과 특별지시 등을 신속하게
전달하기 위하여 설정됨.

- 적용 : SCATANA RULE 유효기간중 사우디 공역에 운항중이거나 진입 예정 항공기

- 절차

A) 상황발생시 ADNC (AIR DEFENCE NOTIFICATION CENTER)에서 JEDDAH ACC에 SCATANA
RULE 발효를 통보.

B) 사우디의 전 ATC 기관은 동 상황을 영공내 전항공기에게 모든 가능한 주파수를 동원
하여 알리고 SCATANA 지시를 위해 대기하라고 INFO.

C) ADNC 지휘하에 전용 ATC 기관은 특별 SCATANA 지시를 각 항공기에게 전달하고,
동시에 가능한 모든 방법을 동원하여 인접/전세계 교통기관, 사우디내 전공항기관에
전파.

D) 상황을 접수한 기장은 모든 SCATANA 지시를 반드시 따라야 함.

- 항로 / 고도의 변경

- 운항중인 항공기는 가장 인접한 공항에 착륙 (매우 위험한 상황일 경우)

- 출발하지 않은 항공기는 지상에 대기 등

E) 관련 NOTAM OFFICE에서 CLASS-I NOTAM 발표

- 참고

O SCATANA RULE 유효기간중 모든 항공기의 운항은 ADNC의 허가를 받아야 하며,
부여된 전시 항공교통 우선순위 NBR 에 따라 운항하게 됨.

O 동기간중 민간항공기 운항이 허가될 지라도 공항에서 운영되는 대부분의 항법
보조시설이 DOWN 될 것임.

- EFF : FROM 19NOV 1990 0001Z - PERMANENT

- 입수 경로: SAUDI ARABIA NOTAM A1002/90 DATED 13NOV 1990

0144

NNNNZCZC YLA141 TSA539
GG RKSSYNYX
130749 DEJDYNYX
(PART ONE OF SIX PARTS)
A1002/90 NOTAMN
2300Z/90 NOTAMN
C5401/90 NOTAMN
A) JEDDAH FIR
B) 11190601Z
C) PERM
D) NIL
E) SECURITY CONTROL OF AIR TRAFFIC AND AIR NAVIGATION AIDS FOR ... DI
   ARABIA ?SCATANA?
   A PLAN CALLED THE SECURITY CONTROL OF AIR TRAFIC AND AIR
   NAVIGATION AIDS SCATANA,HAS BEEN DEVELOPED TO ENSURE THAT,
   SHOULD HOSTILITIES BREAK OUT IN SAUDI ARABIAN AIRSPACE, ALL
   CIVILIAN AIRCRAFT IN FLIGHT SHALL BE QUICKLY NOTIFIED OF THE
   CIRCUMSTANCES AND GIVEN SPECIAL INSTRUCTIONS TO IMMEDIATELY
   VACATE OR AVOIDE THOSE AREAS CONSIDERED TO BE HAZARDOUS.
F) NIL
G) NIL

NNNNZCZC YLA14N /SA533
GG RKSSYNYX
130749 DEJDYNYX
(PART TWO OF SIX PARTS)
A1002/90 NOTAMN
A300Z/90 NOTAMN
C5401/90 NOTAMN
A) JEDDAH FIR
B) 11190601Z
C) PERM
D) NIL
E) IN CASES WHERE THE SAFETY OF A FLIGHT MAY BE IN DIRE JEOPARDY,
   THE AIRCRAFT SHALL BE INSTRUCTED TO LAND AS SOON AS POSSIBLE AT
   THE NEAREST AIRPORT SUITABLE TO THE PILOT.ONCE THE JEDDAH ATS AREA
   CONTROL CENTER (ACC) HAS BEEN INFORMED BY THE AIR DEFENCE
   NOTIFICATION CENTER (ADNC) THAT THE FOLLOWING SCATANA RULES ARE
   ... ... ALL ATS UNITS IN THE KINGDOM SHALL BROADCAST ...
   ALL ... FREQUENCISE THAT ?SCATANA RULES ARE NOW ACTING
   ALL AIRCRAFT STAND BY FOR SCATANA INSTRUCTIONS? AND ...
   ... THE DIRECTION OF ADNC, THE APPROPRIATE ATS UNIT SHALL
   ... ... INSTRUCTIONS TO EACH AIRCRAFT
F) ...
G) ...

0145

안 전 지 출 및 긴 급 파 기 계 획
====================================

주 바레인 대사관   1990. 8

1. 목 적 :

   본 계획은 적의 공격, 화재, 기타의 비상사태에 대비하여 보관중인 각종 비밀
   문서, 암호자재, 장비등을 안전하게 지출 또는 파기하여 국가의 비밀을 최대한
   으로 보장하기 위하여 비상시 당관의 자체 비상대책 계획을 수립, 운영하기
   위한것이다.

2. 직책에 의한 책임 :

   당관의 안전지출 및 긴급파기의 책임은 집무시간(비상소집 했을때를 포함)에는
   보관책임자와 당관의 분임 보안담당관이 지고, 집무시간외에는 당직자가 진다.

3. 서류함의 우선순위 :

   당관의 각 담당별 사무실에 비치된 서류함 및 비밀용기 좌상단에 안전지출
   우선순위를 표시하고, 비상시 동 순위대로 긴급 안전지출토록 한다.

4. 비밀용기및 자재의 위치 :

   비밀용기는 보안상태를 참작, 적당한 곳을 선정, 비치한다.

   비밀용기의 위치가 이동되었을 때에는 지체없이 당관 분임보안 담당관에게 통보
   하도록 한다.

5. 안전지출 및 긴급파기의 절차

  가. 시간적으로 여유가 있을때 :

      보안담당관은 당관에 보관하고 있는 비밀의 안전지출 또는 긴급파기의 범위,
      시기, 방법등에 관한 계획을 수립하여, 공관장의 재가를 얻어 각 담당관에게
      통보하고, 분임보안담당관의 책임(지휘)하에 실시한다.

  나. 시간적 여유가 없을때 :

      상기 '가'항의 절차를 밟을 시간적 여유가 없을때에는 비상시 긴급성의 정도에

0146

따라 집무시간중에는 각 담당관별로 보관중인 서류의 보관책임자 또는 비밀관리 책임자가, 집무시간 외에는 공관장의 승인을 득한후 당직자가 안전지출 또는 긴급파기한다.

다. 초비상시 :

상기 '가' 또는 '나'항의 절차를 거칠수가 없을 정도로 사태가 긴박했을 경우에는 비밀관리 책임자 또는 당직자가 단독으로 안전지출 또는 긴급파기하고 지휘 계통을 통해 사후 보고한다.

단, 이때에는 '가' 및 '나'항의 절차를 밟을수 없었다는 사실을 인정할만한 충분한 이유가 있어야한다.

6. 안전지출 및 긴급 파기조의 편성

긴급파기는 각 담당관별로 하며, 분임보안 담당관이 동 안전지출 및 긴급파기를 지휘한다.

7. 안전지출 또는 긴급파기와 그 방법

가. 당관의 안전지출 장소는 비상시에는 공관청사에서 관저 또는 각 담당별 자택 (공관청사 및 관저의 화재시)으로하며, 초비상시에는 현장에서 소각한다.

나. 동 비밀의 안전 지출후 보관장소는 관저 또는 각 담당별 자택(공관청사 및 관저 화재시)으로하되, 즉시 주재국 경찰의 경호를 요청토록 한다.

다. 지출방법 :

(1). 비상지출대의 비치 : 각 담당관은 비상시 비밀문서를 넣어서 지출할 수 있는 비상지출대를 항상 보관용기 또는 케비넷, 서류함에 보관해야 한다.

(2). 비밀수송조의 편성 : 비밀 수송조는 분임보안 담당관의 책임(지휘)하에 각 담당별로 수송을 담당하며, 수송을 위한 차량편은 일차적으로 각 개인 승용차를 이용토록 한다.

(3). 비밀의 지출 : 비밀지출은 분임보안 담당관 책임 (지휘)하에 비밀문서를 비상지출대에 넣어서 반출하여 각 담당이 수송토록 한다.

0147

9. 최종확인

  가. 안전지출 또는 긴급 파기조에 의해 지출 또는 파기하였을때는 공관장 또는
     공관장의 지시에 의해 분임 보안담당관이 확인해야 한다.

  나. 공관장이 직접 지시하여 지출 또는 파기하였을 때에는 공관장이 직접
     확인해야 한다.

10. 기타 필요한 사항은 공관장 또는 공관장의 지시에 의해 분임 보안담당관과 협의
    하여 정한다.

11. 화재로 인한 비상시에는 별첨 편성 임무에 따라 신속히 조치한다.

0148

방 . 화 조 편 성

주 바레인 대사관   1990. 8

당관 청사 및 관저에 화재가 발생되었을 경우, 다음과 같이 비상시의 방화조를
편성 계획을 수립하여 실시한다.

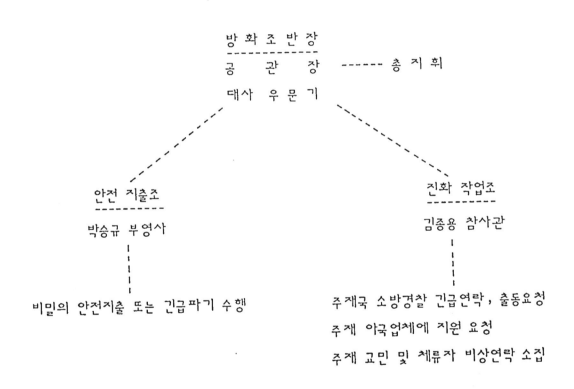

```
                      방 화 조 반 장
                      ----------
                      공   관   장  ------  총 지 휘
                      대 사  우 문 기

        안 전 지출조                        진 화 작업조
        ----------                        ----------
        박승규 부영사                       김종용 참사관
            |                                 |
            |                                 |
            |                                 |
   비밀의 안전지출 또는 긴급파기 수행      주재국 소방경찰 긴급연락, 출동요청
                                         주재 아국업체에 지원 요청
                                         주재 교민 및 체류자 비상연락 소집
```

0149

긴급 파기 계획수립 (암호자재 및 통신보안장비)
===

주 바레인 대사관   1990. 8.

1. 목 적 :

   긴급사태 발생으로 공관에 보관, 운용하고 있는 암호자재 및 통신장비의 안전보호
   또는 안전지출을 할 수 없다고 판단되는 경우 이를 긴급 파기함으로서 적 또는 불순
   분자에게 탈취, 노획되어 외교통신의 암호체계 및 통신 보안장비의 제원이 누설
   되는 것을 방지함에 있다.

2. 정 의 :

 가. '긴급사태' 라함은 내란, 외란, 천재지변 및 기타 사항이 긴박하여 아국 공관
     원과 공관 시설물의 안전보호 및 안전지출이 불가능하다고 판단되는 사태를 말
     한다.

 나. '통신보안장비' 라함은 난수처리기기(501호기)와 본부에서 통신보안장비로 지정
     하는 장비를 말한다.

3. 파기순서 및 파기방법

 가. 암호자재 :

   (1). 긴급사태가 발생하였다고 인정한때에는 우선 과거용을 파기하고, 사태가
        더욱 악화되었을 때에는 미래용을 파기한다.

   (2). 현재 사용중인 암호자재를 계속 사용할 수 없을 정도로 상황이 악화되었을
        때에는 '전공관용'자재부터 차례로 파기한다.

   (3). 암호자재 및 통신보안장비 운용설명서 등의 문건은 암호자재 파기에 앞서
        파기하거나 이와 병행하여 파기한다.

   (4). 난수자재, 암호 프로그램 디스켓 및 환자표 등의 문건 파기는 소각처리한다.

0150

나. 통신보안장비

  (1). 501 호기

    (가). 모니터를 들어내고, 본체 좌우측면 각각 2개의 나사와 뒷면 1개의 나사를 풀어 덮개를 열고, 세로로 꽂혀있는 3개의 카드를 뽑아 파기 함으로써 501호기의 모든 기능은 마비된다.

    (나). 전체 기계의 형을 가능한대로 식별이 불가능 하도록 햄머등으로 강타 파기한다. (이경우는 안전지출이 전혀 불가능한 긴급사태로서, 공관 이 완전 철수후 복귀 불가능하다고 판단되는 최후의 조치임).

  (2). 기타 통신보안장비는 전항에 준하여 파기한다.

다. 문 서 : 긴급사태 발생시 다음 순서로 문서를 파기한다.

  (1). 2급비밀로서 암호자재, 통신보안장비와 관련한 모든 공문 및 전문.

  (2). 3급비밀로서 암호자재, 통신보안장비, 기타 통신실 운용에 관한 모든 공문 및 전문.

  (3). 대외비로서 (1),(2)항에 준하는 모든 공문 및 전문과 기타 일반 공문 및 전문.

4. 보 고

  암호자재 및 통신보안장비를 긴급 파기하였을 때는 다음사항을 장관에게 긴급 보고 하여야 한다.

  (1). 파기 경위.

  (2). 장비명칭 및 수량, 등록번호.

  (3). 파기일시 및 장소.

  (4). 파기자.

예 고 : 신계획 수립시 파기

0151

카탈

수 신 : 내부결재
제 목 : 교민 긴급 비상 철수 계획 수립

<table>
<tr><td rowspan="3">앙
고
지</td><td></td><td></td><td colspan="2">대 사</td></tr>
<tr><td></td><td></td><td rowspan="2"></td></tr>
<tr><td></td><td></td></tr>
</table>

　　　　이라크의 쿠웨이트 침공 관련, 이라크와 다국적군간의 전쟁
돌입 가능성이 커짐에 따라 만일의 사태에 대비하여 당지 거주 아국 교민
의 비상 철수 계획을 별첨과 같이 수립 시행하고자 하오니 재가하여 주시기
바랍니다.

　　　첨 부 : 교민 비상 철수 계획 1부. 끝.

0152

교민 비상 철수 계획

주 카타르 대사관

1. 목 적

   걸프 사태 악화로 인해 전쟁 발발시 당지 거주 아국 교민들은 전쟁의 피해로 부터 보호키위해 신변 안전 확보 및 안전지대로의 효율적인 철수 대책 수립

2. 세부 시행 계획

   가. 신속한 연락 체제 구축

   - 비상 연락망 재정비 : 별 첨
   - 교민 세대별 가족수 까지 상세 파악 : 별 첨

   나. - 한인회를 중심으로 한 비상 철수 대책반 조직 : 별 첨

   다. 세부 행동 계획

   1) 제 1 단계 :
      전쟁 발발 위험이 임박해질때 교민부인과 어린이를 우선 철수

   2) 제 2 단계 :
      전쟁 발발이 거의 확실시 될때 가족은 물론 본인들까지 철수

   3) 제 3 단계 : 전쟁 발발시
      전쟁이 발발하여 카타르 까지 전쟁 피해 지역으로 확대될시 잔류 교민 전원과 공관 직원 가족 철수

      가) 전쟁이 발발하였으나 카바르 까지 피해지역으로 확산될 위험이 없을 시 잔류 교민들은 공관과의 긴밀한 연락 계속 유지 불필요한 외출 자제, 외출이 불가피할때는 대사관이나 인근 교민에게 행선지 및 연락처 통보. 상황에 따라 철수 준비 사전조치로 1차 집결지인

0153

대사관으로 본인 차량으로 이동.

대사관 수용시설 준비 : 지하실, 홍보물 열람실, 2층 자료실
3층 비서실

나) 전쟁이 카타르까지 피해지역으로 확대될 시 : 고민 전원 철수
조치

- 공항 철수 가능시 : 정상적인 항공기 이용 불가시 본국에
비상철수용 특별기 요청하거나 인근 아국
공관과 공동노력으로 KAL 기 비행 순로
등 조정 요청

- 공항 폐쇄 등 공로 철수 불가시 : U.A.E., 오만으로 각자
차량으로 육로 이동 (3개
차량 1개조씩 편성) 출입국
수속과 숙소, 항공편 예약
등 편의 제공 요청

- 공로 및 육로 철수 불가능시 탈출 조치 강구시까지 대사관
영내 체류 각자 비상물품 지참토록하고 대사관 비축분은
대사관 영내 체류가 장기화될 때 사용함.

- 고민 철수 관련하여 미국, 영국, 일본 등 우방국 대사관들과
긴밀한 협조 체제 유지

- 여권 분실 고민을 위해 폴라로이드 사진기와 필름 구비.

3. 행 정 사 항

고민 철수 대상자 실태 파악

자진철수, 특별기편 철수, 최후까지 잔류, 3경우로 구분하여 분류
수시 파악 기록 정비

가. 자진철수 : 대사관 의 권유에 의하여 가족중심철수.
(5명)   나종엽가족 4명 (부인 및 자녀 3명) : 1.9 철수
최태진 가족 1명 (부인)   : 1.11 철수

0154

나. 특별기편 접수 (61명)

특별기가 마련되어 접수하게 될 경우에 접수 희망자 :
명단 별첨

다. 최후까지 잔류 (16명) : 대사관 최종 잔류 인원, 주재국
기관 고용된 자 및 사업등, 기타
사유로 잔류가 불가피한 자
유 내형대사, 김태혁영사,
나종엽, 이은국, 최태진, 최원탁,
최주영, 김대용, 문광일, 김일섭, 신재근,
김충한, 최세현, 박희남, 윤석구, 이원호

첨 부: 1. 기타 고민 유의사항 1부
2. 비상연락망 1부
3. 한인회 중심 비상대책반 편성표 1부
4. 세대별 가족 현황 1부
5. 특별기편 접수 대상자 명단 1부. 끝.

0155

교민 안전 유의 사항

- 여권 분실시에 대비 항상 여권용 사진 2매 비상시 즉시 휴대 가능 장소에 보관

- 거주지역 인근 이웃들과 평소 사소한 시비 자제하고 신빈관계 유지, 특히 치안당국자들과 친밀한 관계 유지하여 유사시 이들의 도움을 받을 수 있도록 함.

- 교민 실태 파악을 위해 본인 및 가족들 해외 출장 휴가등 국외나 국내의 장거리 여행시 반드시 대사관에 통보.

- 전화 불통에 대비하여 공관 및 인근 교민들과의 연락을 위해 비상연락 조별 운용 철저히 시행

- 특히 원거리 거주 교민 외출시 행선지를 가족 및 인근 교민에게 통보

- 전기 공급 차단의 경우에 대비하여 건전지, 까스 등, 초 다량 준비

- 식수 공급 중단에 대비 식수 충분히 준비하고 수도물을 장기 저장할 수 있도록 대형 플라스틱 물통 등 준비

- 비상철수 시 신속한 이동이 가능하도록 반출용 가재도구 정리

- 항공료 준비 (미불 현찰)

- 상호 정보 교환하되 유언비어에 현혹되지 않도록 조심

- 육로에 의한 장거리 차량 운행에 대비, 여분의 연료 및 비상식량 비축

- 응급조치 구급약 상비

비 상 연 락 망

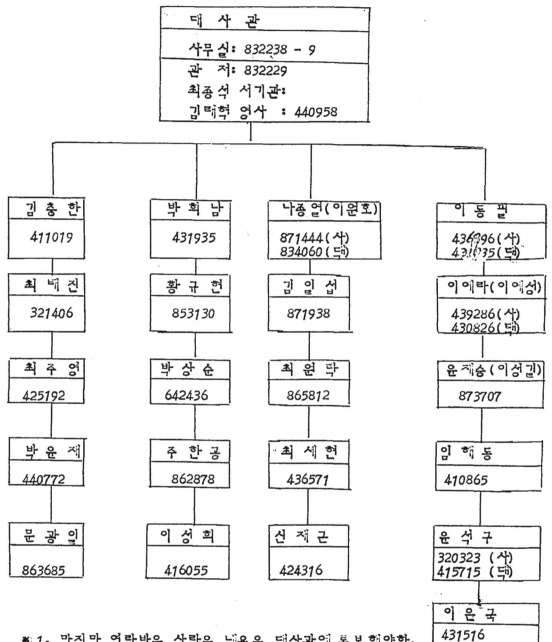

대 사 관
사무실: 832238 - 9
관 저: 832229
최종석 서기관:
김태혁 영사 : 440958

김 충 한	박 희 남	나종업(이원호)	이 동 필
411019	431935	871444 (사) 834060 (댁)	436996 (사) 431935 (댁)

최 배 진	황 규 현	김 일 섭	이에라(이여성)
321406	853130	871938	439286 (사) 430826 (댁)

최 주 영	박 상 순	최 원 락	윤재승(이성길)
425192	642436	865812	873707

박 윤 재	주 한 공	최 세 현	임 해 동
440772	862878	436571	410865

문 광 일	이 성 희	신 재 근	윤 석 구
863685	416055	424316	320323 (사) 415715 (댁)

이 은 국
431516

＊1. 마지막 연락받은 사람은 내용을 대사관에 통보해야함.

2. 다음 사람이 연락안될때는 그 다음사람에게 연락해서 맨 마지막 사람까지 연락이 계속 유지되도록 해야함.

0157

한인회 비상대책반 편성표

반 장 : 박 희 남 (한인회장)

통제조	상황조	연락조	보급조	구급조	예비조
조장 : 나종열	김대용	박상순	이동필	최주영	주한공
임해동	이은국	최원탁	이여라	최대진	이성길
박윤재	문광일	신재근	윤재승	윤석구	이예성
	최세현	김일섭	김충한	이성희	김희원
			황규현		이정현
					이준용
					그형학
					이상로

＊ 각 조원은 해당조 에서의 상황을 통제조 에 수시 통보

0158

카타르 체류자 현황

1990. 12. 27. 현재

구 분	성 명	가 족 현 황	비 고
대사관(14명)	유 내형	김정진	
	최종 석	이종 애, 상윤, 서윤, 혜욱	
	김 래혁	유 한선	
	이 영천		
	황용 순		
	고복 회	김 더용, 김형범	
남송 산업(6명)	윤 재승		
	김 회원		
	이 정헌		1월중순 도착예정
	고 형학		
	이준용		
	이 상로		
런던베커리 (7명)	이 에락	임정숙, 이주 영, 이주 리	
	이 에성	구 은경, 이주 호	
메드 걸프 (1명)	이은국		
비 이 에스 (2명)	윤 석구	엄 저숙	
현대건섭(1명)	이동 필		
코리안베커리 (1 명)	이성길		

0159

벼구코치(18명)	문광일	김은숙, 문승균, 문승민
	최주영	장기선, 최재영, 최재성
	최원탁	박노경, 최재훈
	김충한	삼석정, 김재현, 김건영
	박윤재	
	최태진	부 인

탁구코치(19명)	주한공	조준순
	박희남	김귀자
	박상순	
	임혜동	김희미, 임현주, 임우상
	이성희	이미혜, 이지아
	황규현	오정애, 황보라, 황유미
	최세현	김형숙, 최은선

태권도코치(12명)	나종엽	양경희, 나목화, 나국화
		나혁균
	신재근	최성이, 선동진
	김일섭	정옥, 김태민, 김태현

| 농구코차 (2명) | 이원호 | 이윤기 |

총 체류자 : 83 명
휴 가 : 1명
현 체류자 : 82 명

총 체류 세대주: 35명
부 인 : 20명
자 녀 : 27명

0160

특별기편 첩수 대상자 명단

소 속	본인성명	가 족
대사관 (11명)		김정진 , 유한선
	최종석	이종애, 상윤, 서윤, 혜욱
	이영천	
	황용순	
	고복희	김형범
남송 산업 (6명)	윤재승	
	김희원	
	이정현	
	고형학	
	이준용	
	이상로	
런던베커리(7명)	이억타	임정숙, 이주영, 이주미
	이예성	구은경, 이주호
현대건설 (1명)	이동필	
코리언베커리(1)	이성길	
비에스가족 (1)		임지숙
탁구사범(14)	주한공	조준순
	박상순	
	임해동	김희미, 임현주, 임우상
	이성희	이미혜, 이지아
	황규현	오정애, 황보타, 황유미
탁구사범 (가족 2명)		김형숙, 최은선
배구사범 (1)	박윤재	
배구사범가족 (11)		김은숙, 문승군, 문승민
		장기선, 최재영, 최재성
		박노경, 최재훈
		심석정, 김재현, 김건영
태권도사범가족 (5)		최성이, 신동진
		정옥, 김태민, 김태현
농구사범가족 (1)		이연기

비상사태 대비 공관 철수계획

1990. 11.

예고 : 신계획 수립시 파기

주 사 우 디 대 사 관

0162

1. 목   적

   - 공관 및 직원 철수계획은 주재국 내에서의 비상사태에 대비하여
     공관 및 직원의 안전한 철수를 목적으로 함.

2. 실시 내용

   가. 1단계 : 전쟁 임박시

   1) 철수 계획

   가) 인원 : 본부지시에따른 공관원의 가족, 고용원 및 그 가족

   나) 장소 : 서울, 아테네, 로마등

   다) 수송 : 젯다 발 KAL 또는 SAUDIA

   라) 인솔 : 직원 1명

   2) 안전 지출 및 긴급파기

   o 음어자재, 비밀 서류등의 안전지출 및 긴급파기를 위한 제반
     준비를 하며, 상황이 악화될 경우 동 계획에따라 실시함.

   3) 비상식량, 현금등 확보

   o 직원 및 고용원 각자가 비상식량, 유류, 연료 및 현금등의 비상
     물자를 적의 확보함.

   o 총무는 공관장의 재가를 얻어 공용 비상물자 및 현금을 확보하여
     청사 및 관저에 확보함.

0163

4) 비상 대피소 준비

　ㅇ 장 소 : 청사 지하실

　ㅇ 준비물 : 전원, 취사시설, 비상약품 등

나. 2단계 : 전쟁 발발시

1) 철수 계획

　가) 인원

　　ㅇ 본부와의 협의후, 필수요원을 제외한 전직원

　　ㅇ 필수요원 : 대사, 정무 참사관, 영사, 노무관, 외신관

　　ㅇ 정무 2, 무관은 본국정부 및 공관장과 협의후 별도결정

　나) 장소 : 서울, 아테네, 로마등

　다) 수송 : " 교민비상대피 철수계획 "에 따름

2) 안전지출 및 긴급파기

　ㅇ 안전지출 및 긴급파기 계획에 의거 즉시 실시함

3) 비상식량, 현금등

　ㅇ 전쟁발발 초기에는 개인이 확보한 비상물자를 활용하고,
　　고갈시 공용 비상물자를 지원함

　ㅇ 비상물자의 확보를 계속 추진하며, 필요시 본부 및 인근 공관에
　　지원을 요청함

　　첨　부 : 1. 비상연락망

　　　　　　2. 직원 현황

　　　　　　3. 고용원 현황

　　　　　　4. 안전지출 및 긴급파기 계획

0164

직 원 현 황

직 위	성 명	가족수
대 사	주병국	1
공 사	박명준	2
참 사 관	백기문	3
참 사 관	정우성	3
영 사	양봉렬	3
총 무	백성택	3
외 신 관	이수용	3
공 사	강동연	1
서 기 관	이승국	3
파 견	박 훈	
무 관	이영남	3
재 무 관	노훈건	2
재무관보	천동관	1
재무관보	김성집	1
재무관보	배경훈	3
상 무 관	안잉기	3
건 설 관	서주환	1
건설관보	박화동	2
노 무 관	김정규	1
노무관보	김헌수	3
계	20명	42명

0165

고 용 원 현 황

소 속	성 명	가 족 수
총 무	이 수 길	2
총 무	정 원 태	3
총 무	이 인 희	2
정 무	최 순 길	4
경 제	이 강 석	3
영 사	김 재 완	3
영 사	정 영 우	3
건 설	정 성 수	3
전 공	조 충 근	2
정 원	허 만 국	
경 비	임 경 규	
경 비	이 말 재	1
관 저	박 명 호	2
관 저	권 현 식	
KODCO	오 세 철	
계	15 명	28 명

0166

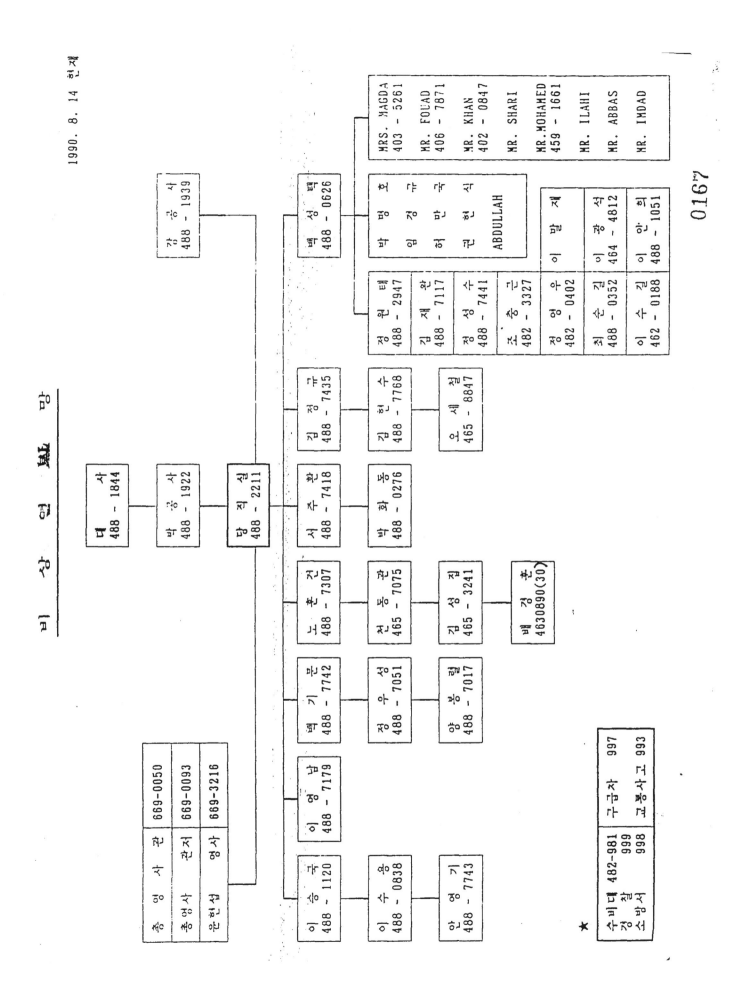

비 상 연 락 망

강문사 488 - 1939

대사 488 - 1844
공사 488 - 1922
참사관 488 - 2211

총영사관 669-0050
총영사 669-0093
영사 669-3216
부영사

MRS. MAGDA 403 - 5261
MR. FOUAD 406 - 7871
MR. KHAN 402 - 0847
MR. SHARI
MR. MOHAMED 459 - 1661
MR. ILAHI
MR. ABBAS
MR. IMDAD

배성택 488 - 0626
ABDULLAH

정현태 488 - 2947
김재환 488 - 7117
정성수 488 - 7441
조중근 482 - 3327
정영아 482 - 0402
최산길 488 - 0352
이수길 462 - 0188
이재림
이광상 464 - 4812
이한희 488 - 1051

정영규 488 - 7435
김현사 488 - 7768
어세철 465 - 8847

서주환 488 - 7418
박화동 488 - 0276

문춘진 488 - 7307
전광동 465 - 7075
김성직 465 - 3241
배경춘 4630890(30)

배기만 488 - 7742
정아성 488 - 7051
양용렬 488 - 7017

이영남 488 - 7179

이순 488 - 1120
이수영 488 - 0838
한영기 488 - 7743

★ 수비대 482-981
참정 999
방서 998
누급자 997
경호사 993

근로자 비상 대피 계획 세부 계획

1. 일반 사항

   ○ 별첨 비상 연락망에 의하여 통보

   ○ 사전에 출국비자를 받아두도록 권고.
      - 이 경우 여권을 본인이 소지하게 됨.
      - 비상시 스폰서의 부재 등으로 여권이 없는 자에
        대하여는 영사과와 협조하여 임시여권 발부.

2. 동부 지역

   ○ 자체 계획에 의하여 리야드로 대피계획을 갖고 있는
      신화건설, 현대산업개발 등을 제외한 나머지 근로자및
      개별 취업자는 구일산업의 어선을 이용하여 인접국인
      카타르, UAE, 파키스탄으로 대피.
      - 구일산업 수용 능력
        · 담맘지역 12척(500명),

      - 이용 대상
        · 개별취업자, 소규모 건설업체지사
      - 제외: 현대산업. 신화건설, 삼성, 현대건설, 유원건설 (494명)
        · 리야드지사로 대피시킨 후 리야드 철수계획에 의함.

      - 구일산업과 협의, 사태발생시 승선지점, 시각을 비상연락망을
        통하여 전파

   ○ 구일산업 선박이나 리야드로 대피하지 못한 교민은 카타르등
      인접국으로 대피 유도.

      ++ 사태가 발생하면 동부지역은 주 전장이 될것이므로 공항을
         이용한 대피는 어려울 것임.
      ++ 사태가 임박하게 되면 사전에 동부지역 철수를 지시하고
         철수하지 못한 교민에 대하여 구일산업 선박을 이용하여
         대피시킴.

3. 리야드 지역

  ○ 리야드지역에 거주하는 교민, 근로자 등은 각자 집, 캠프에서
     비상연락을 기다리도록 함.

  ○ 동부지역, 부레이다, 호푸프 등 인접지역에서 대피한 취업자와
     근로자를 위하여 다음과 같이 캠프를 마련함.

     - 이용가능한 캠프:

위 치	수용능력
현대건설 내무성 공사캠프	600-700 명
현대건설 병원단지	500
삼환기업 지사	300
계	1,400-1,500 명

     - 건설업체 (신화, 현대산업 등) 근로자는 각 회사에서 관리 퇴록 함
  ○ 아국 식품업체로 하여금 동 캠프에 매장을 설치하고 우선 공급
     하도록 함.
     - 정식품(쌀) : 241-1134
     - 권식품 (부식,한국식품) : 463-4101
     - 농심라면 : 478-2441
     - 기타 식품업체

+++ 리야드에서의 철수 계획은 기본 계획에 의함.

0169

4. 의료요원 철수 계획

  ° 사태가 발생하면 당관에서 보건성장관과 아국 의료요원의 전원 근무 종료와 귀국 문제 협의.

    - 사우디 보건성에서 리야드 또는 제다 공관에 수송 요구.

    - 귀국 항공료 부담.

  ° 사우디 보건성의 수송수단이 적절치 못할 경우 다음과같이 시행.
    - 담맘지역 (2) : 구일산업 선박이용
    - 호푸프 : 국제 알하사 현장 및 고민 이정수와 협의 (27)

    - 하일 : 유원건설 하일 현장과 협조(8)

    - 부레이다: 현대건설 RIQAS, ST135, 삼성 우나이자 현장과 협조 (133)

0170

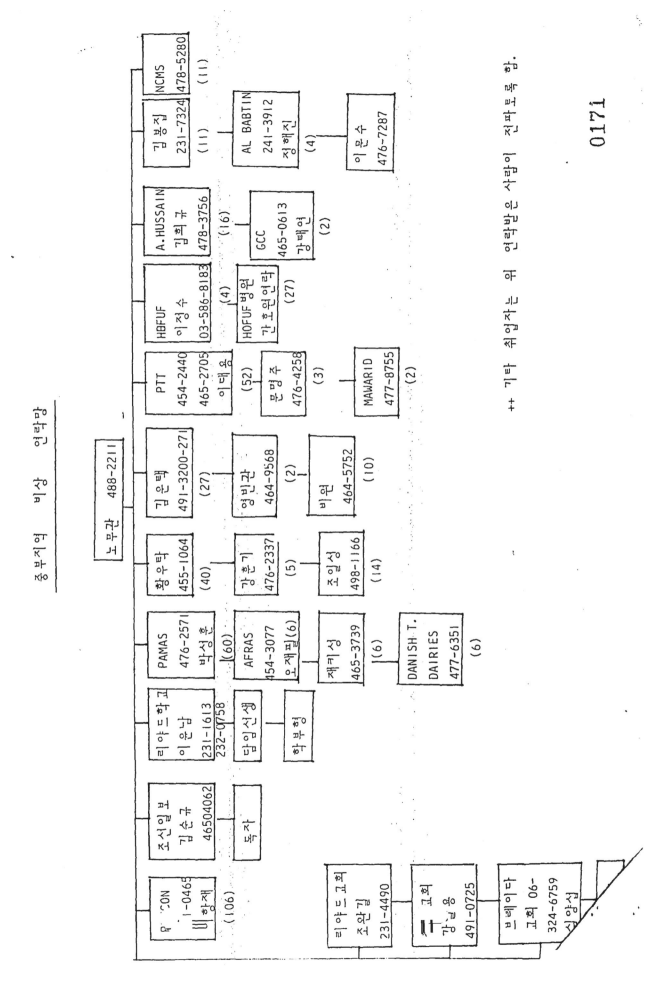

중부지역 비상 연락망

노무관 488-2211

NCMS 478-5280 (11)
김봉직 231-7324 (11)
AL BABTIN 241-3912 정해진 (4)
이문수 476-7287

A.HUSSAIN 김희규 478-3756 (16)
GCC 465-0613 강태익 (2)

HBFUF 이정수 03-586-8183 (4)
HOFUF방면 가호인연락 (27)

PTT 454-2440 465-2705 이대요 (52)
문영주 476-4258 (3)
MAWARID 477-8755 (2)

김운태 491-3200-271 (27)
임비간 464-9568 (2)
비현 464-5752 (10)

황우택 455-1064 (40)
강춘기 476-2337 (5)
조일성 498-1166 (14)

PAMAS 476-2571 박성훈 (60)
AFRAS 454-3077 오재필(6)
제기성 465-3739 (6)
DANISH T. DAIRIES 477-6351 (6)

리야드학교 이운남 231-1613 232-0758
당의선생 급부청

조선일보 김순규 46504062
독자

P.CON 1-0465 비한제 (106)

리야드교회 조현기 231-4490
교회 응규 491-0725
제리야다교회 06-324-6759
한인신

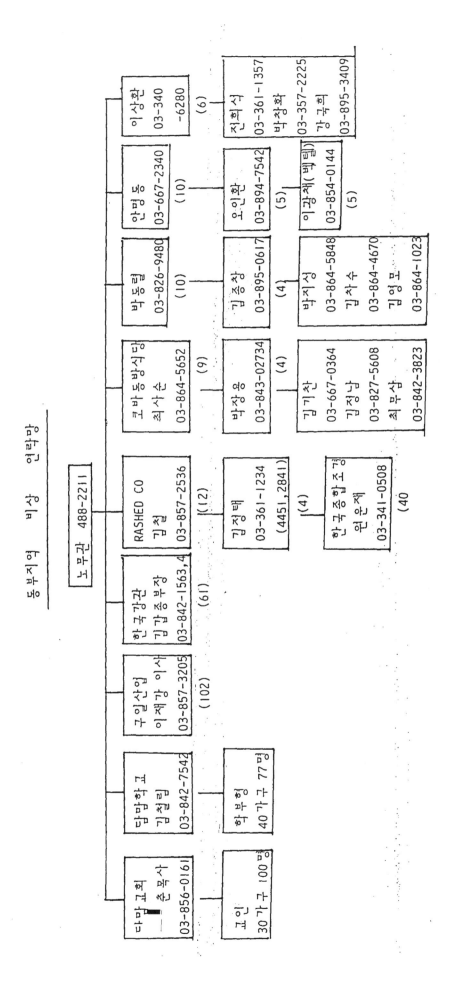

동부지역 비상 연락망

0172

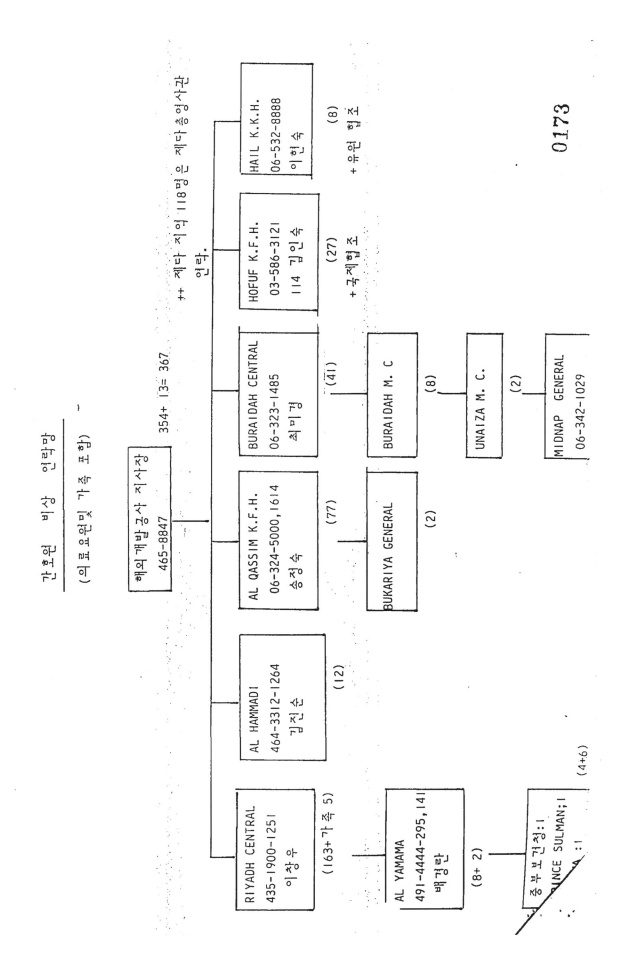

간호원 비상 연락망
(의료요원및 가족 포함)

해외개발공사 지사장
465-8847

354+ 13= 367

++ 제다 지역 118명 은 제다총영사관
 인타.

RIYADH CENTRAL
435-1900-1251
이창우
(163+가족 5)

AL HAMMADI
464-3312-1264
김진순
(12)

AL QASSIM K.F.H.
06-324-5000,1614
송정숙
(77)

BURAIDAH CENTRAL
06-323-1485
최미경
(41)

HOFUF K.F.H.
03-586-3121
114 김인숙
(27)
+ 국제협조

HAIL K.K.H.
06-532-8888
이현숙
(8)
+ 유언 협조

AL YAMAMA
491-4444-295,141
배경탄
(8+ 2)

중부보건청:1
PRINCE SULMAN;1
        :1
(4+6)

BUKARIYA GENERAL
(2)

BURAIDAH M. C
(8)

UNAIZA M. C.
(2)

MIDNAP GENERAL
06-342-1029

관리 번호				분류번호	보존기간

번   호 : WBG-0636   901231 1531 FK 종별 : 지급

수   신 : 주 이라크 대사. 총영사 (조태용 서기관, 박종순 서기관)

발   신 : 장   관 (김의기 중근동과장)

제   목 : 업   연

　　　本部 형편이 급박하게 돌아가고 있는 사정을 감안 향후 일정은 황기수
중대장에게 맡기고 가능하면 일정을 단축 1.4. 까지 귀국하여 주시기 바람. 끝.

예 고 : 독후 파기

	보 안 통 제	7h

앙 고 재		기안자 성 명		과 장	신비아 전결	국 장		차 관	장 관		외신과통제
				7h							하

0174

외 무 부

종 별 :

번 호 : BGW-0001   일 시 : 91 0101 1900

수 신 : 장관(중근동과 김의기과장님)

발 신 : 주 이라크 대사(박종순)

제 목 :

1. 1.1 바그다드에 무사히 도착후 SVC 잘접수하였읍니다.

2. 가장빠른 항공편 주선중이며 항공편 예약되는대로 귀국일자 알려드리겠읍니다.

끝

독후파기

중아국

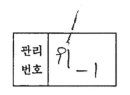

관리번호 외 무 부 　　　　　　　　　　　　원 본

종　　별 :

번　　호 : BGW-0002 　　　　　　　　　일　　시 : 91 0101 1900

수　　신 : 장관(중근동)

발　　신 : 주 이라크 대사

제　　목 : 직원출장

　　　대:WBG-604

　　　대호관련, 박종순서기관, 황기수사무관은 1.1 당지에 무사히 도착하였음. 끝

　　　(대사 최봉름-국장)

　　　예고:91.6.30

중아국

PAGE 1 　　　　　　　　　　　　　　　　　　　91.01.02　　07:37

　　　　　　　　　　　　　　　　　　　　　　　외신 2과　통제관 DO

　　　　　　　　　　　　　　　　　　　　　　　　　0176

외 무 부

관리
번호 │ 9/6

종   별 :

번   호 : BGW-0009   일   시 : 91 0103 1200

수   신 : 장관(중근동)

발   신 : 주 이라크 대사

제   목 : 직원출장

    대 WBG-0604

    연:BGW-0004

    연호, 동인들은 당지 일정을 마치고 1.3.09:00 IA 169 편 요르단으로 향발하였음.

끝

    (대사 최봉름-국장)

    예고:91.6.30 일반

중아국

출장 결과 보고서

1. 출 장 자 : 박종순 서기관   (중근동과)
   황기수 별정직 5급 (비상계획관실)

2. 출 장 지 : 사우디, UAE, 바레인, 카타르, 이라크, 요르단

3. 출장기간 : 1990. 12. 25 - 91. 1. 5.

4. 출장목적 : ○ 걸프전쟁 발발 경우 화학전에 대비한 방독면등
   장비 사용 시범 교육
   ○ 체류 교민 안전 실태 파악

5. 활동사항

   가. 출장 일정

날짜	시간	내용
90.12.25.	17:10	서울 출발
	00:50	바레인 토착
12.27.	12:40	바레인 출발
	13:50	사우디 도착
12.29.	20:30	사우디 출발
	23:00	U.A.E. 도착
12.30.	17:40	U.A.E. 출발
	17:30	카타르 도착
91. 1. 1.	07:00	카타르 출발
	09:50	요르단 도착
	10:30	이라크 출발
	13:00	이라크 도착
1. 3.	09:00	이라크 출발
	12:30	요르단 도착
	20:30	요르단 출발
1. 5.		귀 국

0178

나. 주요 활동 내용
  1) 화학전 대비 방독면등 화학장비 사용 시범교육 실시
    가) 교육 실시일자 및 피교육자 :
      - 90.12.26-91.1.3.
      - 주재 공관원 및 가족과 진출업체 대표등
    〈세 부 내 역〉

공관명	교육 실시 일자	피 교 육 자	장 소
바 레 인	90.12.26. 10:00-12:00	공관원 4명 및 고용원등	
사 우 디	90.12.28. 11:00-12:30	24명	각 공관 회의실
U. A. E.	90.12.29. 10:00-12:00	공관원 5명 및 가족 5명	
카 타 르	90.12.31. 10:00-12:00	공관원 3명 및 가족 3명	
이 라 크	90.1.2. 10:00-12:00	공관원 및 가족, 고용원 9명, 업체 대표 6명	
요 르 단	90.1.3. 14:00-15:00	공관원 4명	

    나) 시달 조치 사항
      A. 교민 담당 영사로 하여금 체류교민에게 동 화학장비 사용
         시범 별도 교육토록 시달
      B. 주재국 화생방 경보체재 파악, 사전 숙지하여 체류 교민에게
         통보토록 시달
      C. 화학전 대비 주재 우방국과의 사전 협조 체재를 구축토록 시달등
  2) 체류 교민 안전 실태 점검
    가) 주재 공관별 자체 비상철수계획 수립 여부 파악
      - 각 공관별 자체 비상 철수 계획 기수립
    나) 체류교민 신변안전 대책 강구 여부 파악
      - 각 공관별로 교민 신변 안전대책 기수립
      - 주재국 진출 아국업체별로 소속 직원 안전대책 방안 수립
    다) 주재공관과 교민과의 비상 연락망 체재 구축상태 점검
      - 각 공관별로 관.민 협의회 구성을 통한 비상업무 협조체재 유지

0179

3) 최근 걸프사태 정세 현황 및 전망 설명

    가) 대 상 자 : 주재 공관원과 가족 및 진출업체 대표

    나) 소요시간 : 각 공관별로 약 1시간

4) 걸프사태 정세에 대한 주재국내 반응관련 의견 교환

    - 대다수 중론이 전쟁이 일어나지 않을 것이라 하며, 그러나
      후세인의 예견치 못한 돌발적인 행동에 의해 사태가 악화될
      수 있는 가능성도 배제할수 없다는 반응

6. 종합 평가 및 건의

  가. 종합 평가

    ㅇ 현지에 출장, 아국 공관원 및 가족을 대상으로 화학장비 사용법
      교육을 실시함으로서 만일의 전쟁 발발 경우에 화학전에 대비한
      사전 신변 안전대책을 강구토록 하는데 기여함

    ㅇ 체류교민의 안전 실태를 점검함으로서, 현지 실정에 맞는 교민
      비상철수 대책을 수립할수 있음

    ㅇ 걸프사태 정세에 대한 주재국의 반응을 파악함으로서 사태를 분석
      하는데 도움이 됨

  나. 건 의

    걸프전쟁 발발에 대비한 체류교민의 신변안전 보호조치를 위해 아래 사항을
    건의함

    1) 사태가 악화 되기전 주재 공관원 가족 전원의 조기 철수(1.15. 이전)

    2) 체류교민의 신속하고 안전한 철수를 위해 KAL 특별기 투입

    3) 진출업체 자체 비상 철수계획과 연계 현지 공관장 판단하에 교민
      철수업무 추진

    4) 효율적인 철수 업무 추진을 위해 주재공관에 91년 1/4분기 배정
      예산의 긴급 영달

  첨 부 : 걸프지역 주재 공관별 교민 비상철수 계획서 각 1부. 끝.

		담 당	과 장	심의관	국 장	차관보	차 관	장 관
		박종순						

0180

정 리 보 존 문 서 목 록					
기록물종류	일반공문서철	등록번호	2012090039	등록일자	2012-09-03
분류번호	772	국가코드	IQ/IR	보존기간	영구
명 칭	이란.이라크 전쟁 후속조치, 1990-92				
생 산 과	중동1과/국제연합1과	생산년도	1990~1992	담당그룹	
내용목차	* 1990.1.6 Hussein 이라크 대통령, 대이란 평화협상 제의 　　1.11 이란, Sevardnaze 소련 외무장관 중재에 의한 평화협상 제안 수락 　　8.16 이라크, 이란에 평화조약 제의 　　9.10 이라크, 이란과 외교관계 재개 합의 　1992.1.15 주한이란대사, 이라크의 대이란 배상 이행 관련 한국 지지 요청 * 1989년 문서 일부 포함				

0001

UN, 이란·이락 平和協商 再開 推進 초외원인경보
('89. 1. 27.)

1. 「케야르」UN事務總長의 <u>個人特使인 「엘리아슨」(UN駐在</u>
   <u>스웨덴大使)</u>이 이란·이락 平和協商 再開를 論議하기 위해 1.24
   부터 이란을 訪問中에 있으며 1.27에는 이락을 訪問할 豫定임.

2. 이란·이락 兩國은

   가. 休戰發效(88.8)以來 UN仲裁下에 제네바 및 뉴욕에서
      3次에 걸친 協商(88.8.25~9.13, 10.1~8, 10.31~
      11.11)을 開催하였으나

   나. 「케야르」 UN事務總長이 提示(88.10)한 軍隊撤收,
      捕虜交換, 페르샤灣 自由航行, 샤트알아랍水路 掃海 등의
      4個 議題를 圍繞하고
      ○ 이란側은 國際的으로 認定된 國境線으로의 軍隊撤收를
         優先 實施할 것을 主張한 데 반해
      ○ 이락側은 自國의 唯一 海上 出口인 샤트알아랍水路
         掃海와 이란側에 의한 페르샤灣에서의 通行船舶 檢索
         中止를 優先的으로 要求하는 등의 意見對立으로 完全
         終戰을 위한 協商 進展을 보지 못해 왔음.

31-30

0002

3. 이번 「엘리아슨」 特使의 兩國 問訪은

　가. 最近 파리 開催 國際化學武器會議(1.7~11)에서 「케
　　　야르」 UN事務總長이 이란·이락 兩國外相과 個別會談
　　　을 가진 바 있고

　나. 이락側이 同 特使의 兩國 巡訪 開始直前 一方的 捕虜
　　　釋放을 斷行(1.23~24間 255名)함으로써 協商再開를
　　　위한 肯定的 雰圍氣가 造成되고 있는 가운데 이루어지
　　　고 있다는 점에서 注目됨.

31-31

0003

외 무 부

종 별 :

번 호 : UNW-0180 일 시 : 890207 1530

수 신 : 장 관 (국연,중근동)

발 신 : 주 유엔 대사

제 목 : 이. 이전 종전 (1)

　　2.7. 유엔 사무총장 대변인 발표에 의하여 이란-이락간 평화협상 계속을 위해 이락 및 이란 외무장관이 2.7 과 2.9 각각 뉴욕 도착 예정이라고함. 끝
　　(대사 박상용-국장)

국기국　　중아국

PAGE 1

89.02.08　　10:27
외신　1과　통제관

0004

외 무 부

종 별 :

번 호 : UNW-0207 일 시 : 890210 1820

수 신 : 장 관 (국연,중동,정일,기정)

발 신 : 주 유엔 대사

제 목 : 이란-이락 외무장관 회담

　　금 2.10 15:30 유엔본에서 사무총장 주재로 이란-이라크 외무장관 회담(3차 회담)이 개최되었음. 정오 브리핑시 사무총장 대변인에 의하면 동 회담에서 차기 이란-이라크간 휴전협상의 재개일자 및 방법등이 협의될 것으로 예상된다고 하는바, 동 회담 내용등 결과 파악되는대로 추보하겠음. 끝

　　(대사 박쌍용-국장)

국기국　　1차보　　중아국　　정문국　　청와대　　안 기

89.02.11　10:06
외신 1과　통제관

0005

외 무 부

종 별 :

번 호 : UNW-0230   일 시 : 890214 1820

수 신 : 장 관 (국연,중동,정일,기정)

발 신 : 주 유엔 대사

제 목 : 이란-이라크 종전 협상 (2)

    연: UNW-0207

    금 2.14 사무총장 대변인실이 배포한 자료에 의하면 연호 사무총장과 이란, 이라크
의무장관간 3자 협의는 동 3자협의를 <u>3월 하반기 유엔본부</u> 부근에서 재개하기로하고
그때까지 유엔과 이란. 이라크 대표단간 실무회담을 진행하는것에 합의하였다고함. 끝

    (대사 박쌍용-국장)

국기국   중아국   정문국   청와대   안 기

PAGE 1   89.02.15 10:34
                                                 외신 1과   통제관

                                                    0006

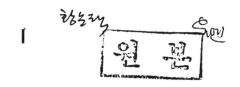

외 무 부

종 별 :

번 호 : UNW-0604

일 시 : 89 0413 1600

수 신 : 장관(국연,중근동)

발 신 : 주유엔대사

제 목 : 이란-이락 외상회담

4.13 유엔 사무총장 대변인은 4.20 부터 제네바에서 사무총장 주재로 이란-이락 외상 회담이 개최된다고 성명을 발표한바, 동 성명문을 별첨 송부함.끝

(대사 박쌍용-국장)

별첨:동 성명문 UNW(F)-030

국기국 1차보 중아국 정문국 정와대 안기부

PAGE 1

첨부 UNW(F)-03 ८
지관 (국연)
UNW-0604 (3매)

Statement by the Secretary-General

13 April 1989

Following consultations with the Governments of
the Islamic Republic of Iran and of Iraq and preparatory
talks between the UN delegation led by Ambassador Eliasson
and an Iranian delegation (2 - 3 March and 6 - 10 April)
and an Iraqi delegation (8 - 9 March and 30 - 31 March) in
New York, agreement has been reached to convene a new
round of direct Ministerial talks under the auspices of
the Secretary-General in Geneva starting 20 April. The
talks will be attended by the two Foreign Ministers and
will be chaired by the Secretary-General.

The Secretary-General hopes that these intensive
discussions at a high level will provide an important
opportunity to move towards full and rapid implementation
of resolution 598, the achieving of good neighbourly
relations and lasting peace between the two countries.
This task should be pursued with urgency, determination
and goodwill.

0008

- 2 -

The discussions which have so far taken place have
focused on the manner in which the resolution can be
implemented. In particular, the Secretary-General and his
Personal Representative have emphasized the need for
withdrawal without delay to the internationally recognized
boundaries, the release and repatriation of the prisoners
of war and the speedy beginning of the mediation efforts
to achieve a comprehensive, just and honorable settlement
of all outstanding issues in accordance with the Charter
of the UN. In this context, pragmatic arrangements,
particularly with regard to the economic life of the two
countries, may well be needed to hasten the return to
normality.

The discussions of the Secretary-General and his
Personal Representative have underlined the urgent need
for the implementation of the resolution in conformity
with principles of international law as they pertain to
respect for territorial integrity, non-acquisition of
territory by force, the inviolability of internationally
recognized boundaries and non-interference in the internal
affairs of other States. The underlying principle is of
course the fulfilment in good faith of international
obligations.

2

0009

- 3 -

As we approach a new round of direct talks in
Geneva, it is the hope of the Secretary-General that both
countries will exercise maximum restraint in order to
create the proper atmosphere and continue to make gestures
of goodwill.

At this stage, it is essential that time be
devoted by both sides in Geneva to discuss the fundamental
questions which pertain to their respective intentions and
to their future relations.

3

0010

외 무 부

종 별 :

번 호 : BGW-0008   일 시 : 90 0106 1000

수 신 : 장 관 (중근동,정일,기정)

발 신 : 주 이라크 대사

제 목 : 주재국 대통령, 대이란 평화협상 제의 (자료응신 제 1호)

　　HUSSEIN 대통령은 1.6 제 69회 국군의 날을 맞아 행한 성명에서 다음 요지의 대이란 평화협상제의를 함.

　　1. 유엔후원하에 바그다드와 테헤란에서 번갈아 가며 양국대표간 직접대화에 '한 화회담을 개최할것을 제의하고 본회담은 이란측의 동제의 수락으로부터 3개월 이내에 개시되어야 한다고 시한을 부여함.

　　2. 국제적십자사를 통해 병상자포로 전원을 즉각 송환할 것을 제의하고 동 포로송환도 이란측의 수락으로부터 2주이내에 이루어져야 한다고함.

　　3. 양국민간 신뢰회복 및 평화분위기 조성을 위해 종교인의 상대국 성지순례 교환과 가족의 억류중인 포로방문을 허용할것을 제의함.

　　4. 양국 민항기의 상대국 영공운항 및 공항사용을 허용토록 제의함.끝

　　(대사 최봉름-국장)

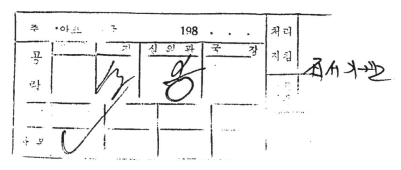

중아국　　1차보　　정문국　　청와대　　안기부

외 무 부

종 별 :

번 호 : BGW-0012   일 시 : 90 0109 1400

수 신 : 장관(중근동,정일)

발 신 : 주이라크대사

제 목 : HUSSEIN 대통령 대이란 평화제의

연: BGW-0008

연호 HUSSEIN 대통령의 평화제의에대한 역내제국의 반응을 다음 보고함.

1. 사우디 FAHD 국왕은 각의에서 금번 이라크 평화제의를 이.이간 평화정착을향한 진일보조치로 평하고 이란측이 동 제의에 주의를 기우려 주기 바란다고함.

2. 이집트 MEGUID 외상은 본제의에 이라크가 이.이간 평화달성을 갈망하고 있음이 잘 나타나고 있다며 이란측의 동 제의 수락거부에 실망을 표하고 아랍제국에 대해 이라크의 평화입장에 공동 보조를 취하도록 촉구함.

3. 요르단 WASSIM 부수상겸 외상은 JORDAN TIMES 회견에서 동 평화제의를 지지하고 불안정한 이지역의 평화정착 필요성에 대한 국제적 주의를 환기시키는 계기가되었다고함.

4. 쿠웨이트 JABIR 부수상겸외상은 동 제의가 이.이 양 국민에게 평화에 대한새로운 희망을 안겨 주었다며 이란측의 긍정적 반응을 기대함.

4. 팔레스타 DOHA 에서 ARAFAT 대통령은 동 제의를 통해 이라크가 평화입장을더욱 공고히 하였다며 전쟁포로를 인도적 견지에서 다른 정치협상과 분리하여 조속 실행할것을 촉구함.

6. 아랍연맹 KLIBI 사무총장은 동 제의를 환영하고 이란측이 상응한 조치를취할것을 촉구함. 끝.

(대사 최봉름-국장)

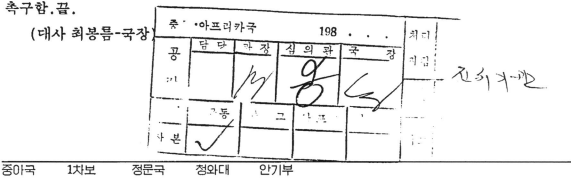

PAGE 1   90.01.09   22:21

                                          외신 1과   통제관

                                                    0012

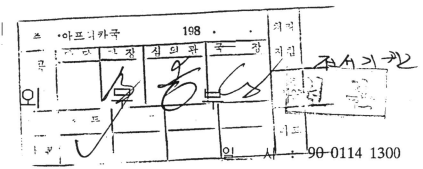

종   별 :

번   호 : BGW-0022

수   신 : 장 관(중근동,정일)

발   신 : 주이라크대사

제   목 : HUSSEIN 대통령 대이란 평화제의(자료응신제2호)

    주재국 외무성은 1.10 공한으로 1.5 제 69회 국군의날에 있었던 HUSSEIN 대통령의 대 이란 평화제의 내용을 주재외교단에 알려오면서 각기 본국 유관기관에 봉보하여 줄것을 요청하여온바, 본내용 전문 (영문번역 FULL TEXT)을 별첨 타전함.첨 부: 동 TEXT. 끝.

    (대사 최봉름-국장)

    (UNOFFICIAL TRANSLATION)

    FIRST: REPRESENTATIVES OF THE LEADERSHIP OF BOTH COUNTRIES SHALL MEET ALTERNATELY, IN TEHRAN AND IN BAGHDAD, UNDER THE AUSPICES OF THE SECRETATIAT OF THE UNITEDNATIONS, IN ORDER TO CONDUCT A DIALOGUE BETWEEN THEM, AND WITH THE LEADERSHIP OF THE TWO COUNTRIES DIRECTLY, WITH AVIEW TO REACHING A COMMON UNDERSTANDING OF THE PROVISIONS OF SECURITY COUNCIL RESOLUTION 598 AND THE PROCEDURES AND TIMINGS FOR THEIR IMPLEMENTATION, IN ACCORDANCE WITH THE AGREEMENT OF 8 AUGUST, 1988. THE MEETINGS SHALL TAKE PLACE AND COME TO AN END DURING APERIOD NOT EXCEEDING THREE MONTHS AND IRRESPECTIVE OF THE RESULTS THEY LEAD TO. THERE SHOULD BE THREE MEETINGS IN BAGHDAD AND THREE SIMILAR MEETINGS IN TEHRAN, I ORDER TO SPREAD AN ATMOSPHERE THAT SERVE SPEACE, AND TO PLACE THE PUBLIC OPINION IN BOTH COUNTRIES WITH IN THE FRAME WORK OF THE DESIRE FOR PEACE AND TO ASSIST IN FINDING THE BEST MEANS POSSIBLE FOR IT.

    SECOND: IN ORDER TO CONTRIBUTE TO THE CREATION OF A PROPITIOUS CLIMATE FOR THE PEACE PROCESS, AND IN AFFIRMATION OF THE HUMAN ITARIAN AND LEGAL CONCEPTS AND HUMAN RIGHTS AND IN CONFORMITY WITH THE MINIMUM REQUIRED BY THE THIRD GENEVA CONVENTION RELATING TO THE PRISONERS OF WAR AND IN THE FRAME WORK OF

중아국   1차보   정문국   청와대   안기부

PAGE 1

THE DESIRE TO RELEASE ALL POW'S COMPREHENSIVELY AND COMPLETELY BY THE TWO PARTIES, PRESIDENT SADDAM HUSSEIN PROPOSED:

1-AN IMMEDIATE EXCHANGE OF ALL SICK AND WOUNDED PRISONERS OF WAR THROUGH THE ICRC.

2-AN EXCHANGE OF ALL PRISONERS OF WAR WHO HAVE SPENTA VERY LONGTIME IN CAPTIVITY AND IN PARTICULAR THOSE WHO FELL INTO CAPTIVITY BETWEEN THE BEGINNING OF THE WAR ON 4 SEPTEMBER, 1980 AND THE END OF 1982. SUCH AN EXCHANGE SHALL BE COMPLETED WITHIN A MAXIMUM PERIOD OF TWO WEEKS FROM THE DATE OF IIRAN'S ACCEPTANCE OF THIS PROPOSAL. NATURALLY, THE EXCHANGE SHALL BE DONE IN ACCORDANCE WITH THE CONCEPTS AND THE BASES OF THE THIRD GENEVA CONVENTION SIGNED BY BOTH PARTIES AND WHICH NEITHER PARTH HAS ANNULLED ITS PUBLICLY STATED LEGAL RECOGNITION OF IT. THIS SHALL ALSO TAKE PLACE THROUGH THE ICRC. THIS REQGUIRES THE REGISTRATION OF ALL PRISONERS OF WAR OF THE TWO DIDES FOR THE PERIOD FROM SEPTEMBER 1980 TO THE END OF 1982 INCLUSIVE.

3-REGISTERING ALL PRISONERS OF WAR HITHER TO UNREGISTERED BY THE ICRC, IMMEDIATELY AFTER THE COMPLETION OF THE EXCHANGE OF POWS FOR THE YEARS 1980, 1981 AND 1982, AS MENTIONED IN PARAGRAPH SECOND(2), AND TO BEGIN THEIR RELEASE IN ACCORDANCE WITH A TIME-TABLE DRAWN BY THE ICRC.

4-ARRANGEING VISITS TO THE POWS BY THEIR FAMILIE SIN THE CAMPS IN BOTH COUNTRIES IMMEDIATELY.

THIRD: INAFFIRMEATION OF THE PEACE APPROACH, IN RESPONSE TO A DESIRE TO OPEN UP WAYS FOR THE PEOPLES OF BOTH COUNTRIES TO DEAL WITH THE FACTS AS THEY STAND, AND IN APPRECIATION OF, AND RESPECT FOR, RELIGIOUS BE LIEF AND RITES, WE PROPOSE THE EXCHANGE OF ORGANIZED RELIGIOUS VISITS BY THE PEOPLES OF BOTH COUNTRIES TO EACH OTHER IN ORDER TO VISIT SACRED AND RELIGIOUS SHRINES AND PLACES. THE VISITS SHALL TAKE PLACE BY LAND AND BY AIR. IN ORDER TO ACHIEVE THIS AND WHAT ISMEN-TIONED IN PARAGRAPH SECOND (4), AND TO SPREAD THE AT MOSPHERE OF PEACE, WE PROPOSE THE OPENING OF AIRLINE OFFICE SIN BOTH COUNTRIES AND TO PERMIT CIVIL AIRCRAFT TO USE THE AIRSPACE AND THE CIVILIAN AIRPORTS OF BOTH COUNTRIES EQUALLY. -END-

PAGE 2

0014

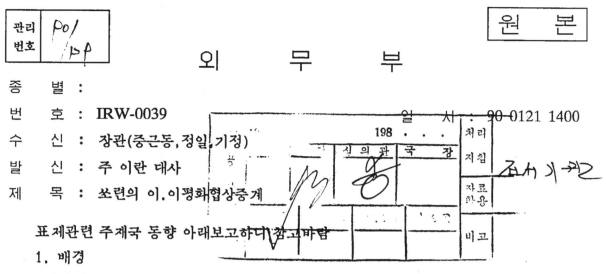

외 무 부

종 별 :

번 호 : IRW-0039

수 신 : 장관(중근동,정일,기정)

발 신 : 주 이란 대사

제 목 : 쏘련의 이.이평화협상중계

표제관련 주재국 동향 아래보고하니 참고바람

1. 배경

-이란정부는 지난 1.11 세바르드나제 쏘 외무장관의 중재에의한 이.이 평화협상 개최 제안을 수락한다고 밝혔으며, 이라크 외무장관및 유엔 사무총장도 이를 환영한 것으로 알려짐

-정확한 일자는 아직 발표되지 않았으나, 이.이 외무장관이 모스크바를 방문, 세바르드나제 장관의 환영하에 회담을 갖게될예정임.

2. 최근동향

-KHARRAZI 주유엔대사, 유엔사무총장면담시 (1.11) 이라크 대통령의 최근 제안은 안보리의 활동을 방해, 평화정책 노력을 저해하고있다고 비난

-VAEZI 외무부차관보 쏘련방문 VELAYATI 장관 친서전달시 (1.10)쏘련측 평화협상 중재 제의에 긍정적회신

-KHARRAZI 주유엔대사 외신기자회견시 (1.12) 동 중재수락 및 추가 50 명의 이라크 포로 석방발표, 대 이라크 국제적 압력을 호소

-라프산자니 대통령 (1.12) 상기 이라크측 제의 강력비난

-VELAYATI 장관(1.14) 쏘련측 중재제의가 이란측 요청에의한 것이라는 일부언론보도 비난

-KHARRAZI 주유엔대사 (1.15) 유엔 사무총장앞 서한에서 이라크의 안보리결의 수락을 위한 이사국들의 노력촉구

-VELAYATI 장관(1.20) 쏘련의 중재제의 수락재확인

3. 주재국입장

-1958 년이래 이라크에 대한 주요 무기공급원인 쏘련은 이라크에대해

종아국   장관   차관   1차보   2차보   구주국   정문국   청와대   안기부

상당한영향력을 행사할수 있는 위치에 있으며, 이란또한 쏘련과 현재 좋은관계를 유지하고 있으므로 일부 회의적 시각이 없는것은 아니나 대체로 쏘련의 중재를 환영함.

  -서방측은 쏘련이 이.이협상 중재를 통해 역내에서 외교적으로 유리한 고지를 점하는 것에 반대할 것으로 보이며, 이는 장애요인의 하나임

  -이.이평화협상은 유엔 안보리결의 598 의 범위내에서 행해져야하며, 이러한 점에서 유엔 사무총장의 참석은 필수적임.

  4. 분석평가

  -이란은 동 쏘련측 중재제의 수락을 통해 이라크측의 최근제안을 무마할수있게 되었으며, 쏘련의 영향력기대라는 관점에서 당지 유력언론인은 동 수락을 긍정적으로 평가하고있음

  -그러나 모종의 획기적인 조치가 없는한 동 중재의 성공전망을 매우 불투명한 것으로 당지 관측되고있는바 (이란측 전제인 이라크군 철수를 쏘련이 효과적으로 유도하지 못할 것이므로) 일부 인사는 동 중재 노력실패시 쏘련측의 동 지역내 위상의 실추를 가져올것으로 보고있음.

  5. 상기관련 회담일시 및 쏘련 입장등 파악 가능한대로 추보예정임.끝
  (대사 정경일-국장)
  예고:90.6.30 까지

직권으로 재분류 (1990. 6. 10)
직위   성명 박중손

Embassy of
The Republic of Iraq
Seoul

PRESS OFFICE

No. 3/90

```
┌─────────────────────┐
│                     │
│      PRESS          │
│    RELEASE          │
│                     │
└─────────────────────┘
```

S E O U L, April 5, 1990

0017

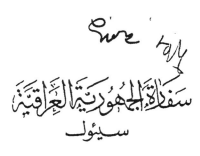

Embassy of
The Republic of Iraq
Seoul

STATEMENT

The Arab Ambassadors accredited to the Republic of Korea have met today and discussed what the International News Agencies said concerning the Republic of IRAQ in its efforts to get some materials related to the atomic bomb.

The Council of the Arab Ambassadors would like to state that IRAQ has declared, more than once, that it has no intention absolutely to obtain the nuclear weapon, and its nuclear centre, which is exclusively for peaceful purposes, is under routine check up by the International Agency for Nuclear Energy.

In accordance with the statement issued by the Council of the Arab League in this respect, the Council of the Arab Ambassadors in Korea, condemns, strongly, the unjust campaign which is launched against IRAQ in order to hinder its scientific progress.

They recalled the Zionist "Israeli" aggression on the IRAQI Nuclear Centre on June, 1981, and declare their stand with their IRAQI brothers to stand against these fabricated and false allegations.

April 6th, 1990

0018

The informative media in Korea and other countries spoke much about the sentencing to death of the Iranian nationality spy who was bearing British certificate of identity, because of his spying on Iraq for the interest of the Israeli and British intelligence. Then that was followed by what was mentioned in the newspapers that Iraq tried to smuggle materials which can be used in manufacturing the nuclear bomb.

We would like to declare here that the din raised concerning the first issue was needless, because Bazoft who had been sentenced to death confessed a tangible acts of spying against Iraq and for the interest of Israeli and British Intelligence and in such acts he endangered the Iraqi national security, and it is only today, April 5th, 1990 the British authorities officially confessed that the spy Bazoft was its agent, accordingly needless to say anything more.

For the second issue which concerns what was allegedly called smuggling of some materials used in manufacturing atomic bomb, we would like to declare the following facts ;

1. To fulfill the needs of the University of Technology, Baghdad, for a power supply to the CO_2 Laser System, different companies were contacted by the Ministry of Industry for high voltage capacitors to be used in this unit. An offer was accepted from a British-based company(EUROMAC) in May, 1989, and an official order was placed in June, 1989 (ANNEX 1) for a total of 85 of these capacitors at a total cost of U.S. 10,500 dollars.

2. These H.V Capacitors, in addition to their capability to be used as detonation devices as has been alleged, have many scientific and industrial applications such as ;
    - Power Supply for Laser Systems (Ground or Airborne)
    - Power Supply for Plasma Metal Cutting Machines
    - Separation of Missile Stages for Satellite Launching

    However, our sole purpose as has been confirmed in the End-User Certificate (ANNEX 2) is for the CO_2 Laser System (Ground and Airborne Usage).

3. Many open telexes were exchanged with the supplier (EUROMAC) and the sub-supplier (CSI) regarding technical details and follow-up of the order.

4. By doing so, the Iraqi side did not break any contract or regulations regarding the export of prohibited materials or goods, and has fulfilled its obligations by signing the End-User Certificate and providing the supplier and his sub-suplier with all the technical information requested by them openly.

0019

2

5.   It is also well-known that it is the supplier's responsibility (in accordance with the 1980 INCOTERM as amended and issued by the I.C.C. of Paris) to provide the export license and perform all the formalities required for the shipment of goods to their destination.

6.   However, it would seem clear from the review of some of the telexes by (CSI) that a deliberate attempt was made by official American authorities to frame the Iraqi side in an illegal position, as is explained below ;

- A request by (CSI) to meet our specialists in London where the specifications of the items were agreed upon, and later confirmed by us in a telex upon CSI request (ANNEX 3), but approaches were made by Mr. Saunders (allegedly from CSI who appears to be an F.B.I. agent as the American sources confirmed to edquire about the need for other materials such as switches and special triggering devices which relate to nuclear detonation devices a telex dating January 11th, 1990, stating the possibility to offer EBWS and neutron generators (allegedly in response to a request from the supplier on our behalf) with reference to problems of exposure to us authorities and the necessity for protection and safety in handling these materials and asking for U.S. delivery point which was in fact overstressed (ANNEX 4).

- The Iraqi side was shocked by the contents of the above telex and protested to the supplier by the ELE telephone. When (CSI) received no answer, another telex was followed by (CSI) to the Iraqi side which dealt on the 23rd of January, 1990, (ANNEX 5) with the subject of capacitors as in the order this time but referring at the end to an offer (of other equipment) and warning exposure to U.S. authorities.

- This telex was answered routinely regarding the capacitors, but it was also stated ((if we are going to buy anything from you, we will do so according to your ordinary formalities.)) (ANNEX 6)

We are awaiting the confession of these parties that have accused Iraq to announce the fact of what we have mentioned exactly as what happened in the case of the spy "Bazoft", and then the public opinion could have known the facts.

0020

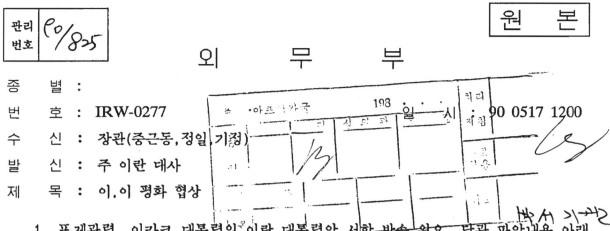

관리
번호 EO/825

외 무 부

종 별 :

번 호 : IRW-0277

수 신 : 장관(중근동,정일,기정)

발 신 : 주 이란 대사

제 목 : 이.이 평화 협상

1. 표제관련, 이라크 대통령의 이란 대통령앞 서한 발송 위요, 당관 파악내용 아래
보고하니 참고바람.

- 이라크 외무장관은 5.14 이라크 대통령이 라프산자니앞 평화서한 (LETTER OF
PEACE)을 발송하였으며, 이란측으로부터 고무적인 회신을 받았다고 지적하였는바,
이는 주재국 정부에 의해서도 사실임이 확인되고 있음.

- 현재까지 동서한 내용은 공식적으로 공개되지는 않았으나, 당지 관측봉 및
언론은 하기 6 개항을 이라크측 서한의 주요 내용으로 추정하고 있음.

. 양국 정상 회담 개최 제의

. 향후 양국 관계 전망 (교역, 문화, 종교적 차원의 협력)

. 3 개월 이내에 평화 정착 방안 수립 (시한 설정에 의의가 있음)

. 75 년 알지에 협정을 기초로 국경 및 SHAT-AL-ARAB 수로문제에 대한 직접 협상을
추진 (관측봉들은 이라크측이 알지에 협정은 무효라는 과거의 입장에서 양보하므로써
가장 중요한 문제의 하나인 동건 해결 전망이 밝아졌다고 평가함)

. 포로 교환

. 대 이스라엘 이란, 이라크 군사 협정 체결 검토

- 상기 정상회담 개최 가능성에 대해 이란측은 공개적인 관심을 표명하였으며,
라프산자니 대통령및 의회도 이를 긍정적으로 평가한다고 언급한바 있으며 나아가
주재국 언론도 이러한 입장을 지지한바 있음. 다만 이란측 회신 내용은 상금 파악되고
있지 않으나, 우선 이라크측이 동제의 GOOD WILL 을 입증하기 위해 이란 영토로
부터 먼저 철수해야 할것이며 이.이전 책임은 이라크가 부담하여야 할것이라고
회신한것으로 알려지고 있음.

2. 한편 GOULDING 유엔 사무차장이 현재 당지 체류중인바, KHORASSANI 주재국

중아국	장관	차관	1차보	2차보	정문국	청와대	종리실	안기부

PAGE 1

90.05.17   18:07

외신 2과 통제관 DK

0021

20

국회 외무위원장은 5.15 동 사무차장 접견시 이란 영토로 부터의 이라크군 철수를 위해 유엔측이 관련문서 배포등 국제적 영향력을 행사해줄것을 요청한바 있음.

3. 상기건 및 이.이 평화 협상 관련 본부 입수 정보있을시 송부바람. 끝

(대사 정경일-국장)

예고:90.12.31 까지

90. 12. 31. 인터넷 2

관리
번호 eo1835

외 무 부

종 별 :

번 호 : IRW-0282   일 시 : 90 0520 1530

수 신 : 장관(중근동,정일)

발 신 : 주 이란 대사

제 목 : 이.이평화협상

연ZIRW-0277

연호관련 이라크측에서 공개되거나 언론보도된 사한교환내용등 본부입수정보
있을시 당관에 참고로 알려주시기 바람. 끝

(대사정경일-국장)

예고 90.12.31 까지

중도 • 아프리카국		198 . . .		처리 지침
공		심 의 관	국 장	
사 본				비고

90. 12. 31.
인미지

중아국   차관   1차보   정문국

0023

외 무 부

종   별 :

번   호 : IRW-0293   일   시 : 90 0527 1400

수   신 : 장 관(중근동,정일,기정)

발   신 : 주 이란대사

제   목 : 이.이평화협상

　　1. MOTTAKE 주재국 외무부 국제담당차관은 5.24표제와 관련된 이라크측 서한에 언급, 이란측의긍정적 회신사실을 확인하며, 아래요지설명하였는바 참고바람.

　　-이라크는 외채부담등 다양한 국내.외문제로인해 과거와같은 국제적 지지를 향유할수없다는 인식하에 양보적인 서한을 발송하게된것으로봄.

　　-이란은 GOODWILL 의 표시로 이라크측 서한에긍정적으로 회신한바있으며, 이라크측이 양국간평화정착을위한 정치적결단을 갖을수있기바람.

　　-이란은 안보리결의 598 및 이를위한 UN 의중재와 관련한 어떠한 노력도 환영함.

　　-이란은 이라크와 질병또는 부상중인 포로의상호교환을 희망하며, 이를위해 노력중임.

　　2. 한편 당지 언론은 라프산자니 대통령주재국가최고 안보회의(5.26개최) 에서 이라크측 제2차서한에 대해 협의하였다고 보도하였는바,진전사항 파악되는대로 추보예정임.끝

　　(대사정경일-국장)

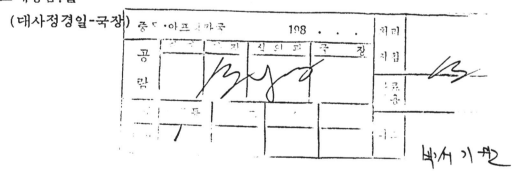

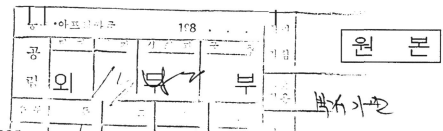

종   별 :

번   호 : IRW-0305 √   일   시 : 90 0603 1500

수   신 : 장관(중근동,정일,기정)

발   신 : 주이란대사

제   목 : 이.이 평화협상 전망

　　　1.최근 바그다드 아랍정상회담을 위요 이.이전관련 당지 반응을 아래보고하니
참고바람.

　　　가.외무부 성명

　　　- SHAT-AL-ARAB 수로가 이라크에 배타적 귀속된다는 동정상회담의 결의는
불법,무효이며 이.이 양국간 지속적 평화및 역내 안정을 해하는 무책임한 자세임.

　　　-또한 동결의가 이.이 포로교환만을 요구하며, 이라크군의 이란영토로부터의 철수
에 대해서는 침묵하고있는바, 이는 안보리 결의에 위배됨.

　　　나.외무부 MUSAVIAN 국장 논평

　　　-이라크 대통령의 이란 대통령앞 서한으로 이.이정상회담 개최 가능성이 높았으나,
동결의로 전망은 불부명함.

　　　- PLO 측은 아라파트의장이 이.이 정상회담 주선을 위해 곧 이란을 방문예정이라고
밝힌바있으나, 동결의의 서명자인 동인의 중재는 의미가없음. (아라파트의장의 방이는
이란정부도 공식 부인한 것으로 알려짐)

　　　다.언론

　　　-당지 언론들도 상기 입장을 지지하는 내용의 기사를 계제하며, 이.이전 같은
민감한 사안에 대해 아랍국가들이 무책임한 결의를 행함으로써 이.이 평화협상의
전망을 어둡게하고 있다고비난함.

　　　2.한편 라프산자니 대통령은 최근 주유엔이란대사를 통해 유엔사무총장의
방이를요청하며, 안보리 결의 이행을 위해 유엔이 계속 노력하여 줄것을 요청한것으로
알려짐.끝

　　　(대사정경일-국장)

중아국　　　1차보　　　정문국　　　안기부

90.06.03   21:56 CG

　　　　　　　　　　　　　　　　　　　　　　　　외신 1과 통제관

0025

Iran, Iraq Hold First Direct Talks, Signal Moves Toward Peace in Gulf

By Caryle Murphy
Washington Post Foreign Service

CAIRO, July 3—The foreign ministers of Iran and Iraq, who have refused to speak directly with each other since their countries signed a cease-fire agreement nearly two years ago, today met for talks in Geneva.

The brief meeting between Iraqi Foreign Minister Tariq Aziz and his Iranian counterpart, Ali Akbar Velayati, is the most significant indication so far that the two neighbors have launched a serious effort to draw up a peace treaty ending their eight-year-long war.

"It is in some way a psychological breakthrough," said United Nations Secretary General Javier Perez de Cuellar, who sponsored the meeting. Since their August 1988 cease-fire, Perez de Cuellar had been unable get the two sides to implement the truce's provisions for negotiations.

Today's highly publicized meeting followed an exchange of letters between Iraqi President Saddam Hussein and Iranian President Ali Akbar Hashemi Rafsanjani, in which a meeting between the two was discussed. Rafsanjani has indicated interest in the idea, first put forth by Saddam Hussein.

The meeting today also was preceded by secret diplomatic contacts between the two countries, according to an Iraqi official. In an interview in Baghdad June 24, Iraqi Foreign Ministry Undersecretary Nizar Hamdoon said Iran and Iraq "have established [direct] diplomatic contacts, which is significant." He declined at that time to elaborate on the contacts.

Hamdoon indicated that his government views the proposed presidential summit as aimed at a comprehensive settlement.

"What is the purpose of a summit meeting if not to discuss all outstanding issues, strike a deal and complete a package?" Hamdoon said.

Asked whether Iraq was prepared to compromise on its claim of sovereignty over the disputed Shatt al Arab waterway between the two countries, Hamdoon said: "I don't think it's advisable at this point to complicate the issue by putting preconditions on the meeting.

"This is the essence of our position from the beginning: that everything should be discussed in direct talks . . . in order to achieve common understanding in order to achieve a peace package," Hamdoon said.

In 1980, Saddam Hussein withdrew Iraq's agreement to a 1975 pact with Iran that divided the Shatt al Arab along the middle, giving each country control of half.

Both countries have strong motivations for seeking a final peace treaty.

Iraq's Saddam Hussein is turning more of his attention to inter-Arab affairs and would like to see his eastern border with Iran secure. Also, Iraq wants the Shatt al Arab cleared of its war debris so it can be used again for oil exports.

Tehran's main concern is to get a withdrawal of Iraqi troops from pockets of Iranian land they still hold along the border. A peace treaty also would boost Rafsanjani's lagging efforts to gear up his country's economy.

A peace treaty would also free at least 70,000 and possibly as many as 100,000 prisoners of war believed held by both sides since the end of the war. They have not been repatriated because of the two countries' mutual distrust.

July 4
WP

0026

외 무 부

종 별 :

번 호 : IRW-0371　　　　　　　　일 시 : 90 0705 1400

수 신 : 장관(중근동)

발 신 : 주이란대사

제 목 : 이.이평화협상

1. 표제관련 제네바 이.이 양국 외무장관 직접협상(종전후처음개최)에 참석중인 VELAYATI 주재국 외무장관은 이란측 수행기자들에게 아래 요지 언급한것으로 알려지는바 참고바 람.

　-이.이 양국은 안보리 결의 598 이 협상의 기초가 되어야하며, 동결의 이행을 위한 유엔 사무총장의 감독기능을 지지한다는데 합의

　-양측은 이후 계속해서 유엔 특사 ELLIASON 의 중재하에 전문가회의를 개최하는데 합의

　-양국 대통령간 서한교환은 매우 긍정적이었으며, 이것이 바로 금번 직접협상을가능케 하였음.

　-금번회의는 과거 협상과는 다른 분위기속에서 개최되었음.

2. 한편 라프산자니 대통령은 7.4 기자회견을 통해 이.이 양국간 평화협상 전망은그 어느때보다도 밝다고 언급함.

3. 특기사항있을시 추보예정임.끝

(대사 정경일-국장)

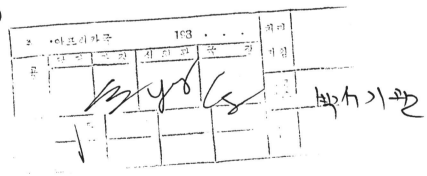

중아국　김문국　(차민　안기부

발 신 전 보

	분류번호	보존기간

번   호 : **WIR-0225**   900706 1342 ER   종별 :

WLY -0238

수   신 : 주 수신처 참조   대사(아프리카)

발   신 : 장 관   (중근동)

제   목 : 이란•이라크 외상 ~~직접 평화~~ 회담

　　　　이란, 이라크 외상간 직접 평화회담이 90. 7. 3. 제네바에서 개최 되었
다고 외신에 보도된 바, 동 주요 회담내용등 관련사항을 파악하고, 익에 대한
분석 및 전망도 함께 보고 바람. 끝.

　　　　　　　　　　　　　　(중동아프리카국장 이 두 복)

　　수신처   : 주 이란, 이라크 대사

	보안통제	
	외신과통제	

앙고재	90년7월6일 중근동	기안자성명	과장	심의관	국장		차관	장관

0028

외 무 부

종 별 :

번 호 : BGW-0337

일 시 : 90 0710 1200

수 신 : 장관(중근동,정일)

발 신 : 주이라크대사

제 목 : 정세보고(응신자료 42호)

1. 이라크, 이란에 구호물자 전달

- 이라크 적십자 대표단은 이란의 지진 희생자를 위한 구호물자 (의류, 식품,의료장비, 의약품등)를 전달하고 7.8 귀국 하였다고 발표된바, 이는 80년 전쟁발발후 처음으로 이라크의 공식 대표단이 이란을 방문하게 된것임.

- 이란의 지진을 계기로 양국간 화해 분위기가 조성되고 있는바, 이란의 라프산자니 대통령은 훗세인 대통령이 보낸 조전과 구호원조 제의에 대하여 7.6 감사의전문을 보냈으며, 7.3 제네바에서 양국 외상이 직접회담을 가지고 <u>양측이 제네바에서 계속 접촉할것에 합의하는등</u> 평화회담에 밝은 전망을 보여주고 있는바, <u>양국수도를 상호 방문, 회담을 가질 가능성도 시사되고 있음</u>

2. 파키스탄 수상 방이

파키스탄의 부토수상이 아랍국가 순방의 일환으로 7.10 이라크를 공식 방문함.

끝

(대사 최봉름-국장)

중아국 정문국

90.07.10 21:16 DA

외신 1과 통제관

0029

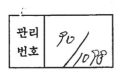

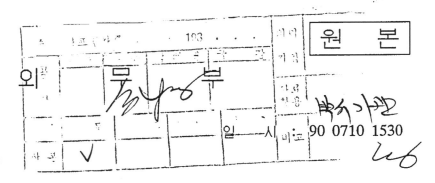

종 별 :

번 호 : IRW-0385

수 신 : 장관(중근동)

발 신 : 주 이란 대사

제 목 : 제네바 이.이 외무장관회담

연:IRW-0371

1. 표제 VELAYATI 외무장관은 라프산자니 대통령주재 각의에참석, 동회담결과를 보고하였음. 이자리에서 동장관은 연호 기자회견내용을 재확인하였으며, 대통령도 동회담성과를 긍정적평가한것으로 알려짐.

2. 한편 양국 외무장관회담 후속의일환으로 제네바에서 양국전문가회의가 7.6 부터 ELLIASON 유엔복사중재하에 개최되었는바, 동회의에서는 특히 유엔사무총장의 이.이양국 방문문제및 안보리결의 598 의 제 6 조(전쟁책임당사자 규명문제)가 집중거론될것으로 보임.

3. 동회담 위요 당관 평가를 아래보고함.

가. 긍정적요인

양국대통령간 서한교환등 일련의 고조된 분위기속에서 이루어진 금번회담은 양국 외무장관간 천 공식회동이라는 점과 양측이 과거경직된 입장에서 벗어나 유연한 태도를갖고 회담에 임하였다는점에서 우선 그의의가 큼. 특히 동회담과 때를 마추어 라프산자니 대통령은 7.6 이라크측의 이란 지진구호지원에대해 감사전문을 발송하였으며, 이에앞서 7.3 이란측은 이라크 포로들에게 가족접견기회를 허용하였는바, 이는 간접적으로 평화회담분위기 증진에 기여할것으로 보임. 더욱이 평화협상에 대해서는 주재국내에서도 강.온파간 의견이 어느정도 일치하고있으므로 국내적 장애요인도 거의없다고 할수있음.

나. 부정적요인

그러나 당관이 그간 조사파악한바에의하면, 이.이평화협상의 최대장애요인은 이라크가 미국의 지원을받고있는 이란반정부 조직인 MKO 구룹의 동국내 활동을 묵인하고있는데 대해 이란정부가 동구룹의 추방을 요구하고있는데서 야기되는 정치적

중아국   장관   차관   1차보   정와대   안기부   90.12.31 일반

PAGE 1

마찰인바, 이는 동 MKO 를 이란과 국경을 접하고있는 이라크 영토내에 그대로 용인함으로써 이를 이란에대한 LEVERAGE 로 이용하려는 미국의 의도와 연계되어있어서 동건에대한 모종의 양보와 타협이 선행되지않는한 평화협상의 단기적 해결전망은 불부명할것으로 사료됨. 나아가 최근 이.쿠웨이트관계 호전등은 상대적으로 이.이관계에 대한 부정적 요인으로 작용할수도있을것임.

　　다. 이와관련, 제 2 차 외무장관회담은 현재 진행중인 전문가회의 결과의 추이를 보아 결정될예정인바, 동제 2 차 회담에서 더욱 구체적인 결과가 나타날수있을것으로 보임.끝

　　(대사정경일-국장)

　　예고:90.12.31 까지

외 무 부

종 별 : 긴 급

번 호 : BGW-0509   일 시 : 90 0815 1200

수 신 : 장관(중근동,정일,기정)

발 신 : 주이라크대사

제 목 : 훗세인대통령 이란제의 수락발표(74호)

    훗세인대통령은 8.15.11:00 전국라디오, TV 를통하여 이란대통령에게 보낸 성명을 발표한바 우선 동 요지를 아래 보고함

    1.이란측의 90.8.8 제의 수락함.(90.7.30 이라크제의에 대한 이란의 회신임)

    2.75년 AGREEMENT 를 인정하며,특히 전쟁포로 교환및 안보리 결의 6-7항의 원칙을 수락함

    3.수락내용

-양국 수도에 상호대표 파견

-90.8.17 부터 이란국경으로부터 모든 이라크 군대의철수

-양국에 억류되어있는 모든 전쟁포로의 즉각적인 교환.끝

    (대사 최봉름-국장)

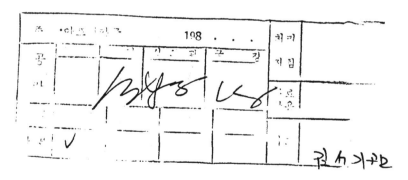

중아국   1차보   정문국   안기부

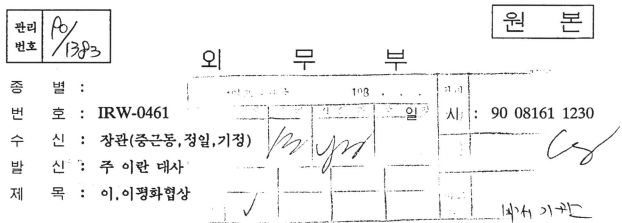

원 본

외 무 부

종 별 :

번 호 : IRW-0461

수 신 : 장관(중근동,정일,기정)

발 신 : 주 이란 대사

제 목 : 이.이평화협상

시 : 90 08161 1230

1. 이락 사담대통령의 8.15 자 이란-이락간 75 년 ALGIER 협정및 88 년 유엔 안보리결의 598 의 수락표명관련, 주재국정부, 언론인등은 일제히 이를 이란의 외교적 승리로 보며, 일단 긍정반응을보이고있음. 현재까지 주재국은 이락측으로부터 공식입장을 통보받지 못한것으로 알려지는바, 국가최고안보회의(대통령주재) 대변인 및 SARMARDI 외무부대변인은 이란의 공식입장은 동사실 공식접수, 검토후에야 발표될수 있을것이라고 언급하였음. 이와관련 VELAYATI 외무장관은 동 공식통보문서가 이란측에 전달중인것으로 알고있다고 설명하며 동수락이 사실일경우 이락대표단의 당지방문은 조속 실현될수 있을것이라고 언급하였음을 참고바람.

2. 한편 당지언론은 이락의 쿠웨이트침공으로 야기된 최근의 역내정세가 이락으로 하여금 동조치를 취하도록 유도하였다고 설명하며, 이란은 이란의 국가이익과 페만역내문제 해결위한 이란의 역할을 명확히 구별해야 할것이라고 강조하였음.

3. 당관이 당지 외교관및 언론계인사와 접촉 파악한 당관 관찰은 다음과같음.

 - 이락은 쿠웨이트침공과 관련 국제적고립 탈피를 위해 이란과의 관계발전을희망

 - 쿠웨이트병합이 기정 사실화되는경우 이란은 페만에의 ACCESS 가 가능해지는바 이는 샤트-알-아랍수로에 대한 이락의 이해를 감소시키게 되며 결과적으로 알지에 협정의 수락을 인정할수있는 여권을 조성함.

 -그러나 쿠웨이트를 통한 이락의 자유로운 페만접근은 이란에대한 주요위협요인이되므로, 이란측은 이락의 쿠웨이트병합 반대라는 기존입장을 견지한 가운데금후 이.이평화협상에 임할것으로 전망됨.

4. 동건 진전사항 계속 추보예정임.끝

(대사정경일-국장)

예고:90.12.31 까지

90.12.31. 일만

중아국   장관   차관   1차보   2차보   정문국   안기부

관리 번호 Po /13A

외 무 부

종 별 : 지 급

번 호 : BGW-0519

일 시 : 90 0816 1630

수 신 : 장 관(중근동,정일)

발 신 : 주 이라크 대사

제 목 : 이라크 대이란 평화제의(응신자료 75호)

1. 훗세인 대통의 8.15 대이란 평화제의에 대하여 이란측은 환영을 표시하였다고 하면서, 이라크는 동제의에 대한 호의의 표시로 일방적으로 8.17 부터 국경에서의 이라크 군대철수 개시와 함께 수천명의 이란포로를 석방할것 이라고 발표함

2. 동평화제의 수락으로 이.이 국경에 배치된 이라크의 30 사단 병력이 사우디 국경으로 이동배치가 가능하게 되었다고 보도됨

3. 본 이.이 평화협상 타결은 이라크의 쿠웨이트 침공이전에 합의한바 있으며 구체합의를 위한 실무회담을 거쳐 8.16 종결 발표한것임. 따라서 이라크 정부는 대이란 관계를 거의 전부 양보하는 조건으로 종결한후 쿠웨이트 침공을 감행한 것으로 평가됨. 끝

(대사 최봉름-국장)

예고:90.12.31.까지

90.12.31.일반

중아국 대책반   장관   차관   1차보   2차보   통상국   정문국   청와대   안기부

PAGE 1

90.08.17   00:30

외신 2과 통제관 DL

0034

Embassy of
The Republic of Iraq
Seoul

NO. 21-90   **PRESS RELEASE**   August 16th, 1990

Iraq has decided to withdraw its forces from the areas facing Iran as from Friday, August 17, 1990, and to start releasing the Iranian prisoners of war (POWs) as from the same date.

This was contained in a message sent by President Saddam Hussein to Iranian President Ali Akbar Hashemi Rafsanjani, and which included a comprehensive settlement to the relations between Iraq and Iran.

The message said that within the frame of confirming desire of Iraq and his people for peace and as a result to the direct contacts made between Iraq and Iran following the president message to messrs:
Ali Khameini and Ali Akbar Rafsanjani on April 21, 1990, and in conformity with the spirit of the president initiative and as a final and clear solution we decided the following;

One. Approving your proposal which was contained in your reply message dated August 8th, 1990 and which was received by our representative in Geneva, Mr. Barazan Ibrahim Al-Tikriti from your representative Mr. Syros Naseri on endorsing the agreement of 1975 linked with the bases included by our letter on 30th July, 1990, especially as concerns the exchange of POWs and articles 6 and 7 of the Security Council Resolution No. 598.

Two. On the bases of what was included in para one of this letter and your letter of July 30, we are ready to despatch a delegation to Tehran or that an Iranian delegation visits us in Baghdad to arrange agreements and getting prepared for signing them on the level to be agreed on.

Three. As an initiative of good intent, our withdrawal will start as from Friday, August 17, and we will withdraw our forces facing Iran along the borders with the exception of what would be token forces together with the police and borders guards for implementing daily duties in normal circumstances.

Four. An immediate and comprehensive exchange of all POWs in both Iraq and Iran will take place and across the land borders along Khanaqin-Qasr Shireen Road and other outlets to be agreed upon. We will take the initiative and start that as from next Friday.

President Hussein's message added that in our decision, everything has become clear and everything you wanted was realized and nothing has remained but to exchange documents from a position overlooking new life prevailed by cooperation in the shade of principles of Islam and to respect each other rights and also to distance those of bad intentions from our coasts, and maybe we will cooperate for keeping the gulf a lake of peace and safety free from foreign threats and forces which are after us.

The President message expounded that after removing all what could obstruct the path for brotherly relations with all moslims and for opening the way for a serious interaction with all believers for confronting evil forces which are after harming Muslims and the Arab nation and for keeping Iraq and Iran away from the blackmail and games of the evil international forces and their lackeys in the region and in conformity with the spirit of our initiative announced on August 12, 1990, in which we wanted the realization of lasting and comprehensive peace in the region and so that to remove any pretext that could prevent interaction and maintain precaution and also for boosting Iraq's potentials in the field of the great duel and mobilizing them towards the objectives which all Muslims and honourable Arabs were unanimous that they were right so that good people could find their way for normal relations between Iraq and Iran), this decision was made.

0035

Embassy of
The Republic of Iraq
Seoul

No. 109-90

The Embassy of the Republic of Iraq presents its compliments to the Ministry of Foreign Affairs of the Republic of Korea and has the honour to enclose herewith a letter of H.E. President Saddam Hussein's, addressed to the president of the Islamic Republic of Iran, H.E. Ali Akbar Hashemi Rafsanjani.

The Embassy of the Republic of Iraq avails itself of this opportunity to renew to the Ministry of Foreign Affairs of the Republic of Korea the assurances of its highest consideration.

S E O U L, August 17, 1990

TO THE MINISTRY OF FOREIGN AFFAIRS
OF THE REPUBLIC OF KOREA

0036

In the name of god the compassionate, the merciful
His Excellency, President
Ali Akbar Hashemi Rafsanjani
President of the Islamic of Iran

Having relied on almighty Allah, and with a view to removing all obstacles which prevent the establishment of brotherly relations with all moslems, and with those moslems, in neighbouring Iran, who will choose brotherhood, to opening the door for serious interaction with all believers in the confrontation with the evil-doers who harbour evil intentions towards moslems and the Arab nation, to distancing Iraq and Iran from the extortions and the games of the evil world powers and their followers in the region, and in conformity with the spirit of our initiative of 12/8/1990, by which envisaged the achievement of a comprehensive and durable peace in the region, in order not to leave any pretexts for anyone not to respond and to maintain his apprehensions and concerns, in order not to leave any of Iraq's capabilities out of the great confrontation, and to mobilize these capabilities for achieving the goals which the moslems and honorable Arabs have unanimously accepted as the truth, to separate the interlocking of trenches, remove the supicions and missings in order that the good people may find their way to establish normal re- lations between Iraq and Iran, and as the outcome of our dialogue which has continued directly since we sent our letter of 21/4/1990, and until your last reply to us dated 8/8/1990, as a clear and final settlement which leaves no excuse for anyone, we have decided the following;

1. The acceptance of your proposal, stated in your reply of 8/8/1990, which Mr. Barzan Ibrahim Al-Tikriti, our representative in Geneva, received from your representative, Mr. Cyrus Nassiri, to adopt the agreement of 1975, together with the bases contained in our letter of 30/7/1990, particularly in respect of the exchange of prisoners 0037

of war and paragraph (6 and 7) of Security Council Resolution No. 598.

2. On the basis of paragraph (1) of this letter, and what was mentioned in our letter of 30/7/1990, we are ready to send a delegation to Tehran, or to receive a delegation from your side in Baghdad, to prepare the agreements to be signed on a level to be agreed upon.

3. As a gesture of good-will, our withdrawal will commence on Friday 17/8/1990. We shall withdraw our forces, confronting you along the boundries, and only symbolic units will remain together with frontier guards and police to fulfill the daily tasks in normal circumstances.

4. To start an immediate and comprehensive exchange of all prisoners of war, held on both Iraq and Iran. This exchange is to be carried out across the land boundries by way of Khanaqin, Qasr Shirin, and through other crossings to be agreed upon. We shall take the initiative in this regard as from Friday 17/8/1990.

My brother, President
Ali Akbar Hashimi Rafsanjani,
By this decision of ours, all is now clear. All that you wanted and concentrated on has been accomplished. Nothing remains but the preparation of the documents so that we can clearly survey from a vantage point new life of cooperation in which the principles of Islam and respect for the rights of each other shall prevail. Thus we shall keep those who fish in troubled waters away from our shores. We may also cooperate so as to keep the gulf a lake of peace and security, free from foreign fleets and foreign powers which are always looking for opportunities to harm us. This in addition to our cooperation in other fields of life.

God is great, and god be praised.

Saddam Hussein
President of the Republic of Iraq
August 14, 1990   0038

長 官 報 告 事 項

1990. 8 . 17.
中東.아프리카局
中近東課(29)

題目 : 이라크, 이란에 평화 조약 제의

8.16. 이라크는 이란에 평화 조약을 전격 제의하였는바, 관련 사항을 다음과 같이 보고 드립니다.

1. 경 위

88.8-89.4	이.이전 종결후, 4차례의 유엔 후원하 이.이 평화 협상 전개, 상호 이견 노출로 별다른 성과무
90.1	이라크, UN 후원하의 이.이 평화 회담 제의
90.5	이라크 대통령, 이란 대통령간 직접 평화 회담 제의
90.6	이란 대통령, 이라크 대통령과의 정상 회담 용의 및 예비 회담 제의
90.7	이.이 외상 직접 회담 개최(제네바)
90.8	이.이 평화 협상 타결

2. 제의 내용

○ 75년 양국간 국경 조약 수락

- 샤트알 아랍 수로 중간 기점으로 양국간 국경선 획정

0039

○ 점령지 철군

  - 8.17. 이란 국경으로부터 모든 이라크 군대 철수

○ 전쟁 포로 교환

  - 양국 억류 모든 전쟁 포로의 즉각적 교환

○ 양국 수도에 상호 대표 파견

3. 분석 및 전망

○ 이라크의 쿠웨이트 침공 관련 국제적 고립 탈피

○ 이.이 국경 주둔 대규모 이라크 병력의 사우디 접경 이동 배치 가능

○ 쿠웨이트 점령을 기정 사실화 하여 걸프 지역 진출 보급로 확보

○ 최근 미국의 대이란 화해 시도에 제동

○ 10년간 지속된 대이란 분쟁 종식을 통해 이.이 관계 진전이 예상되나 국경
  조약 수락의 실질적 이행 어부 불투명

4. 향후 조치 계획

○ 이.이 평화 협상 합의에 의거한 실행 진전 추이 파악.   끝.

0040

長 官 報 告 事 項

題 目 : 이라크, 이란에 평화 조약 제의

8.16. 이라크는 이란에 평화 조약을 전격 제의하였는바, 관련 사항을
다음과 같이 보고 드립니다.

---

1. 경 위

88.8-89.4 이·이전 종결후, 4 차례의 유엔 후원하 이·이 평화 협상
　　　　　　전개, 상호 이견 노출로 별다른 성과무

90.1.　　　이라크, UN 후원하의 이·이 평화 회담 제의

90.5.　　　이라크 대통령, 이란 대통령간 직접 평화 회담 제의

90.6.　　　이란 대통령, 이라크 대통령과의 정상 회담 용의 및 예비 회답
　　　　　　제의

90.7.　　　이·이 외상 직접 회담 개최(제네바)

90.8.　　　이·이 평화 협상 　 타결

2. 제의 내용

ㅇ 75년 양국간 국경 조약 수락

　- 샤트알 아랍 수로 중간 기점으로 양국간 국경선 획정

ㅇ 점령지 철군

　- 8.17. 이란 국경으로부터 모든 이라크 군대 철수

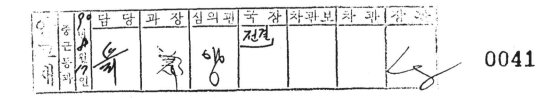

ㅇ 전쟁 포로 교환

  - 양국 억류 모든 전쟁 포로의 즉각적 교환

ㅇ 양국 수도에 상호 대표 파견

3. 분석 및 전망

ㅇ 이라크의 쿠웨이트 침공 관련 국제적 고립 탈피

ㅇ 이·이 국경 주둔 대규모 이라크 병력의 사우디 접경 이동 배치 가능

ㅇ 쿠웨이트 점령을 기정 사실화 하여 걸프 지역 진출 보급로 확보

ㅇ 최근 미국의 대이란 화해 시도에 제동

ㅇ 10년간 지속된 대이란 분쟁 종식을 통해 이·이 관계 진전이 예상되나 국경 조약 수락의 실질적 이행 여부 불투명

4. 향후 조치 계획

ㅇ 이·이 평화 협상 합의에 의거한 실행 진전 추이 파악. 끝.

0042

외 무 부

종 별 :

번 호 : UNW-1547   일 시 : 90 0817 1530

수 신 : 장관(중근동,국연)

발 신 : 주유엔대사

제 목 : 이라크의 대이란 화해조치

　　표제 90.8.14 이라크의 대이란 화해 조치 발표와관련, SADDAM HUSSEIN 이라크 대통령의 상기 이란대통령앞 서한 및 TARIQ AZIZ 이라크 부수상겸 외무장관의 유엔사무총장앞 서한이 유엔문서로 배포되었기 이를 참고로 보고함.

　　첨부: UNW(F)-133. 끝

　　(대사 현홍주-국장)

중아국　　1차보　　국기국

외신 1과 통제관

0043

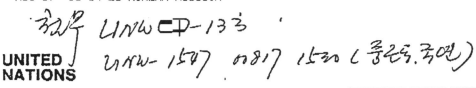

UNITED NATIONS

Security Council

Distr.
GENERAL

S/21528
15 August 1990
ENGLISH
ORIGINAL: ARABIC

LETTER DATED 15 AUGUST 1990 FROM THE PERMANENT REPRESENTATIVE OF IRAQ TO THE UNITED NATIONS ADDRESSED TO THE SECRETARY-GENERAL

On instructions from my Government, I have the honour to transmit to you herewith a letter dated 15 August 1990 addressed to you by Mr. Tariq Aziz, Deputy Prime Minister and Minister for Foreign Affairs of Iraq, enclosing two letters, dated 30 July 1990 and 14 August 1990 respectively, from Mr. Saddam Hussein, President of the Republic of Iraq, addressed to the President of Iran.

(Signed) Abdul Amir A. AL-ANBARI
Permanent Representative

90-19268 1676i

/...

10—1

S/21528
English
Page 2

<u>Annex</u>

<u>Letter dated 15 August 1990 from the Deputy Prime Minister
and Minister for Foreign Affairs of Iraq addressed to the
Secretary-General</u>

    Iraq has always been assiduous in urging and in striving sincerely and
persistently for the establishment of a lasting and comprehensive peace with its
neighbour Iran that will guarantee the rights of the two countries and the
permanency of relations of good-neighbourliness between them.

    As you know, Iraq has given proof of this well-established position since the
establishment of the Islamic Republic of Iran in 1979. It continued to affirm this
position in various ways and on various occasions during the armed struggle between
Iraq and Iran, in particular by means of the many letters addressed by
Mr. Saddam Hussein, President of the Republic of Iraq, to the Iranian peoples, some
of which were distributed as documents of the General Assembly and of the Security
Council (documents A/38/113-S/15636, A/38/268-S/15825 and S/18258).

    You are also aware that Iraq did not hesitate throughout the period of the
conflict to adopt positions that brought opportunities for peace nearer and that it
was the initiative of President Saddam Hussein of 6 August 1988 which led to the
declaration of a cease-fire.

    After the entry into force of the cease-fire and the start of the meetings
held under your auspices, Iraq presented a set of initiatives and ideas for the
achievement of peace. Among the most prominent of these were the proposals
submitted by us in Baghdad on 13 November 1989 to your Personal Representative,
Mr. Jan Eliasson. That was followed by the comprehensive peace initiative of
Mr. Saddam Hussein, President of the Republic of Iraq, of January 1990, which was
communicated to the United Nations and circulated in document S/21070.

    Iraq then adopted a historic and courageous position when
President Saddam Hussein took the initiative of establishing direct contact with
the Iranian leadership. This was done by means of the peace message sent by
Mr. Saddam Hussein, President of the Republic of Iraq, to Mr. Ali Khamenei and to
Mr. Ali Akbar Hashemi Rafsanjani, President of the Islamic Republic of Iran, on
21 April 1990, whose tenor met with a positive response enabling the two countries
to pursue their contacts. It should be noted that, in this context,
Mr. Saddam Hussein subsequently sent a number of letters, dated 19 May, 16 July,
30 July, 2 August and 3 August 1990, to President Rafsanjani. The direct contacts
continued to be maintained throughout this period by two accredited representatives
of the leaders, namely Mr. Barzan Ibrahim al-Takriti and Mr. Cyrus Naseri, the
Permanent Representatives of Iraq and Iran respectively to the United Nations
Office at Geneva. In the course of these contacts, we presented numerous proposals
and initiatives aimed at facilitating the process of achieving peace.

    In keeping with this well-established position of principle to which Iraq has
remained committed and in keeping with its sincere desire actually to enter into

/...

0045

S/21528
English
Page 3

the process of achieving peace and resolving all the outstanding issues between it
and Iran, on 14 August 1990 Mr. Saddam Hussein addressed a historic letter to
President Ali Akbar Hashemi Rafsanjani that included the following decisions:

"1.   To agree to the proposal [i.e. that of the Iranian side] contained in
your letter of reply dated 8 August 1990 and received by our representative in
Geneva, Mr. Barzan Ibrahim al-Takriti, from your representative,
Mr. Cyrus Naseri, that the 1975 Accord should be used as a basis while
standing in close relation to the principles set forth in our letter of
30 July 1990, particularly with regard to the exchange of prisoners and to
paragraphs 6 and 7 of Security Council resolution 598 (1987).

"2.   On the basis of paragraph 1 of the present letter and of the tenor of our
letter addressed to you on 30 July 1990, we are prepared to send a delegation
to you in Tehran or to be visited by a delegation from you in Baghdad in order
to prepare the agreements and make ready for their signature at the level at
which agreement is reached.

"3.   As an earnest of good faith, our withdrawal will begin as of Friday,
17 August 1990 and we shall withdraw the forces opposing you along the borders
so that only a token presence will remain, with border guards and police and
no more, in order to carry out the day-to-day duties required in normal
circumstances.

"4.   There should be an immediate and comprehensive exchange of all prisoners
of war, the full number held in both Iraq and Iran, to take place across the
land boundaries and by way of the Khanaqin - Qasr-e Shirin road and other
crossing points to be agreed upon. We shall take the initiative in this
matter and shall put it into effect as of Friday, 17 July 1990."

By means of this historic initiative, Iraq, by its noble and historic stance,
is laying the foundations for a comprehensive and lasting peace between it and Iran
and is achieving the object of the endeavours of the international community and
the United Nations and meeting the desire of all the peoples of the world.

I must once again call attention to the historic initiative proclaimed on
12 August 1990 by Mr. Saddam Hussein, President of the Republic of Iraq, addressing
the issues of the region. We hereby affirm the sincerity of our intentions and the
rigour of our position on the solution of a dangerous and complex regional issue
and one whose continued existence poses a threat to international peace and
security.

In order to carry out the withdrawal with effect from the date set in the
letter of President Saddam Hussein, namely 17 August 1990, I request you to
instruct the Chief Military Observer of the United Nations Iran-Iraq Military
Observer Group, Major-General Slavko Jovic, to co-operate with the competent Iraqi
authorities in carrying out the task.

/...

3

0046

S/21528
English
Page 4

I enclose herewith copies of the letters dated 30 July 1990 and 14 August 1990
from Mr. Saddam Hussein, President of the Republic of Iraq, addressed to
Mr. Ali Akbar Hashemi Rafsanjani, President of the Islamic Republic of Iran.

(Signed) Tariq AZIZ
Deputy Prime Minister and
Minister for Foreign Affairs of Iraq

/...

4

0047

Enclosure I

**Letter dated 14 August 1990 from the President of Iraq addressed
to the President of the Islamic Republic of Iran**

    Having placed our trust in Almighty God; for the purpose of removing the
obstacles to the establishment of fraternal relations with all Muslims and with our
worthy brothers the Muslims of neighbouring Iran; in order to open the way for
vigorous common action with all Believers in confronting the evil doers who wish
calamity on the Muslims and on the Arab nation; in order to extricate Iraq and Iran
from the blackmail and intrigues of malicious international forces and their
adjuncts in the region; in keeping with the spirit of the initiative announced by
us on 12 August 1990 through which we aspired to the achievement of a comprehensive
and lasting peace in the region, so that we may leave to those who have a pretext
nothing that may prevent their involvement or perpetuate misgivings and suspicion;
so that none of Iraq's capacities shall remain unutilized away from the field of
the major clash and can be mobilized for the goals on whose validity the noble
Arabs and Muslims are unanimous; in order to keep mutual interference out of the
trenches and remove suspicions and misgivings so that the worthy may find their way
to establishing normal relations between Iraq and Iran; as a result of our direct
dialogue extending from the time of our letter addressed to you on 21 March 1990 up
to the latest letter from you addressed to us on 8 August 1990; and as a definitive
and unequivocal solution that will leave an excuse to none;

    We have decided as follows:

1.   To agree to the proposal contained in your letter of reply dated 8 August 1990
and received by our representative in Geneva, Mr. Barzan Ibrahim al-Takriti, from
your representative, Mr. Cyrus Naseri to the effect that the 1975 Accord should be
used as a basis while standing in close relation to the principles set forth in our
letter of 30 July 1990, particularly with regard to the exchange of prisoners, and
to paragraphs 6 and 7 of Security Council resolution 598 (1987).

2.   On the basis of paragraph 1 of the present letter and of the tenor of our
letter addressed to you on 30 July 1990, we are prepared to send a delegation to
you in Tehran or to be visited by a delegation from you in Baghdad in order to
prepare the agreements and make ready for their signature at the level at which
agreement is reached.

3.   As an earnest of good faith, our withdrawal will begin as of Friday,
17 August 1990, and we shall withdraw our forces opposing you along the borders so
that only a token presence will remain, with border guards and police and no more,
in order to carry out the day-to-day duties required in normal circumstances.

4.   There should be an immediate and complete exchange of all prisoners of war,
the full number held in both Iraq and Iran, to take place across the land
boundaries and by way of the Khanaqin - Qasr-e Shirin road and other crossing
points to be agreed upon. We shall take the initiative in this matter and shall
put it into effect as of Friday, 17 July 1990.

/...

S/21528
English
Page 6

   Mr. President Ali Akbar Hashemi Rafsanjani:

   With this decision of ours all has become clear, and thus all that you have
desired and all that you have stressed has been achieved. It remains only for the
instruments to be circulated before we can look down together from a commanding
position onto a new life in which co-operation holds sway under the aegis of the
principles of peace. Each of us will respect the rights of the other, we shall
dismiss from our shores those who fish in troubled waters, and we shall perchance
co-operate both in ensuring that the Gulf remains a lake of peace and safety, free
of foreign fleets and the forces of the foreigner which lie in ambush to our
misfortune, and in other spheres of life.

/...

6

0049

<u>Enclosure II</u>

<u>Letter dated 30 July 1990 from the President of the Republic of Iraq
addressed to the President of the Islamic Republic of Iran</u>

Following careful consideration of that which must be considered and a
thorough review of the evolution of relations between - and the situation in - Iraq
and Iran, as well as of the dangers encircling and encompassing the region, and
with a view to maintaining our practice of launching initiatives which afford
greater opportunities for the achievement of peace, we find ourselves confronted -
in accordance with our national responsibility and with the humanitarian
responsibility which our great principles place upon our shoulders - with the
responsibility of launching a fresh initiative. Since our initiative this time
addresses all the essential issues contained in the provisions of Security Council
resolution 598 (1987) at one time, in a single context and in detail, we hope it
will receive the attention which is its due. We hope that the initiative will be
treated with sufficient seriousness to prevent our two peoples' being denied the
opportunity of enjoying their right to live in conditions of peace whose every
detail is agreed, as well as to ensure they are spared from the schemes of enemies
of peoples, who endeavour - God forbid - to turn back the clock in our two
countries to the situation as it was before August 1988. In that event, losers
will be losers, without any evident gain.

The forces of darkness, which pry into corners and bear the instruments of
death, are capable - under the influence of a feeling that the war between the two
countries is not yet legally over - of causing the spark of war to be lighted once
again. As you are aware, war can spring from beginnings that seem at first to be
of only minor importance, just as a massive fire can spring from a single spark.
Those evil beings who lie in wait to waylay us may, as a result of their inability
to achieve their aims without engaging the two countries - or either one of them -
in war, of their concern at the quantity of weapons accumulated by the two parties
to the dispute, and of their desire to test the effectiveness of those or some
portion of those weapons, be driven to light the spark by their own vile means. In
this they may encounter little difficulty, given a front which - on land alone -
stretches for some 1,200 kilometres, and for about 800 kilometres at sea. On these
fronts, where it is quite possible - and probable - that sparks may fly from the
mouths of weapons, it is hardly necessary that many should fire their weapons in
order for hostilities to begin. If just one of them does this for any reason, and
at whatever prompting, then many will fire as a consequence. The loss will then be
the greater for all; only the wicked will gain; and, as we have said before, it
will be our peoples who suffer the consequences.

Since this is the objective of neither Iraq nor Iran, as is evident from the
statements of those who represent them, it is thus imperative not only to achieve
peace but to do so as rapidly as possible, in order to ensure that our area is
spared any practical application of the dreams of darkness and the oppressors.

In accordance with all the above, I advance the following initiative:

/...

7

S/21528
English
Page 8

1.   I again raise the idea of holding a prompt meeting between the Heads of the two States, at a place to be agreed upon, where they may discuss the issues which, if the subject of an agreement, may serve as the basis of a comprehensive and lasting peace.

2.   The discussion and agreement should cover all outstanding issues. Once a comprehensive agreement has been reached, no new issue may be raised by one side, without the agreement of the other: to raise any such new issue shall constitute an evasion of the agreement. The rubrics of the agreement shall be drawn from the provisions of Security Council resolution 598 (1987). The agreement shall be concluded on the understanding and assurance that the fundamental objective of resolution 598 (1987) is none other than to bring about a comprehensive and lasting peace by means of dialogue, that the elements of the agreement constitute an indivisible whole, in the form of an integrated and inter-related transaction, and that an infringement of any one of its provisions is an infringement of every one of them.

3.   The starting-point for the dialogue and agreement on the issues is not important. However, agreement on any one or more components of the subjects under discussion shall remain dependent on agreement on the other items, in conformity with all the contents of paragraph 2 above.

      Accordingly, either party to the dialogue shall be entitled to reply as it sees fit to any individual declaration made by the other party: this shall include the right to repudiate a partial agreement on any one of the agreed subjects of the dialogue.

4.   Withdrawal shall take place within a period of no more than two months from the date of the final ratification of the comprehensive agreement concluded by us, though if the period is shorter, so much the better. The agreement should be based on an inseparable relationship of interdependence between each step to be taken by the parties to the conflict, with respect to the commitment of each side under the agreement to take an appropriate or equivalent step such as will correspond to the commitment of the other side.

5.   We continue to consider that the subject of prisoners of war should be governed by the Geneva Convention. We therefore assume that their release should be based on the provisions of that Convention. Two years have passed since the time when prisoners should have been released in accordance with the Convention, i.e. from the cease-fire until the present. Nevertheless, in order to facilitate the peace process, we have no objection, in conformity with the principles and concepts referred to above, to accepting a timetable for the release of prisoners based on the period specified in paragraph 4, namely, on a maximum period of two months from the date of the final ratification of the agreement. If agreement can be reached on a shorter period, so much the better.

/...

8

0051

6.   The dialogue concerning the Shatt al-Arab must be based on the three following rubrics:

    (a) Full sovereignty over the waterway belongs to Iraq, as is its legitimate historical right.

    (b) While Iraq shall have sovereignty over the Shatt al-Arab, it shall apply the concept of the thalweg line in respect of navigation rights between Iraq and Iran, including right of passage, the right to fish and the right to join in the control of shipping passing through the waterway and distribution of profits arising therefrom.

    (c) The Shatt al-Arab issue shall be referred to arbitration on the basis of a formula to be agreed upon by the two parties, each one undertaking in advance to accept the results of such arbitration. Until such time as the issue is decided by arbitration, a start will be made on operations to clear the Shatt al-Arab, in accordance with a formula to be agreed upon by the two parties, to make it viable for shipping and other uses.

    The agreement will be based on the supposition that the two sides will jointly select any of the three above rubrics, on the understanding that the first rubric represents the right of Iraq and that the other two rubrics represent the wishes of Iran.

7.   There must be an agreement to drop paragraph 6 of Security Council resolution 598 (1987) from the discussion and finally to set it aside, because it obstructs rather than promotes progress towards peace. Its consequences may give rise to rancour and hatred, and to revenge in the future, while peace could serve as an alternative path for the Iranian and Iraqi peoples. In this connection, the Secretary-General of the United Nations should be informed, officially and in writing, of the agreement which we conclude.

8.   No start should be made on any of the aforementioned steps, as included in the peace agreement to be concluded by us between Iraq and Iran, before the completion of all legal measures for its ratification as required under the Constitutions of the two countries, in order to ensure that the agreement is final from the legal and constitutional point of view and does not admit any total or partial retraction whatsoever, and that its provisions are effective. The instruments of ratification of the agreement are to be deposited with the Secretary-General of the United Nations simultaneously in accordance with an agreement between the two parties.

9.   The new peace agreement between Iraq and Iran should include all matters upon which agreement is reached. There shall be no objection, with a view to facilitating the rapid conclusion of the peace agreement, to the inclusion therein - apart from new issues, land border questions and other rights which may be agreed upon - of some of the contents of previous agreements from the history of relations between our two countries, and of that which was formerly agreed upon, provided that the provisions contained in the present letter are not thereby infringed.

/...

9

0052

S/21528
English
Page 10

10. The agreement must include clear principles concerning the establishment of good-neighbourly relations, non-intervention in internal affairs and respect on the part of each country for the political, economic and social system which may be chosen by the other country, as well as an unequivocal affirmation of the rights of passage for all forms of shipping through the international waters of the Gulf and the Strait of Hormuz.

11. It may be appropriate for proper implementation of the agreement to be guaranteed by an accepted international body (the Security Council).

12. Although we recognize that the international situation does not allow us to set great hopes on the provision of assistance to us for reconstruction, we consider that the international assistance which is to be provided under paragraph 7 should be divided equally between Iraq and Iran.

13. With a view to facilitating communications between us, and in light of the positive evolution of our relations, we believe that our embassies at Tehran and Baghdad should be opened once again, particularly since they remained open during the war and closed only in September 1987.

     This, Mr. President, is what we think will bring about a lasting and comprehensive peace between Iraq and Iran. It is an integrated proposal, the elements of which are interdependent and indivisible. This is what our experience has helped and even inspired us to seek, and it at the same time reflects the contents of the talks held between our representatives in Geneva, Mr. Naseri and Mr. Barzan.

     Everything is thus made clear, leaving no room for any contrary interpretation: what we seek is a genuine, comprehensive and rapid peace.

     God is most great.

                                        (Signed) Saddam HUSSEIN
                                        President of the Republic of Iraq

관리
번호 : Po/1405

외 무 부

종 별 :

번 호 : IRW-0464

일 시 : 90 0818 1100

수 신 : 장관(중근동,정일,기정)

발 신 : 주 이란 대사

제 목 : 이란.이락관계

연:IRW-0461

1. 연호 구체적조치의 일환으로 이락은 8.17 이란인포로석방및 점령영토로부터의 철수를 시작하였으며, 주재국 외무부대변인은 이에대한 상응조치로 이락포로들을 조속 석방예정이라고 밝혔음.

2. 상기와같은 급진전된 양국관계에도불구 당지 유력영자지(정부입장대변)TEHRAN TIMES 지 (8.18 자) 는 이락의 쿠웨이트철수를 강조하는 기사를 게재하고, LARIJANI 외무장관고문이 이락의 쿠웨이트침공이 정당화될수 있는지에 회의를표하는 발언을 행하는등 이락에대한 비난을 간접적으로나마 늦추고 있지 않음이 감지되며 다른한편에서는 이락의 쿠웨이트 침공에 대한 이.이간 묵계소문이 사실었으며 따라서 이란의 대이락비난은 형식적인것에 불과하다는 시각이 있음을 참고로 보고함. 끝

(대사정경일-국장)

예고:90.12.31 까지

90. 12. 31. 일반 In

| 중아국
대책반	장관	차관	1차보	2차보	통상국	정문국	청와대	안기부

PAGE 1

90.08.18   17:18

외신 2과 통제관 EZ

0054

외 무 부

종 별 : 지 급

번 호 : BGW-0530

수 신 : 장 관 (중근동,정일)

발 신 : 주 이라크 대사

제 목 : 전쟁포로 송환 (77호)

일 시 : 90 0818 1100

　　이라크는 8.17 이란군 포로 1,000명을 이라크 북부모슬에서 바그다드경우, KHOSRAWI 국경을 통하여 이란측에 인도함. 이라크당국은 앞으로 매일 2,000명씩 송환하기를바라고 있으나 현 19명의 ICRC 대표로서는 동인원의 송환절차를 처리하는데 어려움이 있어 당분간 매일 1,000명씩 송환하게 될것이라 함. 이에 대응하여 이란당국도 이라크 포로 1진을 이라크에 송한하기 위해 국경지대로 인도되었다고 말하고 있으나 석방될 포로규모에 대해서는 언급이 없음.끝

　　(대사 최봉름-국장)

중아국　　1차보　　　정문국　　　안기부　　　대책반

90.08.18　　18:24 FC

외신 1과　통제관

0055

외 무 부

종 별 :

번 호 : IRW-0515

일 시 : 90 0909 1600

수 신 : 장관(중근동,정일,기정)

발 신 : 주 이란 대사

제 목 : 이락 외무장관 주재국 방문

1. AZIZ 이락 외무장관이 석유장관대동 주재국 공식방문을 위해 금 9.9 오전당지 도착하였음. 장관은 VELAYATI 장관과 만나 안보리결의 598 이행문제 포함현 이락-쿠웨이트사태(이락측의 식.의약품등 인도적 물자제공 요청등)에 대해 협의 예정인것으로 알려짐.

2. 주재국 언론반응

-이락 외무장관의 방이목적은 양국간 평화수립및 주재국에 대한 식, 의약품등 물자제공 요청임. 이란은 상기 이락측 요청을 페만국가들의 이해증진및 긴장완화라는 측면에서 검토할것임.

-이란의 대이락. 쿠웨이트사태 입장은 이락의 쿠웨이트 침공비난, 미국의 페만 주둔반대, 분쟁의 역내국가간 협의에 의한 처리임.

3. 동건 상세 파악되는대로 추보예정임.끝

(대사 정경일-국장)

예고:90.12.31 까지

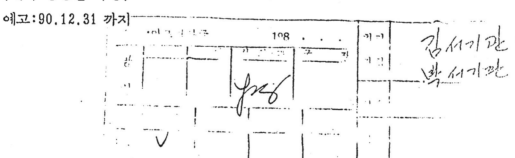

중아국-- 장관   차관   1차보   2차보   정문국-- 정와대   안기부   대직반

PAGE 1

90.09.10   00:16

외신 2과 통제관 CW

0056

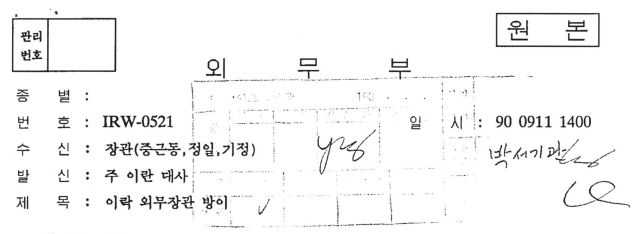

관리
번호

외　무　부

종　별 :

번　호 : IRW-0521

수　신 : 장관(중근동,정일,기정)

발　신 : 주 이란 대사

제　목 : 이락 외무장관 방이

일　시 : 90 0911 1400

연:IRW-0515

1. 연호 이.이 양국간 협의내용 파악 우선아래보고함.

　-메시지전달: 사담대통령의 라프잔자니 대통령앞 서한전달(내용미공개)

　-이.이평화협상

　이락측,75 년 알지에협정및 안보리결의 598 에 대신하는 새로운 평화협정체결 제의, 이란측은 이에대해 조심스럽게 부정적입장피력

　이.이 외교관계 정상화 조속추진

　POW 완전교환을위한 협의기구구성

　-폐만사태

　이란측, 이락의 쿠웨이트침공 및 미군의 폐만주둔 동시비난

　이락측 요청내용(식, 의약품지원요청으로추정)은 미공개

　-메카성지순례(이란측 언급사항)

　중동전역에서의 이스람문화 유지발전

　사우디소재 메카의 역내국가간 공동관리

　PLS 지원및 쏘련거주 유태인의 이스라엘 이주반대

　-기타

　VELAYATI 외무장관의 이락방문초청

2. 당관관찰

　-이락외무장관의 방이는 폐만사태관련 외교적고립을 벗어나기 위한 노력의 일환으로 양국간 관계정상화추진, 식, 의약품등 물자제공요청을 주목적으로 하고있음(동요청은 미공개 협의사항 및 사담대통령의 메시지에 포함된 것으로추정)

　-상기 이락입장에 대한 이란측 입장은 아직 불투명한바 이란은 국제사회

중아국	장관	차관	1차보	2차보	정문국	정와대	안기부	대책반

구성원으로서의 의무와 이락의 관계증진이라는 국가이익의 조화를 위해 부심하고있는 것으로 관측됨.

-이와 관련 이란의적(미국)의적(이락)이 반드시 이란의 친구는 아니라는 당지언론 사설이 있음을 참고 보고함. 끝

(대사정경일-국장)

예고:90.12.31 까지

長官報告事項

1990. 9. 11.
中東.아프리카局
中近東課(34)

題目 : 이라크, 이란 복교 합의

이라크는 이란과 9.10. 외교관계를 재개하기로 합의하였는 바, 관련
사항을 다음과 같이 보고드립니다.

1. 경 위

○ 87.10.   이.이 양국간 외교관계 단절

○ 88.8.-89.4.   이.이전 종결후 4차례의 UN 후원하 이.이 평화 협상

                     전개, 별다른 성과무

○ 90.5-6   . 이라크 대통령, 이란 대통령간 직접 평화 회담 제의

                     . 이란 대통령, 이라크 대통령과의 정상회담 용의 및

                       예비회담 제의

○ 90.7.   이.이 외상 직접 회담 (제네바)

○ 90.8.   후세인 이라크 대통령, 이란에 평화 조약 체결 제의

○ 90.9.10.   이라크 외무장관, 이란 대통령과 외교관계 재개 합의

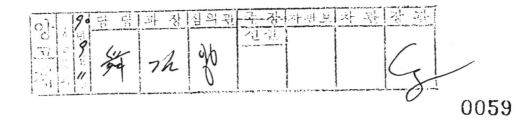

0059

2. 배 경

○ 이라크의 쿠웨이트 점령이후 국제적 고립 심화

● 경제 제재, 특히 봉쇄에 대한 대응 방안 모색 필요 관련성

○ 서방측의 대이란 화해 움직임

3. 합의 내용

○ 이.이 양국 조속한 관계 정상화

- 양국 공관 업무 재개

※ 걸프사태에 대해서는 이견 노출

● 이란:-이라크의 쿠웨이트침공 비난 및 쿠웨이트에서의 즉각 철수 주장

- 유엔의 대 이라크 제재 조치 준수

4. 분석 및 전망

○ 걸프사태 관련, 서방 국가들과의 현 대치 상태인 이라크가 이란을 자기편

으로 끌어드리려는 전략

○ 이라크 식량난에 대비 이란으로부터의 보급로 확보 의도

○ 이.이 관계 정상화로 당분간 양국관계 발전 증대 예상되나, 걸프사태 진전

여하에 따라, 관계 변화 가능성

5. 향후 조치 계획

○ 이.이 양국 관계 정상화 이후 관계 진전 추이 파악. 끝.

0060

長 官 報 告 事 項

1990. 9 . 11.
中東.아프리카局
中近東課(34)

題目 : 이라크, 이란 복교 합의

> 이라크는 이란과 9.10. 외교관계를 재개하기로 합의하였는 바, 관련
> 사항을 다음과 같이 보고드립니다.

1. 경 위

- 87.10.   이.이 양국간 외교관계 단절

- 88.8.-89.4.   이.이전 종결후 4차례의 UN 후원하 이.이 평화 협상
                  전개, 별다른 성과무

- 90.5-6   . 이라크 대통령, 이란 대통령간 직접 평화 회담 제의
                  . 이란 대통령, 이라크 대통령과의 정상회담 용의 및
                    예비회담 제의

- 90.7.   이.이 외상 직접 회담 (제네바)

- 90.8.   후세인 이라크 대통령, 이란에 평화 조약 체결 제의

- 90.9.10.   이라크 외무장관, 이란 대통령과 외교관계 재개 합의

0061

2. 배 경

o 이라크의 쿠웨이트 점령이후 국제적 고립 심화

o 경제 제재, 특히 봉쇄에 대한 대응방안 모색 필요 절실

o 서방측의 대이란 화해 움직임

3. 합의 내용

o 이.이 양국 조속한 관계 정상화

- 양국 공관 업무 재개

※ 걸프사태에 대해서는 이견 노출

. 이란, 이라크의 쿠웨이트 침공 비난 및 쿠웨이트에서의 즉각 철수 주장

4. 분석 및 전망

o 걸프사태 관련, 서방 국가들과의 현 대치 상태인 이라크가 이란을 자기편
으로 끌어드리려는 전략

o 이라크 식량난에 대비 이란으로부터의 보급로 확보 의도

o 이.이 관계 정상화로 당분간 양국관계 발전 증대 예상되나, 걸프사태 진전
여하에 따라, 관계 변화 가능성. 끝.

0062

관리
번호 90/1143

외 무 부

종 별 :

번 호 : BGW-0828

일 시 : 90 1008 1000

수 신 : 장관(중근동)

발 신 : 주 이라크 대사

제 목 : 주재국 실무대표단 이란방문

1. 10.8 바그다드 옵서버지는 주재국외무성 실무대표단 일행이 10.9 부터 이란을 방문할 예정이라고 보도함

2. 입건 방문에서는 상호대사관 개설문제를 비롯하여, 지난 5 월 당지에서 개최된 양국 외무차관 회담시 협의되었던, 포로교환 문제, 국경개방문제, 주재국 식량 도입및 석유판매 지원문제등 제반 현안문제들에 대한 실무협의가 진행될 예정인것으로 알려짐

3. 참고로 최근 주재국 북부 국경지역에서는 양국 관리들 묵인하에 쿠르드족에의해 이란, 이라크간 국경 밀무역형태로 쌀등 생필품이 주재국으로 계속 반입되고있다고함. 끝

(대사 최봉름-국장)

예고:90.12.31

중아국

외 무 부

종 별 :

번 호 : IRW-0586

일 시 : 90 1014 1530

수 신 : 장관(중근동,정일,기정)

발 신 : 주이란대사

제 목 : 이.이대사관 개설

(자료응신:90-8)

이란,이락 양국은 최근 이락 외무차관의 방이중 합의에따라 금 10.14 을 기해 양국 수도에 대사관을 개설(CHARGE D'AFFAIRES 급) 할 가능성이 매우 크다고 당지 언론이 보도하였으니 참고바람 (사실여부 미확인). 끝

(대사 정경일-국장)

공람	담당	과장	심의관	국장	처리 지침	
수무	중근동					
사본	✓				비고	

중 ㆍ아프리카국   190 . . .

중아국   장관   차관   1차보   2차보   정문국   안기부

PAGE 1

90.10.14   23:41 CG

외신 1과 통제관

0064

관리
번호 90/1923

외 무 부

종 별 :
번 호 : BGW-0949   일 시 : 90 1115 1000
수 신 : 장관(중근동,기정)
발 신 : 주 이라크 대사
제 목 : 이란외상 주재국방문

1. 벨라야리 이란 외상을 단장으로하는 이란 대표단 일행이 11.14 2 일간 주재국을 방문하기 위해 당지에 도착, 훗세인 대통령을 예방한후 양국 대표단간 제1 차 회담을 개최했음

2. 이번 이란외상의 주재국방문은 지난 9.8-10 간 아지즈 주재국 외상의 이란 방문에 대한 답방 형태로 이루어진것으로서 양국간 상호 대사관 재개 합의(10.14)이래 양국관계 증진과 포로교환 재개및 평화협정 체결등 전후 처리 현안문제들을 협의하기위한것임

3. 주재국은 쿠웨이트 침공 직전부터 동부 국경지역 안보 위협 부담을 해소하기위해 대이란 관계개선에 주력, 샤트 알 아랍 수로에대한 영유권 사실상 포기등 이.이전 발생 이전 상태로의 대이란 관계 원상회복을 급속히 추진함으로서 내부적으로 8 년 전쟁 희생 결과에대한 국민들의 불만이 내연되고있는바, 동 방문결과및 양국관계 발전동향 에의 파악 추보하겠음. 끝

(대사 최봉름-국장)
예고:91.6.30

중아국   차관   1차보   2차보   정문국   청와대   안기부   대책반

주 국 련 대 표 부

주국련 2031334- *143*   1991. 3. 7.

수신 장관

참조 국제기구조약국장, 중동아프리카국장

제목 UNIIMOG   임무종료 (91.2.)

　　　　표제 관련 안보리문서를 별첨과 같이 송부합니다.

　　첨 부 : 상기 안보리문서 (S /22263, 22279-80, 22286).　　끝.

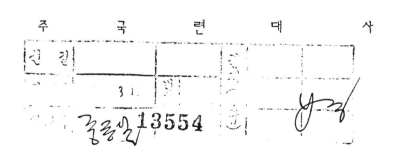

0066

UNITED NATIONS

S

Security Council

Distr.
GENERAL

S/22625
21 May 1991

ORIGINAL: ENGLISH

LETTER DATED 17 MAY 1991 FROM THE CHARGE D'AFFAIRES A.I. OF
THE PERMANENT MISSION OF THE ISLAMIC REPUBLIC OF IRAN TO THE
UNITED NATIONS ADDRESSED TO THE SECRETARY-GENERAL

Upon instructions from my Government, I have the honour to submit, for the purpose of registration, a list of further violations of the terms of the cease-fire by Iraqi forces. These violations had been reported to the United Nations Iran-Iraq Military Observer Group (UNIIMOG) at the time they had taken place. The numerical sequence of these violations follows the sequence of those previously reported and circulated as Security Council document S/22268.

3186. On 17 December 1989, during one hour, Iraqi forces fired 40 rounds from heavy machine-guns and Dush-K from Sivagaz towards Champara.

3187. On 19 December 1989, Iraqi forces fired two rounds of mortar from Sivagaz towards Champara.

3188. On 19 December 1989, a base was constructed by Iraqi forces at the geographic coordinates of NE 571-818 on the map of Garmab.

3189. On 20 December 1989, a Dush-K firing position was constructed by Iraqi forces at the geographic coordinates of ND 483-107 on the map of Kharatha.

3190. On 20 December 1989, a firing position was constructed by Iraqi forces at the geographic coordinates of ND 484-088 on the map of Kharatha.

3191. On 20 December 1989, during one hour at night, Iraqi forces fired two rounds of mortar from Sivagaz towards Champara.

3192. On 20 December 1989, at night, Iraqi forces fired 30 to 40 rounds from Dush-K from Sivagaz towards Champara.

3193. On 21 December 1989, during one hour, Iraqi forces fired about 30 rounds from Dush-K from Sivagaz towards Champara.

3194. On 22 December 1989, during one hour, Iraqi forces fired 60 to 70 rounds from Dush-K and heavy machine-guns from Sivagaz towards Champara and Aseman Bin.

91-16459 2459j (E)

/...

3195. From 22 to 26 December 1989, a bunker was improved by Iraqi forces at the geographic coordinates of NF 296-017 on the map of Sardasht.

3196. From 23 to 28 December 1989, 50 Iraqi commandos opened fire in the vicinity of Shiler Valley.

3197. On 24 December 1989, during one hour, Iraqi forces fired four rounds of mortar from Sivagaz towards north-west Shakh Eshkout and Champara.

3198. On 25 December 1989, a 25-metre-long embankment was constructed by Iraqi forces at the geographic coordinates of NC 559-958 on the map of Kharatha.

3199. On 25 December 1989, a 50-metre-long embankment was constructed by Iraqi forces at the geographic coordinates of NC 555-956 on the map of Kharatha.

3200. On 27 December 1989, a bunker was constructed by Iraqi forces at the geographic coordinates of PD 05-90 on the map of Nosud.

3201. On 27 December 1989, Iraqi forces in two instances demolished rural houses with explosive materials in the Sivagaz area.

3202. On 27 December 1989, during one hour, Iraqi forces fired 50 rounds from heavy machine-guns from Sivagaz towards the south-east of Aseman Bin.

3203. On 27 December 1989, Iraqi forces fired three rounds of mortar from Sivagaz towards the south-east of Aseman Bin.

3204. On 28 December 1989, during two hours, Iraqi forces demolished houses by explosive materials in the Sivagaz area.

3205. On 28 December 1989, at 1400 hours, one Iraqi helicopter landed on Soor Kouh height at regiment base for 15 minutes and flew away at the geographic coordinates of NR 962-693 on the map of Baneh.

3206. On 28 December 1989, two accommodation shelters were constructed by Iraqi forces at the geographic coordinates of NE 299-966 on the map of Sardasht.

3207. On 28 December 1989, five prefabricated bunkers were installed by Iraqi forces at the geographic coordinates of NF 266-014 on the map of Sardasht.

3208. On 28 December 1989, an observation post was constructed by Iraqi forces at the geographic coordinates of NE 271-989 on the map of Sardasht.

3209. On 29 December 1989, during two hours at night, Iraqi forces fired 200 rounds from Dush-K and heavy machine-guns from Sivagaz towards lower Shakh Eshkout and the opposite area.

3210. On 29 December 1989, during two hours at night, Iraqi forces fired six rounds of mortar from Sivagaz towards Aseman Bin.

/...

0068

3211. On 29 December 1989, Iraqi forces fired with mortar and heavy machine-guns in and around the geographic coordinates of NE 728-639 and NE 700-640 on the map of Baneh.

3212. On 29 December 1989, a bunker was constructed by Iraqi forces at the geographic coordinates of NE 914-397 on the map of Marivan.

3213. On 29 December 1989, a base was constructed by Iraqi forces at the geographic coordinates of NE 960-625 on the map of Nanoor.

3214. On 29 December 1989, a base was constructed by Iraqi forces at the geographic coordinates of NE 943-628 on the map of Nanoor.

3215. On 30 December 1989, during one hour, Iraqi forces fired 20 rounds from Dush-K from Sivagaz towards Champara.

3216. On 30 December 1989, a shelter was constructed by Iraqi forces at the geographic coordinates of NE 271-888 on the map of Sardasht.

3217. On 30 December 1989, a bunker was constructed by Iraqi forces at the geographic coordinates of PD 088-941 on the map of Nasoud.

3218. On 30 December 1989, a light machine-gun was deployed by Iraqi forces at the geographic coordinates of NC 554-964 on the map of Kharatha.

3219. On 30 December 1989, three RPGs-7 were deployed by Iraqi forces at the geographic coordinates of NC 559-958 on the map of Kharatha.

3220. On 31 December 1989, a communication pylon was installed by Iraqi forces at the geographic coordinates of QB 181-005 on the map of Dehloran.

3221. On 31 December 1989, a road with a length of 100 metres was constructed by Iraqi forces at the geographic coordinates of NC 546-525 on the map of Sumar.

3222. On 31 December 1989, a trench was dug by Iraqi forces at the geographic coordinates of QA 27-96 on the map of Nahr-e-Anbar.

3223. On 1 January 1990, six bunkers were constructed by Iraqi forces at the geographic coordinates of NC 77-24 on the map of Halaleh.

3224. On 2 January 1990, a guard post was constructed by Iraqi forces at the geographic coordinates of NC 619-331 on the map of Kani Sheikh.

3225. On 2 January 1990, an observation post was constructed by Iraqi forces at the geographic coordinates of PB 149-768 on the map of Mehran.

3226. On 2 January 1990, a row of barbed wire was set by Iraqi forces at the geographic coordinates of TQ 81-33 on the map of Talul.

/...

3227. On 2 January 1990, a firing position was constructed by Iraqi forces at the geographic coordinates of NC 611-327 on the map of Kani Sheikh.

3228. On 2 January 1990, a 20-metre-long trench was dug by Iraqi forces at the geographic coordinates of NC 621-334 on the map of Kani Sheikh.

3229. On 2 January 1990, two observation posts were constructed by Iraqi forces at the geographic coordinates of NC 693-265 on the map of Kani Sheikh.

3230. On 2 January 1990, Iraqi troops reinforced their forces with the strength of 20 soldiers at the geographic coordinates of ND 678-212 on the map of Ghasr-e-Shirin.

3231. On 2 January 1990, at 1130 hours, a bunker was constructed by Iraqi forces at the geographic coordinates of NE 892-312 on the map of Panjwain.

3232. On 2 January 1990, at 2225 hours, Iraqi forces reinforced their troops with the strength of 20 soldiers at the geographic coordinates of NC 678-212 on the map of Kani Sheikh.

3233. On 3 January 1990, two group bunkers were constructed by Iraqi forces at the geographic coordinates of PB 151-767 on the map of Mehran.

3234. On 4 January 1990, a bunker was constructed by Iraqi forces at the geographic coordinates of QB 703-396 on the map of West Jofeir.

3235. On 4 January 1990, at 0930 hours, Iraqi forces set up a 10-metre-long mine field at the geographic coordinates of NC 511-692 on the map of Sizdeh.

3236. On 4 January 1990, at 1530 hours, an observation post was constructed by Iraqi forces at the geographic coordinates of NB 142-802 on the map of Mehran.

3237. On 5 January 1990, two bunkers were constructed by Iraqi forces at the geographic coordinates of QA 064-987 on the map of Gotbeh Mountain.

3238. On 5 January 1990, a row of barbed wire was removed from the top of a spring by Iraqi soldiers at the geographic coordinates of NC 52-56 on the map of Sumar.

3239. On 5 January 1990, at 1230 hours, three Iranian soldiers (Alamdad Shaygan, armed, Ghadam Ali Karimi, unarmed, and Nader Kabootar Ahang, unarmed) were taken captive by Iraqi forces at the geographic coordinates of 91-32 on the map of Marivan.

3240. On 6 January 1990, at 1500 hours, a trench was dug by Iraqi forces over height 654 at the geographic coordinates of ND 692-216 on the map of Ghalmeh.

3241. On 7 January 1990, at 2300 hours, Iraqi forces replaced their frontline troops from the geographic coordinates of TP 315-566 to TP 293-581 on the map of Khorramshahr.

/...

0070

3242. On 7 January 1990, Iraqi forces began training their troops at the geographic coordinates of TP 2675-6155 and TP 2675-6100 on the map of Khorramshahr.

3243. On 8 January 1990, at 1010 hours, an observation post was constructed by Iraqi forces at the geographic coordinates of QA 60-49 on the map of Chananeh.

3244. On 8 January 1990, at 1530 hours, a trench was dug by Iraqi forces at the geographic coordinates of QA 58-45 on the map of West Jofeir.

3245. On 9 January 1990, at 1130 hours, a group bunker was constructed by Iraqi forces at the geographic coordinates of NE 97-52 on the map of Marivan.

3246. On 9 January 1990, at 1615 hours, an Iraqi helicopter was seen patrolling at the geographic coordinates of TQ 15-30 on the map of Hosseinieh.

3247. On 10 January 1990, at 1025 hours, a bunker was constructed by Iraqi forces at the geographic coordinates of NE 304-868 on the map of Sardasht.

3248. On 10 January 1990, at 1025 hours, a row of barbed wire was set up around a mine-field by Iraqi forces at the geographic coordinates of NE 304-868 on the map of Sardasht.

3249. On 10 January 1990, at 1230 hours, a 15-metre-long trench was dug by Iraqi forces at the geographic coordinates of NC 501-633 on the map of Sizdeh.

3250. On 10 January 1990, a trench was dug by Iraqi forces at the geographic coordinates of NC 78-23 on the map of Halaleh.

3251. On 10 January 1990, at 1530 hours, a bunker was constructed by Iraqi forces at the geographic coordinates of QA 401-831 on the map of Ein-Khosh.

3252. On 11 January 1990, a missile was installed over a tank by Iraqi forces at the geographic coordinates of QA 252-986 on the map of Nahr-e-Anbar.

3253. On 11 January 1990, at 1050 hours, a bunker was constructed by Iraqi forces at the geographic coordinates of ND 523-003 on the map of Kharatha.

3254. On 11 January 1990, at 1400 hours, a bunker was constructed by Iraqi forces at the geographic coordinates of NC 881-124 on the map of Halabeh.

3255. On 11 January 1990, at 1600 hours, a 15-metre-long trench was dug by Iraqi forces at the geographic coordinates of NC 532-998 on the map of Kharatha.

3256. On 11 January 1990, at 1100 hours, a 10-metre-long trench was dug by Iraqi forces at the geographic coordinates of NC 530-996 on the map of Kharatha.

/...

3257. On 11 January 1990, at 1300-1900 hours, mines were planted by Iraqi forces at the geographic coordinates of NE 780-599 on the map of Baneh.

3258. On 11 January 1990, Iraqi forces opened fire at Iranian positions at the geographic coordinates of TP 1675-9560 on the map of Nim Istgah Navad.

3259. On 12 January 1990, an Iraqi diver was observed penetrating Iranian territory at the geographic coordinates of TP 1730-9225 on the map of Nim Istgah Navad.

3260. On 12 January 1990, a sandbag bunker was constructed by Iraqi forces at the geographic coordinates of ND 705-464 on the map of Azgaleh.

3261. On 12 January 1990, a bunker was constructed and a trench was dug by Iraqi forces from the geographic coordinates of NC 921-114 on the map of Halaleh to NC 931-102 on the map of Serni.

3262. On 13 January 1990, at 1650 hours, a row of barbed wire was set up around a base by Iraqi forces at the geographic coordinates of NE 994-504 on the map of Marivan.

3263. On 13 January 1990, a row of barbed wire was set up by Iraqi forces at the geographic coordinates of ND 756-614 on the map of Azgaleh.

3264. On 13 January 1990, mines were planted by Iraqi forces at the geographic coordinates of ND 756-614 on the map of Azgaleh.

3265. On 13 January 1990, an Iraqi boat was observed patrolling at the geographic coordinates of TP 1730-9225 on the map of Nim Istgah Navad.

3266. On 13 January 1990, nine Iraqi forces penetrated the no man's land at the geographic coordinates of ND 617-223 on the map of Ghasr-e-Shirin.

3267. On 13 January 1990, nine Iraqi forces demolished an Iranian observation post on their way back at the geographic coordinates of ND 617-223 on the map of Ghasr-e-Shirin.

3268. On 13 January 1990, at 2230 hours, an inactive bunker was demolished by Iraqi forces at the geographic coordinates of ND 618-221 on the map of Ghasr-e-Shirin.

3269. On 13 January 1990, at 2230 hours, a 10-man reconnaissance patrol party approached Iranian positions at the geographic coordinates of ND 618-221 on the map of Ghasr-e-Shirin.

3270. On 13 January 1990, a group bunker was constructed by Iraqi forces at the geographic coordinates of NC 953-102 on the map of Serni.

3271. On 13 January 1990, an observation post was constructed by Iraqi forces at the geographic coordinates of PB 016-981 on the map of Saleh-Abad.

/...

3272. On 14 January 1990, at 0650 hours, an Iraqi helicopter was observed patrolling at the geographic coordinates of NC 50-95 on the map of Kharatha.

3273. On 14 January 1990, a bunker was constructed by Iraqi forces at the geographic coordinates of TP 566-194 on the map of Faw.

3274. On 14 January 1990, a bunker was constructed by Iraqi forces at the geographic coordinates of TP 568-192 on the map of Faw.

3275. On 14 January 1990, a trench was dug by Iraqi forces at the geographic coordinates of ND 478-110 on the map of Kharatha.

3276. On 14 January 1990, a 30-metre-long trench was dug by Iraqi forces at the geographic coordinates of ND 485-091 on the map of Kharatha.

3277. On 14 January 1990, an individual bunker was constructed by Iraqi forces at the geographic coordinates of ND 484-089 on the map of Kharatha.

3278. On 15 January 1990, at 0845 hours, an observation post was constructed by Iraqi forces at the geographic coordinates of PB 135-744 on the map of Mehran.

3279. On 15 January 1990, at 0845 hours, a group bunker was constructed by Iraqi forces at the geographic coordinates of PB 135-744 on the map of Mehran.

3280. On 15 January 1990, at 1000 hours, four individual bunkers were constructed by Iraqi forces at the geographic coordinates of NE 977-528 on the map of Marivan.

3281. On 15 January 1990, at 1030 hours, a bunker was constructed by Iraqi forces at the geographic coordinates of NE 89-23 on the map of Shanderi Khoaro.

3282. On 15 January 1990, at 1145 hours, an ambush bunker was constructed by Iraqi forces at the geographic coordinates of QV 869-324 on the map of Talool.

3283. On 15 January 1990, at 1225 hours, a bunker was constructed by Iraqi forces at the geographic coordinates of ND 482-083 on the map of Kharatha.

3284. On 15 January 1990, at 1255 hours, a bunker was constructed by Iraqi forces at the geographic coordinates of ND 483-083 on the map of Kharatha.

3285. On 15 January 1990, at 1400 hours, a trench was dug by Iraqi forces at the geographic coordinates of NE 901-399 on the map of Panjwain.

3286. On 15 January 1990, at 1645 hours, a trench was dug by Iraqi forces at the geographic coordinates of ND 482-083 on the map of Kharatha.

/...

3287. On 15 January 1990, a bunker was constructed by Iraqi forces at the geographic coordinates of ND 802-628 on the map of Azgalah.

3288. On 15 January 1990, Iraqi forces reinforced their troops by 25 soldiers at the geographic coordinates of NE 384-805 on the map of Gak.

3289. On 15 January 1990, Iraqi forces reinforced their troops by 25 soldiers at the geographic coordinates of NE 384-814 on the map of Gak.

3290. On 15 January 1990, a group bunker was constructed by Iraqi forces at the geographic coordinates of ND 805-632 on the map of Azgaleh.

3291. On 15 January 1990, two observation posts were constructed by Iraqi forces at the geographic coordinates of NC 932-096 on the map of Serni.

3292. On 15 January 1990, a row of barbed wire was set by Iraqi forces from the geographic coordinates of ND 808-635 on the map of Azgaleh.

3293. On 15 January 1990, a row of barbed wire was set by Iraqi forces from the geographic coordinates of ND 812-714 to the geographic coordinates of ND 819-691 on the map of Azgaleh.

3294. On 15 January 1990, blockades were set up by Iraqi forces in the no man's land at the geographic coordinates of TP 178-765 on the map of Khorramshahr.

3295. On 15 January 1990, a row of barbed wire was set up in the no man's land by Iraqi forces at the geographic coordinates of TP 177-749 on the map of Khorramshahr.

3296. On 16 January 1990, a communication antenna was installed by Iraqi forces at the geographic coordinates of NF 289-022 on the map of Sardasht.

3297. On 16 January 1990, at 1100-1600 hours, a 60-metre-long trench was dug by Iraqi forces at the geographic coordinates of PE 011-532 on the map of Marivan.

3298. On 16 January 1990, at 1300 hours, a bunker was constructed by Iraqi forces at the geographic coordinates of NC 894-148 on the map of Halaleh.

3299. On 17 January 1990, at 1430 hours, a bunker was constructed by Iraqi forces at the geographic coordinates of NC 953-069 on the map of Saleh-Abad.

3300. On 17 January 1990, a 4-metre-long trench was dug by Iraqi forces at the geographic coordinates of NC 563-493 on the map of Sumar.

3301. On 17 January 1990, an observation post was repaired by Iraqi forces at the geographic coordinates of NC 563-493 on the map of Sumar.

3302. On 18 January 1990, a firing position was constructed by Iraqi forces at the geographic coordinates of NC 595-424 on the map of Sumar.

/...

0074

3303. On 18 January 1990, a flag was installed by Iraqi forces at the geographic coordinates of TP 2250-7325 on the map of Khorramshahr.

3304. On 18 January 1990, five bunkers were constructed by Iraqi forces at the geographic coordinates of TP 227-731 on the map of Khorramshahr.

3305. On 18 January 1990, at 1000 hours, a flag was installed by Iraqi forces at the geographic coordinates of TP 229-733 on the map of Khorramshahr.

3306. On 18 January 1990, at 1100 hours, a flag was installed in the no man's land by Iraqi forces at the geographic coordinates of TP 211-744 on the map of Khorramshahr.

3307. On 18 January 1990, at 1330 hours, a trench was dug by Iraqi forces at the geographic coordinates of NC 486-083 on the map of Kharatha.

3308. On 19 January 1990, two resting bunkers were constructed by Iraqi forces at the geographic coordinates of ND 765-596 on the map of Azgaleh.

3309. On 19 January 1990, at 1030 hours, a row of barbed wire 3 kilometres long was set up by three groups of five Iraqi soldiers from the geographic coordinates of ND 580-232 to ND 610-232 on the map of Ghasr-e-Shirin.

3310. On 19 January 1990, at 1500-1600 hours, a 400-metre-barbed wire was set up by Iraqi forces from the geographic coordinates of ND 677-210 to ND 673-210 on the map of Ghasr-e-Shirin.

3311. On 19 January 1990, at 1640 hours, a group bunker was constructed by Iraqi forces at the geographic coordinates of PE 011-532 on the map of Marivan.

3312. On 19 January 1990, at 1645 hours, an observation post was constructed by Iraqi forces at the geographic coordinates of NE 281-884 on the map of Sardasht.

3313. On 19 January 1990, at 1740 hours, a group bunker was constructed by Iraqi forces at the geographic coordinates of PE 009-531 on the map of Marivan.

3314. On 19 January 1990, at 1745 hours, Iraqi forces fired five rounds of machine-guns at an Iranian boat at the geographic coordinates of TP 280-697 on the map of Khorramshahr.

3315. On 19 January 1990, at 1830 hours, an Iraqi plane was seen patrolling towards the north-west of Sardasht at the geographic coordinates of NE 30-86 on the map of Sardasht.

3316. On 20 January 1990, a flag was set up by Iraqi forces at the geographic coordinates of NC 61-22 on the map of Kani Sheikh.

/...

3317. On 20 January 1990, Iraqi forces reinforced their troops at the geographic coordinates of NC 61-22 on the map of Kani Sheikh.

3318. On 20 January 1990, Iraqi forces reinforced their troops at the geographic coordinates of NC 61-32 on the map of Kani Sheikh.

3319. On 20 January 1990, a bunker was constructed by Iraqi forces at the geographic coordinates of QB 232-005 on the map of Dehloran.

3320. On 20 January 1990, a group bunker was constructed by Iraqi forces at the geographic coordinates of QA 384-876 on the map of Ein Khosh.

3321. On 20 January 1990, at 0950 hours, an observation post was constructed by Iraqi forces at the geographic coordinates of NC 555-945 on the map of Kharatha.

3322. On 20 January 1990, at 1010 hours, Iraqi forces demolished houses in Badelan village at the geographic coordinates of NE 996-537 on the map of Marivan.

3323. On 20 January 1990, at 1030 hours, an Iraqi helicopter was observed shuttling between the geographic coordinates of NC 64-27 and the geographic coordinates of NC 67-27 on the map of Kani Sheikh.

3324. On 20 January 1990, at 1030 hours, a flag was installed over one firing position by Iraqi forces at the geographic coordinates of TP 181-758 on the map of Khorramshahr.

3325. On 20 January 1990, at 1330 hours, two mortar positions were constructed by Iraqi forces at the geographic coordinates of PE 011-532 on the map of Marivan.

3326. On 20 January 1990, at 1330 hours, two mortar positions were constructed by Iraqi forces at the geographic coordinates of PE 008-532 on the map of Marivan.

3327. On 20 January 1990, at 1330 hours, two mortars were deployed by Iraqi forces at the geographic coordinates of PE 008-532 on the map of Marivan.

3328. On 20 January 1990, at 1330 hours, Iraqi forces were reinforced by the strength of a company at the geographic coordinates of PE 0021-5245 on the map of Marivan.

3329. On 20 January 1990, at 1330 hours, two individual bunkers were constructed by Iraqi forces at the geographic coordinates of PE 011-532 on the map of Marivan.

3330. On 20 January 1990, at 1600 hours, two mortars were deployed by Iraqi forces at the geographic coordinates of PE 011-532 on the map of Marivan.

/...

0076

3331. On 20 January 1990, at 1645 hours, a bunker was constructed by Iraqi forces at the geographic coordinates of QB 232-005 on the map of Dehloran.

3332. On 20 January 1990, at 2315 hours, two warning shots were fired by Iraqi forces at the geographic coordinates of NC 54-97 on the map of Kharatha.

3333. On 20 January 1990, at 2315 hours, seven illuminating bullets were fired by Iraqi forces at the geographic coordinates of PB 067-838 and PB 090-820 on the map of Saleh-Abad.

3334. On 20 January 1990, rows of barbed wire were set up by Iraqi forces at the geographic coordinates of ND 667-218, 668-217, 496-185, 642-214, 638-219, 628-226 and 616-227 on the map of Ghasr-e-Shirin.

3335. On 20 January 1990, a row of barbed wire was set up by Iraqi forces at the geographic coordinates of ND 486-137 on the map of Kharatha.

3336. On 20 January 1990, a row of barbed wire was set up by Iraqi forces from the geographic coordinates of ND 494-185 on the map of Ghasr-e-Shirin to the geographic coordinates of ND 494-168 on the map of Kharatha.

3337. On 21 January 1990, engineering activities were carried out by Iraqi forces at the geographic coordinates of TP 4405-5045 on the map of Abadan.

3338. On 21 January 1990, mines were planted by Iraqi forces at the geographic coordinates of TP 4390-5075 on the map of Abadan.

3339. On 21 January 1990, a row of barbed wire was set up by Iraqi forces at the geographic coordinates of TP 4390-5075 on the map of Abadan.

3340. On 21 January 1990, a blockade was set up by Iraqi forces at the geographic coordinates of TP 4390-5075 on the map of Abadan.

3341. On 21 January 1990, a bunker was constructed by Iraqi forces at the geographic coordinates of QA 53-55 on the map of Yebis.

3342. On 21 January 1990, a bath was constructed by Iraqi forces at the geographic coordinates of QA 53-55 on the map of Yebis.

3343. On 21 January 1990, at 0910 hours, a Dush-K was deployed by Iraqi forces at the geographic coordinates of PE 011-532 on the map of Marivan and after being tested, it was carried to PE 994-537 on the map of Marivan.

3344. On 21 January 1990, at 1030 hours, a trench was dug by Iraqi forces at the geographic coordinates of NE 917-389 on the map of Marivan.

3345. On 21 January 1990, a row of barbed wire was set up by Iraqi forces at the geographic coordinates of ND 695-309 on the map of Ghalameh.

/...

3346. On 21 January 1990, at 1030 hours, a row of barbed wire was set up by Iraqi forces at the geographic coordinates of ND 593-239 on the map of Ghasr-e-Shirin.

3347. On 21 January 1990, at 1600 hours, a row of barbed wire was set up by the Iraqi forces at the geographic coordinates of ND 637-215 on the map of Ghasr-e-Shirin.

3348. On 21 January 1990, at 1600 hours, a row of barbed wire was set up by Iraqi forces at the geographic coordinates of ND 662-212 on the map of Ghasr-e-Shirin.

3349. On 21 January 1990, Iraqi forces reinforced their troops at the geographic coordinates of PB 14-54 on the map of Mehran.

3350. On 21 January 1990, Iraqi forces reinforced their troops at the geographic coordinates of PB 14-50 on the map of Mehran.

3351. On 21 January 1990, at 1300 hours, a bunker was constructed by Iraqi forces at the geographic coordinates of QA 348-908 on the map of Nahr-e-Anbar.

3352. On 21 January 1990, a row of barbed wire was set up by Iraqi forces at the geographic coordinates of QA 73-22 on the map of Chazzabeh.

3353. On 21 January 1990, at 1930 hours, an Iraqi helicopter was observed patrolling at the geographic coordinates of TQ 68-28 on the map of Talool.

3354. On 22 January 1990, at 0915 hours, two Iraqi helicopters were observed patrolling at the geographic coordinates of NB 97-63 on the map of Mehran.

3355. On 22 January 1990, at 1515 hours, a long pole was installed for setting barbed wire by the Iraqi forces at the geographic coordinates of ND 49-16 on the map of Kharatha.

3356. On 22 January 1990, at 1515 hours, a row of barbed wire was set up by Iraqi forces from the geographic coordinates of ND 522-228 to ND 524-229 on the map of Ghasr-e-Shirin.

3357. On 22 January 1990, a row of barbed wire was set up by Iraqi forces at the geographic coordinates of ND 713-502 on the map of Azgaleh.

3358. On 22 January 1990, a row of barbed wire was set up by Iraqi forces at the geographic coordinates of ND 715-513 on the map of Azgaleh.

3359. On 22 January 1990, at 1700 hours, Iraqi forces reinforced their troops with the strength of 30 soldiers at the geographic coordinates of NC 555-969 on the map of Kharatha.

/...

0078

3360. On 22 January 1990, at 0830 hours, Iraqi forces were observed moving in and out of a Chinese ship at the geographic coordinates of TP 2800-6590 on the map of Khorramshahr.

3361. On 22 January 1990, a 50-metre-long trench was dug by Iraqi forces at the geographic coordinates of NC 51-59 on the map of Sumar.

3362. On 23 January 1990, at 1000 hours, an observation post was constructed by Iraqi forces at the geographic coordinates of PB 141-762 on the map of Mehran.

3363. On 23 January 1990, at 1000 hours, a row of barbed wire was constructed by Iraqi forces from the geographic coordinates of ND 702-217 to ND 298-218 on the map of Ghalameh.

3364. On 23 January 1990, at 1330 hours, a telephone pole was installed by Iraqi forces at the geographic coordinates of ND 689-239 on the map of Ghasr-e-Shirin.

3365. On 23 January 1990, a row of barbed wire was installed by Iraqi forces from the geographic coordinates of ND 702-217 to ND 698-218 on the map of Ghalameh.

3366. On 24 January 1990, at 1100 hours, a firing position was constructed by Iraqi forces at the geographic coordinates of NC 929-120 on the map of Halaleh.

3367. On 24 January 1990, at 1320 hours, four pipes were unloaded for construction of a bridge by Iraqi forces at the geographic coordinates of NC 558-952 on the map of Kharatha.

3368. On 24 January 1990, at 1600 hours, an observation post was constructed by Iraqi forces at the geographic coordinates of NC 558-952 on the map of Sizdeh.

3369. On 24 January 1990, at 1630 hours, a bunker was constructed by Iraqi forces at the geographic coordinates of NC 557-962 on the map of Kharatha.

3370. On 24 January 1990, a row of barbed wire was set up by Iraqi forces at the geographic coordinates of ND 53-00 on the map of Kharatha.

3371. On 24 January 1990, a row of concertina barbed wire was set up by Iraqi forces at the geographic coordinates of PB 147-795 on the map of Mehran.

3372. On 24 January 1990, a row of 200-metre-long barbed wire was set up by Iraqi forces at the geographic coordinates of ND 531-008 on the map of Kharatha.

3373. On 24 January 1990, a firing bunker was constructed by Iraqi forces at the geographic coordinates of NC 545-996 on the map of Kharatha.

/...

3374. On 24 January 1990, a firing bunker was constructed by Iraqi forces at the geographic coordinates of NC 563-966 on the map of Kharatha.

It would be highly appreciated if this letter were circulated as a document of the Security Council.

(Signed) Mohammad Javad ZARIF
Ambassador
Deputy Permanent Representative

0080

UNITED
NATIONS

S

Security Council

Distr.
GENERAL

S/22637
24 May 1991

ORIGINAL: ENGLISH

LETTER DATED 23 MAY 1991 FROM THE SECRETARY-GENERAL ADDRESSED TO THE PRESIDENT OF THE SECURITY COUNCIL

Following my last report on the United Nations Iran-Iraq Military Observer Group, dated 26 February 1991 (S/22263), and the follow-up exchange of letters, dated 28 February 1991 (S/22279 and S/22280), I have continued my efforts towards the full implementation of Security Council resolution 598 (1987) of 20 July 1987.

In this context I wish to inform you that, in pursuance of the mandate entrusted to me by operative paragraph 7 of resolution 598 (1987), and in consultation with the Government of the Islamic Republic of Iran, I have asked former Under-Secretary-General Abdulrahim A. Farah to lead a team of experts who will make an exploratory visit to Iran towards the end of May.

Under paragraph 7 of resolution 598 (1987) the Security Council "recognizes the magnitude of the damage inflicted during the conflict and the need for reconstruction efforts, with appropriate international assistance, once the conflict is ended and, in this regard, requests the Secretary-General to assign a team of experts to study the question of reconstruction and to report to the Security Council."

It is anticipated that the team will remain in the area for an initial period of two to three weeks.

In the implementation of my mandate under paragraph 7 of resolution 598 (1987) I am, of course, also in contact with the Government of Iraq.

I should be grateful, Mr. President, if you would bring this matter to the attention of the members of the Security Council.

(Signed) Javier PEREZ de CUELLAR

91-17077   2381h (E)

0081

UNITED NATIONS

 Security Council

S

Distr.
GENERAL

S/22637
24 May 1991

ORIGINAL: ENGLISH

LETTER DATED 23 MAY 1991 FROM THE SECRETARY-GENERAL ADDRESSED
TO THE PRESIDENT OF THE SECURITY COUNCIL

Following my last report on the United Nations Iran-Iraq Military Observer Group, dated 26 February 1991 (S/22263), and the follow-up exchange of letters, dated 28 February 1991 (S/22279 and S/22280), I have continued my efforts towards the full implementation of Security Council resolution 598 (1987) of 20 July 1987.

In this context I wish to inform you that, in pursuance of the mandate entrusted to me by operative paragraph 7 of resolution 598 (1987), and in consultation with the Government of the Islamic Republic of Iran, I have asked former Under-Secretary-General Abdulrahim A. Farah to lead a team of experts who will make an exploratory visit to Iran towards the end of May.

Under paragraph 7 of resolution 598 (1987) the Security Council "recognizes the magnitude of the damage inflicted during the conflict and the need for reconstruction efforts, with appropriate international assistance, once the conflict is ended and, in this regard, requests the Secretary-General to assign a team of experts to study the question of reconstruction and to report to the Security Council."

It is anticipated that the team will remain in the area for an initial period of two to three weeks.

In the implementation of my mandate under paragraph 7 of resolution 598 (1987) I am, of course, also in contact with the Government of Iraq.

I should be grateful, Mr. President, if you would bring this matter to the attention of the members of the Security Council.

(Signed) Javier PEREZ de CUELLAR

91-17077 2381h (E)

0082

외 무 부

종 별 :

번 호 : UNW-1386   일 시 : 91 0528 1800

수 신 : 장 관(국연,중동일,기정)

발 신 : 주 유엔 대사

제 목 : 이란-이락 휴전 후속조치(유엔동향)

    1. 케야르 사무총장은 87년 이란-이락 휴전 후소조치관련 안보리결의 (598 호) 에 의거 전후 복구문제조사단 (단장: A.FARAH 전 사무차장)을 5월말경 우선 이란에 파견계획임을 5.23.자로 안보리의장에게 통보하여 왔음. (S/22637)

    2. 사무국측에 문의한바에 의하면, 동 조사단일행 (11 명)은 명 5.29 이란 향발 예정이라고 하며 2-3 주 동국에 체류한다고함.

    3. 상기 안보리결의에 의거 사무총장은 이락측과도 본건 조사단 파견문제를 협의중인 것으로 알려짐.끝

    (대사 노창희-국장)

국기국   1차보   중아국   정문국   안기부

주 국 련 대 표 부

주국련20313- **424**   1991 . 5 . 30 .

수신 장관

참조   국제기구조약국장, 중동아프리카국장

제목   이란-이락휴전 이행(안보리)

표제관련 안보리문서를 별첨과 같이 송부합니다.

첨 부 : 상기문서. 끝.

주   국   련   대

선 결				결재(고·답)		
접수일시	1991. 3					
처리	31046					

0084

**UNITED
NATIONS**

Security Council

Distr.
GENERAL

S/22280
28 Februar

ORIGINAL: E

LETTER DATED 28 FEBRUARY 1991 FROM THE PRESIDENT OF THE
SECURITY COUNCIL ADDRESSED TO THE SECRETARY-GENERAL

I have the honour to inform you that your letter dated 26 February 1991
(S/22279) has been brought to the attention of the members of the Security Council,
who considered the matter in consultations held on 27 February 1991.

The members of the Security Council agree with the observations and
recommendations contained in your report dated 26 February 1991 on the United
Nations Iran-Iraq Military Observer Group (UNIIMOG) for the period
28 January 1991-25 February 1991 (S/22263) and concur with the arrangements
proposed in the report and the letter.

The members of the Security Council express their gratitude to you personally
and their appreciation to the members of UNIIMOG on the successful completion of
their important task.

(Signed)   Simbarashe Simbanenduku MUMBENGEGWI
President of the Security Council

91-06614 2198e (E)

0085

Security Council

Distr.
GENERAL

S/22279
28 February 1991

ORIGINAL: ENGLISH

LETTER DATED 26 FEBRUARY 1991 FROM THE SECRETARY-GENERAL
ADDRESSED TO THE PRESIDENT OF THE SECURITY COUNCIL

I indicated in paragraph 26 of my report to the Security Council of
29 January 1991 (S/22148) that after the implementation of paragraphs 1 and 2 of
Security Council resolution 598 (1987) had been completed, I intended to begin
contacts with the parties on the manner in which I would pursue the other tasks
entrusted to me by that resolution.

These tasks envisage a political role by the Secretary-General. In
particular, some of the remaining paragraphs of the resolution require me to
explore certain issues in consultation with the Islamic Republic of Iran and Iraq.
Another paragraph requests me to examine, in consultation with those two countries
as well as with other States of the region, measures to enhance the security and
stability of the region.

Such tasks would, in my opinion, be facilitated by the establishment in the
region and particularly in Iran and Iraq of civilian offices, which with
appropriate Headquarters support would help me to carry on my work and to have a
better assessment of developments in the area. I believe this is advisable not
only in the context of that resolution but also in the context of the recent
developments in the area.

As you know, for the reasons stated in the Observations Section of my report
of 26 February 1991 on UNIIMOG (S/22263), I have decided to recommend that the
mission's mandate not be extended. At the same time, the continued presence of a
few military observers attached to those civilian offices which would be located in
Iran and Iraq would allow the Organization to respond promptly to any request from
the parties to investigate matters for which military expertise would be required.
I trust that this arrangement will meet with the concurrence of the members of the
Council.

I should be grateful, Mr. President, if you would bring this matter to the
attention of the members of the Security Council.

(Signed) Javier PEREZ de CUELLAR

91-06608 2103i (E)

0086

UNITED
NATIONS

S

 Security Council

Distr.
GENERAL

S/22263
26 February 1991

ORIGINAL: ENGLISH

REPORT OF THE SECRETARY-GENERAL ON THE UNITED NATIONS
IRAN-IRAQ MILITARY OBSERVER GROUP

(for the period 28 January 1991-25 February 1991)

Introduction

1.   On 31 January 1991, the Security Council unanimously adopted resolution
685 (1991), in which it decided to renew the mandate of the United Nations
Iran-Iraq Military Observer Group (UNIIMOG) until 28 February 1991 and requested
the Secretary-General to submit, during February 1991, a report on his further
consultations with the parties about the future of UNIIMOG, together with his
recommendations on that matter.

2.   Accordingly, the present report covers the period from 28 January 1991 to
25 February 1991 and is intended to provide the Security Council with an account of
the manner in which UNIIMOG has carried out the mandate entrusted to it during that
period.

3.   It will be recalled that in paragraphs 23 and 24 of my report of
29 January 1991 (S/22148), I recommended that the mandate of UNIIMOG should be
extended for a period of one month in order to enable the Group to continue to
assist the parties in implementing the agreements reached at their technical
meeting on 6 January 1991.

4.   As a result of the hostilities in the Persian Gulf region, UNIIMOG has
continued to operate in the Iranian part of its area only, but has maintained
regular contact with the Iraqi authorities through meetings on the border.

Composition, command and deployment

5.   The command of UNIIMOG has been exercised by the Acting Chief Military
Observer, Brigadier-General S. Anam Khan (Bangladesh). On the Iranian side
Colonel H. Purola (Finland) has continued as the Acting Assistant Chief Military
Observer and on the Iraqi side, now temporarily relocated in Cyprus,
Colonel P. Grabner remained Acting Assistant Chief Military Observer.

91-06151 2325b (E)

/...

0087

6.   At the beginning of February, 22 military observers from the Iraqi side whose tours of duty were due to expire during that month returned to their home countries. On 4 February the balance of the observers who had come from Iraq were temporarily relocated to Cyprus where a skeleton headquarters was established and the observers remained on standby for an eventual return to Iraq.

7.   On 25 February 1991 the strength of UNIIMOG, including those temporarily relocated in Cyprus, was as follows:

United Nations military observers

Austria (Acting Assistant Chief Military Observer)	1
Bangladesh (Acting Chief Military Observer)	1
Canada	4
Denmark	3
Finland (including Acting Assistant Chief Military Observer)	9
Hungary	15
India	11
Ireland	1
Italy	9
Malaysia	10
New Zealand	1
Norway	1
Poland	1
Sweden	7
Turkey	1
Uruguay	9
Yugoslavia	11
Zambia	1
	96

Military Police Unit

Ireland	16

Medical Section

Austria	2
Total (military personnel)	114

8.   The observers who departed in February were not replaced as normal rotations were suspended for this mandate period. Of the Member States contributing military observers to UNIIMOG, Argentina, Australia, Ghana, Indonesia, Kenya, Nigeria and Senegal remain unrepresented at present.

/...

0088

9.   The Twin Otter aircraft which had been leased commercially was returned to
Canada on 31 January. The Jetstream aircraft, provided as a voluntary contribution
by the Government of Switzerland and now located at Teheran, continues to provide
air support to UNIIMOG.

Operations

10.   The general situation along the internationally recognized boundaries has
remained very calm during the mandate period. Because of the temporary relocation
of the UNIIMOG-Baghdad observers in January, UNIIMOG continued to monitor the
internationally recognized boundaries from the Iranian side only. Ninety-five
patrols, including those investigating disputed positions, were conducted.

11.   The parties continued to implement the agreement reached during their
technical meeting at Teheran on 6 January 1991 (see S/22148, paras. 14-17) and
UNIIMOG provided assistance in this process. On 20 February 1991, UNIIMOG was able
to confirm that the last of the disputed positions along the internationally
recognized boundaries had been withdrawn. Thus was completed the withdrawal of all
forces to the internationally recognized boundaries as described in the Treaty
concerning the State Frontier and Neighbourly Relations between Iran and Iraq 1/ of
13 June 1975 and its protocols and annexes. This enabled UNIIMOG to complete
verification and confirmation of the withdrawal in accordance with its mandate
deriving from paragraphs 1 and 2 of Security Council resolution 598 (1987).

12.   UNIIMOG also coordinated the establishment of joint survey teams whose task is
to survey areas where there is doubt as to the exact location of the
internationally recognized boundaries because of the difficult nature of the
terrain and to determine the location of any positions in these areas.

13.   In accordance with the 6 January agreement the two parties continued their
cooperation with regard to the exchange of information on unmarked minefields.

14.   During the present mandate period, the Iraqi authorities informed UNIIMOG that
the area of separation envisaged by the 6 January agreement had been established on
the Iraqi side of the internationally recognized boundaries. However, due to the
temporary suspension of its operations in Iraq, UNIIMOG has not been able to
confirm this on the ground. The Iranian authorities also informed UNIIMOG that
they had begun to establish the area of separation on their side of the border, but
they did not request UNIIMOG's assistance during this process. Because of the
restrictions on its freedom of movement referred to in paragraph 17 below, UNIIMOG
is not in a position to confirm progress on the Iranian side either.

15.   As a result of developments in the area, the second technical meeting which
the parties had agreed to hold at Baghdad on 28 or 29 January 1991 did not take
place. The two parties have been considering possible alternative venues and dates
for such a meeting.

/...

0089

Relations with the parties

16.   Throughout the present mandate period UNIIMOG's Command Group has travelled from Teheran to the border to hold weekly meetings in Iraqi territory with the Iraqi Higher Committee for Coordination, thereby maintaining contact with the Iraqi authorities at an appropriately high level.   UNIIMOG military observers from the Iranian side have also had regular meetings with Iraqi liaison personnel on the border.

17.   On the Iranian side, UNIIMOG's operations continued as during the previous mandate period with the assistance of the authorities of the Islamic Republic of Iran.   However, UNIIMOG patrols faced increased restrictions on their freedom of movement, which the Iranian authorities said they had to impose as a result of the situation in the region.   These restrictions, which were protested by UNIIMOG, effectively confined the Group's functions in the vicinity of the border to the investigation of the few remaining disputed positions and to border meetings with the Iraqi authorities.

Observations

18.   It is with considerable satisfaction that I report to the Security Council the completion at last of the withdrawal of the two sides' forces to the internationally recognized boundaries as described in the 1975 Treaty. Paragraphs 1 and 2 of resolution 598 (1987) can now be considered implemented. There remains the question of establishing an area of separation and an area of limitation of armaments, which were put forward in my report of 7 August 1988 (S/20093) as arrangements that, pending negotiation of a comprehensive settlement, could help to reduce tension and build confidence between the parties.   Both sides have informed UNIIMOG that, in accordance with the agreement that they concluded on 6 January 1991, they have begun – and, in the case of Iraq, have completed – the establishment of the area of separation.   It had been hoped that UNIIMOG would play a part in monitoring and confirming this process.   But for the reasons described in paragraph 14 above this has not proved possible.

19.   In recent consultations with their Permanent Representatives in New York, both parties were informed of my conclusion that, in the circumstances described in the present report, the time has come to consider paragraphs 1 and 2 of resolution 598 (1987) as implemented and to move forward by converting the United Nations presence in their two countries into one, which will more appropriately assist me in carrying out the remaining tasks entrusted to the Secretary-General by other operative paragraphs in that resolution.   Those tasks are essentially political rather than military and I therefore informed the parties of my intention to recommend to the Security Council that UNIIMOG should be replaced by small civilian offices.   The offices at Baghdad and Teheran would, however, include two or three military observers who would be available to investigate and help resolve any difficulties of a military nature that might arise on the border.   Subject to the Security Council's agreement, the number of military observers could be increased if circumstances were judged to warrant this.

/...

0090

20. I accordingly recommend that the Security Council take no action to extend the mandate of UNIIMOG, which will come to an end on 28 February 1991. I will shortly address to the President of the Security Council a letter setting out in more detail my intention to establish small civilian offices in the area. Meanwhile, remaining UNIIMOG personnel in the Islamic Republic of Iran, together with those from the Iraqi side who were temporarily relocated to Cyprus, will be withdrawn as soon as possible, except for those who will be required for the proposed civilian offices.

21. It remains only to pay homage to those who have contributed to UNIIMOG's successes during the last two and a half years. First, I express my gratitude to the Governments of the Islamic Republic of Iran and Iraq for the cooperation they extended to UNIIMOG and for the friendly relations that, in spite of the difficulties that occurred from time to time, their representatives always maintained with UNIIMOG's personnel. Secondly, I thank the 26 Governments that contributed military personnel to UNIIMOG for their support of this important peace-keeping operation and especially for their patience during recent months, when it was impossible to plan more than a few weeks ahead. Finally, I pay tribute to the men and women, military and civilian, international and locally recruited, who have carried out their tasks with remarkable dedication and professionalism and who have made such an outstanding contribution to the termination of a long and cruel war.

Notes

1/ United Nations, Treaty Series, vol. 1017, No. 14903.

0091

UNITED NATIONS

Security Council

Distr.
GENERAL

S/22286
1 March 1991

ORIGINAL: ENGLISH

LETTER DATED 28 FEBRUARY 1991 FROM THE PERMANENT REPRESENTATIVE
OF THE ISLAMIC REPUBLIC OF IRAN TO THE UNITED NATIONS ADDRESSED
TO THE SECRETARY-GENERAL

Upon instructions from my Government, I have the honour to enclose herewith the text of a letter by His Excellency Dr. Ali Akbar Velayati, Minister for Foreign Affairs of the Islamic Republic of Iran addressed to Your Excellency.

I will be grateful if this letter and its annex were circulated as a document of the Security Council.

(Signed) Kamal KHARRAZI
Ambassador
Permanent Representative

91-06707 2169h (E)

/...

0092

Annex

Letter dated 28 February 1991 from the Minister for Foreign Affairs
of the Islamic Republic of Iran addressed to the Secretary-General

I have received with pleasure and appreciation Your Excellency's report on the United Nations Iran-Iraq Military Observer Group (UNIIMOG) contained in S/22263, which confirms the completion of withdrawal of forces to the internationally recognized boundaries as determined by the Treaty Concerning the State Frontier and Neighborly Relations between Iran and Iraq of 13 June 1975 and its protocols and annexes. As we come to a new phase of United Nations involvement in the process of implementation of Security Council Resolution 598 (1987), I wish to express the thanks and appreciation of my government to Your Excellency, your colleagues, UNIIMOG personnel and contributing countries for the tireless efforts aimed at the implementation of Paragraphs 1 and 2 of Security Council Resolution 598.

My Government also welcomes your decision contained in the above-mentioned report to take practical measures for the implementation of other provisions of resolution 598. The Islamic Republic of Iran has consistently emphasized the necessity of implementation of all provisions of this mandatory resolution of the Security Council as necessary steps to restore peace and stability in the Persian Gulf region. As Your Excellency has indicated in your report of 23 November 1990 (S/21690), I reiterated in our meeting of 26 September 1990 that "paragraphs 1 to 4 were being implemented, while paragraphs 6, 7, and 8, which conferred a mandate on the Secretary-General, still were not implemented." We are confident that through the practical measures that Your Excellency intends to take, the full implementation of these remaining provisions of SCR 598 will be achieved.

With the military stage of the unfortunate crisis in the Persian Gulf coming to a close, the task of ensuring peace and stability in the volatile Persian Gulf region is, as it should have been, the center of international attention. This regrettable crisis has illustrated the wisdom of Security Council Resolution 598 whose implementation in its entirety would have most probably spared our region from yet another aggression. Therefore, the absolute imperative of the full implementation of this mandatory resolution without further delay is vital today.

The realization of lasting security and cooperation arrangements in the Persian Gulf area, as envisaged in paragraph 8 of SCR 598, is only possible through the active participation of the states of the Persian Gulf without foreign presence or intervention.

The Islamic Republic of Iran firmly believes that this process should be undertaken under the auspices of the Secretary-General of the United Nations and with his active contribution. This would ensure compatibility with United Nations principles and objectives, and would provide the necessary global dimension. The

0093

/...

Islamic Republic of Iran reiterates its readiness to cooperate fully with Your Excellency in this vitally important undertaking.

Ali Akbar Velayati
Minister for Foreign Affairs of
the Islamic Republic of Iran

0094

외 무 부

종 별 :

번 호 : UNW-3879 　　　　　　　일 시 : 91 1114 1830

수 신 : 장 관(중동일,연일,기정)

발 신 : 주 유엔대사

제 목 : 걸프사태(안보리)

1. 이란-이락 사태해결에 관한 87년 안보리결의 598호 (7항)에의거 이란-이락전 당시이란의 피해 상황조사를 위해 금월초 A.FARAH 전유엔사무차장이 이란을 방문한 바,이락은 동방문에 관한 입장을 밝히는 하기 요지의 A.HUSSEIN 외상의 케야르 유엔사무총장앞 서한을 안보리문서로 배포하였음. (S/23213)

가. 이란이 이락의 걸프전으로 인한 곤경을 틈타 파괴분자들을 이락에 침부시킴으로써 양국간 휴전을 위반하였으며 수천명의 이락 전쟁포로 미송환 상태

나. 휴전 잠정이행을 제외하고 상기 안보리 결의 이행이 중단된 상황에서, 동결의의 특정조항 적용은 결의를 자기에게 유리하게 조각내려는 이란의 기도에 이용당하는 결과 초래

2. 한편 이락은 지난 10.26-11.2.간 쿠웨이트 항공기 이락 영공침범, 양국간 비무장지대(DMZ)에서 이락군 납치, 해상위협사례가 발생하였다고 주장하면서 쿠웨이트측 위반방지 및 억류 이락인 석방을 위한 조치를 취해줄것을 사무총장에게 요청하여옴(S/23209) 끝.

(대사 노창희-국장)

중아국　　　장관　　　차관　　　1차보　　　국기국　　　외정실　　　분석관　　　청와대　　　안기부

PAGE 1 　　　　　　　　　　　　　　　　　　　　　　　　　91.11.15　　10:00 WH

UNITED NATIONS

S

Security Council

Distr.
GENERAL

S/23246
26 November 1991

ORIGINAL: ENGLISH

REPORT OF THE SECRETARY-GENERAL ON THE IMPLEMENTATION
OF SECURITY COUNCIL RESOLUTION 598 (1987)

1.   In paragraph 9 of Security Council resolution 598 (1987) of 20 July 1987,
the Secretary-General was requested to keep the Council informed on the
implementation of that resolution. In the past, I have, among other ways,
responded formally to this request in my successive reports 1/ on the
activities of the United Nations Iran-Iraq Military Observer Group (UNIIMOG),
which operated from August 1988 until February 1991 in implementation of
paragraph 2 of resolution 598 (1987) and subsequent resolutions. 2/ The last
such report, covering developments until 25 February 1991, was issued on
26 February 1991, shortly after which the mandate of UNIIMOG came to an end on
28 February 1991. The present report is intended to provide the Security
Council with an account of my efforts in the implementation of resolution
598 (1987) since 1 March 1991.

2.   With the completion of the implementation of paragraphs 1 and 2 of
resolution 598 (1987), the remaining tasks entrusted to the Secretary-General
by that resolution are of a political nature. In my reports to the Security
Council of 29 January 1991 and 26 February 1991, as well as in my letter
addressed to the President of the Council, dated 26 February 1991, 3/ I
expressed the view that such tasks would be facilitated by a continuing United
Nations presence in the area, in particular by the establishment of civilian
offices, which with appropriate Headquarters support, would help me to carry
on my work and to have a better assessment of developments in the region. As
expressed in the letter from the President of the Council addressed to me on
26 February 1991, 4/ the members of the Security Council agreed with this
approach and concurred with the arrangements I had proposed.

3.   Accordingly, as a first step, I proceeded, with the agreement of the
respective host Governments, with the setting up of a United Nations Office of
the Secretary-General in the Islamic Republic of Iran (UNOSGI) and one in Iraq
(also referred to as UNOSGI). This initiative had from the outset the full
support of the two Governments which willingly provided all necessary
assistance and facilities. The legal status, privileges and immunities of the
Office at Tehran was the subject of an exchange of letters between the United
Nations and the Government of the Islamic Republic of Iran, concluded on

91-45890 3465a (E)   /...

0096

3 June 1991. An identical exchange of letters between the United Nations and the Government of Iraq with regard to the status, privileges and immunities of the Office at Baghdad was concluded on 27 June 1991.

4.   In my letter of 26 February 1991 3/ I had also indicated to the Council that the continued presence of a few military observers attached to the civilian offices that would be located in the Islamic Republic of Iran and Iraq would allow the United Nations to respond promptly to any request from the parties to investigate matters for which military expertise would be required. Six military observers, provided by six different contributing States, have thus continuously been attached to UNOSGI, three of them based at Baghdad and the other three at Tehran.

5.   As reported to the Council in January and February 1991, the completion of the withdrawal of all forces to the internationally recognized boundaries as described in the Treaty concerning the State Frontier and Friendly Relations between Iran and Iraq of 13 June 1975 5/ and its protocols and annexes took place on the basis of an agreement reached by a technical meeting of Iranian and Iraqi military experts at Tehran on 6 January 1991. This agreement was also intended to govern the modalities for the strengthening of the cease-fire, including, among other things, the establishment of an area of separation of 1 kilometre on each side of the boundary. During the period covered by the present report, both parties have continued to declare to UNOSGI representatives that the 6 January agreement remains valid. Although the United Nations has never had the opportunity to verify completely the actual existence of an area of separation along the entire border, it has been the policy of UNOSGI to encourage the implementation of and continued respect for the 6 January agreement. The good offices of UNOSGI, including those of its expert military staff, have been available to the parties in order to help to solve whatever difficulties they might face in this respect. UNOSGI has also been mindful of the need to foster whatever confidence-building measures might be considered possible in order to ensure quiet and stability in the border area.

6.   Unfortunately, the border area between the Islamic Republic of Iran and Iraq has not been without problems during the past nine months. The long lists of allegations of cease-fire violations submitted by both parties and circulated, at their requests, as Security Council documents bear witness to this. Iraq was the first to request investigations of such alleged incidents by the military observers attached to UNOSGI. Eventually the Islamic Republic of Iran also resorted to this procedure. Most of the alleged violations related to incidents of a temporary nature, however, which do not lend themselves to ex post facto investigations. Up to the date of the present report, UNOSGI at Baghdad was able to respond to 37 Iraqi requests for investigation. In 31 of those 37 instances the investigations carried out by the military observers led to the conclusion that the alleged violations should be confirmed. UNOSGI at Tehran carried out 11 investigations at the request of the Iranian authorities, as a result of which it confirmed eight cease-fire violations. Each report confirming a cease-fire violation by a party was brought to the attention of the authorities of that party for their

/...

consideration. While the number of alleged violations has at certain times been alarmingly high, it should be noted that it has remained considerably lower than during the period before the completion of the withdrawal. The vast majority of allegations related to incidents not involving any firing, but to unauthorized presence on the border or in the area of separation.

7. The situation of relative unrest persisting along the border between the Islamic Republic of Iran and Iraq constitutes a vivid reminder that lasting peace between those two countries is still elusive. The continuing violations of the cease-fire requirement of paragraph 1 of resolution 598 (1987) emphasize the need for all concerned to address in earnest all remaining paragraphs of that resolution and strive without any delay for their full and faithful implementation. As the two parties themselves have repeatedly recognized, resolution 598 (1987) as a whole constitutes a comprehensive peace plan containing all necessary means and assurances for the establishment of genuinely peaceful relations between them. Both the Islamic Republic of Iran and Iraq, as well as other States in the region and the international community as a whole can only stand to gain if the peace-making efforts in the context of resolution 598 (1987) can proceed now without any further delay.

8. The responsibility for the implementation of resolution 598 (1987) obviously rests in the first place with the Governments of the Islamic Republic of Iran and Iraq themselves. One of the areas in which this is most clearly the case is that of the release and repatriation of the prisoners-of-war. Completion of the implementation of paragraph 3 of resolution 598 (1987), which does nothing more than restate clear obligations of the parties under international law, is, more than any other provisions of that resolution, long overdue. I have therefore seen it as my duty to use every possible opportunity to urge the parties to resume their efforts in cooperation with the International Committee of the Red Cross (ICRC) and bring the repatriation process to the desired ending. My Personal Representative, Ambassador Jan Eliasson, has also raised the matter on a number of occasions. The suffering of thousands of human beings during such a protracted period must now come to an end by the strict implementation of the Third Geneva Convention of 12 August 1949. 6/ I hope that the positive step taken by the Islamic Republic of Iran in recent days by releasing 421 prisoners will indeed signal the beginning of the last phase of the implementation of paragraph 3 of resolution 598 (1987).

9. While, as said above, fulfilment of the requirements of resolution 598 (1987) is in the first instance in the hands of the parties themselves and depends to a large extent on their initiatives, the Security Council has given some specific mandates to the Secretary-General. It is obvious that it is to those mandates that I felt I needed to give special attention and ensure that they are on the right track. During the period under review, I have intensified all efforts in this regard. The results of those efforts with regard to those mandates are the subject of the present and additional reports to the Council.

/...

10. In pursuance of the mandate entrusted to me by paragraph 7 of resolution 598 (1987), I asked, in May 1991, former Under-Secretary-General Abdulrahim A. Farah to lead a team of experts to make an exploratory visit to the Islamic Republic of Iran to obtain initial information and data on the nature and extent of damage sustained by that country as a result of the conflict between it and Iraq and on the status of its reconstruction efforts. The Security Council was informed of this initiative by my letter of 23 May 1991. 7/ Mr. Farah and his team visited the Islamic Republic of Iran from 31 May until 21 June where they performed their tasks with the necessary cooperation of the relevant authorities of the Islamic Republic of Iran and the logistic support of UNOSGI at Tehran. The preliminary report of the mission containing details of the reported damage to the Islamic Republic of Iran's infrastructure, the nature and status of the country's reconstruction efforts and the team's observations on the damaged sites and installations inspected was submitted to the Security Council on 31 July 1991. 8/ As indicated in my letter submitting the preliminary report to the Council, Mr. Farah and his team returned to the Islamic Republic of Iran on 5 November 1991 to complete their work. The final report of this mission will be submitted to the Security Council as soon as it is completed.

11. Paragraph 7 of resolution 598 (1987) applies, of course, equally to Iraq. In my letter to the President of the Security Council of 23 May 1991 7/ I indicated that, in the implementation of my mandate under paragraph 7, I was also in contact with the Government of Iraq. It was obvious that the task of a mission of experts such as the one dispatched to the Islamic Republic of Iran would in Iraq be complicated by the additional damage this country suffered during the more recent armed conflict and subsequent events. On the assumption, however, that the Iraqi authorities might have records of damage sustained during the conflict between that country and the Islamic Republic of Iran, as well as of subsequent reconstruction efforts, a study by a team of experts as envisaged by paragraph 7 of resolution 598 (1987) might be possible. The Iraqi Government has been made aware that a team of experts could be made available whenever the Government wishes to proceed with this matter. The views of the Iraqi Government have been most recently expressed in a letter from the Minister for Foreign Affairs, Mr. Ahmad Hussein, addressed to me on 12 November 1991 and, at the request of Iraq, circulated as a Security Council document. 9/

12. The re-establishment of peaceful relations between the Islamic Republic of Iran and Iraq and security and stability in the Persian Gulf region as a whole are closely interrelated. The Security Council, in paragraph 8 of resolution 598 (1987), requested the Secretary-General to examine, in consultation with the Islamic Republic of Iran and Iraq and other States of the region, measures to enhance the security and stability of the region. Subsequent developments in the region have reconfirmed the original wisdom underlying that provision but may also have made the task more complex. Paragraph 8 is essentially forward-looking and the action it envisages constitutes a fitting and essential complement to the comprehensive peace plan formulated in resolution 598 (1987). It would be unrealistic to assume that

/...

faithful implementation of the spirit and letter of that paragraph can be obtained in the very short term. However, considering the possible tragedies against which the region may be permanently safeguarded as a result of a conscientious and painstaking peace-making effort on a regional scale, the time that will need to be invested in this will certainly be worth while.

13. It is essential that a beginning is made, however limited in scope, taking into account what is possible at this stage. A process of consultations with States of the region has started. I myself have had useful exchanges of views with government leaders of the region, upon which further efforts can be built. My visit to the Islamic Republic of Iran and to Saudi Arabia in the beginning of September 1991, at the invitation of both Governments, provided an opportunity for me to review with the two heads of State as well as their foreign ministers possible efforts to enhance friendly relations among all States in the region. At Jeddah I also had an informative exchange of views with the ministers for foreign affairs of the members of the Gulf Cooperation Council (GCC), as well as with the Secretary-General of that Council. Further discussions took place during the visit of the head of State of Bahrain as well as of the foreign ministers of the States of the region to United Nations Headquarters on the occasion of the General Assembly. The consultations thus far have not gone beyond preliminary exchanges of views and information. All participants have expressed interest, however, in continuing this process. I have been encouraged by some of the initiatives and efforts of cooperation within the region that have been brought to my attention. At the same time, I have expressed to my interlocutors my views on the assistance that the United Nations, and in particular its Secretary-General, might be able to provide in a process of gradually developing friendly relations among all States of the Persian Gulf region with due respect for the principle of sovereignty and other principles of international law and the Charter of the United Nations. The idea of a declaration including basic principles of good-neighbourly relations and other practical arrangements may, perhaps, be pursued under United Nations auspices.

Concluding remarks

14. Resolution 598 (1987) was and remains the basic framework through which the Security Council decided to reach a peaceful settlement of the conflict between the Islamic Republic of Iran and Iraq and to which, for that purpose, the parties have been and remain committed. Following the important boost that was given to the implementation process of the resolution as a result of the completion of the withdrawal of all forces, further efforts seem to have run into difficulties mainly because of the complex situation prevailing in the area following the hostilities in Iraq and Kuwait. It also appears that in recent months different views may have developed between the parties on how to proceed with resolution 598 (1987). Nevertheless it is clearly incumbent upon all concerned to move on with the implementation process. In the circumstances which now prevail in the area, fulfilment of the objectives envisaged by resolution 598 (1987) have become all the more important because

/...

0100

they constitute a cornerstone of the re-establishment of security and friendly relations in the region. It is therefore essential that we reach as soon as possible that stage of the implementation process that is concerned with the future and the construction of genuine peace. This concern has guided my efforts in the context of the implementation of resolution 598 (1987) and I hope that they will indeed have brought us much closer to the real peace-making stage of the settlement process.

15. It is essential, in my view, to pursue, in cooperation with the Security Council, the parties and all concerned, sustained efforts towards the full implementation of resolution 598 (1987) as a comprehensive peace plan. The presence of Offices of the Secretary-General in the Islamic Republic of Iran and Iraq, and perhaps in another interested country in the region, will be a continuing requirement. They greatly assist in providing a better understanding of regional interests and expectations and support for the peace-making role of the Secretary-General. Furthermore those Offices have been an example of how, at the appropriate time, a peace-keeping operation can be phased out and replaced by other effective means to assist in maintaining favourable peace-making conditions.

Notes

1/   S/20093 of 7 August 1988, S/20242 of 25 October 1988, S/20442 of 2 February 1989, S/20862 of 22 September 1989, S/21200 of 22 March 1989, S/21803 of 21 September 1990, S/21960 of 23 November 1990, S/22148 of 28 January 1991, and S/22263 of 26 February 1991.

2/   Security Council resolutions 619 (1988) of 9 August 1988, 631 (1989) of 8 February 1989, 642 (1989) of 29 September 1989, 651 (1990) of 29 March 1990, 671 (1990) of 27 September 1990, 676 (1990) of 28 November 1990 and 685 (1991) of 31 January 1991.

3/   S/22279.

4/   S/22280.

5/   United Nations, Treaty Series, vol. 1017, No. 14903.

6/   Ibid., vol. 75, No. 972.

7/   S/22637.

8/   S/22863.

9/   S/23213.

10/   Official Records of the General Assembly, Forty-sixth Session, Supplement No. 1 (A/46/1).

0101

외 무 부

종   별 :

번   호 : UNW-4160　　　　　　　　　　일   시 : 91 1202 2300

수   신 : 장 관(연일,중동이,기정)

발   신 : 주 유엔대사

제   목 : 안보리(이란,이락사태)

　　87년 이란, 이락 사태의 평화적 해결을 위한 안보리 결의 598 호 이행문제와 관련 케야르 유엔사무총장은 92.2월 유엔 이란.이락군 감시단(UNIIMOG) 임무종료 이후 그간의 동이행노력에 관한 보고서를 안보리에 제출해온 바, 동 보고서요지는 아래와 같음.(S/23246)

　　1.UNIIMOG 해체후 유엔사무총장 이란.이락 사무소 (UNOSGI) 가 설치된바 , 계속유지필요: 양 사무소에 군옵서버도 3명씩 배치

　　2.양국 국경지역에서 휴전위반 사례 계속 발생하고 있으나, 총격사태가 아닌 접경 또는 격리지대 무단침범이 대부분

　　3.국제적십자 위원회(ICRC)와 협조하에 양측의 전쟁포로 송환문제(동결의 3항)종결노력 촉구

　　4.이란.이락전에 의한 양측 피해 및 복구문제(동결의 7항):이란에는 A.FARAH 전사무차장파견(91.5월및 11월), 이락측에는 본건관련 협조용의표명(이락 반대입장)

　　5.지역안보 및 안정강화 대책(동결의8항):91.9월 사무총장의 중동순방,지역주요인사와의 금차 총회시 접촉기회에 예비적의견 및 정보교환(선린관계 원칙및 기타실질조 치에 관한 선언을 유엔주관하에 추진하는 방안도 가능)

　　6.걸프전, 상기 안보리결의 이행문제에 관련양측 이견으로 동 결의이행이 난관에부딪히고 있으나 동결의는 표제사태의 평화적 해결을 위한 기본틀로 여전히 유효.끝

　　(대사 노창희-국장)

<table>
<tr><td>국기국</td><td>장관</td><td>1차보</td><td>중아국</td><td>외정실</td><td>분석관</td><td>청와대</td><td>안기부</td></tr>
</table>

PAGE 1　　　　　　　　　　　　　　　　　　　　　91.12.03　　13:45 WH

외신 1과 통제관

0102

외 무 부

종 별 :

번 호 : UNW-4285   일 시 : 91 1210 2400

수 신 : 장관(연이,중동이,기정)

발 신 : 주유엔대사

제 목 : 안보리(이란,이락 휴전후속조치)

이란,이락 사태해결을 위한 87년 7월 안보리 결의(598호) 6항은 유엔사무총장에게이란,이락전 책임조사를 위한 중립적기구 설치문제를 검토토록 요청하고 있는바, 케야르 유엔사무총장은 이와관련 아래요지의 보고서를 안보리에 제출하여옴. (S/23273)

가.추진경과

1)지난 3년간 이란,이락과 본건 협의할 기회가 수차있었으며, 91.8월 양국에게 의견 제시요청하여 91.8월-9월 회신접수

2) 독립적인 전문가들과 별도협의, 관련 유엔문서 참조

나.이란,이락전 책임문제

1)이락의 개전책임: 80.9.22 이란에 대한 공격은 국제법 위반행위(JUS COGENS 인 무력사용 금지위반)

2)동 전쟁중 국제인도법 위반 행위 다수발생: 화학무기 사용, 민간인 지역공격,전쟁포로 학대등

다.결론

1)본건(6항) 계속추진은 무익

2)양국간 평화관계, 전지역의 평화안보 추구가 긴요한문제: 국제법 준수에 기초한 선린관계

첨부:사무총장 보고서: UNW(F)-1006 끝

(대사 노창희-국장)

국기국	장관	차관	1차보	중아국	외정실	분석관	청와대	안기부

UNW(FD-1006 11210 2400
총 304

**UNITED
NATIONS**

S

Security Council

Distr.
GENERAL

S/23273 .
9 December 1991

ORIGINAL: ENGLISH

FURTHER REPORT OF THE SECRETARY-GENERAL ON THE IMPLEMENTATION
OF SECURITY COUNCIL RESOLUTION 598 (1987)

1.   In paragraph 6 of resolution 598 (1987), adopted on 20 July 1987, the
Security Council requested the Secretary-General to explore, in consultation
with Iran and Iraq, the question of entrusting an impartial body with
inquiring into responsibility for the conflict and to report to the Security
Council as soon as possible in implementation of that request.

2.   In the course of the negotiations during the past three years, I have had
several opportunities to consult with the parties on paragraph 6. While those
consultations enabled me to get a certain understanding of the divergent views
held by both sides, they did not come to a stage where it was felt possible to
submit a meaningful report to the Security Council.

3.   Following the completion of the implementation of paragraphs 1 and 2 of
resolution 598 (1987), a renewed effort to fulfil the requirements of all
other provisions of that resolution was called for in order to ensure the
re-establishment of peace between Iran and Iraq in accordance with the
comprehensive peace plan provided for by resolution 598 (1987) and thus to
contribute substantially to the current requirements of peace and security in
the region. Many of the steps I took in order to intensify all efforts in
implementation of resolution 598 (1987) have been outlined in my report to the
Security Council on that subject (S/23246).

4.   For the purpose of paragraph 6, although elements of the positions of the
two parties on that paragraph were known to me, I requested the Governments of
Iran and Iraq, in identical letters dated 14 August 1991, to provide me in the
most comprehensive manner possible with their detailed views on the
subject-matter of that paragraph. At the same time, in order to obtain the
fullest understanding of the subject-matter, I decided to consult separately
some independent experts. On the basis of the replies provided by the parties
dated 26 August 1991 for Iraq and 15 September 1991 for Iran, the
consultations held with the parties in the past, all relevant information
contained in the official documents of the United Nations since the beginning
of the conflict and the information obtained from independent experts, I would

91-48293 2915d (E)   #UNW-4285   3—/   /...
전부

S/23273
English
Page 2

now like, in the light of paragraph 6 of Security Council resolution
598 (1987), to report to the Security Council.

5.   It is evident that the war between Iran and Iraq, which was going to be
waged for so many years, was started in contravention of international law,
and violations of international law give rise to responsibility for the
conflict, which question is at the centre of paragraph 6.   The area of
violation of international law that should be of specific concern to the
international community in the context of paragraph 6 is the illegal use of
force and the disregard for the territorial integrity of a Member State.

      There were of course in the course of the conflict massive violations of
various rules of international humanitarian law.

6.   The Iraqi reply to my letter of 14 August 1991 is not a substantial one;
therefore I am bound to rely on explanations given by Iraq earlier.   That
these explanations do not appear sufficient or acceptable to the international
community is a fact.   Accordingly, the outstanding event under the violations
referred to in paragraph 5 above is the attack of 22 September 1980 against
Iran, which cannot be justified under the Charter of the United Nations, any
recognized rules and principles of international law or any principles of
international morality and entails the responsibility for the conflict.

7.   Even if before the outbreak of the conflict there had been some
encroachment by Iran on Iraqi territory, such encroachment did not justify
Iraq's aggression against Iran - which was followed by Iraq's continuous
occupation of Iranian territory during the conflict - in violation of the
prohibition of the use of force, which is regarded as one of the rules of
jus cogens.

8.   Of the numerous violations of humanitarian law which were committed
during the Iran-Iraq war, many have already been documented by the United
Nations and by the International Committee of the Red Cross.   At the request
of one or both of the parties I have for instance on several occasions
dispatched expert missions to the theatre of war to investigate such
violations as the use of chemical weapons, attacks on civilian areas and the
bad treatment of prisoners of war.   The results of those investigations were
all reported to the Security Council and issued as Security Council
documents.   They referred, sadly enough, to the existence of evidence that
serious violations of humanitarian law had indeed taken place.   On one
occasion I had to note with deep regret the experts' conclusion that "chemical
weapons ha[d] been used against Iranian civilians in an area adjacent to an
urban centre lacking any protection against that kind of attack" (S/20134,
annex).   The Council expressed its dismay on the matter and its condemnation
in resolution 620 (1988), adopted on 26 August 1988.

9.   The events of the Iran-Iraq war, which for many years provided the news
headlines in the world media, are well known to the international community.
The position of the parties, expressed on many occasions in official
documents, are also public knowledge.   In my opinion it would not seem to

3-2

/...

0105

S/23273
English
Page 3

serve any useful purpose to pursue paragraph 6 of resolution 598 (1987). In
the interest of peace and in line with the implementation of resolution
598 (1987) as a comprehensive peace plan, it is now imperative to move on with
the settlement process. It is the careful construction of peaceful relations
between the parties and of peace and security in the whole region that
urgently needs to be tended to. The Security Council, in 1987, already
offered the right approach, including in paragraph 8 of that resolution,
which, if it had been timely implemented, might have spared the region from
the further tragedy that followed. A system of good-neighbourly relations
based on the respect of international law, as was envisaged by the Security
Council, is essential in securing peace and stability in the region in the
future. It is to be hoped that the Council's call will be heeded.

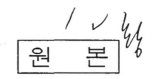

외 무 부

종 별 :

번 호 : UNW-4521　　　　　　　　　　일 시 : 91 1230 1800

수 신 : 장 관(연일,중동이,기정)

발 신 : 주 유엔 대사

제 목 : 이란.이락 휴전 후속조치(안보리)

　　　연: UNW-4285

　　　표제 사무총장 보고서 (S/23273) 가 이락의 개전책임을 명시하고 있는 것과 관련,
이락은 자국책임을 부인하는 한편 총장을 비난하는 요지의 12.13 자 외무부 대변인
성명및 12.22.자 A.HUSSEIN 외무장관의 안보리의장앞 서한을 안보리 문서로
배포하였음. (S/23311)

　　　첨부:이락 안보리문서: UNW(F)-1089 끝

　　　(대사 노창희-국장)

국기국　　1차보　　중아국　　외정실　　분석관　　청와대　　안기부

PAGE 1　　　　　　　　　　　　　　　　　　　　91.12.31　　10:38 WG

　　　　　　　　　　　　　　　　　　　　　　　외신 1과 통제관

　　　　　　　　　　　　　　　　　　　　　　　　0107

P.12

UNW(FI)-1089 11230 180
총 444

Annex

Letter dated 22 December 1991 from the Minister for Foreign Affairs of Iraq addressed to the President of the Security Council

I have the honour to refer to Security Council document S/23273 of 9 December 1991, which contains the further report of the Secretary-General on the implementation of Security Council resolution 598 (1987), concerning settlement of the Iraq-Iran conflict. In that report, the Secretary-General addressed paragraph 6 of the aforementioned resolution.

On this occasion, I wish to add the following remarks to the statement made by the official spokesman for Iraq's Ministry of Foreign Affairs on 13 December 1991, a copy of which is enclosed with this letter. Palpable and authenticated evidence demonstrates that Iran began to shell Iraqi cities and villages in July 1980 and that the Iranian armed forces intensified that shelling on 4 September 1980 when they brought 175-millimetre artillery to bear against the Iraqi cities of Khanaqin, Mandali, Zurbatiyah and Naft Khaneh. The Iranian air force also conducted military operations against Iraq, producing clashes in which aircraft were shot down and ships were sunk and destroyed in the approaches to the Shatt al-Arab. All these incidents occurred before 22 September 1980, in addition to a long series of attacks, threats and violations of Iraq's sovereignty, territorial integrity and internal security committed under the terms of a plan - openly declared by the leaders of the Iranian regime - to take control of Iraq and subject it to Iran's authority. It was as a result of all these operations that Iraq responded, exercising thereby its legitimate right to self-defence. Iraq informed the United Nations and a number of international organizations of these facts and documented them on many occasions. The way the Secretary-General's report belittles the significance of such attacks, violations and threats against the sovereignty and security of a State Member of the United Nations, and the openly hostile intentions underlying such actions, is incompatible with the principles of the United Nations and its obligations to Member States. Neither is it in any way compatible with the manner in which many other international conflicts have been interpreted.

It is also a fact that, as soon as the Security Council intervened in the dispute by adopting its first resolution on that subject (resolution 479 (1980) of 28 September 1980), Iraq announced its acceptance of the resolution and its readiness immediately to declare an unconditional cease-fire. As is well known, Iran rejected the resolution, just as it rejected all the subsequent resolutions adopted by the Security Council, namely resolutions 514 (1982), 522 (1982), 540 (1983), 582 (1986) and 588 (1986), whereas Iraq accepted them all as soon as they were adopted. The report of the Secretary-General ignores this essential aspect, which has a direct bearing on the tasks and role of the United Nations in the maintenance of peace and security. Neither is it any secret that Iran refused to agree to Security Council resolution 598 (1987), which was accepted by Iraq immediately

UNW-4521
첨부

/...

4-1

0108

after its adoption. Iran continued to reject the resolution for almost an entire year, accepting it only after having suffered a crushing military defeat.

Both before and after the outbreak of armed conflict with Iran, Iraq adhered to a principled position of asserting the primacy of good-neighbourly relations, non-intervention in internal affairs and respect for sovereignty. After the outbreak of armed conflict, it also strove to ensure that the dispute was resolved by means of a comprehensive, lasting, just and honourable peace settlement in accordance with the provisions of the Charter of the United Nations and of international law. This consistent position has been documented both in the United Nations and in other international organizations and agencies. Iran, however, adopted a diametrically opposite position. The Iranian Government refused to halt the conflict on the basis of these legitimate provisions, rejected the Security Council's authority to settle the conflict, insisted on continuing its war of aggression and set conditions which were incompatible with the principles of the Charter and of international law. It is a fact that, for the period from the Security Council's adoption of resolution 479 (1980) on 28 September 1980 until Iran's acceptance of resolution 598 (1987) on 19 July 1988, it is Iran alone which bears full international responsibility for the continuation of the war against Iraq and for all the consequences of such responsibility.

I request that you have this letter and its enclosure circulated as an official document of the Security Council.

(Signed) Ahmed HUSSEIN
Minister for Foreign Affairs

/...

4-2

0109

S/23311
English
Page 4

Enclosure

Statement by an official spokesman for the Ministry of Foreign Affairs

On 9 December 1991, the Secretary-General of the United Nations published a further report on the implementation of Security Council resolution 598 (1987), concerning settlement of the Iraq-Iran conflict. The report addresses paragraph 6 of the aforementioned resolution, under which the Secretary-General is required to explore, in consultation with Iran and Iraq, the question of entrusting an impartial body with inquiring into responsibility for the conflict and to report to the Security Council.

Since the Secretary-General's report contains judgements which he has pronounced in his personal capacity, the report is entirely devoid of any legal value and reflects only the personal opinion of Mr. Javier Pérez de Cuéllar. Mr. Pérez de Cuéllar's conduct and behaviour have become evident to all following his adoption of various positions designed to placate the Iranian regime with a view to promoting suspicious deals with that regime on behalf of Western interests, and particularly those of the United States.

Evidence of this fact is provided by the manner in which the report was published. On 26 November 1991, the Secretary-General published a report on Security Council resolution 598 (1987) without addressing paragraph 6, causing astonishment in United Nations diplomatic circles at the time.

A few days after the publication of this report, the Secretary-General issued a separate report on paragraph 6. The date of its publication was clearly linked to the deal made by Mr. Javier Pérez de Cuéllar with the Iranian regime for the release of American hostages in Lebanon, because the report was issued following the release of the last United States hostage on 4 December 1991.

The deal was concluded without regard for those principles of international law and probity which are supposed to be observed when addressing such a highly important issue as the facts of the Iraq-Iran conflict.

Contrary to the observations made in this tendentious report, Iraq has demonstrated - by adducing historical facts and legal arguments based on the provisions of the Charter of the United Nations and of international law - that it was the Iranian regime which initiated the aggression against Iraq by all the means at its disposal and which insisted on continuing the war. For a period of eight years, it rejected all the Security Council resolutions which called for a halt to the war, including resolution 598 (1987), which was accepted by the Iranian regime only after it had suffered a crushing military defeat. These facts, which have an essential bearing on the subject, were deliberately ignored in Mr. Pérez de Cuéllar's report.

/...

4-3

0110

Perhaps the only positive aspect of Mr. Pérez de Cuéllar's report is its correct conclusion that there is no point in pursuing this paragraph. It is a historical fact that the paragraph was originally inserted in resolution 598 (1987) in order to serve as a device and a cover for bargaining with the Iranian regime to restore ties between that regime and the United States. The Iranian side's response to the Secretary-General's statements provides clear evidence of that fact: the Iranian regime quickly took advantage of the cover both for the hostage deal concluded with the United States through Pérez de Cuéllar and for the recently published reports confirming its receipt of weapons from the Zionist entity with the approval of the Reagan and Bush Administrations.

Historical facts cannot be concealed by shady deals arranged under the cover of the United Nations and its agencies by their officials. This report provides further evidence of the Organization's loss of credibility as it is harnessed by the United States and its allies to the service of those countries' political and intelligence interests.

4-4

0111

제1차관보 주한 이란대사 면담록

1. 일 시 : 92.1.15. 15:00-15:45

2. 배 석
   ○ 우리측 : 주복룡 중동1과 사무관
   ○ 이란측 : Moshirvaziri 참사관

3. 내 용
   ○ 신임 인사차 예방, 아래 요지 언급
   - 양국관계에 있어 경제분야에서의 협력은 만족할만하나 정무,문화
     분야에서는 좀더 협력이 증진 되었으면함.
     이를 위해 외무부 고위관리가 이란을 방문해 주었으면 좋겠음.
     특히 Broujerdi 차관은 제1차관보의 이란방문을 기대하고 있는바
     시기등을 정해주면 정식 초청장을 보내겠음.

   - 이란.이라크전 휴전 결의안인 UN 안보리 결의안 598호 제6항의
     이행과 관련, 전쟁도발 책임이 이라크에 있음을 UN이 결정한바
     이에따라 이라크가 성실한 배상을 이행토록 하는데 대하여 한국
     정부가 지지해 줄것을 요청 (동건은 벨라야티 장관의 장관님앞
     멧시지로서 장관님 예방시 요청 예정이었으나 여의치 못했던바
     차관보에 요청하게 되었으며 장관님께도 필히 전달해 줄것을
     요청)

   - ██████████ 이 이란에서 구속된것과 관련, 즉각
     테헤란에 연락, 동인이 석방되는데(1.13)협조했음. 한국에서 출국
     정지중인 이란인 카제루니안 문제의 조속 해결을 위해 외무부가
     협조하여 주기바람.

   - BCCI 은행 파산과 관련, 주한 이란 대사관도 약 50만불이 동 은행에
     예치중임. 곧 회계년도가 끝나가는 상황에서 재정적으로 어려움이
     많은바, 동건의 조속한 해결을 위해 외무부가 협조하여 주기 바람.끝.

0112

EXCELLENCY,

AS YOU HAVE BEEN INFORMED , THAT SECRETARY-GENERAL OF THE UNITED NATIONS, IN IMPLEMENTATION OF PARAGRAPH 6 OF SECURITY ...991 ,, ...THE ATTACK OF 22 SEPTEMBER 1980 AGAINST IRAN, WHICH CANNOT BE JUSTIFIED UNDER THE CHARTER OF THE UNITED NATIONS, ANY RECOGNIZED RULES AND PRINCIPLES OF INTERNATIONAL LAW OR ANY PRINCIPLES OF INTERNATIONAL MORALITY AND ENTAILS RESPONSIBILITY FOR THE CONFLICT. EVEN IF BEFORE THE OUTBREAK OF THE CONFLICT THERE HAD BEEN SOME ENCROACHMENT BY IRAN ON IRAQI TERRITORY, SUCH ENCROACHMENT DID NOT JUSTIFY IRAQ'S AGGRESSION AGAINST IRAN-WHICH WAS FOLLOWED BY IRAQ'S CONTINUOUS OCCUPATION OF IRANIAN TERRITORY DURING THE CONFLICT -IN VIOLATION OF THE PROHIBITION OF THE USE OF FORCE; WHICH IS REGARDED AS ONE OF THE RULES OF JUS COGENS.

IN CONTINUATION, HE STRESSES IN THE SAME REPORT THAT ,, ON ONE OCCASION I HAD TO NOTE WITH DEEP REGRET THE EXPERTS' CONCLUSION THAT CHEMICAL WEAPONS HAD BEEN USED AGAINST IRANIAN CIVILIANS IN AN AREA ADJACENT TO AN URBAN CENTER LACKING ANY PROTECTION AGAINST THAT KIND OF ATTACK.''

IT SHOULD BE RECALLED THAT PARAGRAPH 6 OF SECURITY COUNCIL RESOLUTION 598 MANDATED THE SECRETARY-GENERAL TO INQUIRE INTO THE RESPONSIBILITY FOR THE CONFLICT. HOWEVER, THE IMPLEMENTATION OF THIS IMPORTANT PROVISION OF RESOLUTION 598 WAS REGRETTABLY DELAYED BECAUSE OF IRAQ'S DESTRUCTION OF TACTICS. YET, NOTWITHSTANDING SUCH IRAQI POLICIES AND IN ACCORDANCE WITH PRINCIPLES AND OBJECTIVES ENSHRINED IN ITS CHARTER, THE UNITED NATIONS SHOULD HAVE ADOPTED THE NECESSARY POSITION IN T.SC. TODAY, IT IS EVIDENT THAT HAD THE UNITED NATIONS DISCHARGED ITS RESPONSIBILITIES, IT COULD HAVE PREVENTED NOT ONLY THE MASSIVE HUMAN AND MATERIAL DAMAGE BORNE BY IRAN BUT ALSO THE SECOND AGGRESSION BY IRAQ AGAINST ANOTHER NEIGHBOR, KUWAIT, THUS SPARING THE PERSIAN GULF REGION FROM SO MUCH DAMAGE AND DESTRUCTION.

THE REPORTS OF THE REPRESENTATIVE OF THE UNITED NATIONS SECRETARY-GENERAL, ... IRAN, CONTAINED IN SECURITY COUNCIL DOCUMENTS ... REFLECT ONLY A SMALL PORTION OF THE EXTENSIVE ... BY THE WAR WHICH COULD BE MEASURED ... THE EXTENT OF THE HUMAN AND MATERIAL DAMAGES SUFFERED BY ... AND THEIR MIND - BOGGLING MAGNITUDE ARE PROBABLY THE ONLY DIFFERENCE BETWEEN THE TWO AGGRESSIONS WAGED BY IRA... DURING A DECADE. ONLY CONSISTENT AND EQUAL TREATMENT OF THESE TWO SIMILAR CASES OF AGGRESSION CAN TRULY PRECLUDE THEIR RECURRENCE 0113 ... TOWARDS THIS END WILL BE MUCH APPRECIATED.

THE TEXT OF RESOLUTION 598 (1987) ADOPTED UNANIMOUSLY
BY THE SECURITY COUNCIL AT ITS 2750TH MEETING ON
20 JULY 1987.

QUOTE

" THE SECURITY COUNCIL,
" REAFFIRMING ITS RESOLUTION 582 (1986),
" DEEPLY CONCERNED THAT, DESPITE ITS CALLS FOR A CEASE-FIRE, THE
CONFLICT BETWEEN IRAN AND IRAQ CONTINUES UNABATED, WITH FURTHER
HEAVY LOSS OF HUMAN LIFE AND MATERIAL DESTRUCTION,
" DEPLORING THE INITIATION AND CONTINUATION OF THE CONFLICT,
" DEPLORING ALSO THE BOMBING OF PURELY CIVILIAN POPULATION
CENTRES, ATTACKS ON NEUTRAL SHIPPING OR CIVILIAN AIRCRAFT, THE
VIOLATION OF INTERNATIONAL HUMANITARIAN LAW AND OTHER LAWS OF
ARMED CONFLICT, AND, IN PARTICULAR, THE USE OF CHEMICAL WEAPONS
CONTRARY TO OBLIGATIONS UNDER THE 1925 GENEVA PROTOCOL,
" DEEPLY CONCERNED THAT FURTHER ESCALATION AND WIDENING OF THE
CONFLICT MAY TAKE PLACE,
" DETERMINED TO BRING TO AN END ALL MILITARY ACTIONS BETWEEN IRAN
AND IRAQ,
" CONVINCED THAT A COMPREHENSIVE, JUST, HONOURABLE AND DURABLE
SETTLEMENT SHOULD BE ACHIEVED BETWEEN IRAN AND IRAQ,
" RECALLING THE PROVISIONS OF THE CHARTER OF THE UNITED NATIONS,
AND IN PARTICULAR THE OBLIGATION OF ALL MEMBER STATES TO SETTLE
THEIR INTERNATIONAL DISPUTES BY PEACEFUL MEANS IN SUCH A MANNER
THAT INTERNATIONAL PEACE AND SECURITY AND JUSTICE ARE NOT
ENDANGERED,
" DETERMINING THAT THERE EXISTS A BREACH OF THE PEACE AS REGARDS
THE CONFLICT BETWEEN IRAN AND IRAQ,
" ACTING UNDER ARTICLES 39 AND 40 OF THE CHARTER OF TNE UNITED
NATIONS,
" 1. DEMANDS THAT, AS A FIRST STEP TOWARDS A NEGOTIATED
SETTLEMENT, IRAN AND IRAQ OBSERVE AN IMMEDIATE CEASE-FIRE,
DISCONTINUE ALL MILITARY ACTIONS ON LAND, AT SEA AND IN THE AIR,
AND WITHDRAW ALL FORCES TO THE INTERNATIONALLY RECOGNIZED
BOUNDARIES WITHOUT DELAY SEMICOLON
" 2. REQUESTS THE SECRETARY-GENERAL TO DISPATCH A TEAM OF UNITED
NATIONS OBSERVERS TO VERIFY, CONFIRM AND SUPERVISE THE CEASE-FIRE
AND WITHDRAWAL AND FURTHER REQUESTS THE SECRETARY-GENERAL TO MAKE
THE NECESSARY ARRANGEMENTS IN CONSULTATION WITH THE PARTIES AND
TO SUBMIT A REPORT THEREON TO THE SECURITY COUNCIL SEMICOLON
" 3. URGES THAT PRISONERS-OF-WAR BE RELEASED AND REPATRIATED
WITHOUT DELAY AFTER THE CESSATION OF ACTIVE HOSTILITIES IN
ACCORDANCE WITH THE THIRD GENEVA CONVENTION OF 12 AUGUST 1949
SEMICOLON
" 4. CALLS UPON IRAN AND IRAQ TO CO-OPERATE WITH THE
SECRETARY-GENERAL IN IMPLEMENTING THIS RESOLUTION AND IN
MEDIATION EFFORTS TO ACHIEVE A COMPREHENSIVE, JUST AND HONOURABLE
SETTLEMENT, ACCEPTABLE TO BOTH SIDES, OF ALL OUTSTANDING ISSUES,
IN ACCORDANCE WITH THE PRINCIPLES CONTAINED IN THE CHARTER OF THE
UNITED NATIONS SEMICOLON
" 5. CALLS UPON ALL OTHER STATES TO EXERCISE THE UTMOST RESTRAINT
AND TO REFRAIN FROM ANY ACT WHICH MAY LEAD TO FURTHER ESCALATION
AND WIDENING OF THE CONFLICT, AND THUS TO FACILITATE THE
IMPLEMENTATION OF THE PRESENT RESOLUTION SEMICOLON
" 6. REQUESTS THE SECRETARY-GENERAL TO EXPLORE, IN CONSULTATION
WITH IRAN AND IRAQ, THE QUESTION OF ENTRUSTING AN IMPARTIAL BODY
WITH INQUIRING INTO RESPONSIBILITY FOR THE CONFLICT AND TO REPORT
TO THE SECURITY COUNCIL AS SOON AS POSSIBLE SEMICOLON
" 7. RECOGNIZES THE MAGNITUDE OF THE DAMAGE INFLICTED DURING THE
CONFLICT AND THE NEED FOR RECONSTRUCTION EFFORTS, WITH
APPROPRIATE INTERNATIONAL ASSISTANCE, ONCE THE CONFLICT IS ENDED
AND, IN THIS REGARD, REQUESTS THE SECRETARY-GENERAL TO ASSIGN A
TEAM OF EXPERTS TO STUDY THE QUESTION OF RECONSTRUCTION AND TO
REPORT TO THE SECURITY COUNCIL SEMICOLON
" 8. FURTHER REQUESTS THE SECRETARY-GENERAL TO EXAMINE IN
CONSULTATION WITH IRAN AND IRAQ AND WITH OTHER STATES OF THE
REGION, MEASURES TO ENHANCE THE SECURITY AND STABILITY OF THE
REGION SEMICOLON
" 9. REQUESTS THE SECRETARY-GENERAL TO KEEP THE SECURITY COUNCIL
INFORMED ON THE IMPLEMENTATION OF THIS RESOLUTION SEMICOLON
" 10. DECIDES TO MEET AGAIN AS NECESSARY TO CONSIDER FURTHER
STEPS TO ENSURE COMPLIANCE WITH THIS RESOLUTION. "
UNQUOTE
HIGHEST CONSIDERATION.

J. PEREZ DE CUELLAR
SECRETARY-GENERAL
UNATIONS NEWYORK

0114

報告事項

報告畢

1992. 1. 16.
中東 1 課(3)

題 目 : 이란, 이라크의 「이.이」戰 賠償 履行關聯 우리의 支持 要請

駐韓 이란大使는 1.15. 제1차관보 예방시 이란-이라크戰 休戰 決議案인 安保理 決議案 598(1987.7) 제6항에 의거, 91.12. UN이 이라크의 戰爭 挑發 責任을 명시함에 따라 이라크의 對이란 賠償 履行에 대한 우리의 支持를 要請 해온바, 關聯事項을 아래 報告합니다.

---

1. 駐韓 이란 大使는 本件이 벨라야티 外務長官의 長官님께 대한 멧시지임을 전제, 동 내용을 長官님께 傳達해 줄것을 要請

2. 要 旨

  ○ UN 事務總長 報告書(91.12)는 「이.이」戰 挑發責任이 이라크에 있음을 明示하고 있음.

  ○ 그러나 이라크는 UN의 決定에도 不拘하고 이에 따른 對이란 賠償 履行을 교묘히 回避하고 있음.

  ○ 「이.이」戰 기간중 이란이 입은 被害가 막대하므로 이라크는 당연히 성실한 賠償을 履行하여야 하며 이를 위한 國際社會의 對이라크 壓力이 必要하며 지난번 이라크의 쿠웨이트 侵攻으로 걸프 國家들이 입은 被害와 같은 水準으로 다루어져야 할것임.

  ○ 이와같은 이란 立場에 대한 韓國政府의 支持를 要請함.

3. 言論對策 : 該當없음.

4. 關聯措置 :

  ○ 우리는 本件에 대한 UN 決定을 支持한다는 立場을 이란측에 表明함.
   (사실상 이란측 입장에 同調)

  ○ 추후 UN에서 필요할 경우 우리의 상기 立場 表明. 끝.

공람	주무니거래과전	담당	과장	심의관	국장	차관보	차관	장관
		주		애				

0115

報 告 事 項

報告畢

1992. 1. 16.
中東 1 課 (3)

題 目 : 이란, 이라크의 「이.이」戰 賠償 履行關聯 우리의 支持 要請

駐韓 이란大使는 1.15. 제1차관보 예방시 이란-이라크戰 休戰 決議案인 安保理 決議案 598(1987.7) 제6항에 의거, 91.12. UN이 이라크의 戰爭 挑發 責任을 명시함에 따라 이라크의 對이란 賠償 履行에 대한 우리의 支持를 要請 해온바, 關聯事項을 아래 報告합니다.

---

1. 駐韓 이란 大使는 本件이 벨라야티 外務長官의 長官님께 대한 멧시지임을 전제, 동 내용을 長官님께 傳達해 줄것을 要請

2. 要 旨
   ㅇ UN 事務總長 報告書(91.12)는 「이.이」戰 挑發責任이 이라크에 있음을 明示하고 있음.
   ㅇ 그러나 이라크는 UN의 決定에도 不拘하고 이에 따른 對이란 賠償 履行을 교묘히 回避하고 있음.
   ㅇ 「이.이」戰 기간중 이란이 입은 被害가 막대하므로 이라크는 당연히 성실한 賠償을 履行하여야 하며 이를 위한 國際社會의 對이라크 壓力이 必要하며 지난번 이라크의 쿠웨이트 侵攻으로 걸프 國家들이 입은 被害와 같은 水準으로 다루어져야 할것임.
   ㅇ 이와같은 이란 立場에 대한 韓國政府의 支持를 要請함.

3. 言論對策 : 該當없음.

4. 關聯措置 :
   ㅇ 우리는 本件에 대한 UN 決定을 支持한다는 立場을 이란측에 表明함. (사실상 이란측 입장에 同調)
   ㅇ 추후 UN에서 필요할 경우 우리의 상기 立場 表明. 끝.

0116

주 국 련 대 표 부

주국련 20313- 062   1992. 1. 16.

수신 : 장관

참조 : 국제기구국장, 중동아프리카국장

제목 : 이란.이락전 후속조치 (안보리)

　　표제관련 유엔 이란 복구조사단 (단장 : A. Farah 전 사무차장)의 현지방문
(91.11.7-12.1) 결과 보고서를 별첨과 같이 송부합니다.

첨부 : 상기 문서 (S/23322) 끝.

주 　 국 　 련 　 대

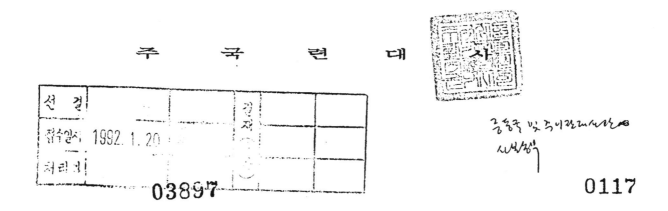

선결

접수일시 1992. 1. 20

처리과

03897

0117

UNITED NATIONS

S

Security Council

Distr.
GENERAL

S/23322
24 December 1991

ORIGINAL: ENGLISH

LETTER DATED 24 DECEMBER 1991 FROM THE SECRETARY-GENERAL
ADDRESSED TO THE PRESIDENT OF THE SECURITY COUNCIL

In my letter of 31 July 1991 (S/22863), I informed you that the team of experts which I had appointed under the terms of paragraph 7 of Security Council resolution 598 (1987) would return to the Islamic Republic of Iran to complete its study of that country's reconstruction efforts in the wake of the conflict between the Islamic Republic of Iran and Iraq.

The team, which was led by Mr. Abdulrahim A. Farah, former Under-Secretary-General, visited the Islamic Republic of Iran from 7 November to 1 December 1991 and has prepared a second and final report containing its findings.

A copy of the report is submitted for the information of members of the Security Council.

(Signed) Javier PEREZ de CUELLAR

91-42367 2860h (E)

/...

0118

<u>Annex</u>

SECOND AND FINAL REPORT OF THE UNITED NATIONS TEAM OF EXPERTS
APPOINTED BY THE SECRETARY-GENERAL PURSUANT TO SECURITY
COUNCIL RESOLUTION 598 (1987), PARAGRAPH 7, PREPARED FOLLOWING
A FURTHER VISIT BY THE TEAM TO THE ISLAMIC REPUBLIC OF IRAN TO
COMPLETE ITS STUDY OF THE COUNTRY'S RECONSTRUCTION EFFORTS AND
NEEDS IN THE WAKE OF THE CONFLICT BETWEEN THE ISLAMIC REPUBLIC
OF IRAN AND IRAQ

7 NOVEMBER-1 DECEMBER 1991

/...

Map 1

MAP NO. 3642.1   UNITED NATIONS
JULY 1991

/...

0120

Map 2

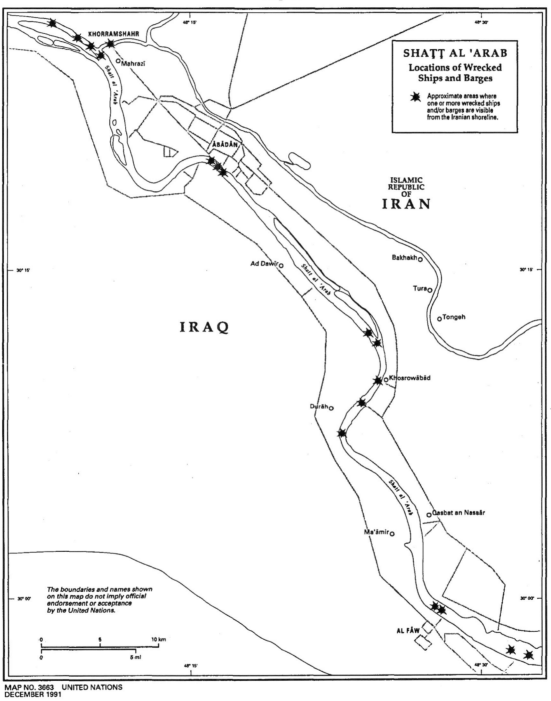

SHAṬṬ AL 'ARAB
Locations of Wrecked
Ships and Barges

✴ Approximate areas where
one or more wrecked ships
and/or barges are visible
from the Iranian shoreline.

ISLAMIC
REPUBLIC
OF
IRAN

IRAQ

KHORRAMSHAHR

Mahrazī

ĀBĀDĀN

Ad Dawīr

Bakhakh

Tura

Tongeh

Khosrowābād

Durāh

Qasbat an Nassār

Ma'āmir

AL FĀW

The boundaries and names shown
on this map do not imply official
endorsement or acceptance
by the United Nations.

0   5   10 km

0   5 ml

MAP NO. 3663   UNITED NATIONS
DECEMBER 1991

/...

0121

EXECUTIVE SUMMARY

The Security Council in paragraph 7 of resolution 598 (1987) recognized the magnitude of the damage inflicted during the conflict between the Islamic Republic of Iran and Iraq and the need for reconstruction efforts, with appropriate international assistance, and requested the Secretary-General to assign a team of experts to study the question of reconstruction and report to the Security Council.

Accordingly, a team of experts was sent to the Islamic Republic of Iran in May/June 1991 on an exploratory mission to obtain initial information on the nature and extent of war damage suffered by the country's infrastructure. The team's first report was issued under cover of Security Council document S/22863. A second and final visit was made by the team of experts in November 1991. Its findings are the subject of the present report.

Government assessment of direct and indirect damage

In order to permit the international community to understand more fully the magnitudes involved, the costs and expenditures which had been expressed in Iranian rials have been converted into United States dollars, using the United Nations assessment rate. On this basis the Government's assessment of non-military war damage, computed at 1988 replacement costs, would be equivalent to $97,200 million.

The report does not discuss the question of indirect losses, which the Government had assessed at Rls 34,535,360 million, because of the difficulty of defining their nature and extent.

Other immeasurable social consequences

In addition to the physical damage to infrastructure and the productive apparatus, the country suffered immeasurable systemic damage to the environment and to social institutions and conditions. Significant human casualties in both dead and permanently disabled were recorded, a large number of the population was displaced and normal education and health delivery services were disrupted with adverse long-term implications.

The macroeconomic environment

During the period of conflict, the focus of the Government was on policies and measures to meet its war mobilization needs. This was achieved to a great extent by diverting resources from otherwise productive uses. Since the cease-fire, the Government has shifted to restoring a peacetime economy. This has involved phasing out the broad system of controls on most economic activities necessitated by the war effort; the privatization of state-owned companies and the contracting-out of certain services hitherto provided from within government; and the establishment of a market-oriented

/...

economy. The Government expects that the new economic policy framework will
provide incentives for private sector development and for private investment
in efficient productive activities, thereby ensuring an increasingly important
role for that sector in reconstruction.

Reconstruction of the oil industry

The economy of the Islamic Republic of Iran is very heavily dependent
upon the production and export of oil for the generation both of domestic
employment and income, as well as government revenue, and of the foreign
exchange needed to pay for imported goods. The oil industry was severely
damaged during the conflict but because of its vital role, immediate (if
temporary) repairs were made to keep the oil flowing. Such repairs were often
undertaken several times because of repeated attacks. The authorities
estimate that 90 per cent of the war-related repair work, owing to its
makeshift nature, will have to be redone. In order to restore the industry to
world competitive standards, large-scale future reconstruction investment will
be necessary.

Sectoral analysis

Throughout the conflict, the industrial sector suffered heavily from
attacks and from the shortage of critical spare parts. The sector is now
operating at close to pre-war capacity through mainly makeshift repairs
despite technological obsolesence. Agriculture in the five war-affected
provinces experienced considerable soil degradation in areas where ground
fighting had been intense and prolonged. The situation has been compounded by
widespread salination caused by the destruction of soil embankments, and
irrigation and drainage systems. Investment in land-levelling and replacement
equipment are needed. The transport sector requires a substantial investment
to replace destroyed equipment such as rolling stock and land vehicles, the
reconstruction of roads which were temporarily resurfaced and the
strengthening of bridges where repair work had been improvised. The ports of
Abadan and Khorramshahr were virtually destroyed. Full restoration of these
two ports depends essentially on the reopening of the Shatt al-Arab (see
below). Damaged or destroyed installations in the telecommunications sector,
particularly in the border areas, have now been rehabilitated. Similarly, the
energy and electric power sector whose installations experienced considerable
damage in the border area, is now operating close to normal levels. However,
the system is somewhat outdated and needs extensive technological upgrading.

The housing and human settlements sector, which suffered far-reaching
direct and collateral damage, requires considerable investment to meet the
needs of the displaced and homeless population (see also below under
resettlement). The education sector was subject to prolonged severe
disruption and its schools and other buildings sustained severe damage,
especially in the war-affected provinces. This situation has slowed
considerably the flow of trained and professional personnel, and has
contributed to the present acute shortage of skilled labor. In the health
sector basic facilities and services in the war zone were heavily damaged. At

/...

the national level, many important urban and rural centres are facing an acute shortage of health facilities caused by the influx of displaced families and by a marked increase in population growth. The disruption in the flow of medical technicians has led to a curtailment in the delivery of normal health services. The <u>cultural heritage</u> sector did not escape damage to many of its world-renowned sites, monuments and museums. A substantial number received severe and, in some cases, irreparable damage. To date only a small fraction of the needed reconstruction work has been accomplished.

Principal characteristics of reconstruction efforts

The report notes that total reconstruction expenditure, from the beginning of hostilities through 1991, is estimated by the Iranian authorities at about $13,000 million. This does not take into account the extensive running-down of stocks and the "cannibalization" of equipment to keep other installations functioning. Moreover, reconstruction costs do not cover losses incurred by the private sector, which has yet to receive some form of compensation. The mission observed that preliminary government forecasts of future expenditure in the achievement of reconstruction targets contain differences among the sectors as to the definition of reconstruction, the time periods covered, and variations in the demand for sectoral services. Owing to the mission's time constraint, the report has not attempted to analyse these data. They will need to be further refined by the Iranian authorities in the future.

Resettlement efforts

The Government has assigned the highest priority to the reconstruction of damaged or destroyed rural and urban settlements in the war-affected provinces, and the return and resettlement of the displaced population. Large numbers of housing units need to be constructed, basic infrastructural facilities established, and employment opportunities created. About 250,000 of the 1.2 million displaced population have returned to their places of origin, and some 2 million square metres of residential, commercial and administrative housing have been rebuilt.

Clearance of Shatt al-Arab

The clearance of the Shatt al-Arab is of utmost importance to permit the reconstruction and functioning of the cities and ports of Abadan and Khorramshahr. Once the political agreement of all parties has been secured, immediate attention should be given to the clearance of this important waterway. On the basis of its discussions, the mission believes that marine clearance operations will require international assistance since the Islamic Republic of Iran possesses neither the resources nor the technical expertise to undertake the work on its own. It is the mission's view that the magnitude and complexity of the task will first require a series of surveys to locate the wrecks, identify the nature of the cargo and determine the best means of clearance. The fact that many of the wrecks are heavily silted and may contain cargo of a hazardous nature increases the need for the utmost care in their removal.

/...

Present economic performance

The recent performance of the Iranian economy has been highly
satisfactory. However, the ability of the economy to sustain its current high
rate of expansion is still doubtful in many sectors, owing to the damage
sustained in the conflict and the inability during the war to channel
resources to reinvestment. Output growth has depended upon short term
measures, including the "cannibalization" of idled facilities and the drawing
down of stocks of spare parts. Unless more permanent improvements to
productive capability are quickly undertaken, the mission fears that not only
will output fall, but serious damage could be done to the basic core of
equipment.

Possible future action

The report notes that the quantity and technical quality of the
reconstruction effort is impressive, particularly since it has been almost
completely undertaken through the domestic mobilization of resources. The
amount of reconstruction so far completed is a relatively small fraction of
what needs to be done. The country's capital stock is depleted in many
sectors, and it is technologically outdated following years of stagnation
caused by the conflict. Since the war ended, the Government has had time to
take stock of the damage inflicted on its economic and social sectors.
Although it has undertaken an impressive programme of reconstruction, it finds
that the losses suffered had reduced its capacity to mobilize domestic
resources in sufficient quantity and within a reasonable time-frame to meet
the remaining costs of reconstruction.

In these circumstances, the Government has expressed its interest in
international assistance in the form of access to external sources for the
renewal and replenishment of capital stock; to export markets; to
international capital markets and investment, and to access to recent
technological advances (including technical assistance).

The Security Council, in its resolution 598 (1987), recognized the scope
of the reconstruction process and the possibility of participation by the
international community. Having made a survey of war damage in the Islamic
Republic of Iran, the Government's reconstruction efforts and its priorities,
as well as the considerable amount of reconstruction work that still needs to
be undertaken, the mission believes that an appropriate mechanism will need to
be devised to provide international participation in the reconstruction
programme. To this end, the mission recommends the convening of a round
table, at which representatives of the Islamic Republic of Iran and States
Members of the United Nations and its relevant agencies and organizations
could meet to discuss ways and means of entering into effective cooperation in
support of the reconstruction efforts of the Islamic Republic of Iran.

/...

0125

CONTENTS

/...

CONTENTS (continued)

/...
0127

INTRODUCTION

A. Terms of reference

1.   A team of experts was sent to the Islamic Republic of Iran in May/June 1991 on an exploratory mission to obtain initial information on the nature and extent of war damage suffered by the country's infrastructure. The team's first report was issued as Security Council document S/22863, annex.

2.   The second visit of the team of experts to the Islamic Republic of Iran (in pursuance of para. 7 of Security Council resolution 598 (1987)) took place from 7 November to 1 December 1991. The team's work was guided by the terms of reference established for the first visit and, in addition, focused on the following tasks:

(a) To complete, where possible, the verification of damage to the country's infrastructure, including the social sectors;

(b) To review economic, social and environmental issues relating to reconstruction and which cannot be dissociated from physical development;

(c) To ascertain reconstruction needs and priorities, and identify sectors covered and type of international assistance required;

(d) To obtain, where possible, a breakdown within each sector of the amount spent so far by the Iranian authorities on reconstruction activities, and on the remaining construction work that needs to be undertaken on restoring damaged sites and installations;

(e) To present a macroeconomic view of the economy to enable an objective assessment of the impact of the reconstruction programme on the national budget to facilitate the identification of areas where the cooperation of the international community could be effective.

B. Official meetings

3.   The mission arrived in Tehran on 7 November and began its work the same day. On the following day the team held meetings with the Vice-President for Reconstruction and Head of the Plan and Budget Organization to discuss its programme of work and to receive additional information on the Government's reconstruction efforts.

4.   During the mission's stay in Tehran, a series of meetings was held at key implementing Ministries to ascertain the priorities of their reconstruction efforts. These included meetings with Ministers or Deputy Ministers of the following Ministries: Economic Affairs and Finance; Industries (Light); Foreign Affairs; Agriculture; Telecommunications; Transport; Oil and Petroleum; Heavy Industries; Power and Energy; Education; Health; and the Interior. In addition, meetings were also held with the Governor of the

/...

0128

Central Bank and senior officials at the Iranian Chamber of Commerce, Industries and Mines, the Environmental Protection Organization, National Iranian Oil Company (NIOC), Ports and Shipping Organization, the Foundation for Displaced People, the Foundation for the Disabled, the Housing Foundation and the Institute for Research in Planning and Development.

5.   The mission has made a record of all documentation received from Iranian authorities containing background information pertaining to damages and losses sustained as a direct result of the war, as well as data relating to national reconstruction.   A detailed list of the documentation submitted to the mission is contained in appendix C.

6.   As a means of supplementing the information obtained during the official meetings, arrangements were made for team members to visit sites in the war-affected provinces to obtain additional data on sustained damage and reconstruction efforts.

7.   The team held official meetings with government representatives at the national, provincial and local levels.   A list of officials met by the team leader and the experts is contained in appendix B.

C.   Procedural matters

8.   In carrying out its task, the team was provided by the Government with information on its assessment of direct and indirect losses caused by the conflict.

9.   The mission obtained all its data and background information on damage and reconstruction from government sources, in the form of documentation handed over by government officials, and information provided verbally either at official meetings or by technical staff who accompanied mission members during on-site visits.   The Iranian authorities had, on their part, conducted a thorough accounting of war losses and reconstruction costs, and supplied supporting detail to the mission for all statements made with regard to actual financial expenditure.   The Government responded fully to requests made by the mission for additional information and clarification.

10.   Because of existing differences between official and non-official exchange rates, the first report of the mission (S/22863, annex) expressed all damage and reconstruction costs in Iranian rials.   Since the absence of a comparable international exchange rate made it difficult for the reader to assess the magnitude of losses of reconstruction cost involved, consultations were held with Iranian authorities and the team to identify an appropriate rate.   In the present report, costs are expressed in both rials and United

/...

0129

States dollars. The exchange rate used, in agreement with the Central Bank, is that accepted by the United Nations for purposes of calculating the Islamic Republic of Iran's membership payments to United Nations bodies. This rate is based on an average of a number of exchange rates calculated by the Central Bank under different statistical concepts. For 1988 the rate would be Rls 237 per United States dollar, while the rate for 1990 would be Rls 300.

11. To achieve a uniform approach in all sectors with regard to the question of reconstruction, the mission endeavoured:

(a) To collect, on a sectoral basis, all information and data pertaining to major war-related damage and to the reconstruction programme;

(b) To carry out on-site inspections of damaged and reconstructed sites and installations;

(c) To describe all visible damage in qualitative rather than quantitative terms, for example, light, moderate, severe and heavy;

(d) To compare the reconstruction work of a particular site with photographs taken at the time the damage occurred or before the work began.

I. GOVERNMENT ASSESSMENT OF WAR-RELATED DAMAGE

A. Overview

12. As stated in the first report, almost 20,000 square kilometres of Iranian territory came under occupation soon after the outbreak of war in 1980. Out of a total of 24 provinces, 5 became active theatres of war (Khuzestan, Ilam, Bakhtaran, Kordistan and West Azarbayjan) while 11 others were repeated targets of attack by aircraft and missiles. (See map 1 above.)

13. In evaluating the economic damage, the Government considered two main categories:

(a) Direct damage consisting of damage to physical infrastructure and to capital stock as the result of direct attack. Such damage was estimated by the Government to amount approximately to Rls 30,811,424 million.

(b) Indirect damage estimated by the Government at Rls 34,535,360 million. This includes facilities and capacities that could have been utilized had there been no war. It also includes resources allocated for defence purposes that would otherwise have been utilized by the economic sectors.

14. A sectoral breakdown with regard to direct and indirect damages is contained in tables 2 and 3 of the first report.

/...0130

B. Assessment of direct damages

15. Following up on the first preliminary estimate of the war-related damages which was presented to the first mission, the Government submitted to the present mission the document entitled Final Report on the Assessment of the Economic Damages of the War Imposed by Iraq on The Islamic Republic of Iran (1980-1988). This document provided details additional to the information previously submitted.

16. The mission believes that, in order to better understand the needs for reconstruction, attention should be focused on the estimates of direct damage in the non-military sectors. For this purpose, therefore, in analysing the total value of the damages, it has excluded armed forces machinery and equipment and materials and goods.

17. The additional information contained in the Government's report provides a breakdown of the value of the damages into two components. The first is the value in rials of domestically supplied materials or equipment while the second is the cost in dollars of imported items. The authorities informed the mission that all such values have been estimated at replacement costs in 1988 prices.

18. In order to present a measure of the damages in internationally comparable terms, the mission has converted to dollars that part of the estimate originally denominated in rials, adding that figure to the part originally estimated in dollars. As explained in the introduction the appropriate rate for 1988 would be Rls 237 per dollar.*

19. The estimate of the value of the non-military damages which are of domestic origin amounts to Rls 12,994,040 million. Converted at Rls 237 to the dollar, the equivalent value is $54,827 million. The estimate of the value of war-damaged items which have been imported, provided in the above-cited report, is $42,421 million. The total of the non-military damages is therefore valued at the equivalent of $97,248 million.

20. Conversely, if the data for war damages of imported items is converted to rials at the same rate of Rls 237 to the dollar, the rial value of this component is equivalent to 10,053,777 million. The total of non-military damages is therefore estimated at Rls 23,047,817 million. For comparative purposes, this total is virtually equivalent to the estimate of gross domestic product (GDP) for 1988, Rls 23,048,200 million.

---

* It should be noted that a trade-weighted conversion rate estimated by the World Bank for 1988 is 178 rials per dollar. The Central Bank rate, calculated in consultation with the United Nations Statistical Office, is an average of a number of rates estimated under different statistical concepts.

/...

21. As indicated in the report of the first mission, these data do not include any estimate for the value of housing or commercial buildings either completely destroyed or partially damaged, given the large number of individual units involved and the disparate conditions under which they were originally built. In the summary of the sectoral reports presented later in this document, estimates are provided of the costs of the replacement houses and buildings which are being constructed under the Government's resettlement programme.

22. The detailed data provided in the tables of the Government's report indicate that no estimates have been made of port damage nor of the losses in shipping and in civilian aircraft which were suffered during the conflict. The Government also informed the mission that additional data on losses sustained by municipal authorities and by private sector manufacturing establishments had been received after the report had been issued.

C. Indirect damages

23. The Government has also provided data on indirect damages, defined as service and productive capacities that would have been exploited if the war had not taken place. This type of damage also includes resources diverted for national defence during the conflict period which otherwise would have been utilized to create extra capacities within the economic sectors (see S/22863, para. 51 (b)).

24. It is apparent that the war as well as the war effort has seriously distorted the pattern of economic activity. It adversely affected the allocation and generation of resources which did not permit even normal capital stock replacement. That distortion in resource use continues to act as a constraint on achieving growth necessitated by the need to overcome the years of neglect. It was also evident that, given the intersectoral and inter-industrial relationship, physical damage suffered by certain key sectors had a wide-ranging negative impact on others.

25. The mission recognized that a large number of possible interpretations could be put on the extent of the indirect damage and that it would be very difficult to reconcile these interpretations during the brief time available to the mission. It was therefore decided to limit the discussion in the report to direct damage and to associated costs of reconstruction and to take note only of the assessment of indirect damage as reported by the Government. These have been given as Rls 34,542,326 million.

II. MACROECONOMIC BACKGROUND

A. Period of the conflict

26. The outbreak of the conflict in September 1980 occurred as the new Government was taking initial steps to assume control of governmental functions and to restore normal economic activities in the wake of the revolution.

27. Oil production and exports play a fundamental role in the performance of the economy of the Islamic Republic of Iran. Not only does the oil sector generate both directly and indirectly substantial employment opportunities but it is virtually the only source of foreign exchange and for many years provided as much as two thirds of government revenue.

28. In international markets, after the second round of oil price increases in 1979, both the decline in world oil consumption and the coming on stream of non-OPEC oil sources led to pressure on prices which began to decline in the course of 1981, from some $36 per barrel in early 1981 to an average of $31 in 1982 and $28 in both 1983 and 1984, but still well above the relatively favourable early 1979 levels. In an effort to stabilize the markets, OPEC member States during the latter period were asked to curtail output and exports.

29. The Islamic Republic of Iran's exports of crude oil in 1980 were below the level of 1 million barrels per day, the lowest since the early 1960s and were well below its OPEC share. This was in part due to the Government's policy of limiting oil exports to the amounts needed to satisfy the country's basic foreign exchange requirements and in part due to the changes in the Islamic Republic of Iran's oil marketing arrangements after the revolution as OECD countries and Japan shifted to alternative sources of supplies. Export levels were seriously affected in late 1980, and especially through 1981, by severe damage to pumping stations and the Kharg Island facilities which were bombed early in the war. This resulted in a level of exports in the latter year which also fell below 1 million barrels per day. But, in 1982 and 1983, exports exceeded 2 million barrels per day as NIOC repaired war damages to its facilities and new markets were developed. War damage constraints, however, once again became more serious in subsequent years, reducing export levels.

30. The low levels of exports in 1980 and 1981 were therefore reflected in the declines in GDP in those years but the recovery of exports and continued relatively favourable oil prices through 1984 led to strong overall economic growth during the period. By 1984, GDP was some 40 per cent above the 1980 level.

31. The substantial expansion in government revenues after 1980, largely from the oil sector, permitted growth of public expenditures, although only a moderate rise was recorded for real capital formation. The sectoral data available to the mission indicate that the relatively small amount of expenditure on reconstruction which was necessary through 1984 was met from

/...

budget allocations for capital expenditure, from the drawing down of stocks of spare parts (particularly, for example, in the oil sector which at the time had suffered the severest damage) and from internal resources available to the enterprises concerned, particularly those which generate revenues.

32. During the course of 1984, heavy damage was sustained by Iran's oil port facilities and tankers throughout the Persian Gulf. Shipping was thereby discouraged from entering the area, resulting in a substantial fall in the volume of exports in subsequent years. At the same time, oil prices sharply declined, from the $28 barrel levels of 1983 and 1984 to $14 in 1986. The combination of the two events had disastrous effects on the Iranian economy. Foreign exchange earnings from oil and gas exports, which had exceeded $21,000 million in 1983, dropped to $17,000 million in 1984, to $14,000 million in 1985 and to $6,000 million in 1986.

33. Although GDP rose slightly in 1985, it declined in each of the subsequent years and by 1988 was 10 per cent below the 1984 level. The impact on government revenues was more severe, a reduction in income from oil and gas in 1986 to less than 25 per cent of the 1982 and 1983 levels. To prevent any further growth in the public sector deficit (and to attempt to limit inflationary pressures), non-oil taxes were increased. But the deteriorating budgetary situation did not permit increases in allocation for capital formation, one of the principal sources of finance for repairing war damaged facilities. In order to free resources for the latter purpose, expenditures on several new projects were, in fact, suspended.

34. However, a number of ongoing projects considered vital to the war effort continued to be implemented. Examples include the ports at Bandar Khomeyni and Bandar Abbas, cited above, which underwent substantial expansion. Given the complete destruction of Khorramshahr, previously the most important port facility, it was essential to proceed with those projects to ensure the functioning of the Iranian economy. (See the discussions in section II.)

35. Other sector reports indicate that strenuous efforts were made to maintain the operational levels of key infrastructural facilities throughout the conflict period. Given budgetary limitations and the difficulties in getting components, some damaged installations were "cannibalized" to keep other units functioning (e.g., power, refinery operations, roads), the financial flows of revenue-producing installations were used to finance some of the ongoing work, and spare parts inventories continued to be drawn down.

36. The loss of foreign exchange earnings also had a significant impact on productive activities as steps were taken to control imports and various measures were taken to control domestic demand and activities. Imports of raw materials and intermediate goods for industry and mining were sharply reduced and priority was given to the production of goods, particularly spare parts and components, needed for the war. Manufacturing activity, which had experienced moderate growth in the 1981-1984 period, declined sharply and by 1988 was some 20 per cent below the 1984 level.

/...

B. Period from the cease-fire to the present

37. With the cessation of hostilities in 1988, the Government rapidly moved to shift from a wartime economy to reconstruction. The task was monumental, given the enormity of the damages which had been sustained. Foremost among the problems were the immeasurable burden arising from the displacement of 2 million people, the casualties from the war, and the urgent need to make up for some eight years of domestic resource allocation essentially oriented towards the war effort and which had entailed the suspension or reduction of many normal economic activities.

38. Immediately after the cease-fire, the Government elaborated its first five-year development plan (1989-1993). The plan was presented to the Majlis (parliament) in early 1989 and adopted on 31 January 1990.

39. The principal concern of the plan is the reconstruction of an economy and, as such, it does not specifically deal with reconstruction of damaged facilities except in so far as those are needed to meet overall objectives. The emphasis in the short run is to take those immediate steps required to restore productive activities in the quickest possible time, so as to establish a flow of goods and services which would permit the generation of resources necessary to lay the basis for sustained economic growth. Moreover, it addresses many of the key socio-economic concerns not directly resulting from the war but rather the consequences of an eight-year time lapse when the principal priority was the conduct of the war. These are spelled out below in section V of the present report.

40. To implement its development plan, the Government announced a series of major macroeconomic policy reforms, the details of which continue to be elaborated. The essential aim is to restore the balance of the economy, moving away from the high degree of state intervention which characterized the war period towards the establishment of an economy relying mainly on market mechanisms.

41. Greater reliance would be put on the private sector and private entrepreneurship. This would include the privatization of many economic activities now undertaken by the Government. Moreover, the authorities indicated that they would be guided once more by the principles established in the Law for the Attraction and Protection of Foreign Investment enacted in 1955 which provides for non-discriminatory treatment of foreign investment.

42. Measures have already been taken to liberalize the financial system, to improve and reform the tax revenue system, to reduce gradually price and distribution controls, to lower the level of protection from tariff and non-tariff barriers, and to move gradually to a unified exchange rate.

43. The Government has assigned highest priority to the voluntary resettlement of the mass of population which has been displaced from the war-devastated areas. This will involve providing adequate housing, basic infrastructural services, employment and income-generating opportunities. The

/...

details of these programmes are contained in the sectoral chapters issued as an addendum to the present report and are summarized in section VI.

44. Economic performance since the end of the hostilities has been highly encouraging. In 1989 GDP grew by some 3 per cent, but rose rapidly by more than 10 per cent in 1990, in spite of a severe earthquake in two northwestern provinces in June 1990 which caused heavy loss of life and considerable damage. The preliminary estimates for 1991 are for continued high growth rates. A major factor has been the strong recovery in the value of oil exports which recovered to $12,000 million in 1989 and rose to more than $17,000 million in 1990. Further improvement in these exports has occurred in 1991 with the current volume exceeding 2 million barrels per day. At the present time, it appears that oil production has reached over 3 million barrels per day, the highest output since 1979. Although there has been some recent instability in oil prices, current levels are 30-40 per cent above the lows recorded in 1985-1986.

45. In other sectors of the economy, the recent changes in the government policy facilitated rapid adjustments towards a peacetime economy. Manufacturing activity increased by 17 per cent in 1990 and the Government reports that the level of capacity utilization in the sector in 1991 reached 80 per cent. The lifting of import controls has improved access to raw materials and intermediate products while the removal of price and distribution controls has encouraged producers to raise output. In general the policy reforms and the improved earnings from oil exports resulted in a substantial increase in imports in 1990 which appears to be continuing in 1991. Recovery of the agricultural sector from war damage has been impeded by the 1990 earthquake and a long period of drought.

46. A significant feature of the economic performance of the Islamic Republic of Iran through this period has been its policy to reduce sharply the level of its foreign debt through timely repayment. The Government has indicated that it has virtually no medium- or long-term foreign debt at the present time. This situation should substantially enhance its creditworthiness in international capital markets.

47. Higher revenue for the Government from oil exports, as well as from tax reform measures adopted earlier, has permitted an expansion in development expenditures and a reduction in the overall budgetary deficit. An additional consequence of these developments has been the decrease in inflationary pressures.

48. Nevertheless, the difficulties in sustaining this productive performance is recognized at many levels since it has depended in many instances on short-term measures to raise output which need to be followed very quickly by more permanent improvements in productive capability. For example, the National Iranian Oil Company (NIOC) reports that 90 per cent of the repairs that it has made to war-damaged facilities will have to be redone in order to avoid serious losses in the future. In addition, the high level of oil extraction at the present time is being achieved by operating wells where war

/...

damage has affected the ability to re-inject associated gases into the oil reservoirs, thus requiring considerable flaring of those gases. It will be necessary to invest in compressing and associated equipment to correct this situation.

49. Similarly, repairs to many of the major roads need to be redone, including a number of war-damaged bridges which require more permanent reconstruction to withstand the loads they are now carrying. Moreover, the entire rail system needs overhaul, in particular, upgrading of rolling stock which had been damaged during the war and which had been repaired using locally produced components.

50. In the case of electric power generation, officials estimate that about one fourth of the repair to damaged facilities will have to be redone in order to ensure safe and proper functioning. In this sector and a number of others, the drawing down of stocks of spare parts at plant sites in order to effect repairs has made the system vulnerable to breakdowns.

III. THE RECONSTRUCTION EFFORT

A. Reconstruction during the conflict

51. The main focus of the domestic mobilization efforts during the period of the hostilities was to provide for strategic and policy requirements of the war. Following the recapture of Khorramshahr in June 1982, the Government authorized the commencement of reconstruction activities in the war-damaged areas in furtherance of that objective.

52. At the national level, reconstruction plans and programmes were limited to short scopes and periods, to enable the damaged facilities to resume their services or production as quickly as possible. Resources available for reconstruction were allocated for projects with immediate feedback, for militarily strategic projects, and for the implementation of urgently needed projects responding to the social and political pressures resulting from the war. In some sectors (e.g. roads and bridges), it was not possible to undertake normal maintenance and repair activities, nor to embark on normal replacement programmes, owing to the limited resources.

B. Post-war reconstruction objectives and organization

53. The Iranian Government elaborated its first five-year development plan in 1989, to provide appropriate orientation for the shift from a war economy to a peacetime economy (see section II). The basic objectives include reconstructing and renovating productive and infrastructural capacities, as well as population centres damaged during the war, achieving economic growth with the aim of increasing per capita production and productive employment, and providing minimum basic needs of the population. In this context, the reconstruction of war-damaged areas was stated to be an integral part of the plan and the specific activities devoted to the various elements making up

/...

0137

reconstruction are defined within the framework of the priorities envisaged in the plan.

54. Within the above-stated objectives the Government has set out the following priorities for action:

(a) Reconstruction of residential, educational, health and commercial units in cities, towns and villages located in the war-damaged areas;

(b) Provision of infrastructure, such as water, electricity and sanitation in war-damaged residential areas, with a view to accelerating the resettlement process and in preparation for the future development of the areas;

(c) Revitalization of the economy through the regeneration of productive employment, particularly through the rehabilitation of agricultural land, and the reconstruction and rehabilitation of industries within war-damaged areas;

(d) Repair and reconstruction of existing communication networks, including roads, bridges and telecommunications;

(e) Repair of damaged historical and cultural sites and monuments.

55. In order to provide top-level supervision over the reconstruction and renovation processes and the return of the displaced, the Supreme Council for the Reconstruction and Renovation of the War-Damaged Areas was created, under the direction of a Vice-President of the Republic. A detailed description of the organization and operation of the Council, its relationships with provincial and local governments and with government ministries, is contained in the first report (S/22863, paras. 64-68). A review of the progress achieved in the resettlement programmes is provided in the summary of the sectoral report on housing and human settlements contained in section VI of the present report; the full sectoral report is contained in the addendum.

C. Role of the private sector

56. The exigencies of the war led to governmental intervention in all sectors of the economy and in the social sectors. Following the cease-fire, the authorities began to seek a more balanced structure by reducing most controls over the economy in order to improve the allocation of resources, reducing public sector involvement and, in general, providing more scope for private sector activity. A major element in this shift has been the privatization of a large number of government enterprises. The macroeconomic policy framework, first outlined in the plan, is designed to provide an appropriate incentive structure for the private sector to establish efficient import-substituting industries and profitable export activities, thereby ensuring an increasing role for that sector in the process of reconstruction.

/...

57. The Government is actively promoting the re-emergence and functioning of private sector organizations, such as the Chambers of Commerce and Industry. These groups can play an important role in dissemination of information on a broad range of topics of interest to the private sector, including technology, government assistance to the private sector and investment promotion. At the same time, the chambers, which are organized on the national, provincial and municipal levels, can serve as channels for private sector views on key elements of government policies. As noted earlier, the authorities have reaffirmed their intention to implement the law on foreign investment originally enacted in 1955, which provides non-discriminatory treatment for such investment.

58. The Government's holding company for small- and medium-sized industries (the National Iranian Industries Organization (NIIO)) has begun the process of privatization by selling shares in some 300 of the enterprises it controls. This is being done through the rejuvenated Tehran Stock Exchange. Trading in these shares accounts for about half of the current level of transactions in that market, which has grown from about Rls 2,000 million in the year immediately following the cease-fire to over Rls 160,000 million in the first six months of 1991.

59. In the areas where hostilities took place, assistance is being provided to small- and medium-sized industries damaged during the war to assist in their reconstruction. Funds have been allocated to the Ministry of Industries to permit it to make grants for rebuilding. These enterprises are also being assisted in arranging financing plans with local financial institutions.

60. The Government is also playing an important role in the development of private construction companies in the war-damaged areas. Grants are being given directly to the owners of damaged houses, who are then responsible for rebuilding. This has led to the creation of many small construction firms in the region which are being contracted for the actual work.

D. Other developments relating to the conflict

61. The reconstruction programme has had to deal with several major socio-economic factors arising from the eight-year duration of hostilities. One of the most striking is the substantial growth in population which exceeded 3 per cent per annum during that period, resulting in a total population size some 50 per cent higher in 1988 than in 1980. The high birth rate has resulted in a demographic profile in which some 45 per cent of the present population is under the age of 14. The provision of social services and educational opportunities for this age group clearly presents major challenges to the authorities in their allocation of resources as they simultaneously cope with the problems of overcoming the damages inflicted in those sectors.

62. The priorities of the war effort made it extremely difficult for the productive sectors to incorporate technological change. This was compounded

/...

by the international political developments associated with the war which limited the country's access to those changes. As a consequence, the Islamic Republic of Iran's basic productive structure and infrastructural framework are by and large technologically obsolete, with a capital stock that is now at least 12 years old, much in fact being considerably older. In these circumstances, the objective of reactivating production or restoring services as quickly as possible may conflict with the need to initiate technological upgrading.

63. Careful assessments will have to be made of proposed repairs or replacements of damaged equipment or system components to ensure that such expenditures do not lock in the existing obsolescence. One example which the mission encountered is the case of telecommunications, where it has been necessary to rebuild completely the network in the war-damaged areas. Some of the replacement has been undertaken with outdated equipment produced by local suppliers, thus saving on foreign exchange. However, the balance of the equipment needed has been imported and this represents more up-to-date technology.

E. Summary of actual reconstruction expenditure

64. Because of the imperative need to keep oil flowing, both for hard-currency exports and to serve the needs of the domestic economy during the conflict, the Government attached the highest priority to repair and reconstruction work in this sector. Maintaining the output of industry - particularly heavy industry to support the war effort - was also a high priority for the Government. The task of rebuilding the fabric of human settlements and of transport were further priority matters for the Government. These priorities are reflected in the actual expenditures made by government ministries for reconstruction over the period from the outset of the conflict to the present. As shown in the summary table below (the data for which were provided to the mission by the Government) these expenditures have to date totalled the equivalent of $17,343 million; all these costs have been met by the Government from domestic resources. Assuming that private sector reconstruction expenditure has been equal to at least one tenth of expenditure incurred by the public sector, an estimate of the total reconstruction expenditure covering both public and private sectors would be about $19,000 million.

65. The expenditures shown in this table are almost certainly a significant understatement of the actual cost of reconstruction carried out to date, because they exclude - inter alia - the extensive "cannibalization" of existing plants and equipment and the running down of stocks of spares, which helped in large measure to keep the wheels of industry turning throughout the conflict, despite the damage from attacks, and the difficulty of obtaining replacement parts through the usual trade channels on account of embargoes.

/...

Table 1. Summary of reconstruction expenditures by government ministries

(In millions of United States dollars)

SECTOR	Cost to 1991 inclusive		
	Foreign Exchange	Domestic Currency	TOTAL in $
Oil and petrochemicals	2 898	214	3 112
Agriculture	520	154	674
Energy	990	310	1 300
Ports	373	110	483
Human settlements	1 143	506	1 649
Heavy industry	1 598	354	1 952
Light industry	3 669	1 084	4 753
Transport	886	262	1 148
Environment	0	0	0
Health	359	159	518
Telecommunications and post	696	84	780
Education	662	293	955
Cultural heritage	13	6	19
TOTAL	13 807	3 536	17 343

Source: Mission estimates based on data provided by the Office of the Vice-President for Reconstruction.

Note: (1) This table is calculated using a rate of Rls 70/$ to convert foreign exchange expenditures.

(2) Domestic currency expenditures are expressed in 1988 prices at Rls 237 to the dollar.

/...

0141

66. The Government has also provided the mission with its preliminary forecasts of spending required in the future to complete its reconstruction efforts in the sectors listed in table 1. As this information was made available to the mission only very late in its second visit to the Islamic Republic of Iran, and after the sectoral experts had completed their reports and left the country, it has not been possible for the mission to examine these forecasts in detail. It can, however, be noted that they involve sums in foreign exchange which are very large, both in absolute terms, relative to the sums forecast to be expended in domestic currency, and by comparison with the expenditures (covering the development of the entire economy) set forth in the current five-year plan. In the mission's view, this could be attributable to the extreme difficulty to be encountered of attempting to separate purely reconstruction costs from development expenditures. Iran's economy is undergoing a major overhaul - particularly with regard to the updating of technology - in the wake of a population explosion and a decade-long absence from international business intercourse.

67. These qualifications having been made, table 2 below is presented for the sake of completeness. It will be noted that the lion's share (56.5 per cent) of the total relates to the oil and petrochemical industry, where the forecast foreign exchange requirements are especially large, given the need to acquire modern plant and equipment from abroad.

/...

0142

Table 2. Forecast of reconstruction expenditures by
government ministries

(In millions of United States dollars)

SECTOR	Expected Cost from 1991 on		
	Foreign Exchange	Domestic Currency	TOTAL in $
Oil and petrochemicals	122 389	1 197	123 587
Agriculture	24 518	2 105	26 623
Energy	15 763	1 513	17 276
Ports	16 733	554	17 287
Human settlements	8 983	3 144	12 127
Heavy industry	3 347	222	3 569
Light industry	8 928	724	9 670
Transport	2 526	376	2 902
Environment	3 403	270	3 673
Health	2 788	336	3 124
Telecommunications and post	2 063	33	2 096
Education	147	145	292
Cultural heritage	211	74	285
TOTAL	211 799	10 711	222 510

Source: Mission estimates based on data provided by the Office of the
Vice-President for Reconstruction.

Note: (1) A rate of Rls 70/$ is used to convert foreign exchange
expenditures.

(2) Domestic currency expenditures in the period from 1991
onwards are expressed in 1991 prices, and therefore a
conversion rate of Rls 300/$ has been used.

/...

0143

IV. THE ENVIRONMENTAL CONSEQUENCES OF THE CONFLICT

68. In the first report reference was made to the environmental consequences of the conflict in the sections on human settlements and agriculture. In the course of its second visit to the Islamic Republic of Iran, the team was provided with more detailed information on the nature of the damage to the environment and the measures that need to be taken to deal with the problem in its various forms.

69. In the case of human settlements the vast destruction of basic infrastructure in many cities and towns that were attacked or occupied during the conflict has created immense problems for the authorities, principally because the displaced population will not be able to return until the sites have been rebuilt. The costs are almost prohibitive, but essential. More details are provided in section V.A of the present report and section A of the addendum.

70. In the south-west provinces, particularly in the coastal region and along the main inland waterways, the scale of environmental destruction is extensive. For example it was stated that along the Karun River, which prior to the conflict was the pulse of the region's economic life, overall economic activities have been severely constrained owing to pollution and contamination. Farmlands were reported to contain dangerous substances resulting from many years of war activities, and these substances are said to have adversely affected the quality of crops. The rural population is reported to have suffered from an unusually high incidence of diseases, especially eye infections, stomach illnesses and skin ailments. These diseases do not occur at comparable levels outside the war-affected provinces. Health authorities are currently unable to offer any explanation as to the exact cause.

71. Along the coast, in particular between Abadan and the Strait of Hormuz, there are more than 250 kilometres of beaches covered with tar or asphalt, threatening the survival of already endangered species and protective vegetation. Leaking oil tankers attacked during the conflict are believed to be the cause of this situation. Oil pollution and oil spills were said to have negatively affected the economic life of more than 20 islands in the Persian Gulf. Mangroves and seagrass cultures have been destroyed, and there is a severe threat to the prawn fishing industry.

72. The section of the present report on agriculture and irrigation provides additional information on the type and extent of damage suffered, together with estimates of related reconstruction costs.

73. The sunken ships and wrecks in and along the river banks of the Shatt al-Arab pose another serious environmental hazard. Naturally, the magnitude of the problem increases commensurate with the time the sunken ships remain in their present position. In the process, the livelihood of fishermen is menaced and a serious danger exists to the ecology of the surrounding environment. No records are available on the nature of cargo carried by the ships at the time they were sunk. Any cleaning-up activity of the Shatt

/...

al-Arab waterway will have to be undertaken with the assistance of the international community and the full participation of the two riparian States.

74. Another type of environmental hazard created by the conflict is the presence of extensive minefields and unexploded ordnance in border areas. The Ministry of Health claimed that at least 10 persons are either killed, maimed or wounded daily by these lethal devices.

75. It is the Government's position that the major environmental problems arising from the conflict need to be studied in detail before preparing a plan to resolve them. Considering the dimension of the environmental degradation and its consequential overall impact, there appears to be a definite role for cooperation at the regional and international levels to address these issues. The Environmental Protection Organization informed the mission that it had so far been unable to carry out any conclusive surveys or studies because of the high cost involved and the level of specialization required. However, the authorities stated that international assistance is required to enable a number of studies highly prioritized by the Government to be undertaken. These include the following: clearance of debris in devastated cities; clearance of tar-polluted beaches; monitoring of Karun River pollution; effects of pollution on Persian Gulf islands; conservation of seagrass and mangrove forests; water quality studies in the war-affected provinces.

V. SECTORAL PRESENTATION (SUMMARIES)

(This section contains summaries of sectoral presentations. A detailed account of each presentation can be found in the addendum to the present report.)

A. Housing and human settlements

76. At the peak of hostilities, over 2 million persons were displaced by the conflict. The influx of large numbers of people over a short period of time placed a very heavy burden on the social and physical infrastructure of the receiving cities. In the process infrastructure, buildings and other facilities of the abandoned areas quickly deteriorated because they were not regularly maintained. Although the Government has placed the highest priority on creating the conditions appropriate for the return of the displaced, the mission was told that economic uncertainties and fear of renewed hostilities keep many of the displaced from returning to their homes in border areas. Thus far, about 250,000 displaced people have left camps to return to their former homes.

77. The loss of shelter for the displaced is the most widespread physical consequence of the conflict. In its field survey of damage, the mission ascertained that few residential or commercial structures in settlements within the areas occupied by enemy troops remained unharmed. The entire housing stock was destroyed in many villages and towns. Cities beyond the immediate area of ground hostilities also suffered varying degrees of damage to their housing stock as a result of missile attacks and aerial bombardment. A revised government estimate indicates that 117,635 housing units were lost;

/...

0145

there was a corresponding loss of commercial buildings in areas where ground action was fought, estimated by the Government to amount to 13,140 commercial units.

78. Water and sewerage systems in urban areas within the theatre of ground combat suffered not only from direct military action but also from collateral damage caused by destruction of buildings as well as by neglect. Networks have become silted and clogged and pumping stations have fallen into disrepair.

79. In areas under reconstruction, owners are responsible for the reconstruction of their own units. However, the Government provides partial compensation for losses and damage sustained by private individuals in the form of grants. In regard to the construction and repair of commercial and residential units, low-cost bank loans have also been made available to owners to cover expenses above the limit of compensation grants. The Government prepares physical development plans and provides technical support and supervision of construction efforts. Other support services include the free transport of building materials to construction sites.

80. The re-establishment of electric power is a prerequisite for the return of displaced populations to the reconstructed cities and towns. With power stations coming back on line and the transmission lines mostly in place, the only remaining element is the reconstruction of distribution networks within the towns and cities. According to the Government, this is being done as part of the overall reconstruction of settlements. Another major requirement for resettlement is the collection, removal and final disposal of waste, scrap and debris. In urban areas the clearing of the debris from damaged and destroyed buildings is well under way, but considerable work still remains to be done. Further, postal services - vital for communications - were greatly affected by the conflict. Some 64 post office buildings were either destroyed or damaged; the total area to be rebuilt is 17,378 m^2, of which 8,807 m^2 have already been rebuilt or rehabilitated.

81. The mission was informed that, for the reconstruction of human settlements, the Islamic Republic of Iran's primary need is for construction equipment. In addition, there are shortages of building materials. Iran possesses a well-qualified body of professionals in the fields related to the physical reconstruction and rehabilitation of war-devastated areas, such as engineering, architecture and urban and rural planning. The existing national capacity provides a good base for the utilization of specialized expertise to augment know-how already available within the country.

B. Petroleum industry

82. The economy of the Islamic Republic of Iran is heavily dependent on the production and export of oil for the generation both of domestic employment and income and of the foreign exchange needed to buy imported goods. The industry was devastated during the conflict.

/...

83. In the "upstream" (oil production) part of the industry, the damage and destruction inflicted covered every aspect of permanent oil/gas high-volume and high-pressure production operations in each of the three operating damaged sectors (south fields, north fields and offshore operations). Kharg Island (part of the south fields operation) warrants special mention because of its unique role in the exporting of Iranian crude oil and the devastation it incurred throughout most of the war by almost daily attacks. Before the war, Kharg was capable of off-loading 14 million barrels per day (b.p.d.), at its 14 berthing facilities, consisting of 10 berths at its T-jetty and four at Sea Island; its off-loading capability is now about 2 million b.p.d. The island had a pre-war crude oil storage capacity of 22 million barrels in 39 tanks; its storage capacity is currently 10 million barrels because 21 tanks were completely destroyed by fires occasioned by the attacks.

84. Table 3 below summarizes the information provided by the authorities on reconstruction costs for the three production areas in the country. It is based on expenditure incurred during the war plus those incurred since the cease-fire, and those expected to be incurred in the future. The authorities estimate that the total cost of "upstream" reconstruction, both past and for the future, amounts to Rls 795,500 million and $18,999 million.

Table 3. Reconstruction costs by production area

(In millions)

Area	TO DATE		IN FUTURE		T O T A L	
	Rls	US $	Rls	US $	Rls	US $
South	30 000	500	640 000	12 000	670 000	12 500
North	20 000	9	18 500	140	38 500	149
Off-shore	17 000	350	70 000	6 000	87 000	6 350
TOTAL	67 000	859	728 500	18 140	795 500	18 999

85. The "downstream" (refining and petrochemicals) operations were also severely affected by the conflict. The outbreak of war in 1980 witnessed attacks on all seven refineries with heavy damage and the widespread disruption of petroleum product supply, particularly at the Abadan refinery. Reconstruction and repairs, together with debottlenecking projects at the Tehran and Esfahan refineries, have brought most refineries back to or above pre-war production levels. However, Abadan is still operating at a little over one third of its original capacity owing to the shortage of crude, although it is capable of operating at one half of its original capacity.

/...

86. The location of the petrochemical industry, along the northern shore of the Persian Gulf meant that the facilities came within easy range of aerial attack during the war. The huge joint venture plant at Bandar Khomeyni was more than 60 per cent completed when the war began. Its products were for the most part to be exported and were expected to provide major revenue for the country. However, as a consequence of the war, the entire project has had to be suspended on account of the damage sustained, and the high cost of reconstruction and risk involved during the war. The damage to the entire sector was such that, for several years during the middle part of the war, production in all chemical plants was virtually halted. This led to a production loss of the order of 30 million metric tons of total petrochemical products over the eight-year period. All the plants, with the exception of the joint venture facility, are once again operating near their pre-war capacity levels. However, much of the reconstruction is of a temporary nature and no major funding has as yet been earmarked for permanent repair of the extensive patchwork.

87. The table below summarizes the information provided by the authorities on reconstruction costs for the seven refineries and seven petrochemical plants in the country, based on expenses incurred during the war plus those incurred since the cease-fire, and those expected to be incurred in the future. The total cost of "downstream" reconstruction, both past and in the future, by the Government's estimate, is thus Rls 218,738 million and $4,098 million.

Table 4. Reconstruction costs incurred on refineries and petrochemical plants

(In millions)

Type	TO DATE		IN FUTURE		T O T A L	
	Rls	US $	Rls	US $	Rls	US $
Refinery	19 034	357	42 298	793	61 332	1 150
Petro-chemical	48 850	915	108 556	2 033	157 406	2 948
TOTAL	67 884	1 272	150 854	2 826	218 738	4 098

Source: Based on documentation obtained at NIOC.

88. In brief, the Government estimates that it has already expended the equivalent of $2,700 million on reconstruction of the oil industry, and expects to spend a further sum equivalent to $24,000 million to complete the task.

/...

Table 5. Reconstruction costs to oil industry

(In millions)

Type	TO DATE		IN FUTURE		T O T A L	
	Rls	US $	Rls	US $	Rls	US $
Upstream	67 000	859	728 500	18 140	795 500	18 999
Down-Stream	67 884	1 272	150 854	2 826	218 738	4 098
TOTAL	134 884	2 131	879 354	20 966	1014 238	23 097

Note: Rls 134,884 million @ Rls 237/$ = $ 569 million;
      Rls 879,354 million @ Rls 300/$ = $ 2,931 million.

Source: Based on documentation obtained at NIOC.

89. The estimate for the oil sector presented to the mission by the
Vice-President for Reconstruction is as presented in the table below. As can
be seen, they are different from those presented to the mission by NIOC.

Table 6. Estimate of reconstruction costs in the oil sector

(In millions of rials)

Name of unit affected	From start of war until approval of resolution	From approval of resolution until first year of plan	Allocations from first year of plan until 1991	Reqd. before end of 1992	Required before completion: foreign currency ($m)	Required before completion: local currency (millions of rials)	Total ($m)	Total (Rm)
NIOC	59 081	25 617	53 613	126 860	99 097	1 618 194	101 085	1 724 262
National Gas Company	2 642	1 763	208	410	125	7 000	160	9,255
National Petrochem. Company	27 394	14 266	69 022	514	2 642	43 000	3 472	759
Ministry of Petroleum (total)	89 117	41 646	122 843	127 784	101 864	1 668 194	104 717	1 734 276

($1 = 80 rials)

Source: Vice-President for Reconstruction, November 1991.

Note: The data on reconstruction obtained from NIOC covers only part of
the reconstruction programme for the industry. The information provided in
the above table is in respect of the industry as a whole.

/...

0149

C. Transport

1. Roads, rail and air transport

90. An impressive amount of reconstruction was carried out in the land and air transportation sub-sector, both during and after the war. It was essential for the war effort to keep transport corridors open in the border provinces; therefore reconstruction of airports, roads and railways was carried out during the war and, where subsequent damage occurred, repeated several times. These multiple repairs are not visible now, but they are reflected in the estimate of the direct loss. The team's inspection confirmed that in most cases the ruins of buildings and pattern of reconstruction, as well as debris and destroyed equipment, were consistent with the damage reports and photographs.

91. The total direct loss in the transportation sub-sector was estimated by the Government at Rls 1,085,600 million. The loss sustained by this sub-sector, compared with other sectors, does not appear to be high, but this is only the quantifiable part of the loss. The war caused a considerable delay in the development of the road and railway network, as well as of port capacities, and this in turn caused serious bottlenecks in the development of other sectors. This part of the loss is not visible in the transportation sub-sector itself. The Government has estimated the costs of reconstruction to date in the transport sector at the equivalent of $1,148 million, and expects the completion of reconstruction already planned to cost the equivalent of a further $2,902 million.

92. The mission has made attempts to verify all severe damage and to assess the extent of the losses suffered by both land and air transportation, as reported by the Iranian authorities. The monetary value of damage caused to buildings and installations in the land and air transportation sub-sector appears to be appropriate except for roads where, in the mission's view, damage to the road network was underestimated. However, the mission was not able to verify the extent of damage caused to railway rolling stock, aircraft, road vehicles and equipment for railway and road construction and maintenance, as these had already been cleared from road sites and depots.

93. Most damage to roads was not caused by direct bombardment, but by overloaded vehicles and/or because of lack of appropriate maintenance during or immediately after the war. Because of the priorities given to the border areas, only relatively small repairs and improvements to the country's road network could be undertaken during the war period, with the result that the overall quality of the road system deteriorated.

94. The reconstruction of land and air transport physical infrastructure was planned and designed by Iranian engineers and executed by Iranian skilled manpower through (mostly privately owned) Iranian companies. The mission observed that the reconstruction work performed meets standard quality requirements even in complicated undertakings, such as bridge construction, or in work with high quality requirements, such as runway construction. Based on

/...

the quality of work observed, the team felt that the Islamic Republic of Iran has adequate and appropriate expertise and manpower for reconstruction work in this sector. However, a considerable amount of foreign currency is needed for the import of equipment and spare parts not manufactured in the country. Reconstruction of railway installations also requires a foreign currency component for materials and parts not locally manufactured.

95. The damage to machinery and equipment in the land and air transport sub-sector (aircraft, railway rolling stock, road vehicles, equipment for railway and road maintenance, as well as other land and air transportation machinery and equipment) was considerably higher than the reported damage to structures and installations. However, because of the restrictions imposed on the country during the war, replacement or repair was, in most cases, of lower quality and considerably more expensive than it normally should have been. Moreover, with few exceptions (railway freight wagons and passenger coaches), these items will need to be imported, thereby causing a heavy foreign currency drain on the economy.

96. A high priority in reconstruction has been given to the rebuilding of the Khorramshahr-Ahwaz railway line, the Abadan and Ahwaz airports, and major bridges in the border provinces. The construction of additional railway capacity to the port of Bandar Khomeyni and new railway capacity to the port of Bandar Abbas, as a consequence of the shifting of port capacities from Khorramshahr, will alleviate the land transportation problems and eliminate some of the bottlenecks. The railway network also needs upgrading and modernization as well as renovation and additions to the rolling stock. The team observed that railways are not carrying a sufficient share of freight although they do have the capacity to do so.

97. All modes of land transport suffered from lack of maintenance and renewal investments during the war and it is critical that such deficiencies be corrected through modernization. In order to upgrade the land transportation infrastructure and to apply a higher level of technology, foreign inputs, mainly foreign exchange, would be needed.

98. The Iranian authorities recognize that it is important to reconstruct and develop the air transportation sub-sector, because there are no viable alternatives to air travel over long distances. However, air transportation facilities have not so far been reconstructed, modernized or developed to an appropriate level. To facilitate this modernization, substantial foreign inputs will be needed.

2. Ports and marine salvage

99. Ports and shipping were major targets during the war years; they are now key factors for the country's recovery and expansion. The Iranian authorities have devoted much effort and expense to emergency repairs, which frequently had to be repeated, followed by restoration and by replacement construction or acquisitions. The work which is still to be carried out will take a considerable period of time to complete.

/...

100. According to information presented to the mission, the repairs to or replacement of shipping tonnage is well under way. The losses of dry cargo tonnage (17 total losses and 18 vessels damaged) amounted to $201 million. The reconstitution of oil cargo tonnage has been completed, at a cost of $498 million.

101. The reconstruction of oil ports has involved substantial repair expenses. Major restoration work under way includes a $225 million project for Kharg Island. Reconstruction of commercial ports during the post-cease-fire years has focused on the reconstruction of Khorramshahr and repairs at Bandar Khomeyni, as well as on landside debris clearance at Abadan and Khorramshahr. A further $57 million has been expended on the dredging of the Bahmanshir.

102. Construction at the major port of Bandar Abbas was continued during the war years, with the result that the overall capacity of Iranian ports is almost at a level with the needs of the present-day economy. However, reconstruction of the ports of Abadan and Khorramshahr, which is planned in the immediate phase to cost the equivalent of $2,468 million, is urgently needed in order to promote a good geographical balance in port location; to ensure a smooth flow of traffic during peak periods; and to meet the needs of future economic expansion, especially in Khuzestan. In addition, the Government estimates that a further $300 million will be required to complete the dredging of the Bahmanshir.

103. The reopening of the Shatt al-Arab is an imperative priority for any undertaking to reconstruct the ports of Abadan and Khorramshahr. The river serves the Iranian ports of Abadan and Khorramshahr, as well as the Iraqi port of Basra. It was reported that during the war, inumerable unexploded shells and bombs landed on the river bed; many vessels were hit and sunk; and a huge amount of silt has accumulated in a channel which used to be dredged regularly. Map 2 indicates approximate areas where wrecked ships and barges are visible from the Iranian shoreline. According to the Government's preliminary estimate, dredging of the waterway would cost $1,800 million.

104. In the course of its discussions, the team understood that once political agreement was reached for the reopening of the waterway international help would be necessary in order:

(a) To alleviate the very heavy financial burden of reconstruction;

(b) To provide, from foreign sources, much-needed specialized machinery, equipment and personnel, hitherto inaccessible to the Islamic Republic of Iran because of export restrictions;

(c) To provide for the clearance of wrecks and unexploded ordnance from the waterway, requiring the latest technology;

(d) To provide the clearance of a number of dangerous wrecks in the Persian Gulf, which require special heavy equipment.

0152
/...

105. Such assistance from the international community would be necessary, despite the proven competence and expertise of the Iranian authorities and personnel, if all the required reconstruction work is to be accomplished within a reasonable period of time.

D. Industry

1. Heavy industry

106. This economic sector comprises the iron, steel and aluminium industries, including their downstream facilities for metal transformation, and the Islamic Republic of Iran's heavy manufacturing industry. A great number of these industrial plants are located in the south of the country relatively close to major Persian Gulf ports and important raw material sources. During the conflict many factories were destroyed either through enemy occupation or by frequent air raids and artillery attacks.

107. According to government estimates, direct damage sustained by the heavy industry sector amounts to approximately Rls 1,102,029 million. Although the mission was not in a position to verify this overall figure, it carried out on-site inspections to 12 major industrial plants which indicated that the damage estimate in the case of the plants visited appeared to be reasonably accurate.

108. Reconstruction expenditure incurred by the Ministry of Heavy Industry has amounted to approximately $1,952 million since the outbreak of the hostilities. In certain instances, some plants were destroyed several times over during the conflict. After each attack, repairs were carried out immediately so that the plants became operational again in the short term.

109. Based on inspection visits to a representative sample of plants in the heavy industry sector, it is the mission's impression that major sectoral constraints include, inter alia, lack of finance for investment, technological gaps, shortage of adequate high-level manpower, and, in certain cases, a lack of sufficiently inexpensive domestic raw materials. Although investment prospects have improved following a decision by Government to encourage foreign participation in joint ventures, matters such as obsolete technology and manpower shortages will need to be addressed in a more comprehensive manner in the long term.

110. Technical staff will need to be exposed to new technologies in other countries by means of study tours and short-term assignments abroad. Moreover, priority will continue to be assigned to the strengthening of national technical institutions and establishment of additional vocational and management institutions.

111. The team believes that for the better and more efficient use of domestic raw materials, the Government - together with the private sector - might wish to revive the important bauxite, alunite and nepheline mines with necessary investments, in order to be able to cut back on expensive imports.

/...

112. Since the end of the conflict, the metal-producing industry has been undergoing a significant transformation which includes a shift away from government ownership. Government is encouraging full private-sector participation both domestically and from abroad. One of the largest privatization efforts being undertaken at present concerns the Arak aluminium plant, where two thirds of the needed investment is expected to be made available by foreign companies.

113. The rehabilitation of heavy industry in the narrowest sense of its meaning can be considered to be complete. Almost all steel and aluminium plants damaged during the conflict are now producing more than in 1980. In certain instances, as for example in the case of the Arak aluminum production plant, the pre-war capacity, which amounted to 45,000 tons per year, was surpassed in 1988 as annual production reached more than 75,000 tons. The future reconstruction programme foresees a further increase in output levels to 120,000 tons per year to satisfy domestic demand in keeping with the overall economic expansion.

114. For the future, the Government has prepared an ambitious programme to modernize its metallurgical industry. This will demand a new generation of engineers, highly skilled specialists, managers and administrators. It is important that the international community be prepared to cooperate in providing technical assistance in the form of highly specialized, short-term advisory services and assist Iranian authorities in advising on research and development programmes, as well as in the identification of equipment and technology.

2. Light industry

115. The light industry sector which comes under the responsibility of the Ministry of Industry covers a wide variety of industrial sub-sectors and includes, _inter alia_, food, leather, textile, paper, chemical, electronics, printing and service industries. Together, these small-, medium- and large-scale industries account for almost 80 per cent of Iranian industry.

116. The mission observed through selected on-site visits that the industrial sector had sustained considerable damage. Damage was severest in the five western provinces where extensive ground fighting took place. The majority of industries destroyed are at present little more than piles of debris and corroded steel. Outside the immediate battle zone, destruction to industrial units was in general less severe, although some installations sustained heavy losses owing to aerial bombardment.

117. The mission also observed that most of the plants are back to what at least superficially resembles normal operation. Physical traces of damage are visible everywhere, many factories continue to suffer from a lack of spare parts, and maintenance facilities and back-up services are limited as a result of the makeshift reconstruction and repair work.

0154
/...

118. Responsibility for the reconstruction of small production units was generally exercised at the local level, with work on medium- and large-scale units being directed from Tehran. In respect of government fund allocation for reconstruction purposes, priority continues to be given to strategic products such as food and building materials. At the plant level, the highest priority was given to the immediate rehabilitation of the most essential production equipment in order to retain a basic production process. The functioning of auxiliary facilities such as maintenance and repair workshops, stand-by generators, safety equipment and administrative buildings which would secure dependable industrial output has yet to be addressed.

119. About 80 per cent of the light industry sector is at present privately owned and, as a consequence of the Government's post-war privatization policy, the share of the private sector is increasing rapidly. Private sector initiative is also a dominating factor in the reconstruction process. Some larger factories managed to finance their reconstruction programmes from their own resources and without any government assistance. Most of the small- and medium-scale units in the war-affected provinces, however, take advantage of the financial incentives offered by the Government.

120. The mission observed that private entrepreneurs are responding positively to the Government's call for new industrial initiatives in the war-affected provinces, especially in the Abadan-Khorramshahr industrial parks, where pioneering industries such as processed meat, fish powder, plastic tubing and textiles are being successfully established.

121. With the exception of the areas where ground fighting took place, most craftsmen have returned to their workshops and nearly all medium- and large-scale industries have reached pre-war output levels. No significant relocation of any medium- or large-size industry has been reported and the reconstruction and rehabilitation process has not been impeded by any reported manpower shortages. At the management level, the lack of awareness of up-to-date technologies has had some adverse effect, but abilities to improvise and the development of mechanical skills have reached impressive levels.

122. Although rehabilitation and reconstruction have brought outputs to pre-war levels, the overall situation is far from satisfactory. Owing to lack of funds, especially the foreign currency components, reconstruction of production lines has often stopped at the bare minimum. As a result, several major plants are, for example, without stand-by generators, proper maintenance facilities or adequate spare part stores. In order to improve this situation and to ensure that no serious work stoppages occur as a result of these shortfalls, it will be necessary to invest large sums of foreign exchange. According to government estimates nearly $3,900 million will be needed in foreign exchange for reconstruction expenditure during the current five-year plan.

123. In the view of the mission the international community could play a major role in providing financial and technical assistance in the completion of the

/...

reconstruction and rehabilitation process. For more than 10 years technology transfer was seriously interrupted. In many instances, industries focused on keeping a basic production process going rather than experimenting with technological innovations. United Nations agencies could be called upon to facilitate the contacts between Iranian industry and relevant technology holders abroad.

E. Agriculture and irrigation

124. The institutional framework relating to the agricultural sector comprises: (a) the Ministry of Agriculture, which is responsible for crop production, on-farm irrigation and other agricultural activities; (b) the Ministry of Energy (mobilization and conveyance of irrigation water); and (c) the Ministry of Construction Jehad (forests, pastures and fisheries).

125. The agricultural sector is reported by the Government to have sustained direct losses equivalent to $7,523 million and to have been the object of reconstruction expenditure to date amounting to $674 million. The Government estimates the cost in the current phase of the present five-year development plan for agricultural reconstruction to be $7,800 million. The farming sub-sector accounts for 80 per cent of the estimated direct losses.

126. The rehabilitation of agricultural land destroyed as a result of the war is accorded the highest priority through land levelling, restoration of the irrigation network and the provision of farm machinery and livestock to resettled farmers. Replanting of destroyed date palms and orchards, reconstruction of agro-industries, replanting of forests and rehabilitation of pastures are given the next order of priority.

127. In the three most affected provinces of Khuzestan, Ilam and Bakhtaran, reconstruction of the farming sub-sector involves land levelling and grading of about 251,000 ha of irrigated farmland and rough levelling of 53,700 ha of rain-fed land. The irrigated areas would also require the construction of irrigation networks comprising 8,500 kilometres of distributary canals and 6,000 kilometres of drainage channels. In addition, about 1,300 kilometres of traditional irrigation canals require reconstruction. Using large fleets of heavy earth-moving equipment, about one half of the above tasks have already been completed. Subject to the availability of foreign exchange resources for replacement of much of the outdated equipment and purchase of spare parts, the remaining work is scheduled for completion before the expiry of the second five-year plan period ending in 1999.

128. Areas dependent on lift irrigation would require reconstruction of 47 large and 300 small pumping stations, as well as 258 deep tube wells and about 200 tube wells of moderate depth. Apart from the deep tube wells, of which some 75 per cent have been reconstructed, very little progress has so far been achieved in reconstructing the remaining units owing to resource constraints.

129. Damage to the water resources sub-sector under the Ministry of Energy would require reconstruction of 126 diversion weirs, 242 pump stations and

tube wells for lift irrigation, about 1,700 kilometres of main canals and ancillary works such as access roads, construction camps and hydro-met stations. Overall progress on reconstruction of the damaged works is estimated at about 20 per cent, with the remaining works scheduled for completion, subject to availability of resources, by the end of the second five-year plan period.

130. About 18 per cent of farm machinery, such as 65 HP tractor units with implements, for resettled farmers, has been supplied so far. Subject to resource availability, the supply of the remaining machinery is scheduled to be completed by the year 1999.

131. More than 3 million date palms and 5,000 ha of orchards were destroyed during the conflict, of which about 15 to 20 per cent have so far been replanted. Reconstruction of damaged farm support buildings, comprising a total area of about 63,000 square metres, has been completed to the extent of about 40 per cent. The remaining work is scheduled for completion by the year 1999.

132. Sugar production at the two major agro-industries in the Ahwaz-Dezful region of Khuzestan is making rapid recovery. In Haft Tappeh it has been restored to about 80 per cent of originally installed capacity of 100,000 tons per year, while in the case of Karun, recovery has reached 20 per cent of its 250,000 ton capacity. Interrupted plans for establishing seven more agro-industrial units in the area have been reactivated.

133. Progress made towards the rehabilitation of some 130,000 ha of natural forests and 753,000 ha of pasture lands in the war zone, together with repair of damage in the fisheries sub-sector, could not be ascertained owing to unavailability of data.

134. The environmental impact of the conflict on the agricultural sector comprises (a) adverse effects on soil fertility due to the removal of topsoil, compaction and flooding of agricultural lands; (b) waterlogging and salinity arising from ingress of saline water into agricultural land, modification in river flow regimes and interruption in the installation of drainage networks; and (c) soil and water contamination, reported by the Government, from the toxic materials emanating from chemical and biological weapons. Comprehensive studies are required to assess the nature and extent of environmental damage caused by the war and to devise remedial measures. The mission noted that the physical constraint imposed by the presence of unidentified mine fields may delay the rehabilitation of some 20 per cent of the affected agricultural land.

135. The principal constraints to completion of the reconstruction programme are (a) the paucity of foreign exchange resources to meet the cost of importing equipment, spare parts and construction materials; and (b) the shortage of skilled manpower and supporting facilities.

136. The expressed needs for external assistance comprise mainly foreign exchange resources for the procurement of (a) heavy earth-moving equipment

/...

such as scrapers, bulldozers, graders, loaders etc. and their spare parts;
(b) civil engineering construction equipment and construction materials such
as well drilling, canal lining, pumping plant, steel and cement, etc.; and
(c) farm machinery and implements with a total capacity of about 250,000 HP.

137. The mission was impressed by progress already achieved in the
reconstruction effort and recommends that, in addition to the expressed needs
for external assistance, technical assistance be provided to assess the
reported environmental damage caused by waterlogging of agricultural lands and
the resulting salinization of the soil.

F. Electric power

138. According to the Ministry of Energy, the major areas of loss in the
electrical sector were (a) the war-zone border provinces of Khuzestan, Ilam,
Bakhtaran and Kordestan, where widespread damage was done to the generation,
transmission and distribution systems; and (b) the transmission network and
principal generating stations in other parts of the country, which were
targeted with a view to disrupting national power supplies.

139. It was evident from the mission's visits to sites in Khuzestan that,
although major efforts had been made to maintain power supplies to consumers,
aided by the installation of temporary diesel generators, significant
reconstruction work remains to be done on the distribution system
(70 per cent, according to the local power authority, over a period of two
years). A number of substations are operating without proper protection
equipment. Two thirds of the reconstruction work has been carried out using
materials diverted from development projects in other areas, and some
10 per cent of the system has been reconstructed only in a temporary manner.
Materials and spare parts valued at some Rls 12,100 million were also
destroyed in the conflict while awaiting distribution from Khorramshahr.

140. In Ilam, Bakhtaran and Kordestan, several small diesel generating units
with an overall capacity of 138 MW were destroyed in isolated networks.
Rather than replace them, the local power authority installed systems
connecting such areas to the major interconnected transmission network.
Substantial damage was also done to the distribution system: 70 per cent of
the reconstruction work remains to be done, over a period of two years. In
the case of West Azerbayjan, which suffered a lesser degree of damage,
80 per cent of reconstruction work has yet to be completed.

141. Most major substations of the transmission system were damaged during the
war, causing disruptions of the power supply to major cities: 50 per cent of
the damage was repaired during the war, but 90 per cent of the repaired
facilities was further damaged in subsequent attacks. Approximately
50 per cent of the physical reconstruction work is now complete: the
remaining work should, in principle, take two years to complete but will
probably take longer owing to financial constraints.

142. According to the national authorities, six thermal power stations and two hydroelectric stations suffered damage during the war: all were restored to service, but in many cases temporary repairs resulted in unreliable operation. The major interconnected system currently has an installed generating capacity of 11,017 megawatts, having doubled - in response to increased demand - between 1980 and 1988. Whereas in 1980 only 7,800 villages were supplied with electric power, that figure rose to 24,000 by 1990, meaning that over 65 per cent of the rural population received supplies.

143. As for nuclear energy, the mission was informed that two 1,200-megawatt units had been under construction (one 85 per cent complete, the other 60 per cent) at the start of the conflict. Both were severely damaged. Neither the nuclear reactor nor nuclear fuel had been delivered.

144. During the war, the Government's policy was to concentrate on the rapid restoration of damaged facilities, achieved exclusively through the use of locally available materials. With the end of the conflict, it has formulated the following immediate objectives: (a) to restore the production capacity of damaged power stations; (b) to ensure that damaged major transmission systems could meet power requirements throughout the country; and (c) to restore the local supply networks in the war-affected provinces to full capacity. Its long-term objectives are (a) to complete the permanent reconstruction of damaged facilities; (b) to implement pre-war development plans for production, transmission and distribution; and (c) to replenish stocks of materials required to ensure the electrical system is not disrupted. The major constraints encountered in meeting such objectives are the time delays involved in ordering equipment from abroad, together with a shortage of foreign exchange with which to make the purchases.

145. Although the situation has improved greatly since the conclusion of the conflict, there are still frequent interruptions to the power supply. In order to overcome these problems, the Ministry has reportedly awarded contracts to construct a further 9,000 megawatts of generating capacity and to expand the associated transmission facilities. In a further attempt to upgrade services, the Ministry has, in principle, agreed to privatize the operation of both regional electric companies and power-generating plants.

146. The Ministry has indicated that international assistance will be required, particularly with regard to the purchase of up-to-date equipment, in order to upgrade the electrical system to a level comparable with that which would have been achieved if the conflict had not affected normal development. There is also a considerable need for assistance in areas relating to management, planning and power systems design, as well as the updating of technology, including dam construction and modern control systems.

G. Telecommunications and broadcasting

147. Estimates of physical damage to the telecommunications sector sustained during the conflict indicate that 172 buildings, 9,000 kilometres of

/...

underground cable and more than 50,000 telephone lines were at least partially destroyed. The value of the damaged assets has been estimated by the Telecommunications Company of Iran (TCI) at a minimum of Rls 115,000 million.

148. The damage observed can be classified into two main categories: damage was total in areas which were occupied by enemy forces, while somewhat lesser damage occurred in those areas outside the war theatre where air and ground artillery attacks took place sporadically. Telecommunication towers are clearly highly visible targets and the exchange and microwave installations could therefore be easily identified. Targeted installations in the interior of the country, however, did not in general suffer serious damage.

149. As regards reconstruction work, the mission believes that the bulk of the restoration of primary services has been completed. A major installation at Khorramshahr, installations of underground cable networks, provision of additional telephone service in the border provinces and the completion of some microwave works are the main items pending.

150. The mission was also informed that the Ministry is currently implementing a five-year reconstruction-cum-development plan, with a view to expanding and modernizing telecommunications systems, that goes beyond normal reconstruction. The plan, which focuses on the border provinces, incorporates both repair and reconstruction of damaged assets, as well as the normal expansion which would have occurred during the period 1980-1988. A total of Rls 139,000 million has been allocated to complete the plan objectives. The mission plan does not separate reconstruction work from development objectives. The mission could not obtain such data.

151. As for the damage to broadcasting installations, the mission was informed that the war had resulted in the destruction of many high-power medium-wave transmitters, FM radio transmitters, buildings and television studios. Their replacement would cost an estimated Rls 19,000 million.

152. The mission noted that in the reconstruction process the general trend is to replace broadcasting equipment with more powerful and technologically advanced components. Moreover, in order to reduce the risk of future damage, new stations are being housed in thick concrete shelters. This has increased reconstruction costs.

153. The mission is impressed with the quality of the reconstruction work in the telecommunications and broadcasting sector. The technical level of Iranian personnel does not call for any outside assistance, with the exception of work relating to the installation and commissioning of transmitters and antennas. Up to now, the Islamic Republic of Iran Broadcasting Corporation (IRIB) has executed all these tasks with its own personnel. However, owing to the increased number of projects to be implemented and the lack of adequately trained engineers, severe difficulties are now being encountered in commissioning some transmitter stations. IRIB in some cases has to call on the services of the equipment supplier which, in general, increases the costs and causes delays.

/0160

H. Education

154. In the five war-affected provinces, 9,300 of the pre-war total of 44,300 classrooms in 2,637 schools were reported as having been damaged or destroyed during the conflict. In addition, 362 schools in other provinces were affected by missile attacks. About 450,000 of the five provinces' 1.25 million pupils and students were forced to flee to other regions, necessitating the introduction of a double-shift system at those regions' schools. Migration of teachers away from the war-affected provinces also continues to pose serious problems.

155. The Government accords high priority to the reconstruction of primary schools and to the provision of teachers in the war-affected provinces. The authorities provide incentives to encourage staff to return to hardship areas where amenities are few and locations remote. It was stated that there was a sufficient number of teachers to staff the schools that had been reconstructed.

156. Over the past three years, more than 50 per cent (1,422) of the damaged schools have been brought back into service. Reconstruction work has been completed on 12 technical and vocational training centres, at a cost of Rls 21,000 million. Work on a further 370 schools is due to be completed within the current budget period. Approximately 20 per cent of the total reconstruction effort has been undertaken by various foundations and trusts working in parallel with the Government, while much of the expenditure (Rls 103,553 million to date, with remaining requirements estimated at Rls 146,400 million) has been covered by voluntary assistance.

157. In the devastated rural areas, school reopenings will have to be delayed until a viable community is re-established. For this reason it is unlikely that later phases of the school restoration programme will proceed at the same pace as has been maintained to date. Thus, only 60 to 70 per cent of remaining reconstruction work is likely to be completed by the end of the first five-year plan period.

158. The major constraint affecting restoration of educational services is a shortage of building materials. In devastated areas, this situation is compounded by the need to replace basic services and infrastructure, including adequate housing. According to the authorities, the problem in the devastated areas is not one of an insufficient number of teachers but of the tremendous need for urban and rural reconstruction.

159. At the national level, there is a shortage of teachers; 40,000 new primary school teachers are required each year, while only 25,000 graduate annually from teacher-training centres; the shortage of secondary teachers is put at 116,000. With a view to easing the pressure on the Government's programme, the private sector has been allowed to set up non-profit-making educational establishments at all levels.

160. With regard to international assistance, the Ministry of Education has expressed interest in expert support for "school mapping" activities. The mission also feels, given the Government's stated policy of reviewing and

/...

0161

modifying the education and training system in accordance with the country's needs and development programme, that expertise in the form of comprehensive human resources analysis might be helpful. Furthermore, it envisages problems in the form of teacher shortages, particularly in rural schools as the resettlement programme gets under way.

161. While current standards of school construction are high, there is no doubt that schools which function equally well could be built at lower costs, for example, by simplifying structures and/or reducing or entirely omitting internal circulation spaces. Area unit costs over the entire range of school types are said to be between Rls 200,000 and 300,000 per square metre (at 1990 prices). The current shortfall in teaching space is now of the order of 160,000 classrooms.

162. The mission was unable to obtain details of the situation regarding institutes of higher education.

I. Cultural heritage

163. Listed archaeological sites, monuments and museums of outstanding significance suffered severe and, in some cases, irreparable damage. Field visits, although necessarily subject to time constraints, permitted an inspection of damage to the well-known national museums, to the principal cultural heritage institutions and to the principal historic cities, monuments and sites affected by the war.

164. Significant damage was done to the excavated monuments at Shush, as well as to the archaeological research centre and exhibits stored within it. One wing of the Shrine of Daniel was partially destroyed, while the mirror decoration of the iwan collapsed. At Chaqa Zanbil, a section of the outer casing of the first and second stages of the ziggurat collapsed, while the Haft Tappeh site was disturbed by trench-digging and the erection of defensive military obstacles. Indirect damage in the Shush area included the illicit removal of objects from unprotected sites and a failure to maintain conservation programmes.

165. In Esfahan, 10 major mosques, 5 religious schools, 3 main bazaars and more than 40 listed historic houses suffered damage, while over 1,000 old houses were totally destroyed. The south-eastern prayer hall of the 'Atiq Congregational Mosque was hit by rockets in 1984, but restoration is now complete. Various restoration and rebuilding work was carried out on the damaged Agha Nur Mosque and its adjacent bazaar, the Masjid Sayyid and the Hammam-e-Wazir. Although no direct damage was inflicted on monuments around Maidan-e-Imam, shock waves from a missile explosion were thought to be responsible for the lifting of faience tiles around the crown of the Imam Mosque's dome. Ongoing conservation work on other monuments was halted to make way for restoration activities.

0162
/...

166. Approximately 15,000 houses and public buildings are said to have been destroyed in Dezful, involving irreparable damage to the urban fabric of the historic city centre. Many historic houses and public buildings were also destroyed or damaged in the old town of Shushtar.

167. Of Iran's 40 museums, 5 in Tehran, 3 in Khuzestan and 1 in Lorestan were all damaged to varying degrees, that of Abadan being destroyed completely. At museums in Tehran, the National, Golestan Palace, National Arts and Glass and Ceramics, nearby explosions caused damage both to exhibits and to the structure of the buildings. In Khuzestan, repairs to the Shush museum building had been completed, while restoration of damage to the collections was still in progress. Despite some repairs to the Haft Tappeh museum, the damaged ventilation system and some showcases need replacement.

168. The Iranian authorities have declared their priorities for the reconstruction and restoration of war-damaged cultural heritage to be as follows: comprehensive revision of plans and objectives; establishment of an adapted organization; provision of adequate legal and financial means; rehabilitation of manpower; rehabilitation and modernization of facilities and equipment; and the reconstruction, restoration and rehabilitation of damaged monuments, sites, museums and collections. The Cultural Heritage Organization estimates that approximately one tenth of restoration work has so far been completed. In monetary terms, that organization estimates that a total of Rls 37,000 million, will be required for restoration work. To date approximately Rls 23,000 million have been spent. That figure does not include overheads or private sector losses. It also excludes the contribution of voluntary groups said to have been organized throughout the country to ensure the protection of heritage sites.

169. With respect to external assistance, the need was expressed for training - both abroad and on-site - of an entire new generation in the conservation, restoration and documentation of cultural property, as well as in the various branches of museology. New technology is required, including, in particular, photogrammetric plotting equipment. Software is needed for the inventory of historic monuments, as well as cultural and intellectual exchanges with overseas institutions and access to specialist publications and reviews.

170. In terms of technical assistance, international advice is sought on methods for the conservation of stone, baked brick and adobe structures. Assistance is also needed for a study of the ancient water mills and irrigation system at Shushtar. A draft United Nations Development Programme project on "Assistance for Training of Personnel and Restoration of Historic Monuments" should be amended to concentrate on the strengthening of the National Research Laboratory in Tehran. Extrabudgetary funding is required to restore a group of historic houses in Esfahan with a view to expanding the facilities of the existing School of Restoration.

/...

171. Despite the commitment of considerable human resources to restoration efforts, and the zeal and competence of traditional craftsmen working under the supervision of talented experts, it is the mission's view that it will take many years to complete the necessary work.

J. Health

172. During the conflict, a total of 102 "health houses", 84 rural health centres, 80 urban health centres and 12 provincial and/or district health centres were destroyed. In addition, 5 quarantine and tuberculosis control centres and hospitals containing 2,076 beds sustained severe damage which will require complete rebuilding. The destruction included medical equipment, supplies, medicines and vehicles.

173. The total cost of infrastructure reconstruction during the period 1983-1990 amounted to Rls 50,848 million for the Ministry of Health and Rls 12,000 million for other governmental bodies and institutions. Infrastructure reconstruction costs for the health sector 1991-1993 are estimated at Rls 295,454 million. War damage to health facilities in the non-government sector was estimated at some Rls 156,943 million, with reconstruction costs expected to exceed the estimated cost of the damage.

174. Health and medical education facilities, which also fall under the responsibility of the Ministry of Health, were severely damaged. They include 3 medical universities, 37 teaching hospitals and 17 educational/research centres in the 5 war-affected provinces. Reconstruction work on 10 hospitals and 10 training centres was completed by the end of 1990.

175. Given its additional responsibility for water supply and sanitation facilities in all villages housing over 150 families, the Ministry incurred costs of some 5,200 million rials in respect of damage to such facilities. The actual cost of reconstruction work so far completed was stated to be Rls 7,346 million.

176. The mission was informed of a latest survey which showed that 593,000 civilians were physically and/or mentally disabled as a result of the war. This is well over the provisional estimates mentioned in the mission's first report. Despite the Government's efforts to reduce the impact of such disabilities, it will be impossible to cover their needs and to meet established health targets in the war-affected provinces without international assistance to help support the launching of an accelerated reconstruction and rehabilitation programme. The programme will need to take into account environmental problems which have proliferated as a result of the interruption of health services during the conflict: the destruction of water and sanitation systems; chemical contamination of the soil; and the threat posed by an alarming increase in health-threatening pests and insects. The incidence of acute respiratory diseases and diarrhoea has risen sharply, resulting in an increase in morbidity and mortality rates.

0164

/...

177. The Government is determined to ensure the earliest possible rehabilitation of interrupted health services and to encourage the return of physicians and other health workers to the border provinces. As a matter of urgency, it hopes for international assistance in securing the following items: 2,000 field vehicles; 1,000 ambulances; 300 prefabricated health houses; 300 prefabricated health centres; and 5 prefabricated 500-bed public hospitals. The establishment of a local facility to produce prefabricated units would be of immense value. The Government also requires up-to-date materials and technical support for environmental monitoring, as well as support in research concerning the conflict's effects on health and the environment.

178. In the medium term, the Health Ministry wishes to obtain access to modern technology in the form of information, modern teaching equipment and laboratory reagents and equipment, as well as training facilities for the disabled and additional means of transport. The transfer of technology should enable the Ministry to reach its long-term objective of self-sufficiency in the production of equipment, reagents and medicines. Meanwhile, the Iranian authorities need links with international institutions offering expertise in disaster management and subsequent reconstruction.

VI. MAIN FINDINGS AND CONCLUSIONS

179. Reconstruction needs for the Islamic Republic of Iran following an eight-year period of hostilities can only be described as substantial when one takes into account the considerable physical damage experienced by the productive sectors, the displacement of large numbers of people, the significant human losses suffered through death and permanent disability, and the economic and social consequences brought about by the diversion of development to satisfy security and military needs.

180. In the three years that have elapsed since the cease-fire agreement, the Iranian authorities have made important progress in defining reconstruction priorities, in mobilizing consensus and widespread public support as to objectives, and in restoring the flow of productive activities essential to resume an economic growth path. Although much of the physical material damage inflicted by the hostilities on the productive sectors has been repaired, it will require many years to overcome the systemic damage to the environment, to the infrastructure, and to social institutions and services in the affected provinces.

181. A mid-term review of progress under the five-year plan is now being undertaken. Although the full results of that review are not yet available, the authorities have expressed general satisfaction with the pace of implementation, particularly as it relates to the achievement of key targets. The growth which has taken place in recent years has been based primarily on the mobilization of domestic resources. Macroeconomic policy reforms have enabled the financial system to capture domestic savings and have encouraged expansion of productive activities by the private sector. At the same time,

/...

0165

improved fiscal performance by the Government has permitted increased allocation of funds for fixed capital formation while reducing the budget deficit.

182. There is consensus within the Government that, at the present time, there are three main barriers to further successful implementation of the plan and to the achievement of its principal objectives. These are: (a) shortage of foreign exchange; (b) shortage of skilled professional and technical cadres; and (c) transportation bottlenecks. In addition, the sector reviews undertaken by the mission indicate the need for substantial upgrading of existing technology and the transfer of new technology.

183. The five-year plan anticipates the acquisition of about $27,000 million from foreign sources to implement specific new projects, which would be in addition to the investments currently being undertaken within the framework of the current development plan. It should be noted that the latter represent largely projects which in the 1980s were in various stages of design or implementation but which had to be postponed because of the war. About $10,000 million of the new funds would be acquired through buy-back arrangements primarily for resource-based activities designed to absorb new technology and to gain access to new export markets. The balance would be for projects in industry, agriculture, oil and petrochemicals. These activities would be import-saving or export-earning to minimize the problems of debt servicing. As noted above, the Government is also actively promoting foreign investment, particularly in the context of joint ventures.

184. Although it was possible to make only a brief survey of the progress in implementing these proposals, the mission was informed that the pace of completion of the necessary arrangements has been slower than anticipated but that this was expected to improve rapidly. A number of important projects are currently being actively negotiated, with prospects for early investments. One example cited was a major aluminium refinery to be financed in great part by European investors which would contain an important export component.

185. An extremely difficult problem to deal with in the short run is the shortage of skills. The Government is making an effort to attract back to the country trained personnel who had emigrated. The new investment projects involving foreign participation which are described in the previous paragraph are expected to involve transfer of skills through on-the-job training of local personnel. Longer-term efforts to fill this gap are in train to re-establish vocational training institutions, expand teacher training and strengthen the university system.

186. Related to the problem of skills is the question of upgrading technology and, in general, raising the technological level of the society. In the past, the Islamic Republic of Iran had demonstrated an excellent capacity to keep abreast of modern technological developments, a capacity which stands it in good stead now as the country seeks to rehabilitate its economy. However, having been cut off for almost a decade from the rapid pace of technological change in a wide variety of fields, special efforts will be required to update

/0166

/...

technologies and to incorporate the newly developed technologies to levels prevailing in modern societies if the economy is to achieve the sustainable growth path its resources, both human and natural, can support. A number of activities are now under way or are being planned to deal with the problem. These include (a) intensive educational programmes for government and private sector officials in the management of technological change; and (b) measures to strengthen the university system.

187. Transportation bottlenecks mainly reflect the problems which have arisen, in part due to the shift in the infrastructure pattern following the closing of Khorramshahr and, in part, due to the war period when it was not possible to undertake normal maintenance and repair of the road and railway networks. The Government attaches high priority to the railway link between the port at Bandar Abbas and the principal cities in the hinterland. Negotiations are under way to secure financing for this project from international sources.

188. The number of persons who are still registered with the relevant government agencies as displaced and requiring resettlement is now of the order of 1.2 million. It is understood that about 250,000 others have resettled with government assistance in their places of origin. Of the 14 million square metres of housing construction which the government estimates is required to meet total resettlement needs, approximately 2 million have been completed.

189. Iran's post-war domestic mobilization effort to deal with the consequences of the hostilities and to reconstruct its economy has been substantial and impressive. Considerable progress has been achieved in what has been essentially a "boot-strap" operation, almost completely dependent upon domestic resources. At the macroeconomic level, a growth path has been established essential to resolving the deep-seated social consequences of the war and the attainment of long-term development targets. The policy framework which the Government has elaborated, with its emphasis on an efficiently functioning market system, is fully consistent with the objective of achieving an optimum allocation of resources.

190. At the same time, the results of the sector reviews indicate the urgency of what may be called a deepening of the reconstruction process. The immediate post-war strategy of rapid recovery of output, often through makeshift methods and improvised technology, appears to be nearing its limits. There is the need to adopt a more thorough approach to the improvement of the physical infrastructure and productive apparatus. Crucial to the change in strategy is an increase in foreign exchange resources.

191. There is little doubt that the international community can make important contributions to accelerating progress in reconstruction. The Islamic Republic of Iran's low indebtedness profile makes it particularly creditworthy for the project financing it seeks, focusing mainly on activities which will generate their own debt servicing capacity. There appears to be a wide range of viable projects in the pipeline, both in the public and private sectors.

/...

0167

Moreover, the policy environment is open and welcomes the establishment of close ties with external partners.

192. In addition, financial assistance, under appropriate terms and conditions, might be provided for activities in the social fields, for example education and health care, where the immediate requirements for investment are substantial but which do not directly generate a capacity for servicing the associated debt. Such financing could be carefully designed within the framework of an overall debt strategy to minimize long-term debt servicing concerns. 1/

193. The need for technical assistance, particularly in the social sectors, are especially acute. For example, given the magnitude of the problems, there is great scope for assistance from private organizations with broad experience in dealing with large numbers of people physically disabled by war or traumatized by displacement or by war.

194. In the economic sectors, technical assistance is needed essentially to strengthen and widen the domestic programmes now planned or under way. Such assistance could best concentrate on filling the gaps currently existing, to overcome the shortage of highly skilled personnel. Major external programmes to support technological development also appear fully warranted in the current conditions of the Islamic Republic of Iran and its past performance in this area.

195. During its meetings with Iranian officials, the mission sought to obtain the views of the Government on the precise forms of international cooperation which would most efficiently assist in the country's reconstruction effort. It was agreed that the latter should be defined in the broad sense of the restoration of the economy to a growth path. Formulated in general terms, the responses stressed three factors: (a) access to recent technological developments (including technical assistance) and to sources for renewal and replenishment of capital stock; (b) access to export markets; and (c) access to international capital markets and investment.

196. Paragraph 7 of Security Council resolution 598 (1987) envisaged a role for the international community in the reconstruction of the two parties to the conflict. Having completed its study of the reconstruction efforts of the Islamic Republic of Iran and being aware of the Government's priorities, the mission strongly recommends that consideration be given to the convening of a round-table conference under the auspices of the United Nations or any other appropriate body at which the Islamic Republic of Iran and States Members of the United Nations and its relevant agencies and organizations could meet to discuss specific measures for cooperation. It is anticipated that a minimum of six months would be needed for the preparation of such a conference. The Iranian Government, with the assistance of the United Nations could arrange for the preparation of the necessary documentation and project profiles, taking into account Iran's substantive need and priorities for reconstruction.

0168

/...

197. In the same connection, the mission believes that the role of the
international community in clearing the waterway at Shatt al-Arab and the
immediately adjacent waters of the Persian Gulf is an economic necessity. It
will be necessary to revive the functioning of the Combined Bureau of
Coordination (CBC) which, prior to the war, administered and coordinated the
operation of the waterway. As detailed in the sectoral report summarized in
section V, the particular salvage work which is needed, its magnitude and
complexity, will require considerable external technical inputs. It will be
necessary to utilize sophisticated and large equipment, not available in Iran,
to deal simultaneously with sunken vessels, a wide variety of ordnance lying
on the river bed, and the extensive siltation which has accumulated as a
result of more than 10 years of neglect. Once the political ground has been
cleared, the mission considers it necessary as a first step, for a series of
surveys to be carried out, as soon as possible, to locate the wrecks and other
obstacles, identify the cargo and to determine the best means of clearance
(including the removal of any hazardous materials and unexploded ordnance).

Notes

1/   In February 1991, the World Bank extended a $250 million loan for an
earthquake recovery project to assist the Government's earthquake
reconstruction programme.

0169

Appendix A

Composition of the team

The team was led by Mr. Abdulrahim Abby Farah, former Under-Secretary-General. Below are the names of the members of the team including their sectoral assignments: Mr. Irwin Baskind (consultant), macroeconomist; Mr. John D. Cuddy (United Nations Conference on Trade and Development), macroeconomist; Mr. Ignacio Armillas (United Nations Centre for Human Settlements), housing and human settlements; Mr. William H. Crowe and Mr. John Thomas (consultants), oil, gas and petrochemical industries; Mr. Vladimir Skendrovic (United Nations Department for Technical Cooperation for Development), rail, roads and air transport; Mr. Andre Pages (consultant) ports and shipping; Mr. Joseph Madeo (consultant), marine salvage; Mr. Christian Beinhoff and Mr. Niels Biering (United Nations Industrial Development Organization), heavy and light industry; Mr. Ali Asghar Abidi (consultant), agriculture and irrigation; Mr. Seamus Kenny (consultant), electrical power; Mr. P. Roychoudhury and Mr. Bernard Humm (International Telecommunication Union), telecommunications and broadcasting; Mr. T. Worku and Mr. J. Sheley (United Nations Educational, Scientific and Cultural Organization), education; Mr. Barry Lane (United Nations Educational, Scientific and Cultural Organization), cultural heritage; Dr. O. Sulieman and Dr. S. Ben Yahmed (World Health Organization), health; Mr. Gerard Fischer (United Nations Conference on Trade and Development) served as Special Assistant and Sectoral Coordinator. Mr. Andrew Brookes (United Nations Secretariat) and Mr. Jafar Javan (United Nations Development Programme) served as translators/interpreters.

0170

/...

Appendix B

Officials met by the team leader and the experts

Mr. Hamid Mirzadeh	Vice-President and Special Government Representative for Reconstruction
Mr. Issa Kalantari	Minister of Agriculture
Mr. Hossein Kamali	Minister of Social Services and Labour
Mr. Reza Malekzadeh	Ministry of Health
Mr. Mohammad Reza Nematzadeh	Minister of Industry
Mr. Hadi Nezhad-Husseinian	Minister of Heavy Industries
Mr. Mohsen Noorbakhsh	Minister of Economic Affairs and Finance
Mr. Abdullah Nouri	Minister of the Interior
Mr. Mohammad Saeidikia	Minister of Transport
Mr. Bijan Zanganesh	Minister of Energy
Mr. Mohammad Hussein Adeli	Governor of the Central Bank
Mr. Mohsen Yahyavi	Deputy Minister, Director of Corporate Planning and Board Member of National Iranian Oil Company, Ministry of Oil
Mr. Ali Khorram	Adviser to the Foreign Minister and Head, Persian Gulf Headquarters
Mr. Mehdi Tabeshian	Vice President, Islamic Republic of Iran Broadcasting (IRIB)
Mr. Behkish	Chamber of Commerce, Industries and Mines

/...

0171

<u>Appendix C</u>

<u>Documentation submitted by the Iranian authorities</u>

1. Final report on the assessment of the economic damages of the war imposed by Iraq on the Islamic Republic of Iran (1980-1988): Plan and Budget Organization

2. Law and Regulations concerning the Attraction and Protection of Foreign Investments in Iran: Iran Chamber of Commerce, Industries and Mines Centre for Economic Research and Analysis

3. Summarized version of the first five-year economic, social and cultural development plan of the Islamic Republic of Iran (1989-1993): Plan and Budget Organization

4. Policies, priorities, functions and experience of nine years of reconstruction in the Islamic Republic of Iran: His Excellency Mr. Hamid Mirzadah, Vice-President in Administrative Affairs, Special Representative of the Government in Reconstruction and Renovation of War-Damaged Areas

5. Statement by the Hon. Mohsen Noorbakhsh, Governor of the Bank for the Islamic Republic of Iran at 1991 Annual Meeting of the World Bank Group in Bangkok, Thailand

6. Telecommunications - War Damage Report - June 1991, received from Telecommunication Company of Iran (TCI)

7. Document defining the credits needed for the reconstruction in the sectors of housing and infrastructure and employment in war-damaged areas

8. Map of Port of Bandar Abas   ) Ports and Shipping
   Map of Port of Bandar Khomeyni) Office

9. Reply from Iranian authorities (in Farsi) to request for information of 13 August 1991 - translation attached

10. A general perspective of the destruction of Iranian villages during the imposed Iraqi war upon Iran and the process of reconstruction: The Islamic Republic of Iran Housing Foundation of Islamic Revolution

11. (a) National Petrochemical Company Information

    (b) National Petrochemical Company Projects

    (c) Answers to <u>Oil and Gas Journal</u>'s questionnaire on current status of crude oil refineries in the Islamic Republic of Iran

0172
/...

(d) NIOC's Petroleum Product Imports (1979-1990)

(e) NIOC: Specifications for gasoline, kerosene, gas, oil and
     1700 sec fuel oil

(f) NIOC: Details of attacks on refinery

12. Central Bank of the Islamic Republic of Iran: Economic Report and
     Balance Sheet 1363 (as at 20 March 1985)

13. Central Bank of the Islamic Republic of Iran: Economic Report and
     Balance Sheet 1366 (1987-1988) (as at 20 March 1988)

14. Implications of the imposed war on the Islamic Republic of Iran Broadcast
     Services

15. Map showing maritime access to Shatt al-Arab ports of Abadan,
     Khorramshahr to Bandar Khomeyni

16. Shipping charts (Ports and Shipping Office)

17. Reconstruction Programme and Development: Director Engineering TCI

18. Ministry of Energy - 1967-1979 Electric Power Industry in Iran; Electric
     Power Industry in Iran 1982; 1989 Electric Power in Iran

19. Brief report on seven damaged Iranian airports during the imposed war -
     Abadan, Ahwaz, Bakhtaran, Hamedan, Orumieh, Sanandadje, and Shiraz (Civil
     Aviation)

20. Document describing priority projects in the field of environment seeking
     assistance from the international communities. Environmental Protection
     Organization

21. Information release - United Nations Environment Programme inter-agency
     consultation on environmental consequences of the Gulf war - attached is
     UNEP document UNEP/GC.16/6, Effects of Chemical Weapons on Human Health
     and the Environment (UNDP)

22. One page - Environment - Costs of projects in rials: Environmental
     Protection Organization

23. Data received from Vice-President for Reconstruction - (tables and
     translations)

24. Statement on reconstruction projects (Ministry of Industry Fund
     Assessment for Reconstruction concerning Ministry of Road and
     Transportation)

25. Data relating to Khorramshahr post office building (Postal Services)

'0173

26. Estimation of necessary machinery for reconstruction (Rural Housing Office)

27. Renovation data relating to ports (NIOC)

28. Educational planning - Data in Farsi: Directorate of Educational Planning and Projects, Ministry of Education (together with handwritten translation)

29. Agriculture - Provincial Statement of Damages, "Summary report on War-damaged areas"

30. Reconstruction programme, including cost of works and external assistance: Ministry of Energy Water Resources

31. Blueprint map of Isfahan: Office for Reconstruction, Iranian Cultural Heritage Organization, Isfahan

32. Document issued by the International Monetary Fund - Statement by Mr. Mirakhor on the Islamic Republic of Iran - Executive Board Meeting, 6 September 1991

33. Two documents of the International Monetary Fund: Islamic Republic of Iran - Staff Report for the 1991 Article IV Consultation (SM/91/145); Islamic Republic of Iran - Recent Economic Developments (SM/91/156)

34. Iranian Cultural Heritage - Damages due to the imposed war. Brief report prepared for Senior Adviser to the United Nations Secretary-General - resolution 598 (1987)

35. The Imposed War - volume 6

36. Agricultural Sector - Khuzistan Province reconstruction programme

37. Miscellaneous documents issued by the Central Bank of Iran

38. Official submission on health sector (Ministry of Health)

0174

주 국 련 대 표 부

주국련20313-　　　165　　　　　　　　1992. 2. 13.

수신　장관

참조　국제기구국장, 중동아프리카국장

제목　이란.이락 휴전결의 후속처리 문제(안보리)

　　　표제관련 안보리문서를 별첨과 같이 송부합니다.

　　첨 부 :　상기 문서. 끝.

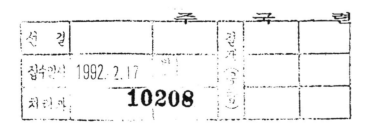

0175

UNITED
NATIONS

Security Council

S

Distr.
GENERAL

S/23322/Add.1
24 December 1991

ORIGINAL: ENGLISH

LETTER DATED 24 DECEMBER 1991 FROM THE SECRETARY-GENERAL
ADDRESSED TO THE PRESIDENT OF THE SECURITY COUNCIL

<u>Annex</u>

SECOND AND FINAL REPORT OF THE UNITED NATIONS TEAM OF EXPERTS
APPOINTED BY THE SECRETARY-GENERAL PURSUANT TO SECURITY
COUNCIL RESOLUTION 598 (1987), PARAGRAPH 7, PREPARED FOLLOWING
A FURTHER VISIT BY THE TEAM TO THE ISLAMIC REPUBLIC OF IRAN TO
COMPLETE ITS STUDY OF THE COUNTRY'S RECONSTRUCTION EFFORTS AND
NEEDS IN THE WAKE OF THE CONFLICT BETWEEN THE ISLAMIC REPUBLIC
OF IRAN AND IRAQ

7 NOVEMBER-1 DECEMBER 1991

<u>Addendum</u>

SECTORAL REPORTS

CONTENTS

91-42467   2862-63h (E)   /...

0176

A. HOUSING AND HUMAN SETTLEMENTS

Introduction

The task of reconstruction and rehabilitation of the human settlements and housing sector will be vast, since ground battles took place for the most part inside the territory of the Islamic Republic of Iran. The Government reports that about 14,000 square kilometres of Iranian territory along the 1,200 kilometre border of the five western provinces were active theatres of ground conflict and the direct effects of the conflict were spread over a 96,000-square-kilometre area. This western third of the country is the most densely populated part of the Islamic Republic of Iran. The population was rather evenly distributed in a settlement pattern centred on cities ranging in population from 1 million down to 350,000, each city in turn having a hierarchical structure of towns and villages within its area of influence.

The amount of damage to human settlements within those areas that saw ground combat is close to total, while cities beyond the front-lines but within reach of the enemy air weapons suffered varying degrees of damage. In order to replace what has been lost, cities, towns and villages, complete with housing, basic infrastructure, services and facilities, as well as industrial and commercial establishments, need to be reconstructed or rehabilitated to accommodate the 1.2 million displaced population in settlements spanning the entire 14,000 km^2 area.

The Iranian Government has assigned the highest priority to the reconstruction and renovation of the cities, town and villages in the war-affected provinces. Apart from facilitating the resettlement of the displaced population, the major investment required to reconstruct the housing sector will contribute in a direct manner to the reactivation of productive capacity and thus the economy of the affected areas and of the country in general.

The priorities set by the Government for the human settlements and housing sector are:

(a) Reconstruction of residential and commercial units;

(b) Creation of productive employment for the people in agriculture and small industries;

(c) Provision of fuel, water, sanitation, electricity, roads and telecommunications facilities;

(d) Reconstruction of factories that produce building materials;

(e) Reconstruction of historic monuments and the preservation of certain symbols of war.

/...

0177

In order to ensure effective popular participation in the reconstruction process, the Government has decreed the following administrative policy:

(a) The owners are responsible for the reconstruction of their own units;

(b) Design and selection of materials is left to the discretion of the owners;

(c) Government support will concentrate on those tasks that individuals can not effectively carry out by themselves or that would be too costly, such as levelling of ground and clearance of debris;

(d) The Government will prepare physical development plans and provide technical support and supervision for the construction efforts;

(e) Support services will be strengthened with respect to available equipment, facilities and technical resources and with respect to their accessibility to war-damaged areas;

(f) The Government will provide for the transport of building materials to construction sites;

(g) The participation of voluntary assistance from other provinces will be encouraged and facilitated;

(h) The resources of the army and the Revolutionary Guard Corps will be employed in the construction of infrastructure and government buildings.

On the financial side, the Government is providing partial compensation for losses and damages sustained by private individuals in the form of grants. Low-cost bank loans have also been made available for the construction and repair of commercial and residential units to cover expenses beyond the compensation grants.

1. Demographic impact of the war

Displaced population

According to government sources, at the peak of hostilities there were over 2 million displaced persons as result of the conflict. The impact of the displaced population in host cities has been considerable. The city of Mahshahr, for example, more than doubled in population during the period 1980-1990 owing, in great part, to an influx of displaced people from cities and towns in the occupied areas. During this same period other cities in the five border provinces, but beyond occupied areas, also showed high indices of population growth owing to the influx of displaced people.

/...

0178

The impact of such demographic movements on human settlements is twofold. On the one hand, the infrastructure, buildings and other facilities of an urban area quickly deteriorate if not regularly maintained. For example, a sewerage system that is not constantly used and maintained becomes clogged with sediment, rendering it useless and difficult to rehabilitate. This has apparently been the case in most of the deserted settlements in the occupied areas. On the other hand, the influx of great numbers of people over a short period of time places an inordinate burden on the social and physical infrastructure of a city. For example, the city of Ahwaz had adequate infrastructure for a population of slightly over half a million in 1980; the city has now close to 1 million inhabitants, and a sizeable portion of the additional population is attributed to the influx of displaced people. As the infrastructure was not designed and built for this level of population, the existing systems have not been able to carry the burden, with a consequent deterioration in services. Moreover, the city's revenues have not grown commensurate with the increase in population since the displaced people are by and large not involved in economic activity that produces revenues for the city.

2. Human settlements

The striking impact of the war on the pattern of human settlement in the Islamic Republic of Iran can be seen from table A.1, which presents population levels for the five border provinces and selected municipalities and cities for the years 1976 (official census) and estimates for 1980 and 1986 and 1990 (official census). The cities marked with an asterisk are outside the areas occupied by Iraq.

/...

0179

Table A.1

Population changes of selected cities
(1976, 1980, 1986 and 1990)

Place	Population			
	1976	1980	1986	1990
Islamic Republic of Iran	33 708 744	39 291 000	49 445 010	56 882 000
Khuzestan Province	2 187 118	2 373 000	2 681 978	3 292 447
* Ahwaz (city)	496 468	569 708	861 970	989 130
Abadan (municipality)	376 911	432 514	0	27 000
Abadan (city)	294 068	337 449	0	19 000
Khorramshahr (municipality)	225 633	258 907	2 098	73 000
Khorramshahr (city)	140 490	166 858	0	6 000
* Mahshahr (city)	89 326	102 503	232 642	266 962
* Dasht Azadegan (city)	100 519	115 348	75 272	88 000
Bostan (city)	6 884	7 900	0	6 000
Susan-Guerd (city)	17 428	20 000	22 776	34 000
Howeyzeh (city)	6 012	6 900	2 246	12 000
* Dezful (city)	303 292	348 034	365 695	419 643
Bakhtaran Province	1 030 714	1 186 000	1 462 965	1 683 000
* Bakhtaran (city)	568 963	652 898	862 378	989 598
Qasr-e-Shirin (municipality)	56 000	62 000	0	8 000
Qasr-e-Shirin (city)	23 000	28 000	0	0
Sar-e-Pol-Zahab (municipality)	49 242	53 000	0	31 000
Sar-e-Pol-Zahab (city)	28 765	25 000	0	6 000
Guilan-e-Gharb (municipality)	45 202	24 000	0	65 000
Guilan-e-Gharb (city)	14 793	9 000	0	12 000
Ilam Province	246 024	294 000	382 091	456 000
Mehran (municipality)	44 351	53 000	29 716	32 321
Mehran (city)	12 133	14 500	0	0
Dehloran (municipality)	51 045	61 000	1 988	21 782
Dehloran (city)	8 786	10 500	0	3 000
Musiyan (municipality)	4 183	5 000	0	0
Kordestan Province	782 440	889 500	1 078 415	1 226 000
Azarbayjan Province	1 407 604	1 610 500	1 971 677	2 256 000

Source: Reconstruction headquarters.

Note: The term city refers to the entity under the city government while the term municipality encompasses the larger urban area.

/...

3. Impact on urban areas

According to reports published by the Government, 50 cities and towns and close to 4,000 villages have suffered varying degrees of damage and many total destruction. The cities of Qasr-e-Shirin, Musiyan, Howeyzeh and Sumar, among others, have been totally destroyed. There is little or nothing above or below ground that can be salvaged or rehabilitated. Other cities such as Khorramshahr, Abadan, Bostan, Susan-Guerd, Naft Shahr and Sar-e-Pol-Zahab have sustained considerable damage ranging from 60 to almost 100 per cent. Many other cities in the country suffered varying degrees of damage. For example, 150 missiles exploded in Tehran alone, the majority during the "war of the cities". Dezful was also shelled by artillery fire and missiles, leaving the city about 50 per cent destroyed.

As an illustration of the extent of devastation the Government provided the following estimates of destruction.

Within the occupied areas

Urban settlements in occupied areas suffered major devastation having been the theatres of battles during the hostilities. They are reported to have been subjected to artillery and other forms of ground fire and explosive charges, aerial bombings and missile attacks and, in some cases, systematic destruction by enemy forces. In addition to the destruction of housing, commercial, government (schools, hospitals, clinics, sports facilities, etc.) and industrial buildings, the infrastructure (water, sewerage, streets) suffered significantly from three sources: (a) collateral damage from the destruction of buildings; (b) heavy war equipment such as tanks circulating in the streets; and (c) lack of maintenance.

The economic viability of these cities was also ruined since the agriculture, industry, services and facilities that supported them were damaged or destroyed. As a consequence, the population in this area has decreased significantly. Most settlements were abandoned at least temporarily during the conflict and municipal governments ceased to function.

Outside the occupied areas

Urban settlements in non-occupied areas, which were nevertheless subject to aerial and missile bombardment, did not suffer total devastation but only partial destruction in varying degrees. In these cases the infrastructure suffered at most occasional damage while only buildings and structures directly hit were significantly affected. During the course of the war, this type of damage added up to a considerable level in some cities. There were also significant demographic changes in the cities closer to the war front. At times, the cities were virtually abandoned by their population, leading to considerable decay in their infrastructure on account of neglect and lack of maintenance; at other times, the great influx of refugees from the war zone led to overdemand for municipal services, causing strain and wear in the various systems.

/...

4. Impact of the conflict on rural towns and villages

Within the occupied areas

Rural settlements in occupied areas suffered from much the same sources as the cities and towns. Because a large number of buildings had been constructed from unbaked mud bricks, some villages which were totally destroyed are quickly reverting to a natural state, leaving few traces of the previous habitation. The destruction of irrigation systems and damage to agricultural and pasture land has totally eliminated the economic base of most of these communities. Those towns and villages that did not suffer directly from the hostilities but were abandoned for safety reasons have also decayed because of lack of maintenance and require rehabilitation.

Outside the occupied areas

Rural settlements in non-occupied areas were only occasionally subject to direct damage from the hostilities, but the destruction of agricultural and pasture land and disruption of irrigation systems adversely affected their existence. Houses that had been abandoned even temporarily by their inhabitants also decayed and now require some rehabilitation.

5. Plans for the reconstruction and rehabilitation of human settlements affected by the war

Urban areas

The reconstruction of settlements ravaged by the conflict necessitates the preparation of appropriate plans. For the larger cities within the occupied areas, plans are being prepared in phases so that reconstruction can commence without having to wait for the complete final plan to be approved. To date reconstruction plans for the following cities have been either totally or partially completed: Khorramshahr, Dehloran, Mehran, Musian, Qasr-e-Shirin, Sar-e-Pol-Zahab, Guilan-e-Gharb, Arvand Kenar, Rufiyeh and Bostan. Plans for Naft Shahr and Sumar have not yet been started since these cities were returned to Iranian control only recently, and clearance of mines and other security operations have yet to be completed.

Rural areas

To date the following three rural reconstruction and development plans have been completed: Abadan Island (rural areas), Dash-e-Azadegan (first phase) and Dehloran. Work is under way in the preparation of the following five physical reconstruction and development plans: Dash-e-Azadegan (second phase), Mehran, Khorramshahr (rural areas), Minu Island (rural areas), and Manuhi District (Abadan Island, subset of overall plan already completed).

/...

0182

All the rural plans completed to date as well as those under preparation
are in the southern part of the zone that was occupied by Iraq. The reasons
for this are that: (a) portions of the central area have only recently fully
reverted to the Islamic Republic of Iran; (b) the land has not all been
cleared of mines and other unexploded ordnance; and, (c) only a small
percentage of the population has returned and, in several instances, local
authorities are only now ready to initiate reconstruction.

6. Housing

Loss of shelter is the most widespread physical consequence of the
conflict. The entire housing stock was destroyed in many villages, and in
several small cities. Moreover, the loss of housing stock was not limited
only to settlements within the area subjected to ground combat. Significant
numbers of dwelling units were damaged or destroyed by aerial bombing and
missile attacks. The Government estimates that 130,611 housing units were
totally destroyed and 190,777 damaged as a direct consequence of the war.

Urban housing

The mission ascertained that few residential or commercial structures in
settlements within the areas occupied by enemy troops remained intact.
Structures had suffered damage either as result of fire power during the
conflict or had been demolished for tactical reasons. In the few instances
where buildings had escaped harm from fire power or demolition they had been
pillaged of all removable items. In major cities, such as Khorramshahr, the
loss of housing stock was very substantial. Smaller cities or towns along the
border area suffered even more drastic destruction. In the cities of
Dehloran, Mehran and Qasr-e-Shirin, for example, the loss of housing stock was
total.

Cities outside the occupied areas also suffered varying degrees of damage
to their housing stock as a result of missiles and aerial bombardment. For
example, in Tehran, 283 housing units were reported to have been destroyed and
an additional 1,212 damaged by missile attacks.

Rural housing

The magnitude of damage to villages in the five border provinces was also
very high. Over 30 per cent of the villages in these provinces were damaged,
many beyond repair. In some villages the destruction was so great that, apart
from debris, there was little evidence that there had once been a settlement
on these sites. The mission visited the village of Islamiyeh which had become
a military camp that changed hands several times during the conflict. Nothing
of the village remains except a few signs of building foundations and some
construction rubble.

/...

According to government estimates, 1,244 villages were completely destroyed and 1,417 villages suffered damages. In terms of housing units, it is estimated that 76,390 rural dwellings were lost. From field visits, the mission could determine that destruction of rural settlements was very extensive in the area from Dehloran up to Qasr-e-Shirin. Most of the destruction observed in this area appeared to be the result of direct military activity. Immediately to the south of this area, around Rafei, part of the destruction appears to have been the result of flooding, which was said to have been induced for tactical reasons. Further south, in Minu and Abadan islands the damage to rural housing seems to result from deterioration as a consequence of the abandonment of dwellings over prolonged periods. As the prevailing construction material in these areas is earth, structures tended to deteriorate more for lack of maintenance. Their repair is not as practical as if they had been constructed of more durable materials such as baked bricks or concrete. For this reason, many structures that are still standing will have to be replaced. In areas beyond the direct theatre of ground war rural housing suffered relatively little since air attacks were concentrated generally on cities.

Commercial buildings

In addition to the massive loss in housing stock, there was a corresponding loss of commercial buildings. It is estimated by the Government that in the areas that saw ground action alone, 13,140 commercial units were destroyed or damaged during the conflict. Beyond the immediate war front, there was also loss of commercial units, most the result of bombing and missile attacks. The Government estimates losses of commercial units in the country at 20,513 units totally destroyed and a further 25,918 units damaged.

Reconstruction needs

The Government has informed the mission that it will make compensation payments for war-related housing losses to up to 117,635 households. In order to encourage and attract displaced families back to their former houses in the war-affected provinces, the Government has decided to assist in the rebuilding and in the upgrading of dwellings by providing funds for rebuilding to a standard surface per family of 120 square metres. This would amount to the rebuilding or rehabilitation of a total of 14 million square metres. In addition, there is a need to build 73,600 housing units as starter homes for new families within the population of the war-affected areas who, because of the war, were not able to build their own houses. Such families will require an additional 8.8 million square metres of housing construction but, of this total, the Government is prepared to cover 40 per cent of the area built for each dwelling. Thus, the total housing area to be constructed at government expense is equal to 17.52 million square metres. The Government estimates the average cost of such construction at 100,000 rials per square metre, which brings the total cost of reconstruction housing in both urban and rural areas to Rls 1,752,000 million.

/...

0184

In terms of commercial space, the Government estimates that 13,140 units will have to be rebuilt or rehabilitated. The Government will provide grants for 15 square metres of construction per commercial unit or 0.2 million square metres of space. Estimating the average cost at the same rate of Rls 100,000 per square metre, the total cost of commercial reconstruction would be Rls 20,000 million.

The Government informed the mission that the total area reconstructed up to the present, including urban and rural housing, commercial units and government buildings, amounts to about 2 million square metres. About half of the total building area reconstructed to date is in the form of rural housing. In urban areas, where housing losses were more extensive and severe, reconstruction has lagged behind proportionately because of the greater expense and difficulties involved in urban reconstruction.

7. Infrastructure

A. Water, sewerage and waste disposal

Water and sewerage systems in urban areas within the theatre of ground combat suffered mainly from collateral damage and neglect. Abadan City is the most striking example of the loss of water and sewerage systems on account of lack of maintenance during the long abandonment of the city. The networks have become silted up and clogged and pumping stations have fallen in disrepair. In cities such as Khorramshahr and Qasr-e-Shirin, in addition to deterioration brought about by abandonment, there was considerable collateral damage caused by destruction of buildings, heavy military vehicle traffic on the streets, which caused considerable damage to pipes underground, and damage from bombing. In Qasr-e-Shirin the mission also saw signs of explosive charges having been detonated in manholes. Most water-treatment plants and pumping stations suffered damage. While rural areas have less infrastructure, the mission was told that most water-supply systems had been damaged during the conflict. The mission had occasion to observe such damage to water supply systems in a number of settlements.

The lack of adequate water and sewerage systems in the larger cities such as Khorramshahr and Abadan is causing some health concerns and is militating against the return of the displaced population to the cities where these problems are being encountered. In rural areas, extensive reconstruction will be required to enable the populations to have access to potable water.

Another major problem engendered by the conflict is the collection, removal and final disposal of waste, scrap and debris. In urban areas the clearing of the debris from damaged and destroyed buildings is well under way, but considerable work still remains to be done. Under ideal conditions some of the debris from buildings could be utilized in some other construction projects (i.e. protective sea walls), but this has been difficult to achieve within a distance that would make the exercise economically viable. The collection and disposal of other wastes, some of which may be toxic, is yet a

further complication of the clean-up of the war-affected area. The problems
of studying and surveying adequate sanitary landfill sites and other forms of
disposal were stressed by the Government. By contrast, the problem of debris
from buildings is much less critical in rural areas. This is due in part to
the nature of construction materials used in the villages (mostly earth
construction), and the much lower settlement densities and smaller
structures. On the other hand, the salvage and recycling of spent war
equipment represents a larger problem, because it is spread over much larger
areas.

Electricity

The re-establishment of electric power is a prerequisite for the return
of displaced populations to the reconstructed cities and towns. The massive
destruction suffered in the electric power sector and specific progress in its
rehabilitation are elaborated in section F: Electric power.

8. Social services

Nature and extent of damage to services

The Government has indicated to the mission that 22.2 million square
metres of public buildings need to be constructed or rehabilitated, in
addition to the residential and commercial construction noted earlier. At the
Government's stated average cost of Rls 100,000 per square metre, the cost of
such reconstruction would amount to Rls 2,200,000 million. Detailed
descriptions of the damage suffered by educational and health facilities are
provided in the relevant sections of the present report.

Postal services, which are vital to the fabric of social life in a
community, were greatly affected by the conflict. The Government has informed
the mission that 64 post office buildings were either destroyed or damaged.
The total area to be rebuilt is 17,378 square metres, of which 8,807 square
metres have already been rebuilt or rehabilitated. These figures include
31 completed projects, 22 under construction and 9 to be started. It should
be noted that the post office in Khorramshahr covered 4,300 square metres, or
about 25 per cent of the total area to be reconstructed. Work on this project
has started.

9. Observations

The task of reconstruction and rehabilitation in the human settlements
and housing sector is vast. The amount of damage to human settlements within
those areas that witnessed ground combat is close to total, while cities
outside the direct war zone suffered varying degrees of damage.
Reconstruction of the entire settlement system within the affected area is now
being undertaken in order to restore the industrial, extractive and
agricultural capacity of the region and to facilitate the return of over

/...

0186

1.2 million displaced people. Considering the degree of destruction to settlements, the Government is giving highest priority to their reconstruction.

The mission believes that the considerable length of time which the displaced people have spent away from their former towns and villages could present complications to the resettlement programme. Some people may find their former homes strange to them; many may have formed families with partners from other areas, and children born since the displacement will need to adjust to what for them will be a new place.

Investment in both public and private construction can be an important element in stimulating the economy, since the construction industry, which is primarily private in the Islamic Republic of Iran, requires mostly internal resources and is labour-intensive. Such reconstruction requires the prior creation or recreation of adequate infrastructure. This is being done as a first priority.

In the mission's view, changes to the environment brought about by the conflict should be carefully assessed in order that in reconstructing human settlements the returning population is not placed in any danger from the long-term effects of contamination. Furthermore, the carrying capacity of some areas, in terms of production and their ability to sustain former activities, may have been altered. In such cases, it is important to ensure that people do not return to land that can no longer sustain them. It should also be pointed out that, on account of the highly seismic nature of the country, all reconstruction efforts should integrate earthquake mitigation considerations. In fact, the building stock in the Islamic Republic of Iran is quite vulnerable to seismic events. This was amply demonstrated in the Manjil earthquake of 1990, where extensive failure of buildings caused over 25,000 deaths. Since most of the war-affected area is also earthquake-prone, it would be advisable that the level of resistance to seismic forces be increased in all new construction and that urban plans take potential seismic disasters into consideration.

10. International cooperation needs

Materials and equipment

In discussing international cooperation needs in the field of human settlements, it is necessary to keep in mind that the Islamic Republic of Iran is reconstructing not only from a long and particularly destructive war, but also from a recent earthquake considered to one of the major natural disasters of the past 25 years. To the numbers of dwelling units that must be rebuilt on account of the war, there must be added 200,000 units destroyed by the earthquake. There were also public buildings, schools, hospitals and infrastructure lost to the seismic disaster.

/...

The mission is of the view that, for the reconstruction of human settlements, the Islamic Republic of Iran, is in need primarily of construction equipment since much such equipment was lost during the war. In addition, there are shortages of building materials, particularly cement and iron. Most, if not all, of the shortfall of other building materials should be made up through the establishment of local building materials industries. International cooperation in setting up building materials industries, particularly ones that can utilize local raw materials, would benefit the reconstruction efforts. Moreover, the task of demolition and removal of debris will add from 25 to 40 per cent of the cost of urban reconstruction. This estimate will vary according to the size of the building, the type of construction, the condition of the building and the method of debris disposal (including distance from the site).

11. Professional requirements

The Islamic Republic of Iran possesses a well qualified body of professionals in the fields related to the physical reconstruction and rehabilitation of war-devastated areas such as engineering, architecture and urban and rural planning. The existing national capacity provides a good base to utilize specialized expertise to augment know-how already available within the country. The particular areas of expertise that would be beneficial to the reconstruction effort include development of building materials and improvements to local construction methods.

/...

B. PETROLEUM INDUSTRY

Introduction

The economy of the Islamic Republic of Iran is heavily dependent upon the production and export of oil for the generation of both domestic employment and income and the foreign exchange needed to buy imported goods. The petroleum industry has, for the purposes of the present report, been subdivided into three closely related but distinct parts: oil and gas production; refining; and petrochemicals.

Table B.1 summarizes reconstruction cost for the three sub-divisions of the petroleum sector.

Table B.1

Subdivision	Expenditure to date (millions)		Planned expenditure (millions)	
	Rls	US$	Rls	US$
Production	67 000	859	728 500	18 140
Refining	19 034	357	42 298	793
Petrochemicals	48 850	915	108 556	2 033
Total	134 884	2 131	879 354	20 966

1. Oil and gas production

The Islamic Republic of Iran's estimated proven petroleum reserves of 93 billion barrels are among the world's largest. However, its present production rate is 3 million barrels per day (b.p.d.), just half its historical peak production rate of approximately 6 million b.p.d. attained in 1976, of which 5.5 million b.p.d. were exported and 0.5 million b.p.d. used domestically as feedstock for its refineries. Similarly, as contrasted with its Organization of Petroleum Exporting Countries (OPEC) quota of 3.5 million b.p.d., the Islamic Republic of Iran's current export rate is but 1.9 million b.p.d. This gap between potential and actual output, and thus exports, arises from the damage inflicted on the country's oil production capacity during the conflict.

The Islamic Republic of Iran is currently producing and exporting at the maximum of its reduced capacity. Of its over 618 wells, 1/ only 360 can be operated without destroying the various reservoirs. Gas is being flared at a

/...

0189

rate of about 1.26 billion cubic feet per day (million mcf/d), the energy
equivalent of 200,000 b.p.d. 2/ Much of this gas could be reinjected into the
reservoirs in order to maintain pressure and the remainder could be used to
produce methanol. However, compressors, turbines, gas-treating production
facilities and equipment necessary to implement such an efficiency-raising
reconstruction operation are not available because of the country's shortage
of hard currency.

Direct damages

General

The problems associated with maintaining, repairing, rebuilding,
relocation and reconstruction of equipment, pipelines, pump/compressor
stations and production facilities during war time and under attack require a
magnitude of effort that is enormous.

The areas of oil production that sustained damage during the conflict
have been classified by the National Iranian Oil Company (NIOC), which has
jurisdiction over all oil-production and export operations in the country,
into three regions: south, north and offshore, which are discussed in turn
below.

2. South production zone

The south fields zone is the main onshore oil production area in the
Islamic Republic of Iran and consists of five fields: Ahwaz, Aghajari, Gach
Saran, Masjid-e-Suleiman and Kharg Island. Most of the oil production in the
south fields (3 million b.p.d.) is pumped to Kharg Island for export via the
T-jetty or the Sea Island loading facilities there. The remainder of
approximately 200,000 b.p.d. is pumped to the Abadan refinery, the products of
which are then pumped north for domestic consumption. A total of
50 facilities were attacked repeatedly during the war. The mission visited 18
of these facilities and performed helicopter fly-overs on a further two
facilities. The damage observed by the mission was generally severe, as
expected given the number of attacks.

The damage and destruction inflicted cover every aspect of permanent
oil/gas high-volume and high-pressure production operations. These included,
but are not limited to, the following: production facilities, oil wells,
natural gas liquids (NGL) plants, pump/compressor stations, pipelines,
desalting plants, control rooms, desulphurization units, manifolds, storage
tanks, gas reinjection plants, loading terminals, housing, offices,
warehouses/stores, hospitals, schools, power plants, machine shops, vehicles,
telecommunication systems, workshops, water/sewerage systems and aircraft.

The mission was informed during its visit to the Abadan Refinery that of
the Refinery's crude storage capacity of 20 million barrels, 15 million
barrels were completely destroyed (over 100 storage tanks). Most of the tanks
are still at their original location in a melt-down condition (caused by the

/...

heat of the fires); it is estimated that the scrap steel they represent amounts to about 2 million tons.

Kharg Island also warrants special mention because of its unique role in the export of Iranian crude oil and the devastation it incurred during the war. It was attacked almost on a daily basis throughout the conflict. Before the war, Kharg Island was capable of off-loading 14 million b.p.d., utilizing its 14 berthing facilities consisting of 10 berths at its T-jetty and 4 at Sea Island. Its off-loading capability is now about 2 million b.p.d. The east and west terminals are still 75 per cent damaged while the trestle (pier) portion of the T-jetty (east) has been reconstructed to about 90 per cent of its pre-war condition. The mission was informed by NIOC that a contract has recently been awarded to a French company for US$ 225 million to reconstruct not only the north and south sections of the T-jetty terminal but also the offshore Sea Island terminal on the west side of Kharg Island. The Island had a pre-war crude oil storage capacity of 22 million barrels in 39 tanks. Its storage capacity is currently 10 million barrels because 21 tanks were completely destroyed by fires occasioned by the attacks. NIOC informed the mission that a contract has recently been awarded to a Korean company to build five 1-million-barrel tanks and one 500,000-barrel tank as part of the reconstruction programme for Kharg Island.

The mission has been informed that the total cost incurred for reconstruction to date in the south fields area amounts to $500 million and Rls 30,000 million, while the remaining cost of reconstruction to return the facilities to pre-war standards is estimated at $12,000 million and Rls 640,000 million. The mission notes that these estimates include the cost of updating technology which is a decade or more out-of-date. It further notes that these estimates include the cost of replacing compressor stations and implanting treating facilities for a gas reinjection programme, neither of which, in the mission's view, should be included in an accounting of strictly reconstruction costs.

3. North production zone

The prime function of this zone is to pump northward for domestic use both petroleum products from the Abadan Refinery and crude from the Marun oil production facilities. Along the Abadan route, crude oil is also picked up at Ahwaz for transshipment to the Tehran Refinery for processing; the Marun route runs to the Esfahan Refinery. A total of 23 facilities were attacked repeatedly during the war. The mission was able to visit five facilities by ground and four facilities by helicopter fly-overs along the two pumping routes. The damage observed was generally severe and in most cases proportionate to the number of attacks.

Pumping stations used in the north fields area consist of the pumps and drives (gas/steam turbines, electric motors or diesel/gas engines), inlet/discharge manifolds, associated piping, boilers, power plants, fuel storage tanks, electrical substations together with switch gear and transformers, pig traps and launches in addition to control rooms and

/...

miscellaneous buildings for stores, workshops, offices, etc. To reactivate such a unit after bombing damage requires not only an extensive reconstruction effort but also (primarily) replacement of damaged or destroyed operating equipment. However, a bottleneck is created by the fact that the high volumetric capacities and pumping pressures required necessitate equipment that can provide sufficient horsepower and strength to withstand the pressure, all of which is costly and must be imported. When such equipment is available, the time necessary to get back on stream is rather short (a few weeks or at most a couple of months), as compared to production and NGL facilities, which normally require several months.

After several attacks, pipelines along the northbound Abadan pumping route were rerouted and buried at two major areas during their reconstruction because of their vulnerability to any future attacks. At most stations, the reconstruction efforts required that most piping, wiring, pig traps and launches as well as manifolds, some equipment and control rooms, electrical substations, etc. be buried or installed underground so as to prevent damage from future attacks. Surface equipment was protected by installing sand-filled reinforced concrete blocks around the equipment. All of these protective measures were costly and time-consuming. Such precautions were also implemented in the south zone.

The mission visited the Naftshahr production facility on the border with Iraq because of the unique circumstances it went through. This entire facility, consisting of oil/gas separators, pump compressor stations, gathering systems, support equipment, piping, etc., was reported to have been completely dismantled and shipped across the border. The Government is committed to rebuilding this facility to its former capacity of 30,000 b.p.d., and reconstruction work has already commenced. When the facility is completed, the crude will be pumped to the refinery at Bakhtaran, which the mission also visited. This refinery was shut down for over three years during the war because it underwent severe attacks. It was originally designed for 15,000 b.p.d. but has been reconstructed to handle 30,000 b.p.d.

The mission has been advised that the total cost incurred for reconstruction in the north fields area to date amounts to $9 million and Rls 20,000 million, while the remaining cost of reconstruction to return the facilities to pre-war standards is estimated at $140 million and Rls 18,500 million. In the mission's view, these estimates are generous, as the main pumping equipment and drives have already been replaced and are included in the cost of reconstruction to date.

4. Offshore production zone

The sole function of this zone is to produce oil for export. It is divided into five areas of production: Kharg Island (four fields), Pazargad Barge (one field), Bahregan Oil Centre (three fields), Lavan Island (three fields) and Sirri Island (two fields). The mission was able to visit three facilities (the Kharg Island onshore production facilities, the Bahregan Oil Centre production facilities, and the Abouzar offshore production/well

/...

protector platform) and to perform helicopter fly-over investigations at four other locations (two drilling/well protector platforms producing from the Abouzar offshore field, well protector platforms producing from the Darius offshore field and the Pazargad Barge/single-point mooring buoy and well protectors producing from the Cyrus field).

The pre-war crude oil production from the five areas was 870,000 b.p.d. Its current production is 242,000 b.p.d., a reflection of the damage inflicted upon the offshore production facilities. Of the 80 installations struck in the whole offshore production area, 32 were completely destroyed.

The Iranian offshore operation includes 139 platforms and 332 wells and involves all aspects of oilfield operations. It is a very costly and complex operation. The mission was advised that over $2,500 million was expended in developing this offshore petroleum operation, most of which is completely destroyed or damaged.

The mission has been advised that the total cost incurred for reconstruction in the offshore production zone to date amounts to $350 million or Rls 17,000 million, while the remaining cost of reconstruction to return the facilities to pre-war standards is estimated by the Government at $6,000 million or Rls 70,000 million. Reconstruction of offshore facilities requires very specialized equipment and marine support vessels. The mission was advised that, because of the war and the vulnerability of all marine vessels and activities, very little offshore reconstruction or any other work has been done except for plugging with cement as many wells as could be done under the circumstances, to protect them from further damage. The mission therefore considers that the damage and destruction inflicted is currently about the same as incurred during the war (50-60 per cent). In the mission's view, therefore, these estimates are generous, even when the cost of marine support facilities is included.

5. Reconstruction costs

Table B.2 below summarizes the information provided by the Government on reconstruction costs for the four production areas in the country, based on expenses incurred during the war plus those incurred since the cease-fire and those expected to be incurred in the future.

/...

Table B.2. **Reconstruction costs by major production area**

(In millions of rials and dollars)

Area	To date		Planned		Total	
	Rls	US$	Rls	US$	Rls	US$
South	30 000	500	640 000	12 000	670 000	12 500
North	20 000	9	18 500	140	38 500	149
Offshore	17 000	350	70 000	6 000	87 000	6 350
Total	67 000	859	728 500	18 140	795 500	18 999

The total cost of reconstruction, both past and future, according to the Government's estimate, is thus Rls 795,500 million or $18,999 million. The worksheet underlying this table has been provided to the mission and is on file for the record.

6. Refining

This section of the report deals with the refining subsector, sometimes referred to, together with petrochemical activities, as "downstream" operations. There are seven refineries in the Islamic Republic of Iran, ranging from Abadan, once the world's largest, to Lavan, a small topping plant on an island off the southern coast. Before the outbreak of the war these seven plants were processing close to 900,000 barrels of crude oil per day, enough not only to supply its domestic needs but also to enjoy the benefits of a considerable export market.

/...
0194

Figure B.1

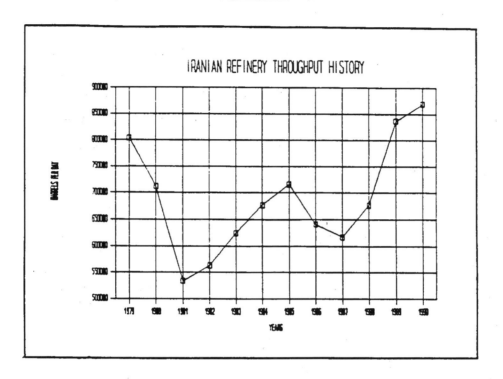

Figure B.1 shows the experience of Iranian refineries spanning the war years, the term "throughput" meaning the quantity of petroleum processed by the plants over a specified period (usually one day).

By far the largest in total throughput was the Abadan Refinery, which had the capability of processing almost 700,000 barrels per day. Only half of this throughput capability was integrated with the full range of secondary facilities needed to produce such products as motor gasoline, kerosene, jet fuel and diesel fuel (so-called "light fuels") for the domestic market, however, with the result that the plant yielded almost 50 per cent "heavy" fuel, a low valued product, most of which was exported. Each of the other six refineries is strategically located to serve a particular area and market: in most cases the topography of the country has influenced the choice of location. The large plants, at Tehran, Esfahan and Tabriz, are the key facilities in the supply network. All three were completely integrated refineries, producing for the domestic market high volumes of the light fuels cited above. The remaining refineries (Shiraz, Bakhtaran and Lavan) are much smaller in capacity and serve smaller speciality markets. Shiraz is worthy of special note in that it anchors a growing and extensive petrochemical complex in a attractive area of the country.

/...

Direct damages

The outbreak of war in 1980 put all seven refineries under attack from the air with heavy damage and widespread disruption of petroleum product supply, particularly at Abadan. This interruption of normal supply grew in intensity and is illustrated by figure B.2. The three historical lines shown are for light fuels, other products (the by-products and residua such as propane, heavy fuel and sulfur) and imports (chiefly motor gasoline, jet fuel, kerosene and diesel fuel) made necessary by the interruptions and shutdowns of refinery production.

Figure B.2

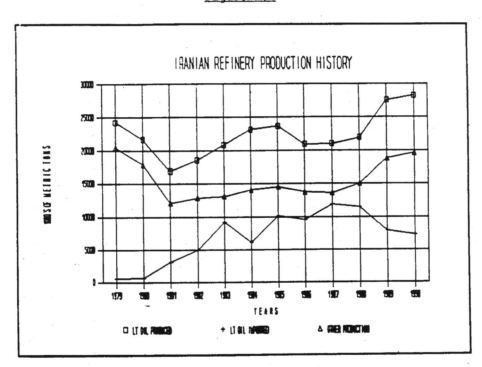

The data show that the import of light fuels reached over 200,000 b.p.d. in the 1985-1987 period. The mission was informed that the import total from 1980 to 1988 was close to 500 million barrels; this would have meant an outlay of over $5,000 million of hard currency. The Government informed the mission that rationing was in force throughout the war period. It further advised that the real demand level was therefore masked and that the import level might otherwise have reached over 400,000 b.p.d. It should be noted however that, except for Abadan, refinery throughput is back to pre-war levels. In fact, at the Tehran and Esfahan refineries, debottlenecking projects have successfully raised the throughput levels significantly beyond pre-war peaks.

/...

0196

Abadan

At Abadan, the recovery has been slow because of the extent of devastation and today throughput has reached only about 350,000 b.p.d., half its original capacity, but it is operating at about 200,000 b.p.d. owing to the lack of crude. The current refining strategy for Abadan is to reach and maintain about 400,000 b.p.d. and develop the secondary units to match this level. Future refining plans for Abadan are not yet clearly defined, although it was hinted that the Government might restore the throughput to its pre-war level. The principal factors influencing planning for the refinery and the area may be summarized as follows:

(a) The desire to maintain a strong and viable refining industry base in the area to anchor the rebuilding of Khorramshahr and Abadan;

(b) The existence of facilities, albeit needing repair and modification, together with a strong base in terms of human resources and technical skills;

(c) The very symbolic nature of Abadan itself.

The statistical record of production and yield for the Abadan refinery (and for each of the other refineries) has been presented to the mission and is on file for the record.

Tehran

This plant is located about 20 miles south of the city and today has a capacity of 250,000 b.p.d. It was attacked on two occasions during the war and lost 247 days of productive capacity in consequence. The extent of the damage, although dramatic at the time, was relatively minor and on each occasion repairs were made with extreme dedicated effort. Today, in addition to maintaining the production level, NIOC has been successful in debottlenecking the refinery to a throughput of close to 300,000 b.p.d.

Esfahan

In 1979, just before the outbreak of the war, Esfahan refinery was a new plant just starting up. Seven attacks during the war resulted in a loss of 364 days of operation, but reconstruction went forward after each attack to maintain productive capability. Recently, the plant has been debottlenecked and has been operating at close to 300,000 b.p.d. Its technology is only 10 years old, but many temporary repairs still need permanent correction.

/...

Tabriz

This refinery is located in the extreme north-west of the country and is about 18 years old. It endured a total of 14 attacks during the eight-year war, which resulted in 238 days of lost production; the mountainous terrain and relative inaccessibility probably saved it from more frequent attack. The interruptions in production were fairly short as the plant was reconstructed after each attack; it operates today at almost 90,000 b.p.d.

Shiraz

Although the Shiraz refinery and its neighbouring petrochemical complex is strategically important, its distance from the war activity precluded frequent attack. Only four attacks were said to have been made on the refinery; these resulted in the loss of only 165 days production in the eight years. The refinery today is operating at the 35,000-b.p.d. level.

Bakhtaran

As the Bakhtaran refinery was situated close to the Iraqi border, it was not only the subject of air attack but was also in proximity to the ground action. The result was 1,400 lost production days; in fact, the refinery was shut down completely during 1981 and 1982, owing to the destruction of the crude pipeline supplying raw material. The refinery is now once again operating at capacity of about 25,000 b.p.d., serving a localized demand in the western part of the country.

Lavan

This small topping plant on the island of Lavan off the southern coast supplies the local needs of the island community and its crude production plant which services several important offshore oilfields. The frequent attacks on these fields and their associated facilities led to two attacks on Lavan plant and 53 days of lost production. Reconstruction of the 20,000 barrel per day plant was relatively minor.

7. Reconstruction costs

The Government provided the mission with the following reconstruction costs for the seven refineries, based on expenses incurred during the war and those incurred since the cease-fire.

/...

0198

Table B.3. <u>Reconstruction costs of refineries</u>

(In millions of rials and dollars)

Place	War time Rls	War time $	Cease-fire Rls	Cease-fire US$	Total Rls	Total US$
Abadan	4 739	89	8 772	164	13 511	253
Tehran	679	13	232	4	911	17
Esfahan	963	18	511	10	1 474	28
Shiraz and Lavan	643	12	509	10	1 152	22
Tabriz	1 114	21	224	4	1 338	25
Bakhtaran	508	9	140	3	648	12
Total	8 646	162	10 388	195	19 034	357

The total cost of reconstruction by the Government's estimate is thus Rls 19,034 million and $357 million. The worksheet underlying this table has been provided to the mission and is on file for the record.

As can be seen, most of the cost is centred in Abadan. In the other refineries, reconstruction has restored capacity to or beyond pre-war levels. However, the status of these plants is acceptable only in 1980 technological and mechanical terms. Ten- to 15-year-old instruments, controls and other equipment leaves the Islamic Republic of Iran technologically behind and operating well below modern efficiency standards. Moreover, the mission was informed that reconstruction costs to date are only 45 per cent of the total necessary to restore pre-war condition and productive capability. Thus, a further sum of Rls 42,298 million and $793 million would be required to complete the reconstruction work. The Government further stated that it was formulating plans to proceed with the balance under a specific time-frame. However, the details have not yet been spelled out.

In connection with these plans for future reconstruction and development, the mission emphasizes that the critical issue is to ascertain what kind of operation the refineries are capable of sustaining. In this regard, the normal indicative criteria are:

/...

(a) Saleable yield;

(b) Percentage yield of light oil versus heavy fuel;

(c) Fuel consumption;

(d) Losses.

The saleable yield record shows quite average values for the industry (94 to 96 per cent). However, the mission was informed that weight percentage losses are close to 0.5 per cent; this is not a good result, for weight percentage losses are real and visible and the refinery closings should be tight except for flare. From the limited data available, it appears that fuel consumption is above average; moreover, the mission observed little evidence of energy conservation equipment (which is hardly surprising with binding financial resource constraints). Most important, it appears to the mission that, as light oil (gasoline, kerosene and diesel) is being imported at high cost, the light oil to heavy oil ratio is far too low. This suggests that the refinery configurations need reexamination.

The mission was provided a list of capital expenditures planned for the next several years, which is on file for the record. Upgrading capital does not appear to be in the planning forecast. In fact, much of the planned work has to do with expanded capacity, lead reduction in gasoline and added lubricating oil production. These are all projects studied and planned in the normal scheme of industry development and are not related to reconstruction due to war damage; they have therefore not been included here. It should, however, be noted that two new refineries at Bandar Abbas and Arak, although already partially built, have been placed on hold on account of shortages of capital; completion is currently planned for 1994 and 1997 respectively.

8. Petrochemicals

Damage

The petrochemical industry was devastated by the war. The location of the majority of the industry along the northern shore of the Persian Gulf meant that the facilities were within easy range of aerial attack. The huge joint-venture plant at Bandar-e-Imam Khomeini was more than 60 per cent completed when the war began. Its products were for the most part to be exported and were expected to provide major revenue for the country. As a consequence of the war, work on this project has had to be suspended, since the damages sustained and the risk and cost of reconstruction during the war was too high. Indeed, the damage to the entire petrochemical sector was such that, for several years during the middle of the war, production at all chemical plants was virtually halted.

The Government has presented the mission with a detailed list of all the petrochemical plants, their feed stocks and products by name and quantity for

/...

the 12 years from 1979 to 1990; this is on file for the record. Figure B.3
shows the historical record and the capacity line emphasizes the production
loss, which is shown to be in the order of 30 million tons of total
petrochemical products over an eight-year period.

Figure B.3

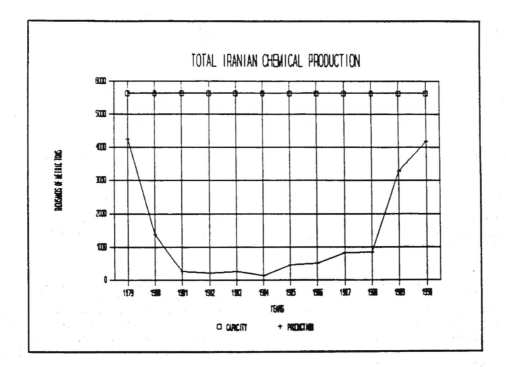

TOTAL IRANIAN CHEMICAL PRODUCTION

    All of the plants with the exception of the joint venture facility are
once again operating near their capacity levels. However, much of the
reconstruction is of a temporary nature and no major funding has been
earmarked for lasting repair of the extensive patchwork.

Reconstruction costs

    The Government has provided the mission with the following reconstruction
costs for the seven petrochemical plants, based on expenses incurred during
the war and those incurred since the cease-fire.

/...

Table B.4. Reconstruction of petrochemical plants

(In millions of rials and dollars)

Place	War time		Cease-fire		Total	
	Rls	$	Rls	US$	Rls	US$
Abadan	1 304	24	3 305	62	4 609	86
Farabi	193	4	130	2	323	6
Imam Port	4 883	92	28 931	542	33 814	634
Raazi	1 542	29	899	17	2 441	46
Shiraz	4 582	86			4 582	86
Pasargad	1 139	21	3		1 142	21
Kharg	1 892	35	47	1	1 939	36
Total	15 535	291	33 315	624	48 850	915

The total cost of reconstruction by the Government's estimate is thus Rls 48,850 million and US$ 915 million. The worksheet underlying this table has been provided to the mission and is on file for the record. The mission was informed that reconstruction costs to date are only 45 per cent of the total necessary to restore pre-war condition and productive capability. Thus, a further sum of Rls 108,556 million or US$ 2,033 million would be required to complete the reconstruction work.

9. Concluding observations

The mission visited many of the refineries and petrochemical plants throughout the country. Analysis of the production data from all these plants confirms that from a purely production standpoint, both refining and petrochemical industries are now able to produce at close to their pre-war output levels.

Table B.5 summarizes the information provided by the Government on reconstruction costs for the seven refineries and seven petrochemical plants in the country, based on expenses incurred during the war plus those incurred since the cease-fire, and those expected to be incurred in the future.

/...

0202

Table B.5. Reconstruction costs

(In millions of rials and dollars)

Type	To date		Future		Total	
	Rls	$	Rls	$	Rls	$
Refinery	19 034	357	42 298	793	61 332	1 150
Petrochemical	48 850	915	108 556	2 033	157 406	2 948
Total	67 884	1 272	150 854	2 826	218 738	4 098

The total cost of reconstruction, both past and future, by the Government's estimate, is thus Rls 218,738 million and $4,098 million. The worksheet underlying this table has been provided to the mission and is on file for the record. This estimate is in line with the mission's own approximate calculation based on the rule-of-thumb accepted in the oil industry of current replacement cost for large plants at $10,000 per b.p.d. of capacity, with a sharply non-linear cost curve as capacity descends below 100,000 b.p.d. On this basis, the mission has very roughly estimated the total outlay of funds necessary for complete reconstruction at $5,000 million. If the rial figure estimated by the Government is converted at the mission's rate of Rls 300 per dollar in 1990 prices, it amounts to the equivalent of $729 million. Adding this to the estimated foreign exchange requirement of $4,098 million gives a total cost for complete reconstruction on the Government's estimate of $4,827 million, which is very close to the mission's rough estimate of $5,000 million.

It is a matter of great concern to the mission that the plants and refineries are technologically at best 10 years out of date. The time and cost of upgrading and of replacing the many temporary repairs soundly and securely is only now being programmed and planned. This work will have a sharp impact on the technological gap and requires careful attention to industry planning decisions. In addition to the obvious drain of such a vast programme on available human resources, money and materials there is the matter of access. The Islamic Republic of Iran must, in order to upgrade in a reasonable time-frame, have easy access to technology and industrial equipment. This will mean either acquiring such technology and equipment on the open market or providing the incentives to attract foreign investment capital into the country in a highly competitive financial environment where the needs are staggering, particularly in the third world.

/...

Notes

1/ 1991 International Petroleum Encyclopedia, p. 297.

2/ World Bank Report No. 9072-IRN-7/30/91, p. 51, and extrapolated by oil production sector mission member.

0204

C. TRANSPORT

1. Rail, roads and air transport

(a) Loss sustained by the transportation subsector

At stated in the first report of the team (S/22863), the Government has estimated the direct loss caused by the war in the transportation subsector at Rls 1,085.6 billions in terms of 1988 replacement costs. The loss sustained by the maritime transport subsector is not included in this total. The war caused a considerable delay in the development of the road and railway networks, as well as of the port capacities, and this in turn caused serious bottlenecks in the development of other sectors. This part of the loss is not visible in the transportation subsector itself.

A breakdown of the estimated direct loss in the subsector is presented in table C.1.

Table C.1. Direct losses in transport sector

(In millions of rials)

Subsector	Buildings and installations	Machinery and equipment	Materials and goods	Total
Land	54 858	965 729	0	1 020 587
Air	13 809	35 331	0	49 140
Storage	10 490	5 331	52	15 873
Total	79 157	1 006 391	52	1 085 600

The loss of machinery and equipment constitutes 92.7 per cent of the total direct loss sustained by this subsector. It is the mission's view that this proportion does not adequately reflect the real relations between the elements of direct loss. Most of the damage sustained by buildings and installations in the transportation subsector were quickly repaired, in many cases several times, during the war. These multiple repairs are not visible now, but they have been reflected in the estimate of the direct loss.

The Government has estimated the costs of reconstruction to date in the transport sector at Rls 124,066 million and expects the future costs to complete the reconstruction already planned to be Rls 63,937 million in foreign exchange and Rls 225,746 million in local currency.

/...

(b) Land transportation

Damage

In 1980 there was a total of 4,570 kilometres of single-track lines and Iranian Railways carried 5 million passengers and 5.7 million tons of freight. By 1988, at the end of the war, the track length had increased to 4,834 kilometres, with 6.8 million passengers carried and 12.5 million tons of freight. During the war period the number of freight wagons increased from 12,150 to 13,312 and the number of passenger coaches increased from 760 to 925. During the same period the number of locomotives increased from 418 to 531.

The direct loss in rail transportation, as presented by the Iranian authorities, consists of the following parts:

 (a) Buildings and installations:

   150 km of railway lines damaged 100 per cent
   118,569 m^2 of buildings damaged from 20 per cent to 100 per cent
   292 bridges and culverts damaged 85 per cent
   3 major bridges damaged 42 per cent
   2 major bridges damaged 24 per cent

 (b) Machinery and equipment:

 (i) Telecommunications and signalling systems:
   120 km damaged 100 per cent
   107 km damaged 55 per cent
   146 km damaged 15 per cent

 (ii) Electrical equipment and network:
   120 km damaged 100 per cent
   107 km damaged 45 per cent
   146 km damaged 20 per cent

 (iii) Wagons and locomotives:
   956 wagons damaged from 35 per cent to 85 per cent
   21 locomotives damaged from 30 per cent to 75 per cent

A detailed list of losses was presented to the mission and is on file for the record.

The direct loss sustained by railways was estimated by the Government at Rls 55,775 millions in foreign currency and Rls 38,932 millions in local currency. These figures include both building and equipment losses. With regard to buildings and installations, most damage was caused to railway stations, marshalling yards and five major bridges. The major damage to rail tracks and associated equipment occurred in Khuzestan Province, in particular to the Ahwaz-Khorramshahr line. This 120-kilometre line is reported to have

/...

been entirely destroyed during the ground war. The bridge at Qotoc near the Turkish border was also damaged and the major line for the flow of goods to and from Turkey was closed for several months. Rail equipment, reportedly in rolling stock, has been estimated as one of the major losses in the transportation subsector.

The mission has made attempts to verify all severe damages and to assess the extent of loss suffered by the rail transportation, as reported by the Iranian authorities. Three major and five minor railway stations, 60 kilometres of track and four major bridges were inspected by the mission. The inspection was aided by photographs taken at the time of the damage. The mission has inspected the following:

Major railway stations: Khorramshahr, Ahwaz and Andimeshk;

Minor railway stations: Hoseyniyeh, Hamid, SarBandar, Haft Tappeh and Tolezang;

The railway line: Ahwaz-Khorramshahr; and

Railway bridges: Ahwaz, Karun river, Tolezang, Souili and Qotoc.

However, the exact number of destroyed wagons and locomotives, as reported by the railway authorities, could not be verified.

Most of damage caused to railway stations, tracks and marshalling yards was temporarily repaired immediately after damage and destroyed rolling stock was replaced either during or immediately after the war. Considerable reconstruction work has been carried out on several railway stations and bridges, thereby leaving no traces of the damage in many places. However, the mission saw evidence of the ruins of destroyed buildings, as well as debris and destroyed equipment. These were consistent with the damage reports and photos. A description of both the damage and the reconstruction work inspected by the mission is contained in the first report of the team of experts.

The monetary value of the damage caused to buildings and installations, as presented by the Iranian authorities, appears to be appropriate. However, the mission was not able to verify the extent of damage caused to rolling stock and equipment, as most of damaged wagons, locomotives and other equipment had already been cleared from tracks and depots.

Roads

As stated in the first report, roads are by far the most important mode of transportation in the Islamic Republic of Iran, for both passengers and goods. There are over 2,000 road transport companies in the country, of which fewer than 6 per cent are government owned. Of total domestic freight, some 85 per cent is by road, whereas only 10 per cent of international freight is

/...

by road. The total volume of freight by road is estimated at 90 million
tons. In 1980 there were about 160,000 kilometres of all-weather roads, of
which 42 per cent was fully paved. By 1989, the road network comprised a
total of 167,156 kilometres outside urban areas. At that time, there were
over 1 million automobiles and nearly half a million trucks and buses.

The direct loss in road transportation as presented to the mission by the
Iranian authorities consists of the following elements:

Buildings and installations

Roads damaged:

Khuzestan province:	1 533 km
Ilam province:	600 km
Bakhtaran province:	845 km
Kurdistan province:	555 km
Azarbayjan province:	330 km

(The above figures include main and feeder roads, as well as minor
bridges and culverts.)

Major bridges:

Khuzestan province:	11 bridges
Ilam province:	10 bridges

Machinery and equipment for road maintenance:

321 pieces of road maintenance equipment damaged in most cases
100 per cent. The loss is estimated at Rls 6,000 million in foreign currency.

Damage was also suffered by some district road offices and loss of
equipment for road maintenance was reported as follows:

Khuzestan province:	7 offices, total 1,489 m^2
Ilam province:	5 offices, total 940 m^2
Bakhtaran province:	1 office, total 4,000 m^2

A detailed list of losses was presented to the mission and is on file for the
record.

Extensive damage to roads was evident in all border areas, particularly
in sectors where ground warfare and occupation had taken place. Besides these
damaged roads, roads in the cities and towns close to the border also suffered
considerable damage, particularly in Khorramshahr, where it is estimated that
80 per cent of all roads require rehabilitation or resurfacing; and in Abadan,
where 40 per cent of all roads were reported to have been damaged by the war.

/...

The direct loss sustained by roads was estimated by the Iranian authorities at Rls 36,014 million in foreign currency and Rls 79,938 million in local currency. These figures include both building and equipment losses.

The mission has made attempts to verify all severe damage and to assess the extent of the loss to road transportation reported by the Iranian authorities. 1,360 kilometres of roads, 40 major bridges and numerous minor bridges and culverts were inspected by the mission. A further 500 kilometres of roads were inspected by low- flying helicopter. The inspection was aided by photographs taken at the time of the damage. The detail of these inspections is as follows:

Roads: 790 kilometres in Khuzestan Province
230 kilometres in Ilam Province
340 kilometres in Bakhtaran Province

Major bridges: Khorramshahr, Abadan, Ahwaz, Karkheb river, Susan-Guerd, Bostan Town, Djesr Naderi, Changuleh, Zagavi, Kondjancham 1,2,3, Haftdhaneh, Naftshahr, Tangab, Emam Abbas, and other major bridges in provinces: Khuzestan, Ilam, Bakhtaran and Emam Abbas.

The mission also inspected four district road offices in Khuzestan. Although the sites had been cleared and partially rebuilt, there remained evidence of damage.

The mission was also able to observe damage inflicted on roads and bridges in the main theatre of war during the conflict. Damage to roads was caused by both bombardment and abnormal overweight traffic loads. Many of the roads had been resurfaced during the war and the same damage caused by overweight vehicles is again apparent. The roads did not receive normal routine maintenance during the war and this accelerated the deterioration of the road surfaces and structures. There is no doubt that the road network suffered extensive damage over and above normal wear and tear. Damage to major bridges and to most of the small bridges and culverts was caused by direct bombardment, but in many cases there were also damages reported to minor bridges from overweight vehicles.

Reconstruction work has been carried out on roads and bridges. Many roads have already been resurfaced and bridges rebuilt or repaired. For this reason, the damage is not evident in many places. However, the inspection confirmed, that in most cases the reconstruction was consistent with the damage reports and photos. A description of the damage and of reconstruction work inspected by the mission may be found in the first report of the United Nations team of experts.

The monetary value of the damage caused to roads and road bridges, as presented by the Iranian authorities, appears to be underestimated. Most damage to the roads was not caused by direct bombardment, but by overloaded vehicles and/or due to lack of appropriate maintenance during or immediately

/...

0209

after the war. In many cases, damage has been caused not only to the road pavement but also to the lower courses of the road structure. This will require both rehabilitation and resurfacing. Moreover, roads outside the border areas suffered deterioration owing to indirect war-related causes. Because of the priorities given to the border areas, only relatively small repairs and improvements to the country road network could be undertaken during the war period. This has resulted in a deterioration of the overall quality of the road system. This general damage to the road system, as well as the necessity to rehabilitate roads in the areas of war operations does not, in the mission's view, appear to be reflected in the estimate of war damage. The mission was not able to verify the extent of damage caused to equipment for road maintenance, as damaged equipment had already been cleared from road sites and depots.

Reconstruction work observed by the mission

An impressive amount of reconstruction has already been carried out in the land transportation subsector, both during and after the war. It was essential for the war efforts to keep transport corridors open in the border provinces so that reconstruction work on roads and railways was executed during the war and in many cases repeated several times. However, this repair work was in most cases of a temporary nature, and more thorough reconstruction needs to be undertaken. The task of reconstruction is immense and it will take many years before it can be completed.

The severely damaged railway line Ahwaz-Khorramshahr has been repaired and reconstructed, but the work carried out was only of a temporary nature. The mission was informed that the transport capacity of this line before the war was seven to eight freight trains (2,000 tons' load) per day. Because of poor track conditions, the capacity at present is only two trains per day, with a limited speed of 45 km/h. It is planned to upgrade the railway line to allow a maximum speed of 100 km/h and trains of 5,000 tons load. The present Khorramshahr station has been rebuilt in the vicinity of the destroyed station. The station has at present only 6 operative tracks compared with 11 operative tracks before the war. A new station complex is proposed to be built 300 metres up-line. The Ahwaz station has been rebuilt and is now operable.

Reconstruction of roads damaged by shell fire or overloaded vehicles was effected only by resurfacing or applying an overlay on the damaged pavement. The authorities are quite aware of the real magnitude of the problem and resurfacing is considered as a temporary measure only. Because of an apparent lack of funds, no proper reconstruction has yet been undertaken, and many recently paved roads will need to be resurfaced. In most cases, only full rehabilitation of the road structure can be considered as an appropriate way of reconstruction of damaged roads. Moreover, a great deal of repair and rehabilitation of road drainage, shoulders, markings and signs is also required.

/...

Many bridges were reportedly damaged and repaired on several occasions during the war. Circumstances made it necessary to use Bailey and pontoon bridges to bridge rivers, and simple steel plates and steel beams have been used to bridge damaged areas. In general, a more permanent form of reconstruction is needed to be undertaken.

Reconstruction plans and needs

The reconstruction of the transportation sector is recognized by the Iranian authorities as one of the prerequisites for the reconstruction of other sectors. Unfortunately, it has not been possible to reconstruct, modernize and develop land transport facilities to the extent needed, and this has caused serious bottlenecks in the execution of reconstruction work in other sectors. As mentioned above, much of the reconstruction carried out during or immediately after the war was only temporary. The Iranian authorities have now prepared sectoral reconstruction plans showing priorities and time schedules. The plans were presented to the mission and are on file for the record. Although part of the reconstruction programme has been implemented, enabling transport flows on the most important lines, a much greater part remains to be implemented.

With the exception of railway tracks, the reconstruction of land transport physical infrastructure has been carried out by Iranian construction companies, the majority of which are privately owned. Railway track reconstruction is carried out by Iranian Railways. All work has been planned and designed by Iranian engineers and executed by Iranian skilled manpower. Some types of construction plant and machinery used in reconstruction work are manufactured in the country, but a great deal of plant has been imported. The mission observed that the reconstruction work performed is of high quality, even in complex undertakings such as bridge construction.

The mission noted that a large proportion of the construction plant and machinery needed is not manufactured in the country. Consequently, a considerable amount of foreign currency is required to cover the cost of imported items. Reconstruction of rolling stock and railway equipment also requires a foreign currency component for material and parts not locally manufactured. While railway freight wagons and passenger coaches are manufactured locally, their wheels and axles as well as some types of bogies have to be purchased abroad. Moreover, maintenance equipment for roads and railways, as well as locomotives and heavy trucks also need to be imported. Since the damage to machinery and equipment in the land transportation subsector was considerably higher than the reported damage to structures and installations, replacement of this equipment also requires a significant amount of foreign currency. Taking all factors into account, it is envisaged in the reconstruction plan that foreign currency will be needed for 45.8 per cent of the budget to meet remaining reconstruction work in the land transportation field. This estimate appears to the mission to be reasonable.

The Government has established priorities in the reconstruction of land transport facilities. The main priority is given to the full reconstruction

/...

0211

and upgrading of the line Ahwaz-Khorramshahr and to the building of a new
railway station at Khorramshahr. The construction of additional railway
capacity to the port of Bandar Khomeyni and new railway capacity to the port
of Bandar Abbas, as a consequence of the shifting of the former capacities of
the Khorramshahr port to these two ports, will alleviate the land
transportation problems and eliminate some of bottlenecks. The railway
network also needs upgrading and modernization as well as renovation and
additions to the rolling stock. This is considered urgent since railways will
be expected to carry a considerably higher share of freight than at present.
The country has the technical expertise and skilled manpower to carry out this
immense and complicated task, but a considerable amount of foreign currency is
needed for implementation of this plan.

In regard to roads, priority is given to the rehabilitation and improved
maintenance of the main roads and reconstruction of the main bridges in the
border provinces. The Government has estimated that the foreign currency
component needed for the remaining road reconstruction work will be
30 per cent of the total budget. This money will be needed mostly for the
procurement of equipment not manufactured in the country.

(c) Air transportation

Damage

Airports

In 1980, major international airports at Tehran, Bandar Abbas and Abadan
were supplemented by 10 grade I and 11 grade II airports. By 1988, domestic
services had increased to cover 38 towns. Seven of these airports are for
international traffic and 12 are suitable for large aircraft. The list of all
airports in operation was presented to the mission and is on file for the
record. The number of air passengers in 1988 exceeded 5.6 million; import and
export air cargo amounted to some 23,000 and 22,000 tons respectively.

Air corridors over the Islamic Republic of Iran were closed to
international carriers during the war period, but have now reopened. All
major airports in the border provinces were attached during the war and
suffered varying degrees of damage. The Abadan airport suffered the most
since it came under continuous bombardment by air and by artillery. With the
closure of Abadan airport, the importance of Ahwaz airport increased making it
also the target for frequent attacks by air. The damage to airports, as
presented to the mission by the Iranian authorities, consists of the following:

/...

Buildings and installations:

Airports damaged:

Abadan:	moderate to severe
Ahwaz:	moderate to severe
Bakhtaran:	moderate
Sanandaj:	minor to moderate
Urmiyeh:	minor to moderate
Tabriz:	minor to moderate

Other airports which sustained minor damages are Hamadan, Shiraz and Tehran

Machinery and equipment:

Terminal, control tower, lighting and other equipment was damaged at the airports of Abadan, Ahwaz and Bahtaran. There was also minor damage to the equipment on the other airports that were attacked.

Aircraft destroyed:

Iran Air:	2 Boeing 727
	1 Airbus EP-IBS
Asseman:	3 Fairchild
	1 Shirk commander

Aircraft damaged:

Iran Air:	1 Boeing 747	6 per cent
	1 Airbus	10 per cent

A list detailing losses was presented to the mission and is on file for the record.

Meteorological stations

The Meteorology Organization provides meteorological data to the aviation, shipping, agriculture and energy sectors. During the war, many of its climatological and synoptic stations were damaged. The damaged stations, as indicated by the Iranian authorities, are:

Climatological stations in:

Bakhtaran Province:	1 station	100 per cent damaged
Ilam Province:	1 station	100 per cent damaged
Kurdistan Province:	18 stations	100 per cent damaged
Azarbayjan Province:	2 stations	80-100 per cent damaged
Khuzestan Province:	7 stations	100 per cent damaged

/...

Synoptic stations:

Six stations received damage ranging from 16 to 100 per cent. The detailed list of losses was presented to the mission and is on file for the record.

The direct loss sustained by air transportation, including both building and equipment losses, was estimated by the Iranian authorities at Rls 27,902 million in foreign currency and Rls 30,651 million in local currency.

The mission has endeavoured to verify all severe damage suffered by the air transportation subsector reported by the Iranian authorities. The mission visited four airports and several meteorological stations. As for the other subsectors, the inspection was aided by photographs taken at the time of the damage. Airports visited by the mission are Abadan, Ahwaz, Bakhtaran and Urmiyeh. The mission also visited Ahwaz, Dehloran, Bakhtaran and Susan-Guerd meteorological stations.

Damage inflicted on airports during the war was observed by the mission. Although reconstruction work had been carried out on the airports visited, the inspection confirmed that the ruins of former buildings and the pattern of reconstruction were consistent with the damage reports and photos. Damage said to have been inflicted on Shiraz, Hamadan and Tehran airports could not be verified.

The mission also observed debris of some destroyed aircraft. An additional description of the damage and of the reconstruction work inspected by the mission may be found in the team's first report.

The monetary value of the damage caused to the airport buildings and installations, as presented by the Iranian authorities, appears to be appropriate. The mission was not able to verify the exact extent of damage caused to aircraft and equipment, as most of them have already been repaired or cleared from the sites.

Reconstruction work observed by the mission

The Abadan airport has been reconstructed to the extent necessary to enable inland traffic operations. Domestic traffic will start by the end of November 1991. The main terminal, the control tower and the longer runway are under reconstruction and international traffic operation will begin in January 1993.

The Ahwaz airport is now operable, although the main terminal building, the apron and the runway, as well as the staff housing are still being repaired or reconstructed. Some development of the airport is being carried out in conjunction with the reconstruction.

/...

0214

The damaged structures and installations at Bakhtaran airport have been repaired and the airport is fully operable. The mission also found that the damage caused to the Urmiyeh airport had also been repaired. These latter two airports remained open throughout the war years.

Reconstruction plans

The Iranian authorities have given priority to the reconstruction and development of the air transportation subsector, because there are no viable alternatives to air travel for the vast long distances that need to be covered within the country. However, air transport facilities have yet to be reconstructed, modernized and developed to the level necessary. The Government has prepared a plan for the reconstruction of 18 airports, some damaged, several requiring expansion and a number to be built. Parts of this plan relating to the reconstruction of damaged airports were presented to the mission and are on file for the record. An amount of Rls 13,000 million in foreign currency has been included in the plan for the replacement of destroyed aircraft. Although some repair and reconstruction has already been effected, the greater part of the reconstruction plan needs to be implemented.

Assessment of implementation capability

The reconstruction of airport buildings, installations, runways, taxiways and aprons has been carried out by Iranian construction companies. Most of construction companies are privately owned. The work was planned and designed by Iranian engineers and executed by Iranian skilled manpower. The mission observed that the reconstruction work performed meets quality standards even in undertakings with high technical requirements, such as runway construction. However, although some types of plant and machinery used in reconstruction work are manufactured in the country, a large proportion of capital equipment requires to be imported (for example, control towers and terminal equipment are not manufactured in the country). For this reason a considerable amount of foreign currency will be needed to cover import costs. Reconstruction and replacement of airport signalling and lighting systems, terminal, fire-fighting, meteorological and traffic control equipment will also require a considerable foreign currency component.

The authorities stated that most damaged or destroyed aircraft have already been repaired or replaced. Since the reported damage to aircraft and equipment in the air transportation subsector was considerably higher than the damage to structures and installations, the replacement of aircraft and equipment, as well as provision of spare parts, require a significant amount of foreign currency. The Government estimates that the foreign exchange component needed for the remaining reconstruction work will be 85.6 per cent of the total cost.

The full reconstruction and upgrading of the Abadan airport has been assigned top priority. The next priority has been given to the reconstruction of the Ahwaz airport, to be followed by work on other damaged airports.

/...

(d) Storage

The airport storage subsector embraces all activities relating to and facilities for public and private warehouses and refrigerating chambers engaged in the storing of various categories of goods. Direct loss to the storage subsector consists of the damage to buildings and installations (66 per cent) and of the damage to machinery and equipment (34 per cent). The amount of direct loss as estimated by the Iranian authorities constitutes only 1.3 per cent of the total direct loss sustained by the transportation sector. In most cases, the damage was caused by aerial attacks. The mission was not able to verify the extent and the monetary value of damage caused to storage facilities, as most of them have already been repaired. However, it did observe a totally destroyed building with refrigerating chambers at Abadan. The mission also visited a destroyed silo at Ahwaz.

2. Ports and marine salvage

The Iranian port and marine system plays a key role in the country's economy as a major industry providing employment and as the main agent for foreign trade. Authority over ports and the merchant fleet is exercised by the Port and Shipping Organization (PSO) for all commercial activities, except those involved in the oil industry which are under the authority of the National Iranian Oil Company (NIOC).

Both organizations are extensively involved in reconstruction and rehabilitation of their capacities, following the heavy damage and losses sustained during the conflict.

(a) Damage sustained in the conflict

Commercial ports

Within the system of commercial ports, the ports of Abadan, Bandar Khomeyni and Khorramshahr were the most severely damaged.

Khorramshahr and Abadan

Located alongside the Shatt al-Arab waterway, the ports of Abadan and Khorramshahr had initially been built by the oil industry for the handling of its supplies. Later, Khorramshahr became a major commercial port, for handling general cargo. Prior to the conflict, it could claim adequate nautical access, fairly good rail and road connections to northern and central parts of the country, and the advantages of a highly populated and industrialized location. Abadan played a more modest role as a commercial and oil supply port. Together, the two ports had a rated traffic capacity of 2 to 3 million tons per year, although through maintaining an exceptionally busy schedule, they managed to sustain an average of 6 million tons per year over several pre-war years. The Shatt al-Arab having been the scene of some fierce

/...

0216

ground fighting during the war, the ports of Khorramshahr and Abadan suffered complete destruction of their above-water structures and equipment and significant damage to their below-water installations.

Bandar Khomeyni

Bandar Khomeyni, the Islamic Republic of Iran's most modern port, was built in the mid-1970s. It is located in a highly industrialized region and is served by excellent maritime access and an adequate road and rail system almost equal to that enjoyed by Khorramshahr. The port handles a wide range of traffic, including conventional general cargo, containers, solid bulk (minerals, cereals, etc.) and liquid bulk (edible oils, etc.). It accommodated vessels of up to 60,000 tons dead weight. Although the port was not involved in land combat, it was situated within the range of aviation attack and suffered extensive damage to its above-water installations and equipment.

The ports of Abadan and Khorramshahr have remained closed since the end of hostilities. The reopening of the Shatt al-Arab to floating craft is an imperative condition for the undertaking of any reconstruction or repair work to the infrastructures of the ports. Given the evolution of marine technology since the 1970s, and depending upon the extent to which the river depths are restored (or even increased) following their clearance, the reconstruction of the ports may require some remodelling for new traffic (roll on-roll off, feeder containers, heavy load vessels, etc.) in addition to general cargo. At present, landside clearance of all debris (buildings, sheds, warehouses, mechanical equipment and cargoes deposited in the storage areas) is under way. Repairs to the port of Bandar Khomeyni are nearly complete and the port is now fully operational.

According to information provided to the mission by PSO, the work done on reconstruction of the commercial ports can be summarized as follows:

(a) During the war years, no amount was allocated towards the reconstruction of the above three ports. However, PSO made progress in the construction of a new major port at Bandar Abbas which is located at the entrance to the Persian Gulf, near the Strait of Hormuz. This port has a design capacity of 13 million tons/year, more than double the peak flows handled at Abadan and Khorramshahr combined. The construction was started in 1986 and was essentially completed during the war years at a total cost of $2,000 million;

(b) During the period 1988-1991 the amount allocated to on-site reconstruction was Rls 45,800 million, mainly for the reconstruction of the port of Khorramshahr, the repair of Bandar Khomeyni and, to a smaller extent, for the clearance of landside debris at the ports of Khorramshahr and Abadan. In addition, some Rls 3,000 million were spent on dredging Bahmanshir;

(c) The amount earmarked, or being considered, for war-related reconstruction activities in the future, by PSO is Rls 152,400 million plus

/...

$4,060 million (the latter amount for imported mechanical equipment). This sum will be needed for the ports of Abadan and Khorramshahr, the completion of repairs at Bandar Khomeyni and for the dredging of the Shatt al-Arab and Bahmanshir.

Despite the rehabilitation of capacities which has already been undertaken at Bandar Abbas as a development within the framework of the ongoing plan for the growth and transformation of the country, the Government is committed to the reconstruction of Khorramshahr port because of the additional capacity which would be brought onstream and the effect it would have in increasing the fluidity of the traffic through the Iranian ports of the Persian Gulf. This would enable exporters and importers to claim more favourable freight rates for their cargoes and reduce the waiting time for berths during periods of congestion. Moreover, since transshipment to container feeder vessels, or to roll on-roll off vessels is an easy operation, the port of Khorramshahr could add its services to those of the port of Bandar Abbas, this latter acting as a major container port. This would reduce the need for land transport to central Iran from Bandar Abbas.

Oil ports

The heavy damage inflicted on oil ports was described in the first report of the United Nations mission (paras. 246-262). Nevertheless, a certain flow of crude oil exports was maintained during the war years (NIOC estimates the flow in one of the worst years, 1988, at nearly 90 million tons). In 1991, it is expected that the level of the best pre-war year (120 million tons) will be nearly attained. Concurrently, imports of refined products which became necessary owing to the damage suffered by the refineries have been reduced progressively from a maximum of 13 million tons in 1987 to an expected 7 million tons in 1991. This is attributed to:

(a) The significant margin of capacity of the oil ports system, compared with the pre-war traffic requirements;

(b) The intensive use of available capacities;

(c) The repair activities during the war years;

(d) The final repairs undertaken progressively to complete the provisional repairs.

NIOC has provided the mission with the following summary table of reconstruction and renovation expenditures for damaged/destroyed port facilities from the onset of the war to the present:

/...

0218

Table 1.   Reconstruction expenditure on port facilities
(Millions of Rls and US$)

	During war time		Since cease-fire		Total	
Place	Rls	US$	Rls	US$	Rls	US$
Mah-Shahr and Abadan	386.6	16.6	525.9	22.5	912.5	39.1
Lavan	154.0	6.6	3 887.0	166.6	4 041.0	173.2
Kharg	1 891.0	81.0	9 622.3	412.4	11 513.3	493.4
Total	2 431.6	104.2	14 035.2	601.5	16 466.8	705.7

Despite the very substantial amount of repair work undertaken during the war, major rehabilitation and reconstruction work remains to be performed. Much of the war-related repair work was of a temporary nature, and the continued attacks throughout the war (many installations were hit several times during the conflict) rendered permanent reconstruction work impossible. Planned reconstruction work includes a $225 million contract for the reconstruction of the Kharg terminals (T-jetty and Sea Island). Other minor contracts, for the completion of restoration work at Kharg Island, as well as at Bandar Mah-Shahr are being considered.

Shipping

Although shipping losses in the Shatt al-Arab and the Karun River (discussed in the mission's first report (S/22863)) were substantial, the marine war was not confined to these areas. The Persian Gulf itself became the site of a "tanker war". Attacks concentrated on the approaches to Bandar Khomeyni, as well as on and nearby Kharg Island, Siri Island, Lavan Island and Hormuz. The mission was informed that during the period 1981-1988, 547 vessels are recorded as having been hit in attacks on Persian Gulf waters, 75 per cent of them being tankers, liquefied petroleum gas (LPG) and combination carriers, and the remainder being dry cargo vessels. On average, one in five of the vessels hit was recorded as a total loss. Many of the vessels hit were chartered foreign vessels, covered by international insurance, whilst vessels flying the national Iranian flag were covered by local insurance. Thus even if shipowners were compensated, the burden of loss for these ships fell on the Iranian economy. They have now either been replaced by repaired vessels or by new tonnage.

The direct losses of Iranian commercial cargo vessels - including those blockaded in the Shatt al-Arab - have been reported to the mission by PSO as having amounted to 17 vessels totally destroyed; 18 vessels were completely repaired, for a total cost of US$ 201,164,610.

/...

0219

The national oil fleet is operated by the National Iranian Tanker Company (NITC). During the period since 1981 until the present, its tonnage increased from approximately 5.5 million dead weight tons (28 vessels), to 6.6 million dead weight tons (33 vessels). Ships were bought to replace destroyed tonnage and to provide for the needs of the transshipment system set up between the exposed waters of the north of the Persian Gulf and the safer waters of the Gulf of Hormuz. NITC furnished the mission with the following data stating that a total of $498 million had been allocated for repair and replacement of damaged ships. Details are as follows:

Repairs: a total of Rls 13,600 million, converted by NITC to $170 million, for the purposes of:

- Provisional and minimum repairs to stricken vessels (39 ships)

- Completed repairs to 28 of above ships

- Ongoing repairs to 8 ships to be completed in 1992

New Shipping: a total of $328 million for repairs or replacement of off-shore boats

Indirect losses are estimated at $1,500 million, which includes loss of crude oil either set on fire or which leaked into the sea.

(b) Need for marine clearance operations

Shatt al-Arab and Karun River

The Shatt al-Arab, which forms part of the boundary between the Islamic Republic of Iran and Iraq, is navigable for sea-going vessels for 140 kilometres. The major ports of Khorramshahr (Islamic Republic of Iran) and Basrah (Iraq) are located on the river. Prior to the outbreak of hostilities, the waterway was administered by a joint commission, the Combined Bureau of Coordination, chaired alternately by the Islamic Republic of Iran and Iraq on an annual basis. Costs and revenues were equally shared.

On the Iranian side, Khorramshahr and its surroundings were the focus of intense fighting throughout the war. Initially limited to a conflict of land forces, the war escalated into attacks on shipping in the rivers. Many vessels were sunk and almost all initially damaged. Significant to future reconstruction efforts, several Iranian dredges escaped damage and are employed today.

The continued closure of the Shatt al-Arab and the presence of sunken ships has had grave consequences for the economy and a serious impact on the environment. The waterway is in a continuing polluting state as fuel and cargoes of uncertain composition leak into the water. Moreover, the destruction of the ports of Khorramshahr and Abadan, along with the closure of the waterway has limited the employment possibilities of most of the

/...

inhabitants of the two cities and their surrounding areas, who relied on the shipping and refinery industries for their livelihood. The local fish industry has all but been destroyed since few fisherman will venture out into the present dangerous waters of the Shatt al-Arab.

As the mission was unable to overfly the river, various vantage points on the Iranian shore were utilized to sight the wrecks. From the jetties at Khorramshahr and Abadan, many sunken ships and barges were sighted - on the banks, in mid-river and alongside the jetties. At Khorramshahr in the Sfealieh Canal and on the Karun River, there were also several smaller wrecks. At approximately mile 26 from the mouth of the Shatt al-Arab in the vicinity of the Iraqi town of Al Faw and the military bridges are a total of 11 wrecks of varying sizes. More details on the areas where sunken ships are located in the Shatt al-Arab are provided in map 1 of the main report.

A list furnished to the first mission by the International Maritime Organization, identifies 86 ships that had either been sunk or immobilized in the Shatt al-Arab as of the date of that report (see S/22863, appendix B, item 22 (f). Plots maintained by the Ports and Shipping Organization of the Transport Ministry show the locations of only 35 wrecks. The mission infers from this that some of the ships mentioned in the first report either escaped or have sunk to the river bed.

The mission notes that the rough total of 800 ships mentioned in the first report includes many small barges, tugs, fishing vessels, etc. beached on both banks. Some of the wreckage may even predate hostilities; most pose no great clearance problem and no hindrance to the operation of the river channel.

The mission was concerned by the fact that the waterway could well contain various types of unexploded ordnance, the amount of which may never be precisely determined. Added to this situation is the complicating factor of silt accumulation which tends to bury such material, hampering normal detection and requiring the use of the most advanced and sophisticated detection equipment. It is almost 12 years since the waterway was last dredged. The silt has deepened and, under compression, has become heavy mud, making it difficult to remove, especially within hulls.

Many of the sunken ships may have contained genuine cargo. Although the value of any salvaged cargo and of the scrapped ships may be small in comparison to the cost of salvage, ownership may be contended.

The mission emphasizes that before any clearance work can commence in the Shatt al-Arab, a solution needs to be found to guarantee the safety of any salvage work force. Provision would also need to be made for the full disclosure by all parties of the types of ordnance used or transported in the area, particularly the presence, if any, of hazardous chemicals. Similarly, the cargo manifests of the damaged ships would need to be made available for determination of the presence of all cargoes, and the banks of the river cleared of mines and other dangerous obstacles which could impair salvage personnel and equipment.

/...

0221

The mission was informed that the Government of the Islamic Republic of Iran had received proposals from foreign Governments and private firms to accomplish the clearance of both wrecks and ordnance from the Shatt al-Arab, but no response has yet been made to these proposals. The only available plan relative to the river is a pre-war plan to dredge the Shatt al-Arab to provide for a draft of 30 feet. Furthermore, the mission has been informed by the Transport Ministry that the Iranian Navy has been assigned the responsibility of clearing explosive material from the waters. The mission has not been able to establish the Navy's capacities in this regard. It is not known whether the Navy possesses the state-of-the-art technology or expertise to perform the task.

In the event of international assistance being required to assist in the clearance of the waterway, further discussions will need to be held with the Iranian authorities on the availability of salvage-oriented divers who can perform under the most disadvantaged and hazardous conditions. Additionally, there would be need to know whether the Navy possesses the necessary management skills and job experience to conduct an operation of this magnitude. The private sector does seem attuned to the enormity and complexity of the task, and there prevails a sense of dedication, aggressiveness and ingenuity that could be harnessed to perform first the small tasks and then graduate to the bigger projects as experience broadens and skills improve.

The equipment required for wreck removal is akin to that of the marine construction industry. Heavy and light capacity cranes, dredges, welding machines, generators, pumps and recompression chambers are the major components of the equipment inventory. Tugs, barges, work boats and launches are necessary ancillary equipment. Berthing barges for remote or heavily damaged areas might also be required. Much of this equipment is available in the country (with the exception of heavy lift cranes of 500-1,000 tons). On the other hand, whilst some detection equipment is available, it may not be state-of-the-art. The utmost in current technology will be required to detect and locate the explosives presumably buried under several metres of silt.

The Ministry of Transport has informed the mission that it estimates the clearance of the explosives and wrecks from the Shatt al-Arab to cost $1,600 million and the dredging to cost $1,800 million. These figures are subject to great uncertainty as no realistic figures can be developed without a proper survey and, in fact, the actual cost may not be known until the work is undertaken and completed.

Other rivers

To a lesser degree, the conditions found in the Shatt al-Arab are also present in the Karun, Bahmanshire and the Khour-e-Musa rivers.

/...

0222

510 걸프 사태 대책 및 조치 5

The Khour-e-Musa

The ports of Bandar Imam Khomeyni and Bandar Mahshahr are located a short distance from each other. They survived bomb and missile attacks and today are fully operational, although there are several wrecks in the vicinity. One wreck at Beacon No. 5 lies partially within the channel and should be removed.

The Bahmanshire

Several small wrecks and wrecked bridges are blocking traffic on the Bahmanshire, a small river 80 kilometres long, to the east of Abadan. The Government is considering plans to clear this and dredge it to 4 metres mainly to harbour fishing boats.

Kharg Island

Both the T-jetty and Sea Island terminals at Kharg Island are in use and able to handle the current level of traffic. However, the approaches to the T-jetty at Kharg Island are hazarded by the presence of a partially sunk tanker about 1 1/2-2 miles offshore. At the Sea Island complex, the remains of a burned-out tanker lie close to the shore and pose a problem for berthing ships on the shore side of the island. The removal of both wrecks is therefore recommended by the mission.

Siri and Lavan islands

The mission was informed by the Iranian Offshore Oil Corporation, which has jurisdiction for Siri and Lavan islands, that there remained no real obstruction in the Siri and Lavan waterways. However, the cost of removing the ship wrecks which occurred during the conflict away from the navigation lanes was not yet available at the time of the mission's departure from the Islamic Republic of Iran.

The Persian Gulf

There are many other wrecks in the Persian Gulf but they appear to be the concern of the other sovereign States or the concern of the Regional Organization for the Protection of the Marine Environment (ROPME), of which the Islamic Republic of Iran and Iraq are members.

/...

0223

D. INDUSTRY

1. Heavy industry

The sector comprises in particular the iron and steel and aluminum industry, including their downstream facilities for metal transformation and the heavy manufacturing industry. Because huge quantities of raw materials and energy (electricity, fuel, gas and coal) are required to ensure satisfactory production and output levels, the majority of these industries is located in the south of the country in relative vicinity to the Persian Gulf ports.

During the conflict many factories were totally destroyed, either by enemy attack or through occupation. In other regions outside the war zone, industrial plants were subjected to air and missile attacks.

The damage sustained by the heavy industry sector is well documented by photos, videos and selected on-site inspections. The mission visited the industrial installation in Arak (province of Markazi), which is the country's main aluminium-producing and aluminum downstream industry; further, the mission inspected the steel plant in Ahwaz (province of Khuzestan) with its downstream facilities in the city's vicinity.

(a) Estimate of damage

According to Government sources, the direct damage sustained by the industrial sector is estimated at rials 1,626,860, of which about two thirds, or rials 1,102,029, are attributed to all types of industries under the umbrella of the Ministry of Heavy Industry.

On-site inspection enabled the mission to verify the order of magnitude of damage and the expenditure estimate for reconstruction in respect of 12 installations in the metallurgical and manufacturing sub-sectors affected by the conflict (a description of these industries including general observations, cost estimates, etc. are provided in annex I to the present report).

(b) Government priorities and targets

The development of the metallurgical sector, especially iron and steel, has been one of Government's priorities for many years in its effort to reach self-sufficiency and industrial diversification by developing important downstream facilities.

In 1980, steel accounted for almost one sixth of total imports and annual steel consumption was estimated at 6 million tons. During the years of the conflict domestic steel production was below 1.5 million tons, mainly produced by an old-fashioned, coal-based steel mill at Esfahan. After the conflict,

/...

steel production remained at the same low level, whereas domestic consumption rose owing to an increased demand in the post-conflict reconstruction boom.

In the immediate future steel consumption is expected to be between 7 and 10 million tons per year. Considering the existing gap between domestic production and the consumption estimates, it is evident that Government affords top priority to the development of the iron and steel industry and the heavy industrial sector.

The Government is in the process of increasing domestic steel-making capacity by putting on stream two new steel plants producing directly reduced sponge iron from iron ore pellets by gaseous direct reduction processes followed by metal transformation and metal work shops.

The plants at Ahwaz and Mobarakeh are already in the phase of commissioning and construction, respectively. Together these plants are expected to produce approximately 5 million tons of steel per year. Unlike the Esfahan plant, the two new reduction plants will utilize the most modern European-type technology.

Similarly, in the post-war reconstruction programme, increasing aluminum production has become another priority of the industrial sector. In particular, Government priority has been given to the aluminum production of the Arak plant and to the development of the aluminium downstream industries in and around the city of Arak. The pre-war capacity amounted to 45,000 tons per annum, but during the conflict the Arak plant was repaired and rehabilitated on several occasions so that by 1988 annual capacity had increased to 70,000 tons per annum. Further planned expansions of the plant will bring its annual production level to about 120,000 tons, sufficient for domestic demand.

The importance of aluminum production is underscored by the fact that the Government has decided to build a second aluminum smelter, which at a yearly capacity of 230,000 tons will become operational in 1994 at an estimated cost of $1,250 million.

Development and growth of other sectors within the heavy industry sector do not predict a similar pattern to iron, steel and aluminium. During the period of the conflict, the main priority of industries directly damaged was to repair and rehabilitate them as quickly as possible. With the exception of four plants located in the Abadan area that were completely destroyed, all other plants could be repaired.

The immediate and often improvised repair, necessary to maintain industrial output, resulted, however, in some major problems with long-lasting effect, the greatest handicap being the existing technology gap created by eight years of war. In order to reach the level of present-day technology and thereby make Iranian industry competitive, huge investments will be required.

/...

(c) Implementation of reconstruction programme

Rehabilitation in the heavy industry sector in the post-war period has resulted in a marked increase in output compared to that of 1980. This expansion of capacities is shown in the table below.

	1980	1990	1992	1994
Iron and steel (million tons)	1.5	2.0	6.0	7.0
Primary aluminum (thousands of tons)	45	70	90	350

The status of implementation in the heavy industry can be illustrated by the following figures:

Throughout the war period, the Government spent Rls 16,000 million on the repair and reconstruction of damaged plants. The total expenditures on immediate rehabilitation, often carried out in the form of "band-aid work" of the inspected plants is estimated by the mission at Rls 90,000 million. However, if there had been a full-scale rehabilitation with adequate equipment replacement, including the incorporation of technological updates, the amount required would have been about Rls 200,000 million (according to Government estimates).

To sum up, the mission concludes that reconstruction in the narrower sense has been achieved and can be considered complete as nearly all factories are producing again. For the few not yet operational, the only need is finance.

(d) The role of the private sector

At present, the metal-producing industry is entirely Government owned. As to the capital stock, three quarters of the remainder of the heavy industry is under Government control, representing about 15 per cent of the number of units. In an effort to make factories more profitable, the Government has agreed to make a change in its policies by encouraging the private sector to participate. The Government is actively promoting joint ventures with participation of foreign companies for new investment so as to obtain the needed technology and capital. In the transfer of ownership to the people the Tehran stock market will play a key role. Some companies have already been traded on the stock exchange, and preparations are being made to continue with this promising process.

The mission was informed that in the future private sector involvement in the heavy industry, including the metallurgical sector, would be the main participant in the task of rebuilding the country's industry. Under this

/...

0226

scenario, the long-term policy foresees a fast expansion of the private sector, while the Government's inputs will be confined to strategic areas of the sector.

(e) Major sectoral constraints

The mission has on file a summary of the observations made on 12 inspected sites in the heavy industry sector. The sector suffers from lack of finance, outdated technology, some manpower shortages, especially at the advanced technical skill level, and, in certain instances from non-utilization of available domestic raw materials.

While access to private investment may positively affect the replacement of equipment and further lead to the introduction of new technological elements, the upgrading of the skill level will be a problem that may have a long-lasting impact on the overall development of the sector. It is therefore necessary to expose technical staff to new technologies in other countries by means of study tours and short-term assignments to modern factories abroad; further, the strengthening of existing national institutional facilities and the building up of additional vocational centres should occur as soon as possible.

As to the better and more frequent use of domestic raw materials it will be necessary to revive the affected mines (bauxite, alunite, nepheline, etc.) with large sums of investment. During the years of the conflict practically no investments took place and raw materials, although available domestically, had to be imported from abroad in order to keep heavy industry running.

(f) Expressed need for international assistance

The Islamic Republic of Iran is embarking on very ambitious programmes for the intensive exploitation of its energy and in future of its mineral resources. The Government has further taken decisive steps in the post-conflict years to set up modern metallurgical industry covering iron and steel production from sponge iron.

At the same time, it is well known that the country during the past decade had only very limited access to high-tech developments. The generation of engineers that was trained during the 1980s had only limited opportunities periodically to upgrade their technical knowledge and to keep abreast with the state of the art in their field of activities.

Considering that thousands of new jobs, requiring high level skills, will be created in the reconstruction of the new steel industry, and that the profitability of these enterprises will very much depend on the skills of their engineers and technicians, the creation of higher technical and vocational training programmes for technicians and managers is a priority.

/...

Moreover, research and development facilities at the plant level are often poorly equipped, sparsely funded and, in certain instances, not existent at all. It is, therefore, especially important that the international community provide technical assistance in the form of highly specialized, short-term advisory services with emphasis inter alia on proposing research and development programmes or identification of technology and equipment. At a less advanced level, vocational training courses could be co-hosted with relevant multilateral or bilateral agencies.

Another area where some assistance from abroad is needed relates to the huge amount of scrap steel resulting from the conflict. The setting up of mobile smelters in the war-stricken regions could lead to producing a revenue-generating product that could be used either domestically or abroad. The scrap removal activity, both steel and construction material, will not only be a major input, but also a precondition in the country's efforts to reconstruct the strategically located cities of Abadan and Khorramshahr.

The mission inspected the 12 following sites in the heavy industry sector. Notes made at the time of the visits are on file.

Iranian Aluminium Company (IRALCO), Arak

Asco-Ahwaz Steel Complex, Ahwaz

Pars Wagon Co., Arak

Azar Ab Industries Co., Arak

Hepco Company, Arak

Machine SE

Khuzestan Pipe Manufacturing Co., Ahwaz

Sepanta Industrial Company, Ahwaz

Ahwaz Rolling and Pipe Mills Company (ARPCO), Ahwaz

Kaavian Steel Co., Ahwaz

Shahid Soltani Industrial Company, Ahwaz

Iran National Steel Industrial Group (INSIG), Ahwaz

2. Light industry

(a) Overview of damage

While the mission found clear evidence that the light industry sector suffered greatly from the conflict, the Government was unable to provide a comprehensive damage estimate. This is explained by the fact that the light industry sector comprises predominantly small- and medium-scale private enterprises with relatively few channels of contacts with the Ministry. Moreover, most repair work was initiated and financed from private sources. Some estimates on damage following on-site inspections carried out during the

/...

0228

first visit of the United Nations team has been provided in the report of the mission (S/22863).

Briefly stated, the team observed that the industrial sector had sustained considerable damage varying among individual companies from moderate to total destruction and that the total value of the losses had been significantly raised owing to the frequently encountered cycle of repeated attacks and repairs of the same installation.

Although the plants are back to what at least superficially looks like normal operation, physical traces of the damages are visible everywhere, and most factories continue to suffer from the lack of spare parts, maintenance facilities and backup services and from the consequences of makeshift reconstruction and repair work.

(b) Government priorities and plan-targets

Government reconstruction policy

The fundamental priority established by the Government for the reconstruction process is the earliest resettlement of the displaced population, preferably in the areas originally occupied. The most basic requirements that have to be met for this process to succeed are housing, infrastructure and employment opportunities. Industrial rehabilitation responds to all three requirements and has therefore received correspondingly high priority in the context of the overall reconstruction process.

Reconstruction policies with respect to industry

The mission has not become aware of any comprehensive or structured reconstruction plan for the industrial sector. But this does not mean that the process has in any way been delayed. In keeping with the traditional dynamism of the predominantly privately owned industry it was, in fact, able to lead the way for many other sectors of the economy.

Since the early stages of the conflict, when industrial plants and small-scale manufacturing units first became the targets of enemy attacks, the overriding objective of the Government has been to maintain or resume at least a minimum production process without exposing the personnel to excessive danger. Physical reconstruction of basic production facilities, within the limitations set by available parts and materials or funds for their procurement, was thus an important target throughout the conflict.

Since the cease-fire the all-important objective has been to bring the industry back to its full production capacity, or at least the level achieved before the war, and very considerable financial resources have been made available by the Government for this purpose, backed by a decentralized system for their allocation to the individual production units. The initial emphasis has been on increasing the output through direct replacement of lost or

/...

damaged equipment and parts rather than on improving productivity, technology and product quality.

In respect of funds allocation from Government funds earmarked for reconstruction purposes under the control of the Ministry of Industry, priority has been and continues to be given to so-called strategic products including food, building materials and inputs to other strategic sectors.

The responsibility for the allocation of Government grants to small-scale industries and handicraft units has been delegated to the Directors of Industry in each of the affected provinces, who approve the applications for financial support on the basis of an analysis of local needs for the product(s) in question.

At the plant level clear priority has been given to the rehabilitation of the most essential production equipment allowing the performance at first of a basic production process, while the establishment of auxiliary facilities such as maintenance and repair workshops, stand-by generators, safety equipment and administrative buildings in many cases has been left pending until today.

(c)   The role of the private sector

About 80 per cent of the light industry sector is in the hands of the private sector and, as a consequence of the Government's privatization policy, the figure is increasing. From this background alone it is obvious that the private sector has played a leading role in the reconstruction process.

Older and financially well established privately owned plants such as the Bisotoon Sugar Refinery were able to auto finance the complete reconstruction process without going through the procedures of applying for Government grants or bank credits. Consequently, they could, all other factors being equal, reach full production level within a minimum time-frame, a significant contribution in itself and an inspiring example for other factories.

In the war zone itself where most small- and medium-scale units were privately owned, the total devastation of their property must have been a violent blow to the entrepreneurs. However, the programme designed by the Government to facilitate their earliest possible return to the area, initiated only in 1989, when the zone became safe to re-enter, is now unfolding and apparently proving to be a success.

Private entrepreneurs are responding to the Government's offer of financial support in the form of grants, to permit the rehabilitation of the production units without further delay. Although the area is still in an initial state of post-war recovery they appreciate the scope for financially viable production activities and are now in ever-increasing numbers taking hold of their previous property and of its reconstruction.

/...

They form the spearhead of the return of economic activity to the area, already followed by government-owned factories such as the oxygen plant and the paint manufacture at Abadan, which are in the process of reconstructing, benefiting from the same type of government grants as the private industry.

Also new private entrepreneurs are following the footsteps of those previously located in the area. They are following the Government's call for new industrial initiatives in the area and are accepting the challenge of setting up pioneering industries such as processed meat, fish powder, plastic tubing and textiles in two industrial parks now being created at Abadan and Khorramshahr.

The Government's belief in the competence of the private sector and the advantages of involving it as closely as possible in the reconstruction process is very visibly brought to bear by the assignment of the responsibility for preparing a five-year reconstruction plan for the Abadan-Khorramshahr area to a private company.

(d) General industrialization policies with bearing on reconstruction

Obviously, the reconstruction of manufacturing units has been and continues to be guided by a set of other priorities and basic principles which are common for the entire industrial sector. These include:

Employment generation, the principle of securing a safe work place for all, especially important for the revitalization of the war-stricken provinces through the return of their former inhabitants;

Privatization, a policy recently given new emphasis by the Government following the end of the centralized wartime economy and intended to favour private ownership of present and new production units by the entrepreneur himself or by shareholders;

Environmental protection is given top priority by the Government, as recently stated at the United Nations Industrial Development Organization (UNIDO) Conference on Ecologically Sustainable Industrial Development, and appropriate regulations are being reinforced also in the context of the reconstruction effort;

Industrial estates, of which 80 already have been established across the nation and which facilitate the creation or relocation of artisanal units and small-scale industries and contribute towards both cost-effectiveness and better environmental control;

Safe construction methods, especially in respect of the earthquake resistance of factory buildings and workshops, achieved through requirement of compliance with existing building codes for government-subsidized construction.

/...

0231

(e) The reconstruction effort

Except for the areas where actual ground fighting took place, most craftsmen have returned to their workshops and practically all medium- and large-scale industries have reached approximately the output achieved before the war with further growth indicated for the next few years. In Khorramshahr all but a few of the mechanized production units are still in ruins, but in many cases plans for their reconstruction are well advanced.

No relocation of any significance has taken place except in the case of small craftsmen (tailors, bakers, welders, etc.) who are mobile and require little or no capital investment and who in some cases have preferred to remain in their new home area. Incentives are, however, being offered to attract as many as possible to the previous war zones.

The only noteworthy case of organized relocation is that of some 35 brick makers from Qasr-e-Shirin in Bakhtaran Province whose production units had been demolished by explosive devices and who are now being regrouped in three larger brick-making enterprises under construction nearby.

The rehabilitation process has not been noticeably hampered by shortage of manpower. Most workers have returned and additional personnel has been easily available except in devastated areas such as Khorramshahr, where skilled workers for the newly rehabilitated soap plant had to be brought from Tehran.

At the technical management level the process has been characterized by a lack of awareness of up-to-date technologies, which makes the exposure of senior staff to the newest developments in their field a must for further growth of their enterprises. Mechanical skills and abilities to improvise and solve maintenance and repair problems by available means have, on the other hand, been developed to impressive levels during the past 10 years.

Although rehabilitation has brought production up to pre-war levels, the situation is far from satisfactory. Owing to lack of funds, including government grants in rials but especially convertible currency in general, reconstruction of production lines has often stopped at a bare minimum. Even major plants (for instance Dorud Cement Factory and Pars Paper Factory) are without stand-by generators, proper maintenance facilities, adequate spare part stores, etc. Urgent rectification of this situation which, no doubt, requires considerable amounts of additional foreign capital, is called for to avoid serious future work stoppages.

Due to the urgency of reconstruction, the general lack of funding, especially convertible, and to some extent the unawareness of technological developments which have taken place over the last 10 to 15 years, reconstructed factories have not improved their technological efficiency over the pre-war level. Except for the totally destroyed industries located in the areas abandoned from 1980 to 1989 owing to ground fighting for which reconstruction plans only now are taking shape, most production lines

/...

0232

operating today consist of the original equipment, repaired as well as it was possible, and supplemented as required with new equipment representing only slight improvements over the originals.

Examples of reconstruction scenarios

As a follow-up to the work of the first team during May and June 1991, which focused primarily on a survey of the damage sustained, this mission concentrated its attention on the past, present and future reconstruction effort. In an attempt to collect as many first hand data as possible within the limited time available, the mission spent three days in Khuzestan Province, where the following 17 units belonging to the light industry sector were visited:

Karun Sugar Refinery, Shushtar

Karun Animal Feed Plant, Shushtar

Haft Tappeh Sugar Refinery, Shush

Pars Paper Factory, Shush

Dezful Sugar Refinery, Dezful

FARCIT Asbestos Cement Plant, Ahwaz

Behterin Fibre Board Factory, Khorramshahr

Stone crushing plants, Khorramshahr

Ahmadian Stone Cutting Plant, Khorramshahr

Zarea Ice Making Plant, Khorramshahr

Gerald Date Packaging Plant, Khorramshahr

Nik-Noosh Soft Drink Plant, Khorramshahr

Khorramshahr Soap Factory, Khorramshahr

Abadan Grand Cooling Store, Abadan

Arvandan Shipbuilding Company, Abadan

Khuzestan Sterilized Milk Company, Abadan

Pazargad Chemical Company, Abadan

Owing to limited time, and considering the fact that the previous mission had carried out an extensive programme of field visits, no other plants were inspected by the present mission. The picture of the reconstruction process in the light industry sector was, however, completed through meetings at Tehran with senior representatives of the following additional enterprises:

Dorud Cement Plant, Lorestan

Western Cement Company, Bakhtaran

Bakhtaran Spinning Mill, Bakhtaran

Bisotoon Sugar Refinery, Bakhtaran

/...

0233

These units, which represent a cross-section of the sector, are described in some detail in appendix I, which in addition to basic data on each plant presents its war history as well as its rehabilitation history. For the purpose of providing a clearer overview of what happened in this sector and of the situation it faces today, the following examples have been extracted.

Medium- and large-scale plants outside the zone of ground fighting

This category includes, among the plants visited, not only Karun Sugar Refinery, Haft Tappeh Sugar Refinery and Pars Paper Plant, but also the four factories in Bakhtaran and Lorestan Provinces, which were not visited during this mission, fall within this category.

Typically, they are privately owned industries established before the Revolution, employing between 1,000 and 3,000 persons and processing locally available raw materials such as sugar cane, beet root, bagasse (cane waste) and limestone. The existence of these raw materials and the availability of cheap energy have determined their location.

During the war they were attacked repeatedly through aerial bombardment directed with relative accuracy towards vulnerable and strategic targets including power stations, generators, transformers and other electrical installations as well as spare part and product stores, maintenance workshops, etc. but, obviously, hitting a host of other targets as well. Most air raids were flown against these plants between 1985 and 1987.

Repair was carried out on a continuous basis after each attack and production was only rarely interrupted for more than a few weeks and seems to have remained at around or even above 50 per cent of the pre-war output level on a yearly basis throughout the war period.

This excellent performance was achieved mainly thanks to the ingenuity and improvisational talents of the staff, who managed to keep the production going with makeshift repairs, first using the plants' own stock of spare parts and later by cannibalizing their own machines to keep other equipment going or by obtaining parts from other factories in the country.

Following the end of hostilities, the reconstruction work continued with as much emphasis on the replacement of damaged equipment and parts with original imported items as the availability of foreign exchange would allow. By 1990, or latest by 1991, these factories were, typically, back to the pre-war production volume averaging some 60 to 70 per cent of installed capacity.

The situation of most of these plants is, however, precarious since the procurement of spare parts and the rehabilitation of vital backup services such as maintenance and repair facilities, stand-by generators and control mechanisms has been awarded too low a priority to allow even modest requirements to be satisfied.

/...

0234

Equally serious is the general obsolescence of the production technologies, which were behind international standards for the industry even before the war started and have not been significantly updated in the course of reconstruction. The earlier this problem is seriously addressed, the better.

Larger plants in the actual zone of ground fighting

Only few larger industries were based in the zone along the border, which was turned into a theatre of intense ground battles. They were mostly located in the Abadan and Khorramshahr area, where the vicinity of the Abadan and Khorramshahr harbours and the Abadan refinery provided a fertile environment for industrial growth. The Avadandan Ship Building Company, the Khuzestan Sterilized Milk Company and the Pazargad Chemical Company are the industries among those visited by this mission that fall into this category.

Similarly to the larger industries elsewhere, they were established before the Revolution. However, in other respects their background is different since they are justified more by the needs for their products, especially by the public and defence sectors, than by availability of inputs. Consequently, they are predominantly owned by the public sector or under public sector control.

Given their location in the initial war zone, they were abandoned and occupied by Iraqi forces during the period from 1980 to 1982 and left in a state of considerable destruction. The dairy was left in this state until the area was again safe in 1989, as were most other installations in the area. Starting from 1982-1983, the two other plants engaged in building military vessels and producing strategically important chemicals were already reconstructed and put back into operation under most trying conditions for the staff.

Before the cease-fire they were both back in full operation and have remained so ever since. The shipyard has even expanded its production and the dairy, which is now in the midst of a dynamic reconstruction programme, is aiming for an output four times the installed capacity before the war.

Small-scale production units in the zone of ground fighting

All six units are privately owned and manufacture products or perform services required in the area. They were all totally destroyed during the period of occupation and left in ruins until the owners could return in 1989.

They have all applied for and are in the process of receiving government grants covering the total cost of reconstruction, in rials as well as convertible currency, and will soon be back to full operation as before the war but on a more modern technological level.

They will once more be contributing towards improving the quality of life and strengthening the economic activity of the area and in this respect play a significant role in the overall reconstruction of the previous war zone.

/...

A similar contribution will be made by larger, private industries in the area, including the Khorramshahr Soap Factory and the Nik-Noosh Soft Drink Plant, which have experienced a comparable pattern of occupation, destruction and abandonment and are now in the process of reaching their pre-war capacities with strong support of the Government.

As stated to the mission by the Minister of Industry, the start of production of the Khorramshahr Soap Factory, soon to be followed by several others, is "a light in the dark" giving new hope for this devastated area.

(f) Achievement of priorities and targets

As demonstrated by the above scenarios, no effort has been spared in order to complete the reconstruction process in the shortest possible time.

The priority given to the promotion of the return of private entrepreneurs to the area of ground fighting in an effort to revitalize the zone along the border and the incentives offered in order to achieve this aim are proving to be successful.

Where reconstruction could be initiated before the cease-fire, production is now on average at par with or exceeding the level reached before the war. In the more severely affected areas where reconstruction has only recently begun, there are promising signs that pre-war output levels will be reached by 1993.

However, from the examples given it is evident that progress towards full rehabilitation of all damaged industrial plants, especially in terms of secondary functions and investments, which have only minor immediate effect on productivity, has been slowed down or temporarily halted owing to lack of funds. The Government is aware of this problem and endeavouring to find ways to overcome it.

(g) Contribution of industry to reconstruction in other sectors

Reconstruction of the industrial sector goes well beyond the rehabilitation of enterprises existing before the war. It also means strengthening the industries which are needed for reconstruction in other sectors, notably the resettlement of the largest possible part of refugees and other displaced persons.

Industry provides the major part of the building materials needed for new or reconstructed housing and necessary infrastructure, including schools and other public buildings, which are an important prerequisite for the return of the population and, at the same time, provide employment opportunities, both in the building materials and other sectors.

There are therefore strong arguments for promoting the establishment of new building material industries in the war-stricken areas and to qualify this sub-sectoral activity as an integral part of the overall reconstruction effort.

/...

0236

Particularly small-scale enterprises, conceived so as to make optimum use of strictly locally available raw material resources and to produce for construction in the vicinity of the unit, would not only make a valuable contribution towards improving the population's access to appropriate materials but would also, by reducing the transport routes for raw material inputs and finished products, lead to an appreciable reduction of the cost of the materials and, in turn, of the buildings themselves.

(h) Role of the international community

As described in the preceding paragraphs, the reconstruction process is well advanced in the light industry sector, and the efforts which remain in order to bring the situation back to the pre-war status are with only few exceptions blocked primarily by the lack of resources, in particular foreign currency.

In the view of the mission, a complete rehabilitation process also requires that the technology gap created as a consequence of the war be somehow bridged. For 10 years or more the technology transfer flow was virtually interrupted, and in any case the efforts of most industries were focused on keeping a basic production process going rather than on technological innovations.

The international community could without much delay and at a minimal cost assist in bridging this gap by facilitating the contacts between Iranian industry and relevant technology holders abroad.

Skill development

There is an urgent need for industrial managers to become acquainted with the technological developments which have taken place at the international level in their field of specialization during these years and to become aware of areas in which their plants could benefit from these developments, even at this stage.

The mission has even met a number of high-level technical staff of major production plants who have never seen similar factories outside the country and therefore do not even have a basis for the assessment of their own plant's technological level and efficiency. Even though they have reached an admirable level of proficiency, especially in mechanical repair and trouble-shooting through trial end error, there is no doubt that their performance could be significantly enhanced through just a brief exposure to the technological situation outside the country.

Technological information services

Lack of or delays in technological innovation is often a result of unawareness of the available options. The sectoral advisory units existing in the Ministry of Industry and the relevant national institutions, including the

/...

scientific advisory council in which both industries and universities are represented, should be invited to establish closer links to existing technological data bases abroad.

They would be able to act as an open window to international technologies and provide authoritative advice to industries seeking new technological options.

Investment promotion

The reconstruction process could be completed earlier and more efficiently and at lesser cost to the national economy if foreign joint ventures were more vigorously pursued. Potential partners would include equipment and technology suppliers as well as manufacturers of similar product lines. The international community, including organizations such as UNIDO, has extensive experience in bringing partners together and assisting in the contract negotiations and should be called upon to contribute to the reconstruction process in this respect.

/...

0238

E. AGRICULTURE AND IRRIGATION

1. Institutional framework

Development activities in the agriculture sector fall mainly within the purview of three Ministries, the Ministry of Agriculture, the Ministry of Energy and the Ministry of Construction Jehad.

The Ministry of Agriculture is responsible for crop production, on-farm irrigation and drainage, agro-industries and agricultural support services such as research, extension, training, etc.

The Ministry of Energy is responsible for mobilization of water resources through construction, operation and maintenance of storage, diversion and lift irrigation facilities as well as conveyance of water through main canals and branches. The distribution and on-farm application of water are the responsibility of the Ministry of Agriculture.

The Ministry of Construction Jehad is responsible for the development and conservation of forests and pastures, fisheries, livestock and date palm plantations. Other related agencies concerned with these subsectors are the Environmental Protection Organization, the Organization of Nomadic Affairs, etc.

2. War damage

Agriculture is reported by the Government to have suffered direct losses estimated at Rls 1,783,377 million and indirect losses estimated at Rls 14,173,953 million. 1/ The farming subsector sustained the bulk (86 per cent) of the direct losses whereas 97 per cent of the total indirect losses are attributed to the forestry subsector.

3. Reconstruction

(a) Priorities

While the entire reconstruction programme is accorded the highest priority by the Government, the relative order of priorities for the various subsectors, as indicated to the mission in the various meetings with the Ministry of Agriculture, are outlined below:

Farming

- Land levelling and grading

- Restoration of irrigation network

/...

0239

- Replacement of farm machinery and pumping equipment

- Replanting of date palm and orchards

- Reestablishment of farm support services

Livestock and agro-industries

- Replacement of animals to resettled farm families

- Reconstruction of dairy, sugar and other agro-industries

Forests, pastures and environmental protection

- Replanting of forests

- Rehabilitation of pastures

- Waterlogging and salinization of land

(b) Progress and programme

As envisaged during the visit of the June 1991 mission, the present mission also concentrated on evaluating the progress and programme of reconstruction works in the three most affected provinces: Khuzestan, Ilam and Bakhtaran. Owing to difficulties of travel and shortage of time, the mission was able to visit only the Provincial Departments of Agriculture in Khuzestan and Bakhtaran accompanied by a representative of the Ministry of Agriculture. Data relating to Ilam were furnished by the Provincial Agricultural Department and necessary clarifications were obtained by the mission over the telephone. Data relating to water resources were furnished at Tehran by the Ministry of Energy. A detailed breakdown on reconstruction costs for these three provinces has been placed on record.

Water resources

The areas affected by the conflict relating to the water resources for agriculture, administered by the General Directorate of Water Resources in the Ministry of Energy, are divided into the three regions shown below:

- The West Water Authority Region, comprising the provinces of Ilam, Bakhtaran, Kurdistan, Loristan and Hamedan.

- The province of Khuzestan.

- The province of West Azarbayjan.

/...

0240

The total scope of reconstruction work involved in rehabilitating the damaged diversion structures, pump stations, main canals and other ancillary works is outlined in table E.4. The extent of work completed to the end of 1991 and the schedule for completion during the remaining two years of the ongoing first five-year plan period (1992 and 1993) and during the second five-year plan (1994-1999) are summarized in table E.1 below:

Table E.1. Reconstruction work in water resources

	Quantity completed to end 1991	Scheduled 1992-1993 (Percentage)	Scheduled 1994-1999
Diversion works 126 Nos.	27	20	53
Pump stations 242 Nos.	15	15	70
Irrigation canals 1674 km	16	14	70
Access roads 450 km	50	40	10
Camp sites 2 Nos.	20	20	40
Hydromet stations 185 Nos.	–	10	90

Agriculture

Farmland rehabilitation

Large areas of irrigated and rain-fed farmlands suffered total destruction as a consequence of military manoeuvre of heavy equipment and vehicles, the construction of an enormous amount of revetments and vast stretches of high embankments, trenches and underground tunnels. Rehabilitation of these areas requires intensive land levelling, grading and formation of basins or border strips for irrigation. The average volume of earth required to be moved for rough levelling of rain-fed areas amounts to more than 500 cubic metres per hectare (m3/ha). For levelling and grading of irrigated farmlands, the volumes of earth to be moved range from an average of 1,000 m3/ha in the plains of Khuzestan to between 1,500 m3/ha and 2,500 m3/ha in the undulating lands of Ilam and Bakhtaran for basin and border irrigation respectively.

The equipment used for land levelling and grading comprises mainly heavy duty scrapers, bulldozers and graders, including loaders, trucks and personnel transport. Much of the earth-moving equipment is reported to have outlived its mechanical life, some being more than 10 years old. However, replacement or major overhaul of such equipment is hampered by resource constraints. At the time of the mission's visit, about 70 scraper units were employed on land-levelling operations in Khuzestan. In Bakhtaran, the number of available

/...

0241

units (scrapers, bulldozers and graders) had fallen recently from 53 to
12 owing to recall of the units which had been temporarily loaned by other
provinces/agencies. The land-levelling capacity of the remaining equipment is
reduced to about 400 ha per year, which highlights the need for provision of
additional earth-moving equipment to Bakhtaran province, where some 35,000 ha
of irrigated farmlands await rehabilitation.

The total scope of land levelling, the extent completed to the end of
1991 and the schedule for completion during the remaining two years of the
ongoing first five-year-plan period (1992 and 1993) and during the second
five-year plan (1994-1999) are shown below:

Table E.2. Rehabilitation of farmland

	Quantity	Completed to end-1991	Scheduled 1992-1993 (Percentage)	Scheduled 1994-1999
(a) Land levelling and grading of irrigated farmlands				
Khuzestan	193 425 ha	50	30	20
Ilam	12 500 ha	40	5	55
Bakhtaran	45 000 ha	22	15	63
Total	250 925 ha	44	26	30
(b) Land levelling (rough) of rain-fed areas				
Khuzestan	1 700 ha	50	30	20
Ilam	40 500 ha	50	10	40
Bakhtaran	11 500 ha	100	-	-
Total	53 700 ha	61	8	31

Irrigation network reconstruction

The rehabilitated lands are to be equipped with a modern network of
distribution canals which are designed for varying discharges of up to 1 cubic
metre per second (m3/s). These canals are proposed to be provided with
concrete lining in order to minimize seepage losses which are reported to be
causing progressive increase of waterlogging and salinization of the irrigated
lands. There is also a network of drainage channels which is to be provided
over the regraded lands or rehabilitated over other irrigated lands.

/...

0242

In addition, there are a large number of traditional canals, often drawing water by diversion or pumping directly from rivers, which need major rehabilitation as a result of the damage caused by military action and neglect suffered during the eight years of conflict. In Dasht Azadgan area of Khuzestan, there are 7 major traditional canals with discharges ranging from 20 to 37 m3/s while the largest canal (Hofel) is 38 kilometres long, with discharge capacity of 110 m3/s. On the whole, the large traditional canals, accounting for about 20 per cent of the total, may have discharge capacities ranging from 3 to 4 m3/s; about 50 per cent are of medium size with discharge of 0.5 to 1.5 m3/s; and the remaining 30 per cent are small channels with capacities less than 0.5 m3/s.

The following table shows the total scope of irrigation and drainage canals reconstruction work, the extent completed to the end of 1991 and the schedule for completion during the remaining two years of the ongoing first five-year-plan period (1992 and 1993) and during the second five-year plan (1994-1999):

Table E.3. Reconstruction work in irrigation

	Quantity	Completed to end-1991	Scheduled 1992-1993 (Percentage)	Scheduled 1994-1999
(a) Modern canal network (distributaries and sub-distributaries on rehabilitated lands				
Khuzestan	7 342 km	50	30	20
Ilam	74 km	10	13	77
Bakhtaran	1 125 km	22	15	63
Total	8 541 km	46	28	26
(b) Traditional canals				
Khuzestan	244 km	0	20	80
Ilam	21 km	17	18	65
Bakhtaran	1 050 km	43	27	30
Total	1 315 km	35	26	39
(c) Drainage channels				
Khuzestan	5 850 km	20	20	60
Ilam	50 km	0	20	80
Bakhtaran	110 km	100	-	-
Total	6 010 km	21	19	60

/...

Lift irrigation

A large number of pumping equipment in the affected provinces for lift
irrigation from rivers and canals, have been destroyed or looted during the
conflict. These pumping stations comprised government-owned large units
ranging in size from 150 to 350 HP and privately owned smaller units averaging
35 HP units. In addition, 258 deep tubewells in the northern Ahwaz (Shush and
Dezful) area of Khuzestan and about 200 tubewells in Ilam, used for exploiting
groundwater for irrigation, were destroyed to varying degrees.

The total requirement of pumping equipment to be replaced and tubewells
to be rehabilitated, the extent completed to the end of 1991 and the schedule
for completion during the remaining two years of the ongoing first five-year
plan period (1992 and 1993) and during the second five-year plan (1994-1999)
are shown below:

Table E.4.   Reconstruction in lift irrigation

	Quantity	Completed to end-1991	Scheduled 1992-1993 (Percentage)	Scheduled 1994-1999
(a) Pumping stations				
Ilam				
160-270 HP	15	10	40	50
Bakhtaran				
350 HP	32	0	20	80
5-65 HP	300	0	20	80
(b) Tubewells				
Khuzestan	258	75	25	–
Ilam	195	5	20	75
Total	800	26	22	54

Farm machinery

The farm machinery available to the affected areas for agricultural
purposes ranged from 0.5 HP to 0.7 HP per hectare, which was completely
destroyed or looted during the conflict. The Agricultural Departments believe
that, but for the hiatus caused by the eight years of conflict, the level of
mechanization in the affected areas would have reached at least 1.0 HP/ha.
Hence, the farmers being resettled in the rehabilitated areas are to be
equipped with farm machinery, mainly as 65 HP tractor units, at the rate of
about 1.0 HP/ha.

0244

/...

The total requirement of farm machinery, the extent provided to the end of 1991 and the schedule for completion during the remaining two years of the ongoing first five-year plan period (1992 and 1993) and during the second five-year plan (1994-1999) are shown below:

Table E.5. Replacement of farm machinery

	Quantity	Completed to end-1991	Scheduled 1992-1993	Scheduled 1994-1999
		(Percentage)		
Khuzestan	193 500 HP	16	14	70
Ilam	53 000 HP	30	40	30
Bakhtaran	72 200 HP	15	25	60
Total	318 700 HP	18	21	61

Replanting tree crops

As reported by the first mission, more than 3 million of the 7 million date palm trees that were under production in Khuzestan have been destroyed, mainly in the Khorramshahr, Abadan and Shalamcheh areas. In addition, orchards covering areas of about 400 ha in Ilam and 4,730 ha in Bakhtaran were reported destroyed. The progress of replanting the destroyed tree crops is hampered, among other things, by the limitations on the production of saplings from available facilities. In general, about 15 to 20 per cent of the tree crops are reported 2/ to have been replanted to date, and the remaining are planned to be completed by the end of the second five-year-plan period (1999).

Farm support buildings

Farm support buildings covering a total area of about 48,000 square metres, along with their equipments and materials were destroyed in Qasr-e-Shirin, Korsay and other parts of Khuzestan province. Similarly, about 15,800 square metres of farm support buildings were destroyed in Ilam province. Reconstruction of these buildings has progressed to varying degrees, with overall completion estimated at about 40 per cent in both provinces. Details of progress on various types of facilities in Khuzestan are shown below:

/...

Table E.6. Reconstruction of farm support buildings

Type of facility	No. of units	Percentage completed
Extension Centre	8	50
Input Supply Warehouses	12	25
Agric. Research Centre	1	10
District Agric. Offices	10	50
Quarantine Units	6	0

Reconstruction of the farm support buildings is planned to be completed during the next five years.

Agro-industries

As reported by the first mission, considerable damage (including destruction of about 40 per cent of the machinery) had been inflicted upon the sugar mills at Haft Tappeh with annual capacity of 100,000 tons and at Karun with annual capacity of 250,000 tons in Ahwaz-Dezful region of Khuzestan. In June 1991, the production capacity of these mills had been restored to 80 per cent and 20 per cent, respectively, of their initial installed capacity. The mission was informed that reconstruction of the agro-industries was in progress, and initial arrangements were under way for reactivating the plans to establish seven more agro-industries in the region with land plots of 18,000 to 23,000 ha devoted to production of sugarcane for each unit.

Forestry, pastures and fisheries

As reported by the first mission, about 85,200 ha of natural forests were destroyed and 46,550 ha exploited for military reasons. Similarly, some 753,000 ha of pasture lands in the war zone were reported severely damaged as a result of military actions.

Losses reported in the fisheries subsector comprised 200 wooden vessels of 20 to 80 gross registered tons and 50 steel fishing vessels of 300 registered tons. A considerable number of cold storage facilities were also reported to be damaged.

The progress of replanting the forests and rehabilitating the pastures or reconstruction of the losses in the fisheries subsectors could not be ascertained owing to the inability of the mission to obtain the required data.

(c) Environmental impact

The adverse impact of the conflict on environmental aspects of the agricultural sector is seen by the Government to relate mainly to the following:

Effect on soil fertility due to:

Removal of topsoil caused by excavations for fortification/trenching;

/...

0246

Compaction effects of movement of heavy military equipment;

Flooding of agricultural lands for defence purposes leading to prolonged anaerobic conditions and biological sterility of the soil.

Waterlogging and soil salinization arising from:

Salinization of soils in estuary areas due to uncontrolled ingress of sea water through intake structures designed to draw river flows making use of tidal movements;

Flooding of traditional canals due to lack of control at diversion structures, resulting in frequent overtopping of canal banks and flooding of lands, causing rise in water table;

Drainage constraints caused by modifications in river flow regimes as a result of blockage by military debris, compounded by the consequent increase in rate of sedimentation in the river beds;

Interruption in the installation of drainage networks and the resultant delay by more than 10 years in commissioning the drainage systems, caused by diversion of earth-moving equipment from construction of drainage channels to defence;

Soil and water contamination attributed by the Government to the toxic material emanating from explosives and/or chemical and biological weapons and its ingress into soil, streamflows and groundwater.

The adverse impact on soil fertility due to displacement of top soil alone may be felt to varying degrees by much of the 300,000 ha of land earmarked for levelled and grading. The extent of the actual or potential increase in waterlogging and salinity owing to the effects of the war has not been assessed. It is reported that some 5,000 ha are affected in Khorramshahr-Abadan region alone of Khuzestan province. No specific studies are known to have been undertaken so far in assessing the suspected contamination of soil and water due to the war operations.

4. Constraints

The main constraint to completing the reconstruction programme on schedule is the paucity of foreign exchange resources to meet the cost of equipment, spare parts and materials required to be imported or assembled locally from imported components.

Because of the magnitude and the urgency of completing reconstruction works, the shortage of skilled manpower and the supporting facilities such as personnel transport and surveying equipment, etc., is also deemed to be a constraint to timely and successful implementation of the programme.

/...

A physical constraint to land levelling is the presence of unidentified mine fields left over from the war operations. It is estimated that up to 20 per cent of the lands awaiting development may be affected by this constraint.

5. Expressed needs for external assistance

The most urgent need expressed by the Ministry of Agriculture for external assistance relates to the procurement of heavy earth-moving equipment, such as scrapers, bulldozers, graders, loaders and dump trucks along with spare parts for such equipment to be purchased as well as the equipment already available but not usable owing to the shortage of spare parts. In addition to the considerable need for farm machinery (about 250,000 HP), pumping and well-drilling equipment would be needed for rehabilitation of lift irrigation facilities, whereas steel, cement and civil engineering construction equipment would be needed for canal excavation, canal lining and construction of control structures, etc.

The General Directorate for Water Resources in the Ministry of Energy has enumerated the scope of external assistance deemed necessary for timely completion of the reconstruction programme. The list includes construction equipment for canals and structures, pumping plant, well-drilling equipment, steel and cement, as well as various technical implements and instruments pertaining to the reconstruction programme.

6. Observations and recommendations

In the mission's view, the extent of reconstruction already accomplished during the short span of time since the cessation of hostilities is an eloquent testimony of the will and determination of the Islamic Republic of Iran to overcome as soon as possible the disastrous consequences of the conflict on the agricultural sector of the national economy. It is hoped that this study will help in expediting the reconstruction efforts, with appropriate international assistance, as envisaged in paragraph 7 of Security Council resolution 598 (1987).

In view of the serious concern expressed by the Government on the growing menace of waterlogging and salinity, it would be appropriate to initiate a comprehensive study to examine the causes, extent and potential risks to the agriculture sector. The study should also examine the preventive or remedial measures which should be considered for adoption including the extent and type of cost-effective canal lining 3/ which is proposed, to be adopted on a large scale in the affected areas. The mission recommends that the Government consider including technical assistance in this regard in the list of expressed needs for international assistance.

/...

0248

The mission observed that there is considerable scope for adopting modern irrigation management practices aimed at more efficient use of irrigation supplies 4/ and increase in crop yields through introduction of demand based irrigation. Technical assistance may also be considered to undertake a programme of applied research, drawing upon a wealth of experience which has been generated in recent years in coordination with the Internation Irrigation Management Institute in Colombo, Sri Lanka. In-service training of agricultural extension staff in improved on-farm water management practices would also be required to transfer the results of the aforesaid research to the farm.

Notes

1/ "Final Report on the Assessment of the Economic Damages of the War imposed by Iraq on the Islamic Republic of Iran (1980-1988)", Plan and Budget Organization, 1991.

2/ Progress on replanting date palm in Khuzestan could not be ascertained owing to the inability of the mission to obtain the required data.

3/ Recent studies on canal lining works carried out in developing countries have shown that traditional design and construction methods are not effective in appreciably reducing seepage losses in the long term.

4/ Overall irrigation efficiency in several cases is reported at around 30 per cent, which can feasibly be increased to 50 per cent through improved irrigation management.

/...

0249

F. ENERGY AND POWER

1. Sectoral objectives

As a result of the conflict, the Ministry of Energy followed an approach in the implementation of its programme to address the specific reconstruction needs of the sector. In the immediate sectoral approach, emphasis is given to (a) restoring the production capacity of the power stations damaged in the war; (b) ensuring that the major transmission systems damaged in the war are capable of supplying the power requirements throughout the country; and (c) restoring to full capacity the local power supply networks in the devastated regions of Khuzestan, Ilam, Kordestan and Bakhtaran.

Concerning the long-term objectives of the sector, priority is allocated to: (a) the completion of the construction to permanent structures damaged during the conflict; (b) the implementation of the pre-war development plans regarding production, transmission and distribution (these plans were designed prior to the conflict, but owing to the war their implementation had been halted); and (c) the stocking-up of materials necessary to ensure that the electrical system is not disrupted.

Since the outbreak of the conflict the Ministry adopted a policy of giving priority to maintaining, at the best possible level, the restoration and distribution of damaged facilities. This was accomplished by using exclusively materials that could be made available domestically. By pursuing this approach the damaged power production facilities are now in most cases back to the pre-war production level. The main power transfer (transmission network) is now in operation with the exception of the war-damaged areas in the Khuzestan province. The distribution network in Khuzestan has so far only been partially restored and according to government estimates two years of reconstruction work will be required to repair the incurred damage.

Similarly, the distribution network in the western provinces of Ilam, Khorramshahr and Bakhtaran has also only been partially restored with an estimated two years of reconstruction work to be carried out to reach pre-war levels.

For the period 1990-1998, the Ministry of Energy has also prepared long-term development plans for the electrical production and transmission systems in order to incorporate present power requirements and a predicted growth in demand of 8 per cent for the period.

2. Reconstruction effort

Implementation of the progress of the reconstruction programme is presented below according to its three main components: generation, transmission and distribution.

/...

Generation

All generation facilities which had been damaged during the war are back to serve the communities. However, in many instances only temporary repairs had been carried out with the main emphasis on restoring productive capacity. This patching-up approach has resulted in a certain loss of reliability. The Ministry estimated that up to the present approximately three quarters of the incurred damage to equipment has been permanently reconstructed in the generation sector.

Transmission

The main north-south and western transmission system which had been badly damaged during the conflict is more or less back to normal service. In some areas of Khuzestan and in the western region of Ilam, Khorrambad and Kordestan, supplies have still not been restored. It is estimated that about half of the transmission work is completed.

Distribution

Distribution systems were mainly damaged in the south-western province of Khuzestan, the western provinces of Khorramabad, Ilam and Bakhtaran. Lesser damage occurred in the north-western province of Azerbaijan. In addition to the above-mentioned distribution centres, materials and spare parts, held in bond in Khorramshahr for use in areas outside the war zone, were also destroyed in the conflict, estimated at Rs 12,100 million. Reconstruction work in the war-damaged provinces of Khuzestan, Ilam, Khorramabad and Kordestan is 30 per cent complete. In the case of Azerbayjan, it is estimated that only 20 per cent of reconstruction work has been completed.

3. Constraints

While the Ministry with its own local resources, human as well as financial, has performed to the best of its ability in the implementation of its reconstruction programme, it has, nevertheless, encountered a number of constraints. Some of the reconstruction programme experienced delays due to unavailability of equipment. In certain instances, equipment could not be obtained locally and subsequently, when ordering it from abroad time lags impeded reconstruction work. In addition, the purchase of equipment for reconstruction required allocation of foreign exchange which was, and continues to be, in short supply. Foreign exchange allocations are authorized by the Ministry of Finance on a case-by-case basis. Both factors, the imported equipment and the foreign exchange restrictions, caused lengthy delivery delays and hence retardation to the reconstruction work.

/...

4. Privatization

The power sector is, with few exceptions, controlled by the Government. It consists of one major system stretching from the Persian Gulf to the Caspian Sea, two smaller systems in the north-east and in the south-east respectively, and several minor isolated systems located in the south-east based on diesel generators serving small villages in remote areas.

Major development plans, prepared prior to the war, could not be implemented, and normal developmental activities had to be replaced with wartime measures. Resources to war-affected areas were severely reduced and the rise in demand in other regions unaffected by the conflict could not be met. This shortage situation, although by now greatly improved, is still experienced through frequent interruptions to the power supply.

To overcome these problems the Ministry has reportedly awarded contracts to private companies to construct a further 9,000 MW of generating capacity and to expand the associated transmission facilities over the medium term (1990-1998).

In a further attempt to upgrade generation, transmission and distribution, the Government has indicated that the private sector could play an eminent role in this task. In support of this decision, the Ministry has, in principle, agreed to privatize the operation of regional electric companies as well as the operation of power-generating plants. However, the generation plants would remain under government ownership.

5. Nuclear power

The existing nuclear development programme is under the control of the Atomic Energy Organization in Tehran. The mission was informed that 2 x 1200 MW generating units were under construction at the start of the conflict. As a result of bombardment, both plants were severely damaged even before construction had been completed; at the time of destruction, one unit was 85 per cent complete, the second unit about 60 per cent complete. The mission was informed that neither the nuclear reactor nor nuclear fuel had been delivered.

6. Expressed needs for international assistance

The Government informed the mission that reconstruction and development in the power sector would necessitate international assistance in several areas. Some assistance would be required to upgrade the electrical system to acceptable standards comparable to those that could have been achieved if the conflict had not affected normal development. As a priority, the Ministry mentioned the reconstruction of electrical systems in the Khuzestan and Gharb provinces as a priority. This would require the purchase of foreign equipment, in particular, electrical transmission networks and substations.

/...

It was also stated that there was considerable need for assistance in areas relating to management, planning and power systems design. As to equipment replaced and/or repaired during the time of the conflict, it was mentioned to the mission that some of the equipment would have to be replaced to ensure the efficient functioning of the system.

In both the water and power sectors, the Government emphasized the need for foreign assistance to improve present technology, including dam construction and modern control systems (computerization).

In the paragraphs that follow, a brief assessment is given of the power system at selected sites visited by the mission.

7. Principal power systems affected by the conflict

Interconnected system

The major interconnected electrical system is controlled by 14 regional companies, each of which plans and implements developments in their own area. However, the Department of Energy sets targets for the overall development of the power sector in the country; it further approves and monitors all major capital projects. Because of the war, the anticipated development had to be reduced to provide resources to the war-affected areas.

The major interconnected system of today has an installed generating capacity of 11,017 MW (megawatts) and a transmission system consisting of 400 KV (kilovolts), 230 KV, 132 KV and 66/63 KV systems. The demand for power decreased by about 50 per cent in the first year of the war. Thereafter the demand for power regained its pre-war level and subsequently the generating, transmission and distribution systems were substantially expanded. In fact the installed generating capacity almost doubled in the period 1980 to 1988. The generating system has four types of power plants - hydro, steam, gas turbine and diesel. The growth in capacity for each is illustrated in table F.1 below.

/...

0253

Table F.1. Power production capacity by government-controlled companies

Year	Hydro MW	Steam MW	Gas Turbine MW	Diesel MW	Private companies	Total MW
1980	1 804	3 983	3 058	783		9 628
1984	1 804	5 445	3 271	899		11 419
1988	1 904	5 981	2 935	705	2 865	14 390
1990	1 953	8 086	3 940	824	3 149	17 952

As seen in table F.2 below, the transmission system was also expanded by 100 per cent during the war years (1980-1988).

Table F.2

Year	400 KV KM	230 KV KM	132 KV KM	63/66 KV KM
1980	1 883	6 297	4 699	6 735
1984	4 318	8 266	5 605	11 732
1988	5 714	10 081	7 612	16 883
1990	5 618	10 970	8 532	18 202

The expansion of the distribution system during the war years was similar. In 1980 electric power was supplied to 7,800 villages and by 1990 electric power was supplied to about 24,000 villages; over 65 per cent of the rural population had been provided with electrical supplies. Details regarding the usage of power in the various sectors is set out in appendix III; the increase in numbers of consumers is shown in appendix IV.

Distribution

It was reported that significant damage was done to the distribution system in both the central and western regions, lesser damage in other areas, but that the greatest damage was done in the border provinces of Khuzestan, Bakhtaran, Kordestan and Ilam, which experienced ground fighting and prolonged occupation during the war.

/...

0254

Khuzestan

The south-western area of the Khuzestan province was reported to have been totally devastated. According to the regional electrical authority, several substations had been damaged on a number of occasions by repeated attacks. To restore supplies rapidly in the war-damaged zones, temporary networks were provided over extensive areas in this province. It was evident from on-site visits by the mission that, while major efforts had already been made to maintain power supplies to the consumers, significant reconstruction work remained to be done on the distribution system.

The mission inspected a number of substations in Abadan and Khorremshahr and witnessed areas where restoration of power supplies at this time was not feasible owing to war debris which had not yet been cleared. In addition, the mission witnessed areas where temporary supplies had been installed to provide power to consumers living in the surroundings of their damaged dwellings.

Abadan

In Abadan, the mission observed large areas where the distribution network had been reconstructed and upgraded using locally designed and constructed equipment. In addition, single circuit temporary supplies were also observed in this area.

It was observed that temporary repairs had been carried out only on several substations. It was reported that the main Abadan substation was destroyed in 1981 causing supplies to the area to be significantly reduced until 1988, when a temporary replacement transformer was installed in lieu of the two transformers which were destroyed during the war.

Khorramshahr

In several of the substations, it was noted that priority had been given to restoring power supplies from these stations by replacing only one transformer and connecting this to the transmission or distribution system, through permanent or temporary systems, depending on availability of materials.

In other substations substantial reconstruction work had taken place, but the substations were operating without proper protection equipment, owing to long delays in delivering the equipment.

In the Abadan/Khorramshahr region, it was reported that the maximum demand for electricity had decreased from 240 MW in 1979 to 100 MW in 1991; at one time, as a result of out-migration the demand for electricity fell even below 100 MW.

The Khuzestan Water and Power Authority reported that physical reconstruction of the distribution system damaged during the war was 30 per cent complete. The breakdown of this damage and reconstruction is set out in table F.3 below.

/...

It was further stated that two thirds of this reconstruction had been carried out with materials diverted from development projects in other areas, with the result that other consumers had been deprived of power supplies. The mission was further informed that some 10 per cent of the power supplies had been reconstructed in a temporary manner only.

During the field visit the mission saw a total of eight substations, inspected the distribution networks in Abadan and Khorramshahr, and assessed the interconnecting systems between Bandar-e-Mahshar and Abadan, Abadan and Khorramshahr, Khorramshahr and Ahwaz. This visit confirmed that, while major efforts were being made to reconstruct this devastated area, a lot of work remained to be done, or needed to be redone as large areas had been reconstructed with emergency temporary supply systems.

Table F.3. Khuzestan distribution system

	Damaged		Reconstructed	Outstanding
Medium voltage lines	2 680	KM	800	1 880
Low voltage lines	1 855	KM	600	1 255
Underground cables	151	KM	0	151
Transformers destroyed	3 384		750	2 634
Consumers disconnected	85 586	KM		
Lighting	35 000	KM	3 500	31 500
Vehicles	80	KM	25	55

It was reported that electrical supply is unable to meet the demand in the area 200 times per year in this province and that at the same time total demand for electricity in the Khuzestan province increased by 75 per cent in the period 1980 to 1990, in particular, in the north and eastern areas, owing to a steady flow of returnees from the war zone. Per capita consumption of electricity in this area doubled during the war. As a result of the war, major system developments planned for the Abadan and Khorramshahr area were not implemented.

Kordestan, Ilam, Bakhtaran

The power system for these three provinces is under the control of the Gharb Regional Electrical Authority.

Gharb

The Ministry of Energy reported war damage and reconstruction in these provinces as set out below.

Several small diesel generating units with an overall capacity of 138 MW were destroyed in isolated networks in the region. These diesel units have

/...

not been replaced but the power supplies to the region have been upgraded by
installing transmission and distribution systems which connect these areas to
the major interconnected transmission network. In addition, substantial
damage was done to the distribution system in this area. The extent of this
damage and reconstruction is set out in the table F.4.

Table F.4. <u>Gharb distribution system</u>

	Damaged	Reconstructed	Outstanding
Substations	894	512	382
Lines	3 176 km	1 800	1 376
Buildings	27 100 sq.m.	9 680	17 420
Street lamps	24 300	13 900	10 400
Consumers disconnected	48 400	24 000	24 400

<u>Transmission system</u>

The transmission system consists of 400 KV, 200 KV and 132 KV networks.
The 400 KV network and the overall control of the operation of the network is
carried out by Tavanir Power Generation and Transmission Company. The 230 KV
and 132 KV networks are controlled by the regional electric companies. The
total transmission system was subject to attack in the areas remote from the
war region due to the capability to disrupt energy supplies required for the
war effort by attacking this system. The substations on this system were the
major targets for repeated attacks due to the capability to disrupt energy
supplies by targeting strategic substations for attack. It was reported that
most of the major substations were damaged during the war. This caused
disruptions of the electricity supply to major cities. As a result of the
attacks power had to be supplied on lower voltage networks, with resulting
deterioration in the total power supply and voltage reductions in the affected
areas. Subsequently, this led either to total failure to supply some areas or
to occasional disruptions in the power supply. The major north/south
electrical supply lines were linked at Arak, where the vital 2 x 400 KV
transmission lines converged. This was reported to have been attacked three
times during the war owing to its strategic importance; twice the resulting
damage was severe, while one attack left behind minor damage. This substation
was returned to service after each attack, but much of the repair work done is
of a temporary nature.

In addition, five other 400 KV substations were reported to have suffered
severe damage. The data provided indicates that approximately 50 per cent of
the permanent reconstruction has been completed.

In the Khuzestan area 26 substations and 340 KM of the 230 KV and 132 KV
transmission circuits suffered extensive damage and some of these were totally
demolished. It was evident from the mission's visit to this area that in
spite of the efforts that had been made to restore power supplies, substantial

/...

reconstruction work remained to be done. Damaged material is in service in several areas to maintain supplies as all available spare materials have been used and replacement material is frequently delayed by up to two years from placement of order. The bulk of the transmission equipment required must be imported.

The regional power authorities mentioned that 50 per cent of the damage to the transmission system had been repaired during the war, but that 90 per cent of this was subsequently damaged again. Time required to complete reconstruction work was estimated at two years, but that completion would take longer as the equipment required had yet to be ordered because of financial constraints. The information provided by the Khuzestan Water and Power Authority showed that approximately 30 per cent of the reconstruction work on the transmission system in this area had been completed.

In the Garbh area, the Ministry of Energy reported that 11 substations and the transmission circuits suffered severe damage. The data provided indicate that reconstruction of the substations is approximately 50 per cent complete and that of the transmission circuits is 80 per cent complete.

Generating system

The generating system was subject to attack in areas remote from the war zone to disrupt the power supply systems. At first only the electrical transmission stations at the power stations were attacked, but subsequently the equipment inside the stations was severely damaged.

In meetings with the Tavanir Power Generation and Transmission Company, it was reported that six thermal power stations including Neka, in the north, on the Caspian Sea, Esfahan, in the east, Tabriz, Zargon and Ramine in the south all suffered severe damage during the war and that Neka was attacked three times causing a loss of production of 25 per cent of the output for over four-and-one-half years. It was reported that these power plants have all been returned to service, but in many cases only temporary repairs had been carried out, with resultant unreliability in operation.

In addition, the hydropower stations at Abbas Pour and Dez which were damaged by repeated attacks during the war have been restored to service using temporary measures, particularly in the electrical switchyard.

The Ministry of Energy reported that permanent reconstruction of the power plant is approximately 45 per cent complete.

/...

0258

Appendix

In the occupied provinces of Khuzestan and Gharb electrical systems, the peak power demands in 1980 and 1981 were 391 MW and 348 MW respectively. The peak demand in Tehran was 1,966 MW in 1981.

At that time the predicted power demand for 1987 and 1992 for each province was as illustrated below.

	1982 MW	1987 MW	1992 MW
Khuzestan	588	1 100	1 700
Gharb	348	950	1 585
Tehran	1 966	2 900	4 800
Esfahan	658	1 700	2 770
Azerbayjan	275	820	1 251
Fars	265	780	1 150
Gilan	248	459	695
Mazandaran	340	592	820
*Hormozgan	181	297	454
*Kerman	180	474	680
*Khorasan	298	730	1 112
*Sistan and Baluchestan	40	187	300

---

*   In 1982 these four provinces had isolated networks.

Hormozgen and Kerman have subsequently been connected to the main interconnected system.

/...

G. TELECOMMUNICATIONS AND BROADCASTING

1. Telecommunications

Telecommunication services in the Islamic Republic of Iran are operated by the Telecommunication Company of Iran (TCI). Prior to the war the country had nearly 1 million telephones, whereas currently the number of working telephone lines is over 2.25 million, served by about 600 telephone exchanges interconnected by a network of about 60,000 analogue trunk circuits. The network is almost fully automatized and normal telecommunication services, including subscriber trunk dialling, telex, etc., are offered. The technology used is mainly analogue and electromechanical (some semi-electronic systems are also in use) and for this type of equipment both investment and operating costs are high. There are also difficulties in offering modern services, for example, detailed billing, and there is a clear need to change over to modern technology. A significant part of the plant is locally manufactured at Shiraz in government factories under the Ministry of Post and Telegraph. These factories are likely to change over to digital (electronic) technology in the near future. Studies for the Integrated Services Digital Network (ISDN) are also being conducted by TCI.

As stated in this report, the border telecommunications network was largely destroyed. A total of 50,000 telephone lines with associated buildings, switching equipment, microwave and open-wire carrier links was destroyed and in many cases the external plant network was destroyed or rendered unusable. In some cases the plant had been reconstructed and then was destroyed again. The installed cost of the damaged telecommunication has been estimated by the Government at approximately Rls 115,000 million. TCI, however, had to restore minimum service rapidly with locally produced equipment, and have achieved notable results in achieving their objectives. TCI has intimated that installations in 120 telecommunication centres were damaged or destroyed. A detailed list was furnished in June 1991, which was referred to in the first report. From this a list of towns with heavy damage has been constructed and is available in table G.1. This list includes 15 towns and 20 small centres. Out of the 15 towns, 9 were visited during the two survey missions. A further list of towns where light or medium damage was inflicted is available in table G.2.

Owing to the high priority given by the Government to telecommunication reconstruction, a substantial part of the destroyed assets have been replaced. In some cases, however, plants have not yet been restored to their full capacity, owing to the fact that the inhabitants have not returned to the areas concerned. It was also noted that service has been restored by using the earlier generation of equipment available from local factories and that these may have to be upgraded or replaced if an integrated network capable of providing modern services is to be built up. TCI submitted a reconstruction and development plan for the border areas (November 1991) which is separately available.

/...

0260

(a) Estimate of physical damages

Government estimates

TCI submitted a detailed report of damages sustained during the war.
This was prepared in June 1991 and details damages to 120 centres in 20
provinces. The report indicates partial or heavy damage to 172 buildings,
9,000 kilometres of underground cable and 50,000 telephone lines with the
associated network. The value of the damaged assets has been estimated by TCI
at Rls 115,000 million. TCI, however, indicated that inflation to the extent
of 62 per cent has been observed during the last three years and the above
figure needs to be revised upwards.

Table G.1 lists the installations which were reported as heavily
damaged. These affect 15 towns and cities and 20 villages. According to
government estimate, a network of approximately 50,000 telephones was
destroyed, including buildings, telephone exchanges, carrier and radio
(microwave) equipment, underground cables, subscribers apparatus and
vehicles. Table G.2 indicates 15 towns where light or occasionally medium
damage was reported. In addition, there was a large number of villages where
the telecommunication facilities were destroyed, but the value of these assets
was small. Table G.3 indicates the progress in reconstruction works at the
heavily damaged installations. This has been extracted from the
reconstruction and development programme submitted to the mission separately
(November 1991).

(b) Methodology of verification

The United Nations mission paid two visits to Iran in June and
November 1991 and inspected 15 towns, including 9 of the heavily damaged ones
listed in table G.1. In many cases, direct verification of damage was
possible; in other cases, indirect evidence in the form of photographs and
visible damage to buildings in the nearby neighbourhood was available. The
physical quantity of assets damaged was verified against population estimates,
type of activity and the assets which would normally have been installed in
such cases. In some cases, the assets installed were in excess of immediate
requirements but are not considered unusual as a forward planning procedure.
The preliminary report (S/22863) may be referred to for a description of the
damages in the southern sector.

(c) Observations in the northern sector

Bostan. Before the war, Bostan had a population of 8,000, and a
telephone exchange of 200 lines with an open wire carrier system connecting it
to the main trunk network. The town was occupied and destroyed along with the
telecommunication system. A new building has been constructed, a 100-line
exchange with a 12-channel carrier system has been commissioned and a
60-channel VHF radio system is being installed. It is understood that the
town is being developed for 35,000 inhabitants taking into account the
surrounding area. Reconstruction will therefore require additional telephone
exchange capacity to be set up.

/...

Dehloran. The pre-war population of Dehloran was 10,500 and a 500-line exchange with 12-channel carrier systems provided service. The town changed hands and the exchange was three times replaced and damaged. Currently, a 100-line exchange is operational, but a 1,000-line exchange with a microwave system will soon be commissioned.

Mehran. This was a town with 14,500 inhabitants with a 500-line telephone exchange and carrier/UHF systems. This was totally destroyed and reconstruction has started. At present, an interim 100-line exchange with a 24-channel UHF system has been installed. This will require substantial expansion when the town is fully developed.

Qasr-e-shirin. Prior to the conflict this town, located some 3 kilometres from the border, had a population of 28,000, and some 62,000 within the municipal area. The 1,000-line exchange that was in operation was completely destroyed. Reconstruction work has started and an interim installation of a 100-line exchange completed.

(d) Conclusions relating to damages

The damage observed could be classified in two categories: where enemy forces occupied the town, for example, Khorramshahr, Bostan, Mehran, Qasr-e-Shirin, the damage was total and explosives appear to have been used to destroy the plants. Towns in the vicinity of the occupation, such as Abadan and Dehloran, also suffered heavy damage as telecommunication targets were in range of ground artillery. The second category contains important cities beyond the immediate areas of ground fighting which were targeted during air attacks. Unfortunately, telecommunication towers are highly visible targets and the exchange and microwave installations could therefore be easily identified. However, targeted installations in the interior generally did not suffer serious damage, except the earth station complex at Asadabad which was heavily damaged.

Based on these observations, it is concluded that the physical estimates of damages presented to the mission by TCI are found to correspond to the lists submitted and that the border telecommunication network consisting of 50,000 telephone lines was almost totally destroyed. A part of the underground cable network could perhaps be recovered, but this would require considerable human effort in tracing the telephone conductors and reconnecting them.

(e) Estimate of financial damage

As mentioned, TCI have indicated that the direct financial loss amounts to approximately Rls 115,000 million. However, based on the type of network existing in the border region, it was felt that if modern technology is used for reconstruction and equipment procured in the international market at competitive prices, the cost per telephone line could be reduced. However, this line of action is not immediately available to Iran as they have to depend on the current manufacture from their own factories until these are modernized.

/...

0262

(f) Reconstruction effort

It is observed from the current status of reconstruction shown in table G.2 that the bulk of the reconstruction work relating to the restoration of primary services has been completed. A major installation at Khorramshahr and installations of underground cable networks and provision of telephone service as well as completion of some microwave works are the main items pending. Much of the external plant network and 15,000 telephone exchange lines out of the 50,000 lines destroyed are yet to be commissioned. These works have been carried out by TCI within its own resources, largely with products from the government factories. In some cases, however, interim installations have had to be resorted to until the population returns.

The reconstruction of towns including the provision of telecommunications services is being done to attract not only the original population but in some cases displaced persons from surrounding areas. This policy requires expansion and modernization of services. TCI therefore plans not only to reconstruct to original capacities, but to develop services further in accordance with their five-year plan, as well as to modernize services. The plan incorporates the reconstuction of damaged sites and equipment, and normal expansion that would have occurred in a peace-time scenario. In addition, a reconstruction-_cum_-development plan for the border areas was prepared and submitted to the mission. TCI mentioned that, taking into account the inflation and current prices, they have been allocated Rls 139,000 million to complete the plan at current prices. This would not be adequate to finance the total development plan for the border areas. Unfortunately, it was not possible to separate the reconstruction component from the total development plan as it is being implemented on an integrated basis using modern technology. TCI also indicated that up to now Rls 40,000 million have been used for reconstruction and this has been worked out by them to be equal to approximately Rls 47,000 million at current prices, taking inflation into account.

As far as the first five-year plan is concerned, TCI has indicated that it proposes to install approximately 450,000 lines in the 5 border provinces during the plan period. Part of this network will utilize modern digital technology and part will rely on the existing technology employed by the factories at Shiraz.

TCI has already undertaken a modernization plan and the Government proposes to change over the factory production to digital telephone exchanges and digital microwave links. Optical fibre links are also to be introduced. With these changes, new services and facilities can be introduced and demand for value added services, which can best be provided by the private sector, will increase. The border areas should also benefit from such advances as they have suffered considerably in the recent past. The reconstruction programme should keep all of this in view. Adequately skilled labour is reported to be availble for the reconstruction effort. However, exposure of engineers to new technologies available abroad should be encouraged.

/...

It was understood from TCI that the present requirement of foreign currency was approximately $1,450 per telephone line. This may increase somewhat during the technology change-over period, but should decrease later on when the factories are operating at full capacity. Modernization of the factories seems to be an appropriate area for international assistance for reconstruction.

(g) **Conclusions**

In the telecommunications sector, two stages of reconstruction are envisaged. The first stage involves restoration to pre-war levels and physically about 35,000 out of the 50,000 lines damaged or destroyed have been completed. The second stage of reconstruction seeks to make up for the loss of normal development during the war years and this stage is expected to be completed by 1993. The expenditure on reconstruction has been Rls 40,000 million up to now and a further amount of Rls 139,000 million is expected to be allocated for the residual part of the first stage of reconstruction and the second stage. It is recommended that the second stage of reconstruction should be carried out to the extent possible with modern technology. Adequate training in new technologies should also be planned and organized.

2. Broadcasting

(a) **General observations**

The Islamic Republic of Iran Broadcasting (IRIB) is responsible for producing programmes and providing radio and television services to the country as well as for transmitting short-wave radio programmes to foreign countries.

Two radio programmes currently cover 95 and 80 per cent of the population and two television programmes can be received by 85 and 65 per cent, respectively. The two radio and television programmes are produced in Tehran. However, local contributions are produced by 24 local radio and television centres and incorporated into the second programmes.

Considering that a significant percentage of the population is illiterate, the Government relies on the broadcast media to disseminate a wide variety of cultural, educational, agricultural and health care programmes. IRIB receives, therefore, strong support from the Government.

The overall damage assessment by the mission during visits to the damaged sites confirmed the results of the first mission. Only one medium-wave radio station had been omitted, namely Gilan-e-Gharb. From the visits, the conclusion can be drawn that the IRIB is technically capable of coping with its reconstruction task.

/...

(b)   Estimate of damages

In the western provinces 10 high-power medium-wave transmitters between 50 and 600 kW and 2 provisional 10- and 20-kW transmitters were destroyed, as well as 7 130-m antennas and 8 diesel generators ranging from 800 to 1,200 kW.

In addition 14 10-kW FM radio transmitters and 22 television transmitters between 2 and 40 kW were destroyed or disappeared during the occupation. Four 10-kW FM transmitters and five 10- or 40-kW transmitters were also damaged. The corresponding 8 towers (44 to 220 metres), including antennas, were demolished as well as 11 diesel generators from 50 to 300 kW.

Two television studios and 5 radio studios were completely destroyed, including the equipment. The demolished buildings have a total surface of 20,000 square metres. Table G.4 provides details on destroyed or damaged stations.

Antennas at the Kamal Abad short-wave station were damaged. This station sends programmes to foreign countries. The Gilan-e-Gharb medium-wave station was of a provisional nature to replace the destroyed Qasr-e-Shirin station. This station will, however, not be reconstructed.

IRIB estimates that the reconstruction costs for the entire broadcasting sector will amount to Rls 19,000 million, of which $118 million are in foreign exchange.

(c)   Reconstruction and development

As witnessed during the visits to the sites, IRIB proved to be very active in reconstructing the destroyed stations. In some cases, where the same type of transmitters is no longer available, more powerful transmitters are being used instead. To reduce the risk of damages by bombing or shelling, the transmitter stations are rebuilt in thick concrete shelters and covered with earth. As a result, therefore, building costs are significantly higher compared to previous years. Table G.4 also provides information on the status of completed work and the timetable of reconstruction for the stations that so far have not been rebuilt. The table shows that a significant part of them is still under reconstruction. Owing to the increased number of projects simultaneously implemented and serious manpower shortages, especially the lack of skilled engineers, severe difficulties causing critical implementation delays are encountered in commissioning some transmit stations. IRIB, in some cases, has to call on the services of the equipment supplier for implementation, work which frequently proves to be very costly.

For future projects, the mission is of the view that the installation and commissioning should be part of the delivery contract, especially if domestic capability is limited or unavailable within IRIB. When these components are included in a project from the very beginning, they are being submitted for competition to interested bidders and will compose a small part of the total delivery and therefore offered at costs representing only a small percentage of the total value of the contract.

/...

(d) Validity of estimates

The financial estimates for the reconstruction of war damage have been roughly verified for the equipment on a station-by-station basis. The figures provided to the mission by IRIB seem to be somewhat high compared to the usual market costs. However, considering the difficult conditions prevailing in the country during and after the war, these figures as well as the total estimated costs for reconstruction are credible.

(e) Government priorities and five-year plan

The current sectoral five-year plan (1988-1992) has as objectives to expand the television coverage to 95 per cent and 85 per cent of the population for the first and second programmes, respectively. For both first and second radio programmes, the coverage is aimed at reaching the entire population by the end of 1992.

(f) Status of plan implementation

No overall reconstruction plan seems to have been developed. Damaged stations are reconstructed as quickly as possible. Table G.4 provides details on the level of completion, the equipment and the foreseen year of future operations. All stations should be fully operational by the end of 1993. At present, approximately 50 per cent of the equipment is reinstalled, but only 30 per cent of the stations are in operation. However, most of the remaining equipment is already on order or has been delivered.

(g) Implementation capability and required assistance

Technical level

IRIB's personnel is adequately trained to carry out reconstruction work of the war-damaged equipment; further, it is capable of developing and operating the broadcasting network with the exception of the commissioning of certain transmit systems, as explained above.

IRIB would need some inputs of technical assistance in these areas. However, owing to the high specialization of the work required, recruitment of international experts other than employees of equipment suppliers might be difficult.

(h) Conclusions

The only difficulty is experienced in the installation and commissioning of high-power transmitters. In certain projects currently being implemented, technical assistance could be requested to address this problem and improve for the longer term the domestic skill level. For future projects, a change in the project design may be proposed. The reconstruction costs are estimated at Rls 19,000 million and the reconstruction work is believed to be half completed. IRIB has not mentioned the need for any direct assistance as their funding is from government budgets. The Government may, however, require financial assistance for the reconstruction of the sector.

/...

0266

TELECOMMUNICATIONS

Table G.1. <u>List of heavily damaged telecommunications</u>
<u>installations</u>

Code: B-Buildings MW-Microwave E-Exchange C-Cable Network
O-Other Plant UHF-Ultra high frequency radio

Location	Damaged Installation	Exchange Size	Remarks
KHOZESTAN			
1. Khorramshahr	B/MW/E/C	10,000	Total destruction
	Storeyard		Total
2. Abadan	B/MW/E/C	13,000	Total
	Trunk centre	800	Total
3. Dezful	B/MW/E/C	10,000	Heavy
	Trunk centre	1,000	Total
4. Susan Guerd	B/E/C	300	Heavy
5. Bostan	B/E/O	200	Total
6. Small towns (4)	B/E/MW/O		Total
ILAM			
7. Dehloran	B/E/O	1,000	Total destruction
8. Mehran	B/E/C/O	500	Total
BAKHTARAN			
9. Qasr-e-Shirin	B/E/O	1,000	Total destruction
10. Zarpol-e Zahab	E/C	400	Total
11. Gilan-Gharb	E/O	100	Total
12. Small offices (12)	O		Total
KORDESTAN			
13. Baneh	B		Heavy destruction
14. Marivan	E/C/O	500	Total
15. Sanandaz	B/O		Heavy destruction
16. Miandoab	E/B	10,000	Total
Trunk centre	E	1,200	
HAMADAN			
17. Asadabad	Earth station	Ant 1/2	Total
TOTAL LINES DESTROYED	50,000 Local	3,000 Trunk	

TELECOMMUNICATIONS

Table G.2. List of towns with light or medium damage

Location	Damaged Installation
1. Ahwaz	Buildings, cable network
2. Ilam	Buildings, cable, trunks
3. Islamabad	Buildings, microwave, exchange, cables
4. Bakhtaran	Building, carrier equipment, cable
5. Nehavand	Buildings, cables
6. Khoramabad	Building, exchange (10,000)
7. Lorestan 5 small centres	Building, exchanges (6,500)
8. Shahrekord	Buildings, carrier
9. Zanjan	Cables
10. Kharg	Buildings, cables
11. Arak	Cables
12. Shiraz	Cables
13. Hamadan	Cables
14. Bushehr (Kharg)	Cables
15. Tehran	Building

Note: In addition, there were a large number of villages where
telecommunication facilities were destroyed.

/...

0268

TELECOMMUNICATIONS

Table G.3. Reconstruction of heavily damaged assets

Town	Pre-war Capacity	Reconstruction Completed	Remarks
Khorramshahr	10,000 lines	2,000/600 ch MW	
Abadan	13,000 lines	10,000/1260 ch MW	3,000 lines under construction
Dezful	10,000 lines	10,000	
Susan Guerd	300 lines	2,000	
Bostan	200 lines	100/12 ch carrier	60 ch UHF under installation
Dehloran	1,000 lines	100/12 ch carrier	1000 line/300 ch MW under construction
Mehran	500 lines	100/UHF-24 ch	
Qasr-e-Shirin	1,000 lines	100/12 ch carrier	
Zarpol-e Zahab	400 lines	100/UHF-60 ch	
Gilan Gharb	100 lines	100/MW-drop	
Marivan	500 lines	1,000/MW	
Miandoab	10,000 lines	10,000/MW	
Asadabad	Earth station	Completed	

Note: MW - Microwave radio   UHF - Ultra high frequency radio
       Ch - Channels

/...

BROADCASTING

Table G.4

Stations	Surface (sq.m.)	Damaged Equipment T	A	D	% DEstruction Bldg.	Equip.	% Reconstruction Bldg.	Equip.	Restart Year
High power medium and short wave stations:									
Martyr Chamran	2,300	4	2	1	60	50	100	100	1987
Beit-al-Mogheddas	3,000	2	2	1	90	100	100	100	1987
Abadan	4,200	2	4	2	100	100	95	60	1992
Qasr-e-Shirin	3,000	2	2	2	100	100	20	10	1993
Gilan-e-Gharb	200	2	2	2	100	100	0	0	-
Kamal Abad antennas	-	-	-	-	0	30	100	100	1990
High power TV and FM stations:									
Khosrow Abad	1,200	10	2	1	60	100	100	20	1992
Bostan	1,200	4	1	1	100	100	10	0	1993
Abadan	1,200	10	2	4	80	100	100	50	1992
Shadegan	3,000	9	1	2	20	10	100	80	1992
Kuh-e-Nooh	1,000	5	4	2	80	100	100	30	1992
Nakhjeer	600	5	5	3	100	100	100	80	1992
Studios:		R	TV	D					
Abadan IRIB	7,000	2	2	1	80	100	95	0	1993
Abadan Oil Co.	500	3	-	-	40	100	100	0	1993

Legend:

T - Transmitter   A - Antenna towers   D - Diesel generators   R - Radio   TV - Television

/...

H. EDUCATION

Introduction

The education system of the Islamic Republic of Iran provides free education for its school-age population. The objectives of the Government's policy, strategy and priorities for the educational programme include:

Review and modification of education and training system according to the country's needs and the development programme;

Provision of elementary education and development of education and training at guidance and secondary levels according to the country's needs and development programme.

1. Major problems relating to reconstruction and
    rehabilitation

In order to bring about economic and social development, the substantive aspect of the reconstruction and rehabilitation process will need to ensure a qualitatively improved education programme as well as the availability of skilled/trained manpower in the war-affected provinces. The present system is characterized by a high attrition rate at all levels of education. This problem is being addressed in the Government's first five-year plan, where one of the key issues of the educational programme is to reduce student repetition and the number of drop-outs at all levels.

There is an urgent demand for trained manpower to reconstruct and develop the war-affected provinces. The situation has been exacerbated by the destruction of manpower training facilities destroyed during the war and by the need to create employment opportunities for those leaving school. The Government has accorded a high priority to the revival of the economic life of the war-affected provinces, but this will require an increase in enrolment at vocational/technical/agricultural institutions so as to reduce the shortage of middle-level technicians and skilled workers in the provinces.

(a) The effects of the conflict

Damage to schools

Before the war there were 44,300 classrooms in the five western provinces. Of these some 9,300 classrooms or (21 per cent) in 2,637 schools are reported to have been gravely damaged or destroyed, requiring reconstruction.

In addition, 362 schools located in 12 provinces outside the immediate war zone suffered considerable damage by missile attacks and aerial bombardments. The mission was informed that the total loss of teaching space in all 2,999 schools is estimated at 1,700 square metres.

/...

0271

Table H.1. Number of damaged schools due to the imposed war in different provinces

Province	Primary	Guidance	Secondary	Service/ Vocational	Technical Training	Teachers Training	Gymnasium	Office	Total
Khuzestan	501	134	77	5	6	3	4	2	732
Bakhtaran	382	106	75	3	1	·	·	1	568
Ilam	95	28	87	4	3	3	4	3	227
Western Azerbayjan	900	59	44	·	·	·	·	·	1 003
Kurdistan	54	13	30	5	2	2	·	1	107
Lorestan	55	17	15	2	·	·	·	·	89
Eastern Azerbayjan	45	32	12	·	·	·	·	·	89
Tehran	32	14	6	·	·	·	·	·	52
Fars	·	·	2	·	·	·	·	·	2
Markazi	6	1	2	·	·	·	·	·	9
Gilan	1	·	·	·	·	·	·	·	1
Isfahan	9	8	5	1	·	·	·	·	23
Hamedan	33	19	10	5	·	·	·	1	68
Zanjan	10	6	3	1	·	·	·	·	20
Charmahal	1	·	2	1	·	·	·	·	4
Kuhkiloieh	1	1	·	·	·	·	·	·	2
Bosher	3	·	·	·	·	·	·	·	3
Sub-total	2 128	438	370	27	12	8	8	8	2 999

Migration of pupils/students away from the war area

Prior to the war there were 1.25 million pupils/students enrolled in 44,300 classrooms in the five war-affected provinces. The war forced about 450,000 (or 36 per cent) to flee to neighbouring provinces for safety causing thereby a dramatic increase in enrolment in schools in those areas. The lack of sufficient school accommodation necessitated the use of a double-shift system to accommodate the new students.

With the reconstruction of more schools in the war-affected provinces, students displaced by the war are expected to return to their places of origin. However, their willingness to return may be conditioned by the standard and/or quality of education they can expect in the reconstructed schools.

War casualty and migration of teachers

The number of educational personnel, including teaching and administrative staff was about 55,000 prior to the outbreak of hostilities. Although no estimates of casualties have been made available to the mission, it is estimated that a considerable number of staff as well as students became war casualties.

When examined within the national perspective, migration of teachers away from the war-affected provinces continues to pose serious problems. According to the five-year plan, 40,000 new primary schoolteachers are needed each year but the teacher-training centres can provide only 25,000 graduates annually. At the secondary level, the shortage of teachers nationwide is at present estimated at 116,000.

(b) Reconstruction/renovation

The Government accords high priority to (a) the construction of primary schools and (b) the provision of teachers to the war-affected provinces. The team believes that reconstruction work was carried out as planned. It was also informed that some schools had to be repaired or rebuilt more than once during the war because of repeated damage or destruction.

With regard to staff, the team noted that the number of teachers available was commensurate with the number of schools reconstructed and with the number of pupils/students that had returned. In some cases, special incentives have been provided to encourage teachers to return to various locations in the war-affected provinces. Moreover, because of a shortage of teachers in the Khuzestan province, the authorities had provided some 400 extra teachers to help out in three of its cities.

/...

Number of schools completely reconstructed/repaired up to the present

More than 50 per cent of the affected schools have been brought back into service over the past three years. Of the 2,999 damaged or destroyed schools, reconstruction work has been completed on 1,060 schools in the war-affected areas and on 362 schools outside the immediate war zone.

Reconstruction work costing of Rls 21,000 million has been completed on 12 technical and vocational training centres located at Ahwaz, Boushehr, Khorramabad, Bakhtaran, Ilam, Boraijerd, Sagez, Tabriz and Mahabad, Khorramshahr and West Azerbayjan. In addition, another 16 centres located in provinces adjacent to the war zone have now been reopened. The team was informed that during the war years attempts were made to keep many of the Centres open despite repeated air attacks on some buildings. Table H.2 details the actual achievements in each sub-sector, and shows that the work accomplished has been evenly distributed in each sub-sector.

Table H.2. **Damaged and reconstructed schools**

Sub-sector	Damaged	Reconstructed
Primary	2 124	1 023
Guidance	441	218
Secondary	371	152
Service/vocational	27	15
Technical	12	4
Teacher training	8	3
Gymnasium	8	2
Education offices	8	5
Total	2 999	1 422

The team was informed that various foundations and trusts, working in parallel with the Government, have assisted in the reconstruction efforts. These include Aston Ghods Razavi Foundation, Jahad Sazandergi, Mostazafin Bonyad, Peoples Help, and the Foundation for the Displaced Population. It is estimated that about 20 per cent of the total reconstruction effort was carried out by these and other foundations.

Number of schools where work is in progress

Work is currently in progress on a further 370 schools that are scheduled to be completed within the current annual budget period.

Costs of reconstruction carried out to date

The expenditure to date on rebuilding and repairing educational establishments, including the sums approved for the current fiscal year, are shown in table H.3.

/...

0274

Table H.3. **Expenditure to date on rebuilding and repairing educational establishments**

No.	Sub-sector	Expenditure to date (1991)	Running cost of completion	Total cost (millions of Rls)
1.	Primary schools	35 000	36 000	71 000
2.	Guidance schools	7 161	11 000	18 161
3.	Secondary schools	11 592	15 000	26 592
4.	Service/vocational schools	12 000	14 000	26 000
5.	Technical schools	20 000	40 000	60 000
6.	Teacher training colleges	12 000	25 000	37 000
7.	Sports halls	800	2 400	3 200
8.	Administration buildings	5 000	3 000	8 000
	Total	103 553	146 400	249 953

Note: Considerable expenditure has been in the form of voluntary assistance and is therefore not recorded by the Ministry of Education. The foreign exchange component of items 1, 2, 3 and 8 is estimated to be about 10 per cent; for items 4, 6 and 7, 20 per cent; and, for item 5, 40 per cent - mostly to cover plant and tools.

Future reconstruction programme

Approximately 1,200 damaged or destroyed schools remain to be rebuilt. Many of these are located in war-devastated cities and towns in the western provinces.

In the war-affected rural areas, particularly villages which were totally destroyed, there might be some merit in delaying rebuilding until there is evidence that a viable community will be re-established, or until an estimate of the school-age population of the district can be determined. For such reasons, the future phases of the school reconstruction programme are unlikely to proceed at the same pace as has been achieved to date.

/...

0275

In the team's view it is estimated that about two thirds of the remaining reconstruction work will be completed during the present five-year development plan. The balance will have to be carried over into the next plan period and possibly absorbed into the general education expansion programme which had been in effect up to the outbreak of hostilities.

(c) Constraints

Constraints in relaunching education services in the war-affected provinces relate mainly to the construction as the most severely affected cities and towns suffer from an acute shortage of building materials.

In some locations, mainly in the Ilam and Bakhtaran provinces, where entire communities have been completely destroyed, restoration of education will have to await the necessary replanning and the reconstruction of basic services and infrastructure. Moreover, adequate housing will need to be available at the same time as schools are being built and reopened if teaching is to resume without delay. The mission was informed that the question of an adequate supply of teachers was not a constraint for the present.

(d) The role of the private sector

Prior to the war, the private sector played little or no role in providing for popular education. However, owing to the pressure on the Government's capacity to restore its educational services, the private sector has been allowed to set up non-profit-making educational establishments with strict adherence to nationally accepted standards. While this sector is not involved in reconstruction, its expansion would help to ease the pressure on the Government's school programme. Indications are that private sector schools will continue to expand. At the present time 7,000 private students are attending primary, guidance and secondary schools, in the larger towns.

2. Expressed needs for international assistance

The Planning and Statistics Division of the Ministry of Education is aware that the activities grouped under the name of "school mapping" are an essential basic tool in every aspect of education planning. The Division has begun to look into the feasibility of setting up such an exercise. The Division requires international assistance specifically in:

The design, scope and testing of an appropriate questionnaire;

Methods of data collection in the field;

Acquisition or design of suitable computer programmes to process the data gathered;

/...

0276

Access and handling techniques for all the departments and organizations which will benefit from the availability of the data.

Additionally, a study fellowship to visit another comparable country where these techniques are being used would be of value.

3. Observations

Policy and strategy

The Iranian Government's stated policy and strategy for the development of the educational programme, calls, _inter alia_, for review and modification of the education and training system according to the country's needs and development programme. This activity would be suitable for external assistance geared to providing expertise in conducting comprehensive human resources sector analysis work on the basis of which a new education policy and strategy can be formulated.

Teachers

Serious problems could arise in the near future in attracting teachers to return to the remote war-affected provinces, particularly in the light of the present country-wide teacher shortage of about 25,000 teachers each year. This situation could be further exacerbated by the 10,000 teachers or so who through promotion, retirement or other reasons, leave the rural areas each year. The mission noted that, in some of the principal cities in the war-affected areas (Ahwaz, Susan-Guerd, Khorramshahr) the problem of teacher shortage does not appear to be critical at this stage. However, it is very doubtful whether the same conditions prevail in rural schools such as the ones visited by the mission. In the event that living conditions are not attractive, the shortage of teachers in rural schools could become very acute, thus contributing to the deterioration of the quality and standard of education.

Reconstruction standards

As mentioned earlier, current standards of construction, and some aspects of planning, are high and consequently comparatively costly. If the Government so wished, there is no doubt that schools which function equally well, could be built at lower costs than at present incurred.

For example, simplifying structures in some cases, and/or reducing or entirely omitting internal circulation spaces where climatic conditions are favourable, would substantially reduce costs. Part of the savings thus effected could be used to provide larger and more appropriate teaching spaces; the balance being used to build more schools.

In general, standards of construction and finish are high, but spacial standards in teaching areas are considered marginal by international standards.

/...

It has been difficult for the mission to obtain an accurate view of the cost of building schools, as project cost analysis techniques are not practised by the unit within the Education Ministry charged with the responsibility for building and equipping all government schools.

The team also looked into the reconstruction costs for schools. Over the range of school types, primary to secondary, the area unit costs were said to be between Rls 200,000 and 300,000 per square metre (1990 costs). Applying these costs to standard-type designs, suggests the following indicative costs for a typical range of schools (buildings only):

Primary school   -   6 classrooms rural   61 million rials

Primary school   - 10 classrooms urban   330 million rials

Guidance school - 12 classrooms rural   375 million rials

Guidance school - 18 classrooms urban   720 million rials

Secondary school - 12 classrooms   540 million rials

The apparent wide divergence in some cases is due to there being a broad range of designs for the same school type, some being more efficient and compact than others. The cost of furniture is generally estimated at 15 per cent of building costs and equipment from +5 per cent (primary) to +15 per cent (secondary). Technical school building costs are probably 10 per cent above secondary schools, but furniture, equipment, tools and plant will add a further 80-85 per cent to these costs. All figures exclude any site and infrastructure costs, which will be different for each location.

/...

0278

I. CULTURAL HERITAGE

Introduction

Throughout eight years of hostilities, the five border provinces of Khuzistan, Ilam, Bakhtaran, Kurdistan and Western Azerbayjan were active theatres of war, while the provinces of Esfahan, Tehran, Luristan, Fars, Bushehr, Markazi, Zanjan, Hamadan, Gilan and Mazandaran were subjected to repeated air raids and missile attacks.

The afflicted area contained many listed sites, monuments and museums, which suffered severe and, in some cases, irreparable, damage. A list outlining damage to a total of 48 monuments and sites of major significance was given to the mission by the national authorities.

1. Observed war damage to cultural heritage

(a) Direct damage

Owing to the limited time available, field visits were restricted to the Tehran area and to the provinces of Esfahan and Khuzestan. The mission also visited key institutions responsible for the protection of cultural heritage, principal historic monuments and sites affected by the war, including two sites inscribed on the World Heritage list, namely Maidan-e-Imam and Choqa Zanbil.

Shush and its surrounding archaeological sites

Shush, considered to be the most important archaeological site in the Islamic Republic of Iran, was founded in the third millenium B.C. and flourished until the Islamic period. The site extends over 360 hectares, of which approximately 30 have been excavated. Today it comprises four archaeological sites: Tappeh Acropolis, Tappeh Apadana, the central tappeh (mound) and the eastern tappeh, known as the City of the Artisans.

Within the archaeological zone are the imposing nineteenth century castle built by the French archaeological mission 150 years ago to serve as a centre for research, the oldest of its type in the country, as well as the site museum, and the shrine of the Old Testament prophet Daniel.

According to local officials, enemy forces occupied a site 3 kilometres away from Shush, and also bombarded the area frequently during the conflict.

Eight years of war have inevitably disturbed the site, and significant damage to the excavated monuments can be seen. Notably, the walls of Shahr-e-Panzdahu, or Fifteenth City, bearing traces of 15 successive layers of occupation, the latest being Elamite, have been reduced in height from 2 metres virtually to zero in places. Extensive impact damage was also visible to the walls, pavement and stone columns of the palace of Khashayer II.

/...

0279

The archaeological research centre was particularly heavily damaged by rocket attacks, which destroyed extensive parts of the wall and roof structure. Traces of impact and metal fragments of missiles are visible.

In addition to the damage to the main structure of the castle itself, many inscribed and carved stones and column shafts from the archaeological site stored in the castle were shattered.

The Shrine of Daniel

The Shrine of Daniel, dating in its present form from the thirteenth century A.D., was hit by rockets, causing the partial destruction of one wing, and the collapse of the mirror decoration of the _iwan_. Traces of impact are visible around the entrance, and the noticeable incline of the dome is said to be a result of vibration. Restoration has now been completed, and photographic documentation was available, showing the extent of damage. A master plan exists for the site, prepared by the Ministry of Construction.

Choqa Zanbil

Thirty kilometres from Shush, Choqa Zanbil, dating from the second millenium B.C., is the largest ziggurat in the region, measuring 150 metres by 150, and 50 metres high. It was the temple of the Elamite capital of Shush. The mission observed that a section of the baked brick outer casing of the first and second stages of the monument had fallen, apparently as a result of the shock of a nearby explosion; fragments of metal found nearby support this.

Haft Tappeh

The Elamite site of Haft Tappeh (seven mounds), dating from the second millenium B.C., is situated 10 kilometres to the south of Shush. It contains the earliest known brick vault. The site was disturbed by some trench-digging and the erection of defensive obstacles by military units stationed in the area.

(b) Indirect damage

During the war years, the archaeological sites were closed both to the public and to researchers as they fell within a military security zone. It was also stated that, for the same reason, it was not possible throughout the war period to conserve or maintain the often fragile excavated structures, some of which are in unbaked mud brick. According to the authorities, a number of objects seem to have been illicitly excavated from unprotected sites during that period. The urgent need for greater protection of archaeological sites and site museums was stressed.

(c) Damage to monuments and the historic urban fabric

The types of damage observed have been grouped into three broad categories: first degree (direct hit), second degree (damage caused by

/...

0280

vibration or shock waves) and indirect damage (deterioration of the environment). The latter is in some respects the most serious in the long term.

Esfahan

The damage to cultural heritage in Esfahan was enormous and affected 10 major mosques, 5 religious schools, 3 main bazaars and more than 40 listed historic houses. The mission was informed that more than 1,000 old houses were totally destroyed during the war. A map was handed over to the mission showing bombed sites.

Historic public buildings

In March 1984, the south-eastern prayer hall of the 'Atiq Congregational Mosque, a masterpiece of Iranian architecture, was hit by rockets which destroyed 11 bays of the twelfth century Shabestan and a part of the adjacent 'Araban Bazaar. Fortunately, detailed studies and a photogrammetric survey existed, and it was possible to reconstruct the whole of the destroyed area. Restoration work has now been completed.

The Qajar-period Agha Nur Mosque in the Dardasht quarter and the adjacent bazaar also suffered some direct damage and had been partly rebuilt. At the time of the mission's visit, restoration work to the brick vaults of the bazaar was in progress.

Rockets which fell in the vicinity of the Masjid Sayyid, a Qajar mosque with exceptional tiled "Qatar Bandi" stalactites, caused damage to windows, tile-work and wooden grilles.

Although no direct bomb damage was sustained to Maidan-e-Imam or to the surrounding monuments, the Safavid faience tile decoration of the outer face of the dome of the Imam mosque is uniformly lifting around the crown. This is thought to be due to shock waves caused by a missile which exploded directly overhead.

The monumental task of restoration, which has started, involves stripping the roof and reassembling the tiles on a negative mould.

An indirect result of the war damage has been the suspension of vital conservation work to other monuments, including the consolidation of the upper floor structure and the transfer of floor loads to the bearing walls of 'Ali Qapu Palace.

Hammam-e-Wazir in the Jamaleh quarter was partly destroyed, along with a part of the adjacent bazaar and residential quarter, and is now the subject of an ongoing restoration project.

/...

Historic residential quarters

Ten ruined historic residential quarters were visited in Esfahan. The pattern of destruction was consistent: individual houses or groups of houses were razed to the ground, and the area recuperated for market gardens. The ruined arches and party walls of the destroyed houses are visible all around.

In the immediate vicinity, extensive secondary damage from vibration to the fragile finishings and fittings of adjacent historic buildings was observed.

The historic houses visited in each damaged quarter showed degrees of damage ranging from 5 per cent (broken windows, minor damaged mural paintings, stucco, mirrors or woodwork) to 100 per cent destruction. The mission was able to see examples of both ongoing (Khané-e-Sheikh-al-Islam) and completed restoration projects (restored Qajar mural paintings and coloured glass windows in the Kharazi House).

Dezful and Shushtar

The twin cities of Dezful and Shushtar offer exceptionally intact examples of a form of traditional urban architecture perfectly adapted to a hot and humid climate. Dating in their present form from the twelfth to twentieth centuries, they are almost certainly built on very ancient foundations.

Dezful, which was a central market for the region and was known as the "throat of Khuzestan", was repeatedly attacked during the war by aircraft and missiles. Approximately 15,000 houses and public buildings are said to have been destroyed. The mission observed that irreparable damage had been inflicted on the urban fabric of the historic city centre. Countless fine old houses had been reduced to rubble, while many others had been seriously weakened.

A considerable budget has been allocated by the Ministry of Housing and Urbanism for the reconstruction of housing. The problem of the reintegration of the historic areas is now being dealt with, the priority being to conserve and restore what little remains.

The old town of Shushtar was also bombarded during the conflict, and many historic houses and public buildings were destroyed or damaged.

The mission inspected the Imamzadeh of 'Abd Allah at Shushtar, which was damaged during an air raid. Repair work had already been done to the damaged domes over the entrance, but it was noted that the twin minarets had developed an alarming outward lean. Combined with the evidence of the pronounced inclination of the ground away from the building, the internal fissures and the outward bulging of the retaining wall to the east, this suggested that the surrounding clayey soil is subsiding. The structure is in urgent need of consolidation.

/...

0282

(d) Indirect consequences of the war on historic urban fabric

In the necessity for urgent action to reconstruct damaged cities immediately after the end of hostilities and return them to normal life, large sections of the war-damaged residential quarters of historic city centres have been subjected to uncontrolled reconstruction using modern materials and forms in a way completely incompatible with the organic structure of the traditional urban tissue. Particularly severe examples of the process of deterioration were observed in the listed historic areas of Esfahan, Dezful and Shushtar. This type of cultural loss is arguably more serious and irreparable than direct damage to individual monuments.

(e) Museums

Of the 40 museums scattered throughout the country, 5 in Tehran (Iran Bastan, Golestan, National Arts, and Decorative Arts), the Museums of Shush, Haft Tapeh and Abadan in Khuzistan, the Museum and Fortress of Falak-al-Oflak in Lurestan, were all damaged to varying degrees, and totally destroyed in the case of Abadan. The following were inspected during the mission:

Tehran National Museum

A twentieth-century, stone-faced reinforced concrete frame structure, the National Museum suffered considerable damage from vibrations caused by nearby explosions. Shattered windows and showcases had been repaired, but very severe cracking was still clearly visible throughout the underside of the concrete roof slab and beams, and to the upper walls. Emergency repairs had been carried out to the roof covering, and a structural survey carried out. After the first attacks, the entire collection, consisting of 60,000 objects, was transferred to a basement store, with the exception of those objects too heavy to transport. The mission was shown a number of exhibits which had been damaged, ostensibly as a result of war action.

Golestan Palace Museum

The Golestan Palace and its gardens were built by Nasr Al-Din Shah in a fine Qajar style. Several missiles are said to have fallen within 500 yards of the palace, causing a considerable amount of damage, both to the building and to the museum collections.

Cracks visible in the floors, walls and ceilings confirmed that the structure had been subjected to considerable stress, probably induced by vibration during the bombardment.

A number of windows, including many elaborate coloured-glass and wood panels, had been shattered. During the field visit to Esfahan, it was possible to see a set of five damaged sash-windows from the Golestan being repaired by a traditional master.

/...

0283

Extensive areas of mirror and gesso wall and ceiling decoration in the entrance hall were reported to have collapsed during the war and been replaced three years ago. The difference in colour between old and new work was clearly visible. Further damage was sustained to stucco decoration in the entrance hall.

The alabaster columns of the "Iwan Takht-e-Marmar", and the throne of Agha Muhammad Khan, founder of the Qajar dynasty, were cracked and have since been repaired by a specialist from Shiraz.

Ongoing restoration work could be seen being done to the clock tower, and to the "Salon-e-Badgir", or wind-tower room in the palace. As work had only recently been started, it was possible to appreciate the complexity and extent of the work completed to date in other parts of the palace.

The collections of the museum and library, consisting of some 64,000 objects, were carefully packed and moved underground during the bombardments, thus avoiding significant losses. However, many of the rare carpets, which included a 60-square-metre Tabriz, were cut by falling glass from the ceilings, and some showcases were shattered, breaking many items of china. A laboratory manned by a skilled ceramics restorer had been set up in the palace where restoration work was proceeding at the time of the mission.

Other museums

Similar patterns of damage were observed in other museums visited in Tehran: the National Arts Museum, a fine Qajar pavilion built by Fath 'Ali Shah. A missile landed 100 metres away from the museum, breaking coloured-glass windows and damaging some nineteenth century miniatures; the Glass and Ceramics Museum, designed by Hans Hollein within the former Egyptian Embassy, also sustained damage to its structure from a bomb blast Some rare exhibits have had to be restored.

Archaeological Museum of Shush

Restoration of damage to the museum building from missile attacks had been completed at the time of the field visit. Photographic documentation, however, showed patching work to the walls and roof, and replacement of doors and windows, under way. The museum contains a conservation laboratory, where the restoration of the damage to the collections was in progress.

Site Museum of Haft Tappeh

Rockets were said to have fallen within the archaeological zone on a number of occasions, including the site museum, shattering windows and showcases. Some repairs have already been carried out, but showcases, and the ventilation system need replacement. Fortunately, the museum collection, consisting of objects dating from 1500 B.C. had been removed for safekeeping to the National Museum in Tehran.

/...

0284

2. Reconstruction

The national authorities' stated priorities in the five-year plan for the reconstruction and restoration of war-damaged cultural heritage are as follows:

(a) Revision of plans and objectives;

(b) Establishment of an adapted organization;

(c) Provision of adequate legal and financial means;

(d) Rehabilitation of manpower;

(e) Rehabilitation and modernization of facilities and equipment;

(f) Reconstruction, restoration and rehabilitation of damaged monuments, sites, museums and collections.

The Iranian Cultural Heritage Organization estimated that approximately one tenth of restoration work to war-damaged monuments and sites had been completed to date. In view of the severity of destruction suffered by historic sites and monuments during the war, a new list of priorities for conservation had to be drawn up and a new list of priorities and plans of action prepared.

3. Establishment of an adapted organization

Prior to the outbreak of war, responsibility for the protection of cultural heritage was ensured by 11 organizations under the authority of three different ministries.

During the first years of war, there was no systematic programme or specific annual budget for conservation or restoration.

The Iranian Cultural Heritage Organization was founded by government decree in 1987, with its headquarters in Tehran. It gathers together under one umbrella all disciplines related to cultural heritage, with three main activities in each discipline: research; presentation; and protection.

4. Reconstruction and restoration costs

The following table was extracted from a detailed breakdown provided to the mission by the Iranian Cultural Heritage Organization, of the cost of reconstruction and restoration of direct damage to historic monuments and sites in the affected provinces:

/...

Table I.1. Cost estimate of reconstruction and rehabilitation

Province	Total estimated cost (Million Rls)	Expenditure to date (Million Rls)
A. Khuzestan	12 520	375
B. Ilam	780	120
C. Bakhtaran	382	3 570
D. Kurdestan	760	35
E. W. Azerbayjan	1 400	120
F. Esfahan	15 000	285
G. Tehran	1 750	670
H. Lorestan	420	240
I. Fars	100	10
J. Markazi	400	40
K. Zanjan	300	30
Total	37 000	2 307

Note: The figures quoted in the second column, "Expenditure to date", include neither overheads (administrative and technical staff of the Iranian Cultural Heritage Organization, as well as the organization's own team of skilled craftsmen), for which a further 15 per cent would have to be added, nor private sector losses, nor voluntary efforts, which are evaluated at 2-300 per cent of the cost of restoration.

5. The role of the private sector

The national authorities emphasized the considerable contribution to the work of reconstruction made by volunteers. One example mentioned was the organization of voluntary groups in villages throughout the country in order to ensure the protection of heritage sites. The Cultural Organization was encouraging such groups to participate in presentation and ethnographic research work, and the use of indigenous craftsmen had helped considerably to stimulate local interest and mobilize volunteers.

/...

0286

In Esfahan, the mission encountered three architects teaching at the Pardis University who were also working in a voluntary capacity in the pilot project office for reconstruction of the historic Jamaleh neighbourhood.

The stated aim of the organization is that the private and public sectors will become increasingly responsible for the maintenance and repair of the historic building stock. Various financial and fiscal incentives were planned to this end.

6. Expressed needs for external assistance

Training

The Cultural Organization's highly qualified staff of restorers, curators and technicians were mostly trained in Europe in the 1960s. A new generation needs to be trained to the same level of skill and in the use of new techniques and equipment.

Assistance was requested in terms of training abroad and on-site training in the conservation, restoration and documentation of movable and immovable cultural property, as well as in the various branches of museology. A need was expressed for cultural and intellectual exchanges with similar institutions abroad, as well as access to specialist publications and reviews.

Equipment

The reconstruction effort had thrown into relief the need to replace outdated equipment with new technology. In particular, photogrammetry had proved an essential tool in the restoration of war damage, and plotting equipment was required to complete the National Laboratory's photogrammetric unit.

The national authorities were facing difficulties in buying equipment and chemicals from abroad owing to exchange rate problems.

Software was required for the inventory of historic monuments.

Technical cooperation

A need was expressed for cultural and intellectual exchanges with similar institutions abroad, as well as access to specialist publications and reviews.

The advice of the international conservation community was sought on methods of stone conservation for the ruins of Persepolis, and of baked brick and adobe structures for Shush and Choqa Zanbil. Assistance was requested for a study of the ancient water mills and irrigation system of Shushtar.

The authorities of the National Research Laboratory wished to modify the draft UNDP project "Assistance for Training of Personnel and Restoration of

/...

Historic Monuments", prepared during the May 1990 inter-agency mission to Iran, to concentrate on strengthening the central laboratory in Tehran.

Assistance was also requested in finding extrabudgetary funding for a project to restore a group of historic Armenian houses in the Jolfa neighbourhood of Esfahan with a view to expanding the facilities of the existing school of restoration.

7. Observations

In visits to three affected provinces and on-site inspection of over 60 destroyed or damaged monuments, the mission was able to appreciate the extent of reconstruction and restoration work which had already been achieved and the intricate and time-consuming nature of the restoration methods called into play.

Important human resources have had to be mobilized to meet the crisis, often relying to an important extent on volunteers.

The fact that the government has been obliged to expend Rls 37,000 million of its reconstruction budget on restoration of direct war-damage to monuments, and that according to estimates much more will need to be spent before these structures can be restored to a semblance of their former condition, illustrates the magnitude of the problem. In some cases, no amount of effort will be able to compensate the loss to the national heritage.

In its discussions the mission was very much impressed by the zeal and competence of the traditional craftsmen working under the supervision of experienced and highly talented experts. In the view of the mission, it will be some years before the necessary restoration work can be completed.

/...

0288

J. HEALTH

Introduction

Organization of health services

Health services in the five war-affected provinces of Bakhtaran,
Khuzestan, Ilam, West Azerbayjan and Kurdestan, are delivered through a
network of health facilities and health programmes. The most peripheral
health facility is the health house (HH) which provides local care for about
1,500 people. Each group of five HHs are supervised and supported by one
Rural Health Centre (RHC) which caters for 7,500 people. In each district
there is one district health centre that supervises all RHCs. There are also
Urban Health Centres (UHC) catering for urban population. This network is
supported by provincial health centres, rural, district, provincial and
teaching hospitals.

Situation in war-affected provinces at outbreak of war

At the time of the outbreak of the conflict, the five provinces had a
population of about 4.9 million and a series of health facilities consisting
of 455 HH, 552 rural and urban health centres (HC), 92 hospitals and about 800
physicians. In addition, there was 1 hospital bed for every 630 persons, an
HH or HC for each 4,820 population and if hospitals were included, there was a
health facility for each 4,400 people. Over and above these health facilities
there were many disease-control and health-promotion and health-protection
programmes. Those programmes aimed at vaccination of children, maternal and
child care, nutrition, health education and control of communicable diseases.
Some 40-60 per cent of the population were benefiting from these programmes at
the beginning of the conflict. There were 3 medical universities, 60
midwifery training centers, 280 nursing schools and 13 PHC workers (Behvaris)
training centres in the war-affected provinces.

In 1980, one third of the rural population and almost 98 per cent of the
urban population had access to clean and safe water supplies and were served
with excreta disposal facilities.

1. Health infrastructure

Damage sustained

A total of 102 HHs, 84 RHCs, 80 urban health centres and 12 provincial
and/or district health centres were destroyed. In addition, 5 quarantine and
tuberculosis-control centres were seriously damaged and in the hospitals a
total of 2,076 beds was destroyed. In many instances, all equipment
installations, tools, machines, medicines and ambulances and other material
that constitutes the standard list of supplies and equipment was lost. Some
of these facilities were reconstructed several times as damage was repeated,
often several times, during the hostilities.

/...

0289

Reconstruction

During 1988-1990, 61 facilities were reconstructed and 117 were planned for 1991; 774 hospital beds were replaced and 458 are planned for 1991. Out of 1,296 vehicles lost or destroyed, only 200 have been replaced. The total cost of reconstruction during the years 1983-1990 was reported by the Ministry of Health to be Rls 50,848 million and Rls 12,000 million for other governmental bodies and institutions. During 1992-1993 the reconstruction of 46 Health Houses, 2 District Health Centres, 600 teaching hospital beds, 847 treatment hospital beds is planned. Total reconstruction cost for health infrastructure for 1991/1993 is estimated at Rls 295,454 million.

War damage to other health facilities in the non-governmental sector, e.g. hospitals run by oil companies, banks, etc., amounted to about Rls 156,943 million. The reconstruction cost of these private facilities is expected to exceed the estimated cost of the damage.

2. Health and medical education institutions

Damages sustained

The effect of the war on health manpower development had many facets. With many trained health workers killed or disabled, training programmes were interrupted and training institutions damaged. Some 200,000 students who were enrolled in various training institutions were negatively affected during the war years. Many joined the armed forces and others were unable to continue their studies. The resultant manpower shortage has been accentuated by the diversion of most available physicians and health workers to deal with war casualties and other war-related health problems.

All training and teaching institutions in the five war-affected provinces were badly damaged, including three medical universities, 37 teaching hospitals, and 17 educational/research centres; in addition, 5 other universities sustained damage to a lesser degree. Reconstruction of these facilities was an ongoing process, even during the war years.

By the end of 1990, the reconstruction of 10 hospitals and 10 training centres had been completed. The reconstruction of additional hospitals and training institutions is planned if international assistance can be secured. However, it is evident that much of the teaching/learning material, research projects documents, reference books and libraries will be difficult, if not impossible, to replace.

Government estimates indicate that up to the end of 1991, a multitude of agencies, governmental as well as non-governmental, will have spent a total of $2,770 million, and Rls 5,978,500 million, for reconstruction in the area of health and medical education. For future reconstruction covering the years 1991 and onwards a total of $11,000 million and Rls 10,995 million will be needed. These costs include reconstruction of facilities, replacement of supplies, equipment and installations.

/...

3. Water and sanitation facilities

The Ministry of Health and the Ministry of Education are jointly responsible for the supply and quality of water to all villages with more than 150 families. The total number of water supply and sanitation facilities before the onset of the war in the border provinces, was 3,042. Of this number, 205 units were destroyed but they have since been replaced. The total cost for damage to water and sanitation is estimated at Rls 5,200 million.

The actual cost of reconstruction and rehabilitation work already completed is Rls 7,346 million, which also includes the purchase of water and sanitation supplies and equipment and vehicles. Moreover, it covers the cost of material for environmental and water quality control.

Taking into account the major reconstruction costs mentioned under the preceding subsections, the following table provides an estimate of the total reconstruction costs already incurred and projected expenditure to the end of 1993.

Summary of reconstruction expenditure

(Millions of rials)

Name of unit affected	1980-1988	1988-1989	1990-1992	Required before completion: foreign currency	Required before completion: local currency	Total
Ministry of Health and Medical Education	4,000	7,746	36,000	58,781	64,156	170,683
Administrative buildings under construction (housing sector)	--	1,100	2,000	2,360	3,540	9,000
Other health sub-sectors	2,000	4,000	6,000	66,843	100,265	179,108
TOTAL	6,000	12,846	44,000	127,984	167,961	358,791

The total area of damaged buildings is estimated at 1,700,000 m^2.

/...

4. Effects of the war on the health of the people (the disabled)

In addition to the deterioration of health services that occurred as a result of the conflict, the most distressing problems relate to the psycho-social effects and disabilities. In the opinion of the mission, the Government of Iran is adequately addressing these issues in order to reduce the impact of complications.

The mission was informed that almost 600,000 people were physically and mentally disabled during the war. There are no overall cost figures available relating to the treatment of the disabled since it is national policy to provide humanitarian services without consideration of the actual cost involved.

5. Overall health situation since 1988

Because of efficiently run health programmes, the country in general achieved higher coverage rates by the end of the conflict in 1988, even though the relatively low rates for the five war-affected provinces were included. National health targets, such as immunization programmes, hospital buildings per population, etc. could be accomplished in the war-affected provinces if an accelerated reconstruction and rehabilitation programme is launched. Such a programme will first have to raise the quality of services to pre-war standards and then, through intensified inputs, ensure that the level of service is available throughout the country. In order to meet this challenge, the Government has designed a reconstruction programme with a phased target approach which will require international assistance for its implementation.

The mere reconstruction and rehabilitation of facilities and services will not solve existing problems. The interruption of services, especially in the areas of disease control and care of environment programmes, has adversely affected the general health of the population, morbidity and mortality rates and has led to a noticeable increase in communicable diseases. The impact of war on the environment was especially serious: water and sanitation systems were destroyed; soil has been contaminated by chemicals; salination has increased, pests and insects harmful to health have multiplied, affecting humans as well as food production. All this has led to an increased spread of disease, re-emergence of diseases which were under control prior to the war, malnutrition, and chronic ill-health. As an example, the incidence of acute respiratory diseases and diarrhoea, which are rated as the main causes of death countrywide, have risen sharply. Fortunately, the health programmes established by the Government through the Ministry of Health and the Ministry of Education and non-governmental organization-sponsored programmes have helped to control the spread of diseases.

/...

6. Areas of priorities and international assistance

The Government has made it a priority to have all health services rehabilitated without delay. This should serve as an incentive to physicians and other health professionals, including the private sector, to return to the war-affected provinces. Authorities have allocated appreciable amounts of funds to meet all local costs. In view of the magnitude of needs and the limited funds at its disposal, the Ministry of Health has indicated that it would appreciate international assistance in the following forms:

(a) 2,000 field vehicles for ambulatory visits and follow-up visits;

(b) 500 ambulances for medical hospitals;

(c) 500 ambulances for university hospitals;

(d) 300 prefab health houses;

(e) 300 prefab health centres;

(f) 5 prefab public hospitals with 500 beds each;

(g) Related equipment.

For purposes of its reconstruction programme, in the medium term, the Ministries of Health and Education would like to acquire modern technology in the areas necessary to strengthen its hospital facilities, laboratories and medical universities. Such assistance should be in the form of transfer of technology, the provision of modern teaching equipment, and laboratory reagents and equipment. Training facilities, teaching aids and technical assistance in vocational training for the disabled was also emphasized.

7. Observations

One of the major problems in the reconstruction effort is the acute shortage of health facilities, which if not remedied could serve as a deterrent to would-be returnees to the border areas. Moreover, when reconstruction work intensifies, there will be a greater demand on health services. This demand can be met only by giving the health sector a priority not only in reconstruction and rehabilitation but also in strengthening and expanding its capabilities.

Reconstruction and rehabilitation work performed so far by Iranian authorities is impressive. Their experience should be documented and steps should be taken to consolidate their achievements. Furthermore, in order to ensure that the present efforts continue, supplies and equipment, including essential transport facilities, should be given highest priority.

/...

Reconstruction work could be accelerated if prefabricated buildings could be manufactured locally.

Provision of supplies and equipment should be coupled with training in their maintenance and repair and essential tools and workshops needed for this purpose should be provided.

Although it is relatively easy to observe the physical and immediate effects of war at the present time, considerable research work and studies will be needed to assess the effects of the war in the medium and long term.

Effective coordination and advisory mechanism should ensure that the supplies and equipment provided are suited for the local need and culture. Standardization of such supplies and equipment is essential to facilitate maintenance, repair and replacement in the future.

During the process of reconstruction, some problems may arise in the areas of management, logistics, intersectoral coordination and community involvement. It is essential to strengthen these areas.

The development of an incentive system to encourage professionals, workers and the private sector to work in war-affected areas may be considered.

0294

외 무 부

원 본

종 별 :

번 호 : UNW-1017

일 시 : 92 0406 1930

수 신 : 장 관(연일,중동일,기정)

발 신 : 주 유엔 대사

제 목 : 안보리(이란-이라크 분쟁)

이란공군기가 4.5. 이라크내 이란반군 기지를 공습한데 대해 이라크는 안보리의 즉각적인 사태개입을 요청하였으며, 이에 따라 금 4.6. 안보리는 비공식 회의를 소집,본사태를 심의한 바, 안보리 결의 또는 의장성명 채택대신 안보리 의장이 기자들을상대로 다음과 같이 안보리의 의견을 전달하기로 함

'안보리는 상기사건을 심각히 우려하며, 유엔사무총장으로 하여금 이란 및 이라크 에 소재한 유엔사무소를 통해 사태의 진상을 파악하도록 촉구함

(대사 유종하-국장)

국기국   중아국   외정실   분석관   청와대   안기부

PAGE 1

92.04.07   08:49 WH

외신 1과 통제관

0295

외 무 부

종 별 :

번 호 : IRW-0465   일 시 : 92 0723 1600

수 신 : 장관(중동일,기정)

발 신 : 주이란대사

제 목 : 이란-이라크전 사망자 유해 교환

　　1.주재국과 이라크는 7.22 이란 서부국경 KHOSRAWI 에서 이란-이라크 전쟁시 사망한 이란군 유해 50구와 이라크군 유해 51구를 상호 교환함.

　　2.또한 양국은 이.이전에서 사망한 여타 이란군 유해의 송환을 위하여 이란정부관계자를 이라크에 파견하는 문제를 협의한바, 이라크측에서 이란정부관계자의 활동에 필요한 조치를 취할것에 합의함.끝

　　(대사 이상열-국장)

중아국　　외정실　　안기부

92.07.23　　21:21 DQ

외신 1과 통제관

0296

외교문서 비밀해제: 걸프 사태 10
걸프 사태 대책 및 조치 5

초판인쇄 2024년 03월 15일
초판발행 2024년 03월 15일

지은이 한국학술정보(주)
펴낸이 채종준
펴낸곳 한국학술정보(주)
주 소 경기도 파주시 회동길 230(문발동)
전 화 031-908-3181(대표)
팩 스 031-908-3189
홈페이지 http://ebook.kstudy.com
E-mail 출판사업부 publish@kstudy.com
등 록 제일산-115호(2000. 6. 19)

ISBN   979-11-6983-970-9 94340
       979-11-6983-960-0 94340 (set)